# Lesbian Couples

## A Guide to Creating Healthy Relationships

D. MERILEE CLUNIS, PHD
AND
G. DORSEY GREEN, PHD

Seal Press

Lesbian Couples
A Guide to Creating Healthy Relationships

Published by
Seal Press
A member of the Perseus Books Group
1700 Fourth Street
Berkeley, CA 94710

ISBN-10: 1-58005-131-6
ISBN-13: 978-1-58005-131-6

Library of Congress Cataloging-in-Publication Data
Clunis, D. Merilee.
  Lesbian couples : a guide to creating healthy relationships / by D. Merilee Clunis and G. Dorsey Green.— 4th ed.
      p. cm.
  Includes bibliographical references and index.
  ISBN 1-58005-131-6 (pbk. : alk. paper)
    1. Lesbian couples—United States. 2. Lesbians—United States—Life skills guides. 3. Interpersonal relations. I. Green, G. Dorsey. II. Title.

  HQ75.6.U58C58 2004
  306.76'63—dc22


2004023652

9 8

Cover design by Gia Giasullo, studio eg
Interior design by Margaret Copeland/Terragrafix
Printed in the United States of America by Worzalla

*To our partners*
*Margaret Schonfield*
*and Ann Stever*

## Acknowledgments

Although we have made extensive changes to *Lesbian Couples* throughout the years, we remain indebted to those who helped us create the foundation upon which this revision is built. Thanks again to all who made that first edition possible: the therapists in Washington and California who shared their observations and reflections with us; the readers of early versions, who provided sustaining encouragement and gentle guidance; our writing and word processing coaches and especially our editors at Seal Press, Barbara Wilson and Faith Conlon. We are indebted to Vickie Sears, who generously shared her writing and expertise on the topics of racism and disability, and to our clients, our friends, and our families for all that they have taught us about relationships.

We are indebted to those who helped us shape the changes in our thinking and writing through the years. Liang Tien's thoughtful observations about cross-racial and cross-cultural relationships and Pat Freeman's knowledge of gay and lesbian history were extremely helpful. We are grateful to those at both ends of the age spectrum who educated us about their lives and perspectives: Amy Bollinger, Becca Calhoun, Carolyn Chow, Gabriel Foster, Kristin Pula, Amy Reddinger, Mary Wiltenburg, and Carley Zepeda helped clarify how the world looks to younger dykes. The women interviewed for the Looking Back . . . Looking Forward project enriched our understandings about older gay women.

We appreciate immensely the energy, responsiveness, and guidance of our editors at Seal Press. Jennie Goode's ability to communicate to us how she heard what we wrote was the impetus for our being more inclusive of younger voices in our community. We are grateful to Faith Conlon, who initially invited us to revise *Lesbian Couples,* and whose confidence in us through the years inspired and nourished us. Most recently, our thanks go to Leslie Miller for shepharding us throughout this latest revision.

# Table of Contents

# § Introduction

When Seal Press asked us to revise *Lesbian Couples*, which was first published in 1988, we had no idea how much the lesbian and societal landscapes had changed since then. We knew that we had aged; we are now in our fifties and sixties. Dorsey has gotten divorced and started a new relationship; one son has graduated from college and the other has started (she was pregnant with her younger boy when we were writing the book in 1984). Merilee and her partner, Margaret, have celebrated their twenty-eighth anniversary, attended the weddings of both children, and welcomed their first grandchild into the world.

We had not realized how much we had unconsciously spoken from the perspective of the thirty- to forty-five-year-old age group in writing the first three editions. As we looked around this time, we identified different generations of lesbians. To help us address how issues might affect women of different ages, we divided them into three groups: those under thirty-five, those over fifty-five, and those in between. What emerged was a picture of (at least) three different world views—lesbian style. Hopefully we have done justice to these perspectives.

We tried to be aware of how race, class, physical and mental ability, and geographical location might interact with an individual's age (and when she came out) in creating her experience in the world. Each of us, then, brings

1

our unique self into a relationship with an equally unique other. This is what makes relationships exhilarating and frustrating.

The first edition of *Lesbian Couples* now looks like a snapshot of lesbians in relationships in the mid-to-late 1980s. By nature, a photograph is two-dimensional, and in some ways we think the picture we created with our book was two-dimensional as well. It was a description of lesbian couples as we knew them to be. In the '80s, we needed pictures because most lesbians (and certainly most of mainstream society) did not know what communities of lesbians looked like. We only knew what our own lives were like. We needed reflections of ourselves and information about lesbians as a group. Now as we go to press in 2004—thirty-five–plus years after Stonewall, the symbolic beginning of the modern lesbian and gay civil rights movement—we wanted to provide more than photographs. We tried for more depth and complexity.

This edition of *Lesbian Couples* builds upon the third edition, which was less descriptive and more prescriptive than previous editions. This is partly because we are more opinionated and more willing to state our views. But it is also because we know more about relationships in general and lesbian relationships in particular. The last decade has seen an enormous amount of new research about couples: what contributes to their health and what helps them to improve when there is trouble. Print, movie, television, and computer media have also contributed more information and images of lesbians and our families. This is a good thing; however, public focus is still predominantly on white lesbians and therefore offers a limited picture. We continue to need more material by and about women of color.

There has been an explosion of resources for and about lesbians in the last fifteen years. There have been a few books through the years that explore relationships in general, but it is the diversity of topics that truly underscores the changes in society's recognition of lesbians and bisexual women. Sex between women, as usual, has received much attention, with Felice Newman's *The Whole Lesbian Sex Book* being a good example. Bisexuality, which used to be seen as a stepping stone to a real sexual orientation, is now viewed as a separate and valid orientation. *Bilives: Bisexual Women Tell Their Stories* by Kate Orndorff is one contribution to this growing body of information. As parenting has become more visible in the queer community, books geared toward lesbians, both as single and coupled parents, have become available. Our *The Lesbian Parenting Book* and *The Queer Parent's Primer: A Lesbian and Gay Families Guide to Navigating the Straight World*, by Stephanie Bull, are two examples of the different approaches available. *A Donor Insemination*

*Guide: Written for and by Lesbian Women* by Marie Mohler and Lacy Frazer is as specific as one can get about lesbians' getting pregnant. Janet Wright expanded the discussion on parenting and families with *Lesbian Step Families*. Coming out has moved from how-do-you-tell-your-parents to *Lesbian Epiphanies: Women Coming Out in Later Life* by Karol Jensen. Disability is receiving more attention and titles as more people recognize the importance of the issue. And of course, any perusal of online or progressive bookstores provides plenty of wedding guides for lesbian and gay couples— general legal guides, along with the recent addition of books arguing specifically for the rights of lesbians and gay men to marry legally in the United States. Jonathan Rauch's *Gay Marriage: Why It Is Good for Gays, Good for Straights and Good for America* is one example of the flood of books produced in the last two years. None of these books existed when we first wrote *Lesbian Couples*!

Lesbian novels and mysteries contribute fictional accounts of couples who try all sorts of ways to succeed in their relationships as well as in other areas of their lives. Movies, videos, and documentaries show lesbians, their relationships, and their children in a realistic light. Millions watched Ellen DeGeneres, of television fame, as she came out over an airport loudspeaker and as her personal life splashed over the pages of major magazines. *Queer as Folk* and *The L Word* brought us televised shows with a gay/lesbian focus, with lesbian couples on television becoming more routine, some even including children in their families. Rosie O'Donnell's coming out and subsequent adoption of children brought the reality of lesbian families into millions of homes. Daring for its time, the Hollywood film *Boys Don't Cry* brought transgender issues to a mainstream audience with the tragic story of Brandon Teena's murder. Lesbian and gay magazines and newspapers are sold in large and small bookstores. *Newsweek* and other mainstream magazines routinely run stories, some flattering and some not, about many facets of the lesbian, gay, and bisexual communities. The Internet has hundreds of lesbian and gay sites, allowing anyone with a computer and modem access to more information than any one person could possibly assimilate. We have come a long way from the depressing ending of Radclyffe Hall's *The Well of Loneliness*, in which the heroine's gift to her lover is a heterosexual mate.

Society has matured in other ways as well. Many white people's understanding of racism has expanded to include awareness of their own white privilege. Individuals with more than one racial ancestry are asking for acknowledgment of their multiracial and multicultural heritages. Stepfamilies are beginning to receive the recognition and support they deserve. The AIDS epidemic has become less associated with gay (and lesbian) people and is seen more accurately as a global threat to everyone. The wars in Iraq and Afghanistan, regardless of personal opinion, have forced more American awareness of Islam and enriched the country's conversation in general about the relationship between religion and state. The American Disabilities Act has advanced the rights of people with disabilities to give them more equal access to employment, education, transportation, and housing. Lesbian couples who want their marriage or celebration of commitment recognized by a church or synagogue are able to do that in many areas of the country.

As we write this during the months leading up to the 2004 presidential elections, the country is engaged in a conversation about legal marriage for same-sex couples. The conversation is sometimes respectful and usually heated; it has polarized people from all areas of the country in an extraordinary way. The national debate began when legal marriage for same-sex couples became a reality in some provinces in Canada. Vermont then legislated civil unions and was followed by the Massachusetts Supreme Court, which mandated that same-sex couples in that state be allowed to marry. In California, the mayor of San Francisco issued an order allowing gays to marry and as thousands in San Francisco jubilantly lined up to do so, America saw real lesbian couples flashed across their television screens. Other cities, counties, and states are also wrestling with the possibility of legalizing gay and lesbian relationships. Whatever the outcome, it is clear that lesbian relationships are being taken more seriously than at any other time in our history.

Despite this progress, however, homophobia, racism, ableism, class bias, and sexism live on. A lesbian still has to work very hard to be seen as a complete human being and not just a sexual creature—and often a deviant one at that. Racism and cultural prejudice abound, making it difficult for many people of color and immigrants to claim a piece of the prosperity that the United States government maintains is available to all. Religious intolerance of homosexuality fertilizes hatred, which contributes to many acts of discrimination and violence. Just as we are demanding equal treatment from mainstream society, we need to hold ourselves and our communities accountable for behaving in ways that respect the differences among us.

Respect is, in many ways, the main theme of this book. Recognizing and accepting difference in your partner is fundamental to creating a healthy and satisfying relationship. Now that you have access to the many pictures of ways women can be coupled, you can use these images as a starting place for designing your own relationship. Ask others how they manage the differences and tough spots. We encourage you to take from our book anything that helps, use the resources, and create your own books, articles, support groups, rituals, movies, videos, or conversations.

Every chapter has been revised and some have been almost completely rewritten since we published the original book. We changed the order of the chapters and some of their titles to reflect what we hope is a more helpful progression of the topics and skills involved in developing a healthy and happy relationship. It has been very exciting to discover and think about what has changed in the last sixteen years. It has been a privilege to spend time together, with other women and with great written material, learning about these evolving communities of lesbians. We can't wait to see what comes next.

*D. Merilee Clunis, PhD*
*G. Dorsey Green, PhD*
*Seattle, Washington*
*August, 2004*

## CHAPTER 1

# ᛰ What Is a Healthy Couple Anyway?

One of the questions we asked in the first edition of this book was, "What is a lesbian couple?" In the 1980s this inquiry was about definition—how do we know when two people form a couple? We decided that lesbians are in a couple when they say they are. Lesbian thought has shifted from defining our relationships, and just surviving, to seeing ourselves as deserving to be in strong, happy couples. We are expanding the definition of what makes a healthy relationship even as we defend our right to be in one.

In the time since we wrote our first draft of *Lesbian Couples* in 1983, a lot of research has been conducted regarding what constitutes a good marriage. We will refer to this new information throughout the book. However, comparable as we are to our heterosexual counterparts, lesbian relationships are unique.

Lesbian couples are composed of two women, which means that both partners are similarly socialized: They both have been taught to focus on their primary relationship. Lesbians must always be conscious of homophobia and the damage it can do to individuals and couples. The lack of legal acknowledgment of same-gender relationships, in forty-nine out of fifty states, deprives lesbian couples of the societal support that opposite-gender couples take for granted. This includes the right to marry legally and the privileges that come with it, such as inheritance and insurance benefits. Another important difference between heterosexual and lesbian couples is that the women appear to value equality in the relationship more than other kinds of couples.[1] These variances can translate into different kinds of chore and child-care sharing than might happen in heterosexual or gay male couples. Frequency of sexual contact also varies between different kinds of couples.[2] Because of these disparities it is important to examine research data from married, heterosexual couples with caution. For example, does sexual frequency include intercourse, orgasm, and snuggling, or just intercourse? Does the research on divorce rates consider the privileges that come with legal marriage and societal support?

Often it's in our primary relationships that we discover the joy and exhilaration of loving women; it is here that we experience the magic and rightness of being lesbian. Our relationships define us as lesbians to the world and to each other. It is in our romantic partnerships that we confront some of our greatest challenges—both unique and universal. Will she still love me when she sees me at my worst? Will my parents accept our relationship? Can I keep my heart open when she disappoints me? Is it safe to come out to my coworkers? Can we be unalike and both be okay? Will my children reject us? In large measure it's in our relationships that we learn who we are and become more of who we can be.

Couple relationships aren't for everyone. They are not a requirement for being happily lesbian. Some women decide that they never—or never again—want to be part of a couple. Others find that at certain times in their lives, other interests, goals, or activities take priority over being in a relationship. Still others prefer to be celibate or involved in multiple relationships rather than being with one person. And sometimes a woman may not meet anyone with whom she wants to have a relationship and may choose to put her energy elsewhere.

However, many lesbians live in a couple or would like to. We want to know how to choose good partners and create successful relationships. And relationships do take work, but it doesn't mean endless drudgery. Myriad goals and pleasures in life involve work, such as going to college, raising children, gardening, completing an apprenticeship, working on one's racism, meditation, running a marathon, and resolving conflicts with our partner. But it can be joyful work, done in a spirit of loving kindness for oneself and one's partner.

## Why Are Relationships So Important to Us?

For many lesbians, our primary relationships play a significant role in our lives. We focus a lot of time fantasizing, analyzing, daydreaming, writing, worrying, and talking to our friends about them. And this doesn't count the time we actually spend with our partners.

We are drawn into relationships when we fall in love. We may then find that we love the person beyond that first rush of passion or, as sometimes happens, discover that sexual attraction follows the love of friendship. The Greeks named three kinds of love: eros, agape, and filia. Eros is the physical, romantic, lustful energy of love; agape is unconditional, undeserved love; and filia is sisterly love, what we feel for family. Lesbian relationships have components of all three. One type of love may predominate and others fade at different times in the life of a couple, but given time we can have a rich multidimensional love.

As human beings we desire both emotional and sexual intimacy, and we look to our partners for much of this. Because we are women, we have received strong cultural messages about the value of coupling, and we have learned to prize couple relationships. As lesbians in a homophobic world, we live with oppression, but we give and gather strength from the partnerships that validate our identity and nurture our self-esteem. Many of us want to create something bigger than ourselves. A good relationship can enable us to become something greater than two people. Part of what attracts us to, and makes us fight for, relationships is the transformation that can happen as we live over time as a couple. We are challenged to invent and maintain a "we-ness" that also invites us to grow and become more individually whole.

### Achieving Intimacy

Intimacy is a special type of connection. When we are in an intimate relationship, we feel loved, understood, accepted, known, and appreciated. Intimacy comprises being close emotionally and sexually; it involves sharing thoughts, feelings, and experiences. It also includes negotiating differences and fighting. In the next few pages we offer an overview of intimacy, which creates the context for why lesbians value relationships. We'll explore normal tensions in relationships and how each partner brings strengths and vulnerabilities to the task of managing those tensions. In Chapters Three and Four we widen our definition of intimacy, and we return to intimacy, its development, and its maintenance throughout the book.

There is a natural flow of intimate connection in couple relationships that includes separateness, contact, and merger. Being separate is being apart, focusing on different things; contact is being together, focusing on the same thing; and merger is focusing exclusively on each other. It's common to feel anxiety as we move closer together and farther apart from our partners.

Intimacy is the connection we can achieve when we are able to tolerate our anxiety as we move along this continuum of togetherness and separateness.

Differentiation is the ability to endure emotional discomfort enough to risk moving closer or farther apart—without any guarantee of how the other person will respond. It is a crucial skill for developing intimacy, and it helps us avoid the many ways we accommodate to each other to keep from being anxious. Eventually this accommodation may stifle us until we are chronically resentful or want to leave the relationship.

> Sarah and Margaret always spent the New Year with Sarah's parents and siblings. Every year Margaret felt a twinge of resentment, but the idea of raising the possibility of doing something else so unnerved her that she buried the thought before it was fully formed.

> Lee was surprised to hear herself once again telling Trish that she was willing to have sex. Lee had found that she was not present when they made love because she got bored. But she was scared to say anything to Trish.

Some lesbians have difficulty with intimacy because we fear we have to be close all the time, or that we'll hurt our partners if we pull back at all. We may think that being close means we always have to do what our partner wants or take care of her or be taken care of or always stay the same or never want what she can't or doesn't provide. Knowing that there is a natural ebb and flow of separateness, contact, and merger, and that no one place is permanent, can help partners give each other space. Trusting the process and recognizing what part of it we are in helps to calm such fears as, "I'll never get enough time to myself," or "I'll never get enough of feeling close." Some people want more space, while others want more contact and merger. These wants may fluctuate over time. Although couples often seem to be polarized—one person wants closeness and the other space—it is important to remember that each partner needs both and that anxiety creates polarity. When partners fail to recognize that they each want some separateness and some togetherness, they may feel stuck and unable to resolve their differences. Each woman's discomfort becomes directed toward the stance her partner has taken. Thus, each polarized position may become a personality flaw in the other partner and may be so uncomfortable to one partner that she thinks she needs to leave the relationship.

> Twyla had had it with her partner's clinginess. Camille "whined" when Twyla called to say she'd be late from work. Twyla couldn't take any time for

*herself without Camille's overreacting. Twyla was beginning to think she should end the relationship and find someone who was more independent, the way Camille had been when they first met.*

Ironically, it is often in the sexual arena of our relationships that we polarize the closeness and separateness feelings. Sex is one way of being close; indeed it is the most common place we feel merged. It also can add another dimension to couples' lives and to the ways they can be intimate. Like emotional intimacy, sexual intimacy allows partners to learn how to move toward each other. However, one partner may refuse sex more often than not and the other may become the frustrated initiator. This situation may cause anxiety because the lower frequency of sex can be construed to be rejection, disrespect, or lack of love. Consequently, some women may put up barriers to being close. They may push their partner away the moment that they want to feel close to her.

When we are in a long-term, committed relationship, sex can provide an avenue to enhance intimacy. It is another way to be seen and known deeply by our partner. When we invite sex, we risk that our partner will reject us or not be present for the connection. This risk always accompanies our invitation for intimate connection, and our fear of not being met often keeps us from reaching out to our partner. The gain, however, is the increased intimacy this connection affords us. We think it is worth the risk.

Intimacy grows with time. It takes a while to get to know and trust another person. Time spent together doesn't guarantee intimacy, but closeness over years does mean that a couple has the opportunity to share experiences and changes. "We grew up together" is one expression of this shared history. Often the women in a couple come to know each other more fully than they are known by anyone else.

### Listening to Cultural Messages

Because of the way our society treats girls, as compared to boys, women are more vulnerable to feeling incomplete—of having a gap to fill. Traditionally, boys are told to "go for it," to be all they can be, while girls are encouraged to stay close to home, to curtail their own development in order to support someone else's, to be careful of the male "ego," and to be dependent. By the time girls are eight or nine, they know that eventually they are supposed to find someone and settle down for life. Even though women's interests and careers are taken much more seriously now than in the past, women in general are still expected to coordinate, or subordinate, them to marriage and children. As women, we are constantly deluged with messages that we need someone—a man—to feel complete. Long before we reach our twenties, most women will have started to look for our "other half." Much of what we do is designed to make us more desirable to that "someone" who will complete us.

How does this translate to lesbians who have chosen women as lovers? Quite directly. As girls we are assumed to be heterosexual. We receive similar messages, but instead of looking to a man for completion, lesbians look for a woman: Prince Charming becomes Princess Charming.

There are advantages and disadvantages to this cultural training and emphasis on relationships. One disadvantage is that we may neglect ourselves by overfocusing on our relationship. We may put a partner's wants and needs first and neglect our own. We may put too much energy into making the relationship a good one and not enough into personal growth and development. But there are also advantages: Women are raised to be more emotionally intelligent than men—that is, more sensitive to a partner's needs. Because most women value couple relationships, the women in a lesbian couple likely feel a responsibility for making the relationship work. Both may expect to give as well as receive nurturing and support. Lesbian couples may have the advantage that both partners are willing to invest time and emotional energy in the relationship.

## Finding Support in a Homophobic World

We live in a society in which we may be disliked, feared, and even hated because we are lesbian, gay, or bisexual. These negative attitudes are called homophobia; when we, ourselves, believe them, they are internalized homophobia.

Suzanne Pharr, a feminist writer and activist, best articulates the bind that lesbians, gays, and bisexuals are in as we live our lives. "When we talk about homophobia, we are talking about that particular blend of . . . fear, dread, and hatred that works to keep homosexuals as a hidden (closeted) underclass of society, discriminated against, treated as deviants, sinners maliciously perverted, sick and abnormal. From those who hate us most, we receive the messages that we would be cured or killed; from those who are liberal and tolerant, we receive the messages that we must be quiet and invisible."[3] While homophobic messages may have changed in some large, urban areas, most lesbians are still confronted by these hateful attitudes.

In our daily lives we are faced with subtle and not-so-subtle oppression. Our couple relationships can be a place where we give and get support and energy to deal with the homophobia of the outside world. This need to support each other can pull a couple together, leading to the closeness and security of "you and me against the world." However, it can also strain a relationship. We can become emotionally drained. Or we may avoid expressing differences and working through conflicts because it feels too dangerous to risk losing our partner's support.

### Creating Something Bigger Than Ourselves

When two people decide to be in a couple, they produce a new entity. This creation takes on a life of its own; the couple is different from each individual woman. Their apartment may look unlike their single living spaces did, and their friendship networks may change. Often couples make something outside of themselves: a child, joint business, or remodeled house. Thus, a couple is both an invention of its partners and an inventor fueled by the couple's energies. Sometimes the process of creating brings the two women together in the first place, such as two actors working on a play. Other times the women have been partnered for years before they produce something as a team; indeed, most parents fall into this category.

*Amy and Sonia met while creating a Web page together at work. Their collaboration was so enjoyable that they began dating.*

*Pearl and Barb had been lovers for thirty years when they decided to open a bed-and-breakfast. It was a dream come true for both of them and gave a lift to their relationship as well.*

### Experiencing Transformation

In their research, Judith Wallerstein and Sandra Blakeslee found that the experience of being happily married over time transformed heterosexual partners.[4] Women and men they interviewed talked about how they became different, fuller human beings because of the invitations and demands of their spouses. They developed aspects of themselves that were dormant or unknown.

A happy, healthy relationship encourages and supports both partners to risk becoming more whole. In our experience, lesbian relationships have the same capacity for transformation. In the process of learning to give and take with each other, while not giving away our essential selves, we become a stronger "me" and a better "we."

Being part of a lesbian couple provides opportunities for welcome and challenging learning and growth. The chance to become more fully oneself while also being in a loving couple relationship is one of the most delightful of these opportunities. Differences between partners can provide excitement and stimulation, while similarities can offer warmth and comfort. Creating a successful relationship is an art form. It takes time and motivation; it requires learning and refining specific skills, and it takes patience. Like good art, a couple relationship can bring pleasure to both the creators and those around them.

## CHAPTER 2

# ৯ Relationship Stages

Every relationship is in a process of continual change. External events—moving across the country, getting a promotion, having a baby, or going back to school—require your relationship to shift and stretch. And every good relationship must also adapt to each individual's growth and development. Sometimes these changes seem painstakingly slow. Whatever the pace, in a healthy relationship we use our resources to create and shape a satisfying partnership.

As individuals, we each move through the developmental stages of infancy, childhood, adolescence, and then into the stages of adulthood. Each stage has particular characteristics, tasks, and challenges. As couples, we also move through stages in our relationships. These stages, too, have a typical sequence, tasks, challenges, and skill requirements.

Although there is a growing body of research about what makes a satisfying and enduring relationship, there is still less information available about couple development than there is about individual development. This is especially true of lesbian couples. One way to think about the model of relationship stages, which we outline here, is that it is a rough map. Like explorers, we have a general sense, rather than a complete picture, of the territory. But even a general sense can be useful. Although every relationship is unique, couples face similar tasks and challenges at different points.

As a couple, you will cycle and recycle through these stages. Many of the issues and challenges that you face are expected at particular periods in your relationship. Having even an incomplete road map can be reassuring and helpful. And there are specific strategies you can use to build a strong relationship that can withstand the inevitable stresses you'll come up against as you travel through the different stages.

## Using a Stages Model

We have integrated concepts from different sources into a six-stage model of relationship development for lesbian couples.[1] When you apply this model to your experience—past or present—several cautions are in order.

The first is that relationship development is a process and the stages blend together. No buzzer sounds to announce your passage from the prerelationship stage to the romance stage, or from the conflict to acceptance, or commitment to collaboration stages. However, even though the phases do overlap, and features of one stage can be present in another, each one does have its own special features and developmental tasks. Other cautions relate to how couples move through the phases. No couple does this perfectly smoothly; not every couple starts with the first stage; some couples never go through all the stages, or they move through them out of sequence. There is no rule about how long you may stay in any phase or how often you may recycle through a stage. Also, individual factors, such as your age, experience, comfort with your sexual orientation, and goals for the relationship, impact how this model applies.

In the course of describing these stages, we also discuss ways to create a healthy relationship. Do not be cautious about developing and using these skills and approaches. They are solidly based on research—including research on lesbian and gay couples—about what makes relationships work, and last.

### Stage One: Prerelationship

This is the "getting to know you" stage. Some people refer to it as dating; others describe it as "spending time" or "hanging out." For lesbian couples this phase is typically short. It may be a matter of months, weeks, days, or sometimes even hours, but no matter how long it lasts, the primary task at this point is making choices.

*Maria and Lucy met at a friend's party. Lucy was pleased when Maria called her to go out for coffee. They ended up talking nonstop for hours. Lucy had a wonderful time and wondered if this could develop into something.*

*She didn't want to get her hopes up too high. She worried about whether and how soon to make the next move.*

The first choice after meeting someone is deciding whether you want to invest time and energy into getting to know her. And she, of course, has to make the same decision. This first step is similar for exploring both friendship and romance. In our example, it might be useful for Lucy to look at her attraction to Maria. Is Maria attractive because she is different or because they have a lot in common? Does she remind Lucy of someone else? Does the attraction include a sexual attraction? Is Maria a solution to boredom, dissatisfaction, or emptiness? Might she be a way out of a current relationship that is over, but not yet ended?

Attractions usually integrate a mixture of motives. The decision to pursue a new relationship depends on a combination of what you like about the other person and how well she seems to meet your needs. The important task at this stage is to find out more about who the other person is and to honestly share who you are. The challenge at this point is that both of you are trying to look good to the other—to create a good impression, a positive image. As women, we are often encouraged to be whomever someone else wants us to be, so we may hold back information about ourselves, our wants, and our expectations, for fear that the other person may not like us.

Another choice at this point is deciding whether, or when, to include being sexual in the getting-to-know-you process. Although advice about sex may promote a range of strategies, from abstinence to safe sex, the guidelines women learn early about sexual behavior usually are based on relationships with men. Admonitions to "Save yourself for marriage" and "Just say no" are at the abstinence end of the continuum. Suggestions such as "Don't let him kiss you before the second date" fall in the middle—keep him interested but avoid appearing too eager or easy. At the other end of the continuum, the expectation is that you will have sex, and the focus is on protection from pregnancy and sexually transmitted diseases (STDs)—using birth control and practicing safe sex. Because these rules assume heterosexuality, we may question how well they apply to lesbians. If a woman has newly recognized herself as a lesbian, she may be confused about what rules to follow. This is quite understandable since there really are no rules except the one about protecting yourself from STDs (see Chapter Eight). The best plan is to know your own values about sex and to let these values guide your actions. Do you believe in sex only within a committed relationship? Is having sex a way for you to "break the ice" in a new relationship? Do you prefer to get to know someone pretty well before being sexual?

The key is to be honest with yourself and each other about your values, intentions, and expectations. If you decide to get to know each other better, you have to make choices: how much time to spend together, how often to see each other, and whether or not you will be sexual or whether or not you will be monogamous. Often, these choices don't feel like choices. One or both of you may slide into a "relationship" without being clear with yourself or with the other person about your wants, expectations, and intentions for the relationship. There are at least three factors that get in the way of being clear: making assumptions, mind reading, and being unsure about what is reasonable.

### Making Assumptions

Often we make assumptions about what dating or a new relationship should be like. We may neglect to share these assumptions with our new friend and then feel hurt and betrayed when she violates them.

> After Dawn met Vicky, she was not really interested in dating anyone else. Vicky, on the other hand, wanted to be free to see other people and Dawn agreed, but mostly because she did not want to appear too possessive and "not cool." However, Dawn assumed that Vicky would be sexually faithful to her. Vicky had no such expectation for herself. She assumed that the freedom to see other people included being sexual with them. When Dawn learned that Vicky had sex with someone else, she was upset and disappointed. Vicky was irritated by Dawn's reaction because she had never agreed to monogamy.

Making assumptions can extend to beliefs about behavior other than sex. If you are sure about the right way to look at something, the correct approach to take in a situation, or the best solution to a problem, then you may assume that your partner will agree with you. If she does not go along or behaves counter to your assumptions, you may take it personally and conclude that she is deliberately trying to be difficult.

### Mind Reading

Mind reading is another barrier to clear communication. Women have been taught that mind reading is a loving communication. The lesson goes like this: If you really love someone, you know what she wants and needs without her having to tell you. If she has to tell you, you have failed somehow. On the other side is the belief that, "If you really loved me, you would know what I want. If I have to ask for it, it's not as good." This tendency to mind read, or to expect your partner to read your mind, often leads to mis-understanding, disappointment, and resentment.

Particularly at this early stage in the relationship, clear and straightfor-ward communication is necessary for you both to make good choices about what you want. It is not your partner's job to read your mind (or yours to read hers) and know what you want without your telling her. Actually it is not your partner's job to meet your needs either (see Chapter Four).

## Am I Being Reasonable?

As women we sometimes hesitate to mention our expectations and wants because we are not sure if they are reasonable.

* Is it reasonable to expect a partner in a new relationship to move across the country after you have known each other for eight weeks?
* Is it reasonable to expect that she will stop seeing her old lover because you are jealous of the time they spend together?
* Is it reasonable to expect that you will share expenses equally, even though she makes a lot less money than you do?

The issue here is not what is reasonable as much as it is about what you want. There are no objective rules. What is reasonable to one person is unrea-sonable to another—it's a matter of opinion. So the best strategy is to know what you want and to share this information with the other person. Wanting is not the same as getting. The fact that you want something does not mean that your partner is obliged to do it, no matter how reasonable you think your request is. But you do have the right to ask for what you want.

After you each state what you want, you can negotiate for what will work for you both. Or, you may realize that your wants are too divergent. Discovering that you don't want the same things allows you to change your expectations and plans for the relationship. Whatever you decide, both of you are ahead in the long—and short—run because you can pursue a relationship that will more likely meet your individual needs.

Women have been taught to believe that if we give enough, we will get what we want and need. This reinforces the idea that we do not need to ask or that we shouldn't ask. We continue giving and depleting our energies while not getting what we really want and need. Eventually, we burn out and feel betrayed. It's more effective to establish a practice of acknowledging our needs and wants as early as possible in the relationship and to continue doing so. We increase the potential of getting what we want and reduce the likelihood of losing ourselves in the relationship and becoming resentful. We also get information about the other person and our fit as a couple, which helps us as we choose whether or not to continue dating.

### Stage Two: Romance

The romance stage is a gift. It shows us the possibilities of what could be. Shared dreams and fantasies, and a sense of oneness, harmony, and happiness allow us to imagine what a future together would be like.

Contact and merger are both the goal and the reality in the romance stage. There is a feeling of being completely understood, accepted, loved, and appreciated. There is also a lot of exciting, hot sex. As new lovers, you focus on each other while neglecting friends; you feel made for each other. Each of you puts her best foot forward, and potential irritations are overlooked or minimized as you bask in the glow of perfect harmony.

*Pat and Cheryl met at a support group for married lesbians. They became friends immediately and supported each other through some very difficult times as they dealt with divorce, coming out to their children, and learning to be lesbians. They were clear from the beginning that they were so different that anything other than a friendship was out of the question. And then they fell in love.*

*Rosie and Yvonne met during the summer they both worked as counselors at a camp for disabled children. Rosie was immediately attracted to Yvonne's sense of humor and her playfulness. Yvonne was taken by Rosie's warmth and confidence in handling even the most difficult kids. Needless to say, both were thrilled to discover another lesbian at the camp. Before long, they were spending almost all of their free time together, and that was not nearly enough. Yvonne canceled plans to meet friends on her weekends off. Rosie's drawing projects went untouched. They were delighted to find that they had so much in common; they liked the same sports, music, and books. Both felt wonderful about themselves, each other, and their relationship.*

A danger of the romance period is that in putting your best foot forward, you may end up trying to maintain an image, rather than being yourself. And your new partner may collude with you in this.

*Based on her comments, Tracy knew that her new lover, Rene, admired Tracy's confidence and "take charge" approach. While Tracy liked that Rene appreciated these qualities, she knew that she didn't always feel as confident as she appeared. How would Rene feel about her if she knew how scared she felt sometimes? Tracy wasn't sure she wanted to find out.*

Honesty and taking the risks to be known are required to counteract people's tendency to cling to images. The getting-to-know-you process, which continues into this stage, needs to include quirks and foibles, strengths and vulnerabilities, endearing qualities, and those that are less than endearing.

### What's the Rush?

For numerous reasons, the togetherness of the romance stage is typically very intense for lesbians. In heterosexual relationships just being physically unalike helps establish boundaries. Differences caused by cultural conditioning also keep boundaries in place. Men are trained to be independent and separate from their relationships. Women are encouraged to be relationship-focused and to want more intimacy. These gender influences in heterosexual relationships create an awareness and an expectation that lesbian couples may not experience. In lesbian couples, it may be easier for partners to assume that there are no differences because they are both women. Another factor that contributes to lesbian couples' merging at this stage is that there are no, or few, rituals of courtship; there is no "going steady," engagement, or legal marriage. Without the pacing that these rituals provide, lesbian relationships can move very quickly. Lesbians may get confused about where they are in the relationship process.

Our culture encourages us to view love, sex, and marriage, or commitment, as chain-linked. In the absence of other rituals, for lesbians sex can become the sacrament and living together the marriage vows. It is hard for us to tolerate not knowing whether a new romance will become a long-term relationship. Many of us want the security of a commitment as soon as possible. We are house hunting after we have known each other for four weeks, or we start living together when one of us leaves our current lover and needs a place to stay. We move in with our new lover and instantly are in a "Relationship."

Our primary suggestion for lesbians in the romance (or the prerelationship) stage is to slow down. Get to know the other person and be clear about wants and expectations. In the rush to be in a relationship with a capital R, you may not give yourselves enough time to assess whether the vision you have can become a reality. However, your vision of what could be may not be wrong. What *may* be invalid is the idea that it will all come to pass as easily and quickly as you hoped.

A main challenge during this stage is building togetherness *and* creating autonomy. You need to establish the psychological identity of your relationship—"what we want our relationship to be"—and, at the same time, create room for each of you to be individuals.

The following strategies, which you can initiate in this stage, serve to strengthen the friendship that is the heart of every relationship.

### Healthy Relationship Strategy #1: Enhance Your Love Maps

In his book, *The Seven Principles for Making Marriage Work,* John Gottman describes how emotionally intelligent couples are intimately familiar with each other's world.[2] His first principle for fostering such intimacy is to create and update a richly detailed love map. A love map is a way for partners to chart each other's hopes, goals, preferences, and worries as well as the significant events in each other's history.

Start creating your love map at this early stage and keep adding to and revising it. Make space in your head and your heart for your lover. Notice whether she takes her coffee with double cream, is worried about an upcoming presentation at work, or likes her back scratched lightly. Make it your business to know that she values her independence, likes her routines but wants to be more spontaneous, and regrets that she hasn't traveled more. Attention to these details is like money in the bank when the hard times hit. The more you know about each other, the easier it is to stay connected as your lives shift and change. And it makes the good times more loving and full, too.

### Healthy Relationship Strategy #2: Nurture Your Fondness and Admiration

Developing a relationship that will weather the inevitable conflicts and storms of life requires nurturing your fondness and admiration for each other.[3] The fundamental sense that your partner is worthy of being respected, honored, and liked is a critical ingredient in a satisfying relationship. And to truly have and trust having this feeling for each other, you need to know and be known. If your partner doesn't really know you, how confident can you be that she really likes and respects you? Your confidence is always tempered with the question, "But how would she feel if she really knew me?"

Of course, this cultivation of fondness and admiration for your partner needs to be ongoing throughout your relationship. Remind yourself of her sterling qualities, even as you struggle to accept her imperfections. Pay attention to what you admire and cherish about her and tell her so—frequently. Work as hard for her success, her moment, as you do for your own. Among other advantages, couples with well-developed love maps and the habit of nurturing their fondness and admiration for each other are better prepared to handle conflict.

## Stage Three: Conflict and Disillusionment

You know you have arrived at the conflict stage in your relationship when you discover that your lover is not the person you thought or hoped she was. You may look at her and wonder, "What am I doing in this relationship?" You begin recognizing your disappointment at not getting everything you want or expect to get from her. You disagree about some issue that seems fundamental. She may have let you down in some specific way. You see her flaws and imperfections, and you may feel hurt, resentful, and even betrayed. And she is going through much the same experience.

### Why Don't Some Relationships Survive This Stage?

One reason could be that the women did not get to know each other well enough in the prerelationship stage to realize their incompatibility. They may be poorly matched. As differences in temperament, values, goals, or lifestyles become apparent, they may be too great to be resolved in a mutually satisfactory way. Couples may regret that they didn't figure this out sooner; however, they can console themselves with the knowledge that they did eventually realize it.

Another reason may be that partners are not skilled—or well matched—in analyzing and handling conflicts. One or both of them may end the relationship rather than face the conflict and work through it. Their style of fighting may be so destructive and painful that breaking up seems to be the only alternative. (Improving your capacity to resolve conflicts and come to terms with differences is the subject of Chapter Seven.)

A third possibility is that the women were not attentive enough to the strategies we outlined in the previous stages. If they did not construct good love maps and were remiss in nurturing their fondness and admiration for each other, then there is little to counteract the negativity they will experience in the conflict stage. Those who have practiced these strategies are more likely to see their partner's irritating behavior against the backdrop of her admirable qualities rather than as a fatal flaw or a deliberate attempt to make their lives miserable. It's then easier to keep a clearer perspective.

### Getting Past Stuck

Each partner brings her individual values, opinions, preferences, and experiences to the relationship. It should hardly come as a surprise that even in very good relationships, couples will encounter a myriad of issues. Some conflicts are about minor sources of irritation; others are major. At times, the conflict, disappointment, or disillusionment may feel overwhelming and threaten to engulf the relationship.

Gottman distinguishes between resolvable and perpetual problems in relationships. His research indicates that 69 percent of all couple conflicts fall into the category of perpetual problems.[4] These are the ones that keep coming up over and over again.

*Lin wants to have a baby, but Mona isn't sure that she wants to be a parent.*

*Terry wants sex far more often than her partner, Toby, does.*

*Sara balances her checkbook to the penny. Her partner, Alice, forgets to record the checks she writes and almost never knows what her balance is. They fight over how to manage their joint household account.*

*Ann thinks that Theresa is too strict with their daughter. Theresa is convinced that her approach is best.*

*On the weekends, Eve wants to work together on projects around the house. Her partner, Sandy, wants to go out and have fun.*

The trick is to figure out which problems are resolvable and which ones are perpetual, resolve the first type, and learn to cope with the second kind. You can have a very satisfying and healthy relationship without resolving all of your conflicts. In fact, you can't resolve them all; no one can. Your relationship will be successful to the degree that the differences you choose— partly determined by your selection of a partner—are ones you can cope with. If you get stuck in what Gottman calls gridlock,[5] perpetual problems can kill the relationship. You keep going over and over the same ground, spinning your wheels, and getting nowhere. Eventually you are so hurt and frustrated that you emotionally disengage from each other and head toward having parallel—and lonely—lives. At that point the relationship is likely headed for a breakup.

In the conflict stage, you have an opportunity to clarify which problems are resolvable. Out of these struggles come basic ground rules and communication patterns for the relationship. You test out and establish your conflict styles, decision-making processes, communication channels, and relationship agreements. You can also identify the perpetual problems and learn how to cope with them and avoid making them worse. It's also important to learn to live with them good-naturedly and with humor.

We will talk more about how to tackle solvable problems as well as work with perpetual problems in Chapter Seven. But before we get there, we want to mention a strategy that can help in any conflict situation.

### Healthy Relationship Strategy #3: Let Your Partner Influence You

You need to take your partner's feelings and ideas into account when evaluating your opinions and making your decisions. This is what accepting her influence means. Research indicates that women in heterosexual relationships are much better at doing this than their husbands are,[6] so lesbian couples are potentially in very good shape to use this strategy. As women, our socialization inclines us toward the relationship skills that allow us to accept a partner's influence.

Letting yourself be influenced does not mean giving up everything, giving in completely, or sacrificing your integrity. When you and your partner are at loggerheads over something, you need to be willing to compromise. So find something in your partner's request that you can agree to.

*When she realized how important it was to her partner, Nora, Marnie agreed to get a second dog as long as it was an older one that didn't have to be housebroken.*

*Sue always spent Christmas Day with her parents, siblings, and extended family. Traditionally, that was the one time every year when they all got together, and her partner, Cedar, was welcome as part of the family. Cedar enjoyed spending time with Sue's family, but she wanted a Christmas with just the two of them—maybe to go away to someplace warm. They finally worked out a plan in which every third year they spent Christmas Eve with Sue's family and then left on Christmas Day for a vacation in the sun.*

As you navigate the conflict stage, you are making a place in your relationship that's safe to deal with your differences and disagreements. This requires maturity and sensitivity to one another's needs, the ability to remain connected even when you are angry, a sense of fairness, and having your internal brakes in good working order. Developing and using these capacities and skills moves you into the next stage.

### Stage Four: Acceptance

This stage can be described as the calm after the storm. There is a sense of stability—even of contentment and deep affection. If experience has taught them how to let go of unimportant differences, older women are often able to move to this point more quickly than their younger counterparts. In this stage, each partner has accepted that the other is a separate human being with shortcomings and faults as well as strengths and virtues.

The conflict stage usually involves a lot of finger pointing and blaming, and common accusations include "If only you would spend more time with me, then everything would be fine" or "I would be more affectionate if you weren't so critical."

Instead of accusing and blaming each other, partners in the acceptance stage look at themselves and try to see the ways they contribute to the situation. Disagreements and discomfort are seen as opportunities to learn about themselves and each other rather than chances to keep score. A couple at this stage more easily recognizes solvable and perpetual problems. As the same conflict, or the same pattern, arises again and again, partners can learn to address these issues more effectively. In turn, the experience of successfully managing perpetual issues and resolving solvable problems builds confidence. A couple is no longer afraid that the relationship is in danger of ending each time there is a disagreement or argument.

In the acceptance stage, you can each acknowledge the history and personal quirks you contribute to the conflicts and power struggles. You can then examine and understand how your individual past experiences connect to your pattern as a couple. This puts you in a better position to change the pattern and create the kind of partnership you want.

> Bonnie and Tameeka argued endlessly about how much Tameeka worked. Tameeka's point was that she was working hard to make a better life for them both—so they could buy their dream house. Bonnie's point was that they hardly got to see each other and "quality time" was nonexistent. Eventually, Bonnie acknowledged her fear that they would grow apart, like her own parents had when her father accepted a very demanding job. Tameeka shared how important it was for her, partly because she grew up poor, to own her own home. When they were able to stop blaming each other and look at their own contributions to the situation, they felt a lot closer.

Now this couple can get down to the business of talking about how to buy a home *and* have quality time together. The understanding and acceptance of each other in this stage allows for negotiating agreements that really address your wants and needs.

The acceptance stage is also a good time to be conscious of another of the relationship strategies. This one helps you stay connected with your partner and in so doing is both a cushion to stress and the key to long-lasting romance.

*Healthy Relationship Strategy #4: Turn Toward Each Other Instead of Away*

Movies and romance novels often paint unrealistic pictures of relationships, particularly of what makes for passion. Real-life romance is kept alive by letting your partner know on a daily basis that she is valued.

- When your partner tries to chat with you at breakfast and you aren't fully awake, do you try to respond with interest?
- When you complain about your boss treating you unfairly, does your partner offer you support and understanding?
- When you are headed out and your partner tells you she had a difficult phone conversation with her sister, do you tell her that you are running late now and ask if you could talk about it with her when you get home after the meeting?
- When you ask which earrings look best with your outfit, does your partner give you her full attention and even compliment you on how you look?

The responses to these everyday examples illustrate what we mean by turning toward your partner rather than away. Couples periodically make requests for their partner's affection, attention, humor, or support. Partners either turn toward each other or away after these requests. Turning toward each other is another way to build up an emotional bank account that serves as a cushion during stressful times. Turning toward our partner in little ways is also the key to long-lasting romance. We may think that the way to rekindle passion is a romantic dinner or vacation getaway. However, according to John Gottman's research, the real secret is to turn toward each other in little ways every day. "A romantic night out really turns up the heat only when a couple has kept the pilot light burning by staying in touch in the little ways."[7]

Often couples turn away from each other more out of distraction than malice. They take each other for granted. Realizing the importance of the little moments and paying more attention to them is often enough to solve the problem. However, turning away from each other could be a sign of a festering conflict or other problem. In that case, the underlying conflict or issue needs to be addressed (see Chapter Seven).

### Stage Five: Commitment

What does commitment in a relationship mean? To some it means a guarantee of forever or the security of feeling that "There won't be anyone else as special to you as I am."

We suggest that commitment requires making deliberate choices about your relationship and being responsible for them. It means letting go of the search for the perfect partner, the guaranteed future, the happily-ever-after. In her book, *Love Matters: A Book of Lesbian Romance and Relationship*, Linda Sutton describes her concept of a "good enough relationship." We need to let go of the idea of having a perfect relationship but not of the idea of a relationship in which the "mistakes, the imperfections, the problems are more than compensated for by the many instances in which the relationship feels right, happy or satisfying."[8] Her three ingredients for achieving this kind of relationship are:

1. You feel that your partner is truly worthy of your love.
2. You feel a deep and abiding love and connection for each other.
3. You have a clear desire to have a permanent partnership and the willingness to work through obstacles—namely, a commitment.

You don't need to have each of these ingredients present all of the time. That would be unrealistic. You just need to have them present enough of the time.

Commitment cannot come effectively before the power struggle and disappointment of the conflict stage or before the understanding of the "me" in the "we" patterns of the acceptance stage. In commitment, you accept the reality of change, you accept your partner as basically trustworthy, and you do not experience differences as threats or changes as losses. The stability and familiarity you have developed mean that the rough spots aren't so frightening. "This too shall pass" is easier for you to believe during the hard times.

This does not mean that you never have doubts. Even with commitment, a couple may feel doubt, uncertainty, or regret at a *particular* moment. You can intend to stay on the bus until the end of the line, but that does not mean you won't experience bumps along the way. Sometimes you may even want to get off altogether.

In the commitment stage, a couple comes to terms with opposing individual wants and needs. These contradictions usually turn out to be part of a larger whole. Opposites—such as autonomy versus connection, emotionality versus rationality, or spending versus saving—may appear to be housed exclusively in one or the other partner. Particularly in the conflict stage, partners can become polarized.

*Kendra wants emotionality and expression of feelings in her interactions with her partner, Robyn, but Robyn prefers a calm and objective approach to discussions.*

*Dusty thrives on lots of social time with friends and family. Her partner, Lila, likes a lot of solitude.*

During the acceptance stage, you recognize both of you have needs for each of the seeming opposites—although perhaps to a different degree. In the commitment stage, you realize that these various aspects are not mutually exclusive. It is possible for there to be both separateness and togetherness in a relationship; spending does not exclude saving; thinking as well as feeling can occur in discussions. Each partner recognizes that she needs both aspects and that the relationship requires a balance of the two. When partners become polarized, they are backed into a corner. It's much easier to negotiate getting needs met when the couple recognizes that each wants some of both, and that the relationship benefits from a balance.

*Mary Ann loves the outdoors—camping, skiing, fishing. Her partner of three years, Dora, prefers books and movies. Every time she wants to get out of the city, Mary Ann has to decide whether to encourage Dora to go or invite others who share her interests. When Mary Ann pressures Dora, they fight and it feels like they are so different they'll never be able to stay together.*

Ideally, Mary Ann and Dora can negotiate some kind of arrangement so that they are both satisfied. If they can talk about the issue openly, a resolution may be easier to reach than they think. It may be that Dora is a city person who has had very little experience of the outdoors. She doesn't enjoy camping because she has never really tried it. She may be willing to go camping under certain conditions. Mary Ann may decide that she likes skiing more than camping; she may do less camping and spend that time with Dora, doing things they both like to do, while retaining her skiing friends. They may find places that cater to their different interests. For example, they could look for a ski resort that has a movie theater nearby and cozy places to read. The key to working out a satisfactory agreement is for both women to be clear about their own wants and concerns and to express those. Then they can move toward a creative solution that will address the needs of both.

Whatever the result, the couple is searching for a balance between shared and separate interests and activities. Not allowing for disparate interests can burden the relationship with too many expectations and get in the way of each partner's individual growth. Pursuing individual interests all the time may lead to drifting apart.

Commitment means choice. It implies an expectation about the future, but it does not guarantee the outcome. You make agreements with each other. You know that these agreements can be changed and may even be broken. You don't plan on that happening, but you are aware that it might.

*Elizabeth agreed that she would relocate to wherever her partner, Maya, got into graduate school. But when the time came, she really didn't want to leave her job and friends.*

*Sharon and Rita agreed to be monogamous. Then Rita went to visit her ex in another state and was sexual with her.*

Many relationships grow stronger in the process of dealing with broken agreements. Others do not survive even one violation of an important understanding. If an agreement is broken over and over again, there are serious consequences for a relationship. The one who does not abide by her agreements may lose respect for herself, and her partner may cease to trust her at all.

### Healthy Relationship Strategy #5: Creating Liberating Structures

In the commitment stage, couples need to seek out and create arrangements—liberating structure⁹—so that they can each meet their individual needs as well as enhance their relationship.

*Faith and Sheila lived together for ten years. Then Faith got a promotion at work. The new job brought with it a one-year rotation to a city 350 miles away from their home. Their careers were very important to both women, but so was the day-to-day contact they had enjoyed for the past ten years. Fortunately, they had enough financial resources to support a solution that was a liberating structure for them. Faith rented an apartment in the new city and traveled home to be with Sheila at least every other weekend. This allowed for a balance between freedom for Faith to accept the new job, and security for them both in the relationship.*

*For the six years they had lived together, Adele and Fran split household tasks fifty-fifty. This arrangement worked well until Adele took a second job to pay off her bills. Adele then had less time and energy to keep up her end of the housekeeping bargain. Without talking about it with Adele, Fran did more than her share of housework. Adele felt grateful, but guilty, and Fran felt resentful.*

*Finally, after discussing various options, Adele and Fran decided to try a short-term agreement. They changed their split to seventy-thirty and reduced the number of household tasks. For example, instead of sweeping the kitchen every other day, they settled on once a week.*

Other liberating structures may be rituals or activities that you use to maintain or recapture passion and excitement in your relationship. After the romance stage, partners often settle into familiarity and comfort. They may take each other for granted. Variety and excitement may be missing. Liberating structures might include keeping interest alive by taking your partner out on a date, going away for a weekend, or changing your lovemaking routine.

Some couples decide to have a commitment ceremony or marriage to celebrate their relationship. Although lesbian and gay couples have been excluded from the heterosexual privilege of a legally recognized marriage in almost all states, many couples have been asking their religious groups to hold weddings and other rituals as a way of publicly acknowledging their commitment. Other couples design their own ceremonies.

*Healthy Relationship Strategy #6: Putting the Relationship First*

Judith Wallerstein and Sandra Blakeslee's research[10] on happy heterosexual couples identified a number of tasks that couples need to attend to. One of these—separating from the family of origin—applies in particular ways to lesbian couples at this juncture. Women in committed relationships need to realign themselves as partner first, daughter second. That's part of what the "primary" in primary relationship means.

It can be very difficult to do this if you are not out to your parents and family. If they expect single children to come home for holidays, they are not likely to understand or support your staying in another state with your "roommate." It is much easier to define your partner relationship as primary when your parents know about and support your being a lesbian. But even when they do not agree with your "lifestyle," you need to find ways to assert that you are a responsible adult in a committed relationship, who does not always behave the way your parents want.

*Four years into the relationship, Tanya finally took her lover home to meet her parents and brother. Tanya's parents insisted that the two women sleep separately, Tanya in her old room and Lynnell in the guest room. Neither woman wanted this separation, so Tanya told her parents that they either shared a room or would stay at a nearby motel.*

Couples in the commitment stage are working on balancing opposing needs: freedom versus security, familiarity versus variety, and stability versus change. At this point, you have come to a basic trust of each other and acknowledge that there are no guarantees. Neither of you is isolated. You clarify your needs and figure out ways to meet these needs, both within your primary relationship and in the outside world.

### Stage Six: Collaboration

Collaboration is the stage of a relationship where partners focus on creating shared meaning in their relationship and on producing something bigger than the two of them to share with the world. Couples have found that they can have conflict without ending the relationship; each partner recognizes her own part of the "we" patterns; and partners have both made a commitment to the relationship. Now they may have energy available to direct beyond the twosome into some kind of joint project.

*Yolanda and Tess took the lead in organizing a Gay/Lesbian/Bisexual/ Transgendered Pride Rally in their city.*

*Grace and Joan moved forward with their dream of opening a veterinary hospital together.*

*Melinda and Jenny decided to have a baby together.*

*Kirstin and Sima did all the work on their fixer-upper house themselves.*

Each of these couples is involved in creating something together—a political event, a baby, a business, a home. This collaboration usually enhances the relationship, but the main purpose is to produce something in the world outside of the relationship. Even though lesbians continue to experience oppression in the outside world, we still do some work together that brings the relationship into a broader context. We may choose to be in the gay and lesbian world or in the larger community. For example, Grace and Joan may locate their veterinary hospital in the heart of the gay and lesbian area of their city, or they may locate in the suburbs and not focus on developing a gay and lesbian clientele except by word of mouth. The point is that the couple is creating something together that extends beyond the relationship.

As you shift from an exclusively "us" focus to collaboration, you may go through "miniversions" of the earlier stages of the relationship. You may re-experience romance, conflict, acceptance, and commitment as you work on your project. Collaboration, then, can be like starting the relationship anew. However, this renewed relationship has a history of survival and is more resilient and stable than it was the first time around.

## CHAPTER 3

# ᛦ The Challenge of Separateness and Togetherness

In Chapter One we mentioned that there is a flowing nature between separateness, contact, and merger in healthy couple relationships. All couples must find the balance between separateness and togetherness that meets their needs. When the romance stage winds down and the individual women re-engage in their before-relationship activities and friendships, couples sometimes discover that they are out of balance. Lesbian couples may face a different challenge in balancing these needs than gay or heterosexual couples because women have been conditioned to focus on togetherness. As a result, each member of the couple may be quite sensitive to distancing behavior in her partner.[1] This can amplify the anxiety that may occur when one or both partners returns to her pre-romance life in the world.

In this chapter we explore how the experiences of separateness, contact, and merger can both stir our anxieties and also increase intimacy in our relationships. We give particular attention to expanding our capacity to calm ourselves when our feelings are uncomfortably intense, and to recognizing and making peace with the inevitable disappointments in our relationships.

## Personal Boundaries

Connection or contact is when two people touch each other in some way: physically, cognitively, or emotionally. A handshake, a heated debate, and a

shared emotional experience are all examples of contact. The only requirement for this connection is that each person have some sense of the "other-
ness" of the other person. We need to make contact with someone separate
from ourselves to experience the connection. If there are not two people present, it might be like shaking our own hand, arguing with ourselves, or standing alone watching a beautiful sunset. Fine activities, but they are not
connections with another person. What, then, makes each of us a separate
person—and capable of connection? This is where personal boundaries enter
the discussion.

Our boundary is an intangible bubble that surrounds each of us at our
core. This bubble contains our sense of self and separates what is "me" from
what is "not me."

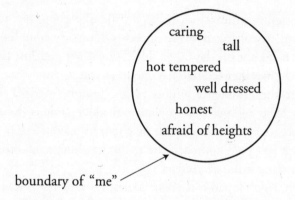

boundary of "me"

The outside world, skills and traits I don't have, other people, and even
their thoughts and feelings about me are all "not me." Someone who is not
afraid of heights is different from me—not me.

When two people are involved in a couple relationship, it is rather like
two bubbles moving through the flow of contact, merger, and separateness.
One bubble contacts the other, edge meets edge, differences are recognized
and appreciated (or not). In the merger experience, there is often the wonderful feeling of "losing oneself." However, the boundaries of the individual
bubbles remain intact, rather than disintegrating, even when the couple is
merging for a time.

Separateness looks like this: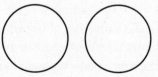

Contact looks like this: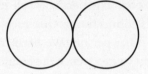

Merging looks like this: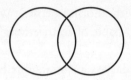

We think of initiating intimacy as being a little like going out to the backyard fence (point of contact between the two boundary bubbles) and calling over to your neighbor on the other side. Sometimes you just talk to the neighbor about the weather (contact); sometimes you intensely focus on each other and share the experience almost as one person (merger); other times you might say hello and go back to your individual gardens (separateness). In each instance you have invited your neighbor to make contact, with no guarantee that she will even approach the fence, let alone talk with you. This is the risk of inviting intimate contact.

If a person has not developed clear boundaries, it's as if her bubble has weak spots. When this is true, the motion between contact, merger, and separateness can be uncomfortable, even terrifying. People may then unconsciously try to keep the relationship in one place to minimize their anxiety. (It is important to acknowledge that other cultures may define good boundaries in very different ways. In some places the boundary line is drawn around the entire family, so to someone raised in white America it might look like a person from another perspective does not have good boundaries. Someone from a less individualistic society might see our definitions of boundaries as selfish or isolationist.)

Boundaries and the sense of self begin to develop early in life. The most accepted theories in Western psychology posit that healthy development is supported by meeting a child's physical needs—food, sleep, shelter, touch, and warmth—as well as tending to her psychological needs—love, nurturance, limit setting, and mirroring of behavior and feelings. A child's healthy development of boundaries can be violated by a range of experiences, from physical and sexual abuse to having to parent her parents and being treated as an extension of a parent. How society treats different groups of people, i.e., in racist or sexist ways, can also make it more challenging to develop a solid sense of self.

When boundaries are not well developed, the person feels vulnerable to pressures from both inside and outside. Outside forces include the expectations and demands of others, which the individual may feel unable to resist or respond to. Pressures from the inside typically are feelings. If her boundaries are not resilient, an individual may not trust that they will contain her feelings, especially intense ones. In extreme cases, she may avoid feeling as much as possible, for fear of "blowing up" or being overwhelmed.

When an individual does not trust her boundaries, she may avoid intimate relationships entirely. She may not want to risk letting anyone inside; it feels too risky, too vulnerable, too exposed. At the other extreme, a person may ease the discomfort of shaky boundaries by merging with a partner and blurring the differences between them. The partnership allows a person with incomplete boundaries to feel whole temporarily. But the wholeness is an illusion, because that person can feel complete in a relationship only when the boundaries are blurred.

This sense of wholeness involves being fused, rather than being able to move. If partners are fused, what one woman feels is experienced by the other as her own feeling, and what one does is regarded by the other as a reflection on her. Partners become emotional extensions of each other. A woman in this situation may see her only options in this relationship as muffling her own wants enough to dampen her anxiety (fear, hurt, anger, etc.) or getting her partner to change. Because of her anxiety, she is not able to allow the flow of contact, merger, and separation that naturally comes with having different feelings from her partner. This may translate into being afraid of losing her lover or herself. In most cases, the lack of fluidity builds up so that one or both of the partners has to break out of the relationship to retrieve a sense of self or safety.

### Calming Yourself

What should you do when your feelings seem to be threatening to burst your bubble? Since feelings really cannot break down your boundary walls and since emotions are always present in life and relationships, you have to develop your ability to tolerate your feelings. Self-soothing, self–hand holding, self-calming, getting a hold on yourself, or not becoming reactive all refer to ways to contain uncomfortable feelings and still move on with what you want to do. (When we use "contain" in this context we are referring to the ability to notice and experience an emotion without having to take action to get rid of it.) Whatever you choose to call it, the goal of calming yourself is to be able to engage constructively with someone you love—even when it stirs up strong feelings.

For instance, if Gert is anxious because her partner is working with a very attractive woman, yet everything she knows tells her that her partner is faithful and very in love with her, Gert needs to find a way to calm herself. Otherwise her feelings may leak into the relationship and cause damage. She can self-soothe by reminding herself that her partner is faithful and has worked with attractive women before. She can take a walk or a relaxing bath, do housework, read love letters her partner has written her, or any other activity that helps calm the worry. Gert can ask herself what the worst outcome could be and remind herself that she can survive even a breakup, although she might be in a lot of pain. If she is not sure she could survive, Gert needs help to become secure enough to know that she can survive. She may need to talk about her anxiety with her partner as a soothing technique and ask for reassurance that nothing is going to happen. Talking to her partner may also bring them closer together as Gert risks being vulnerable and her partner listens without being defensive or dismissive.

In the context of separateness and togetherness, self-soothing is the ability to calm your feelings when your partner moves closer or farther away emotionally. If your anxiety signals a problem that you two need to discuss, and you can self-soothe enough to talk about it, you are more likely to be emotionally present for that conversation. If your reactive feeling is triggered by the past and is not really about your partner, self-soothing and containing gives you time to figure out what is really going on. If you cannot hold on to yourself emotionally and you become reactive, it is very difficult to interact constructively with your partner.

How close or distant you are physically from a partner is often a catalyst for the internal pressure of your feelings. When your partner (or you) moves away, such as going out of town for work, or moves closer, like coming home from visiting her family, you may feel comfort, distress, or nothing. How secure you are in yourself and your ability to calm your anxiety determines the appropriateness of your reaction to this movement. Your feelings and reactions need to match the reality of what is happening. It is important to sort this out with your partner so that your actions are about the present. If you discover that your reaction is based on memory from a hurtful past, you are in a better position to heal.

*Jeri used to get freaked out when her partner would call and say she'd be late from work. Somehow it always felt like a rejection. Finally, she worked up the courage to tell Marta what was happening and asked directly if Marta was trying to tell her something. Marta reassured her that her job was just unpredictable and that she actually really missed Jeri when she had to come home later than usual.*

As adults we can learn to strengthen our boundaries and calm ourselves enough to trust our capacity to contain our feelings. This can happen in a relationship with a partner who is not afraid of closeness and distance. With her we get to practice over time being a separate individual who can be together and apart in an intimate relationship, survive, and even thrive.

## Disappointment

One of the most challenging and least talked-about feelings is disappointment. A crucial task each member of a couple faces is adjusting to disappointing her partner and being disappointed in her. One colleague of ours says getting to know each other, getting used to the disappointments, and learning how to live with each other are the three big-ticket items for committed couples who live together.[2] It is much easier to work on these sequentially and not all at once.

Disappointment is a feeling like anger, happiness, sadness, or excitement and, as with all feelings, arises in relationships that last more than a few months. In many families disappointment is a closet feeling. People are often so uncomfortable with being let down that before we recognize it, disappointment changes into hurt, anger, or some other more familiar feeling. (What we change it into depends on each person's own comfort range.) Some parents punish their children with "I'm so disappointed in you" or "You've disappointed me, and I'm so hurt I don't know what I'll do." As a result many of us grow up terrified of feeling or causing disappointment. We can tie ourselves in knots trying to avoid behaving in a way that will let down our partner. It does not take too long before the disappointments take on mythical power. They can come to represent a fatal flaw in our partner (she can't meet my needs). Or out of our fear of being let down we dampen our feelings and curtail our behavior. Either way the relationship is in trouble.

Disappointment ranges from mild to severe, and it comes from three sources. When we expect something with good reason and it does not happen, we are let down. When we expect something to happen with no good reason, we get disappointed. When we hope or long for something and do not get it, we get disappointed.

*Janel and her partner had agreed to meet for lunch at 1:00 P.M. Mackie still had not shown up at 1:30 P.M. Since Janel had been looking forward to the time together, she was very disappointed and a little worried about Mackie.*

*Kristin had expected to run into her lover at the hospital where Carol worked. Kristin had had an unexpected break in her work routine and had thought how fun it would be to surprise Carol with a latte. She was very disappointed to find that Carol was out visiting a patient.*

*Charlene wanted so badly for her girlfriend to enjoy cooking dinner together but Donna did not like sharing the kitchen with another cook. Charlene was disappointed that the woman she loved did not share her passion for twosome cooking.*

It is important to learn to recognize when you are disappointed and to get support for it. In the first example, support could come in a variety of ways. Janel could name the disappointment, allow herself to feel it, and go to a friend for support. Her friend could sympathize without making it a bigger issue than it really is. Support is neither siding with the disappointee that the disappointer is terrible nor talking a person out of her feelings. It is acknowledging the disappointment as reasonable and supporting the person as she feels it.

In the second example Kristin could self-soothe and support herself by recognizing her feeling of disappointment and reminding herself it was a good idea anyway. Carol could be supportive by saying, "Great idea, sorry it didn't work." Charlene, in the third example, could identify her disappointment and remind herself it is okay to want what she wants. She could share her feelings of being let down with Donna, who could be supportive by listening nondefensively.

Support for disappointment, whether coming from oneself or another person, is about naming the emotion, offering validation, and not trying to make it go away or turning it into a disaster. Often, lovely intimate contact happens in the process of sharing and getting support after being let down.

*Charlene told Donna how different their living together was from her fantasy, especially about the cooking differences. Donna put down the spoon and listened to Charlene. She said that it was hard for her to disappoint Charlene, but that she did love her and loved having her keep her company in the kitchen. Both of them felt very close to each other even while they acknowledged the difference between them.*

When we are able to calm our anxiety as we move through contact, merger, and separateness and can just feel disappointed when our partner does not match our expectations, we are freed up to acknowledge the differences between us as just that—differences. This creates the potential for deeper connections with each other.

## Accepting Differences

There are many ways to experience the particular connection that we call intimacy. In Chapter One we defined intimacy as being close, sharing, and feeling loved, understood, accepted, known, and appreciated. Sometimes this translates into feeling warm and cozy, and other times it doesn't. Intimacy can feel hot and agitated, and it can also include negotiating differences and fighting. Many of us were reared to believe that confrontation and intimacy could not go together. Consequently, we may avoid confrontation out of discomfort or fear of losing what closeness we have. To comfortably experience warmth and coziness as well as argue and disagree (at least most of the time) we must be able not only to be ourselves, but also to allow our partner to be herself. This capacity for acceptance depends in part on the ability to tolerate separateness and togetherness.

Our acceptance cannot be conditional on our partner being who we want her to be, or on her doing what we want her to do. However, acceptance does not necessarily mean changing what we value or liking everything about our partner's behavior. For example, we may not like it that she hates concerts and never wants to go hear music with us, but we can acknowledge and understand her feelings and attitudes without judging or putting her down for having them. To meet our own needs, we can arrange to go to these events with other people or by ourselves. In accepting our partner for who she is, we can give her understanding, freedom, and support for being herself. We can encourage our partner to grow and change, but in ways she chooses for herself, rather than in ways that we might want. We need to resist trying to make our partner be the way we want her to be. We have every right to have wants that are different from our partner's, but we do not have the right to make her live by them.[3]

Being comfortable with ourselves and resisting the urge to try to change our partner requires the ability to self-soothe. We need to find a way to let our partner's dislike of classical music be about her taste in music, not an indication that something is wrong with her or the relationship. A quick way to evaluate whether our discomfort is an early warning sign of a potentially serious problem with the relationship is to ask whether we would be bothered if this were a friend, not a lover. We tend to be less anxious about our differences from a friend than about a partner's.

> *During the first year of Louise and Pam's relationship, Louise felt more loved, understood, and cared for than ever before. She had never loved anyone as much as she loved Pam, so it was very confusing to her when she found herself being critical of Pam. She never mentioned anything out loud, but she found herself thinking that Pam didn't take good enough care of herself or care enough to dress up when they went out. Louise felt deeply disappointed, and even betrayed, because of their differences.*

Louise is having a crisis of disappointment, which surfaced when the romance period ended and she again saw her partner more clearly. The wonderful sense of connection she felt the first year was threatened by the reemergence of her awareness of their differences. All relationships have disparities between partners, and even when there is little initial difference, the women often change as the relationship progresses.

In her relationship with Pam, Louise has blurred the boundaries between herself and her lover. She is very concerned about how Pam appears to other people. If others think Pam is sloppy, Louise feels vulnerable and devastated. It is as if Pam is an extension of Louise, rather than a separate person. In Louise's eyes, what Pam says and what others think of her is a reflection on Louise, rather than on Pam. The only option Louise can see at this point is to get Pam to change.

However, if Louise can calm herself enough to remember that Pam has always dressed this way, and that *she* thought Pam was attractive the way she dressed, then Louise has the chance to move toward accepting Pam as she is. Louise can then view their two styles as differences rather than right and wrong. It might free Louise up to talk to Pam about her worries and even to ask Pam to get dressed up for a special evening on the town. Pam may then feel less defensive and able to support Louise's disappointment, and she may dress up for Louise occasionally.

Neil Jacobson and Andrew Christensen's research supports our experience that confrontation or disappointment that is handled in respectful ways can actually enhance the quality of intimacy a couple experiences.[4] The process of exploring the differences brings the couple closer together as they feel compassion and empathy for and from each other.

## When Do You Need Professional Help?

Struggling with allowing your partner to be different is not necessarily a sign of needing counseling. It is frequently a developmental issue that couples learn to master as they work on their relationship. You may benefit from couples counseling if you have tried and not succeeded at becoming more accepting of your differences.

However, when your sense of self and ability to trust your own boundaries has been seriously damaged, you may need to seek professional help. If you find yourself repeatedly being left or leaving relationships because of intense discomfort with closeness or distance, it may be a clue that it is time to seek such help. If you find yourself in relationships where you feel verbally or physically abused, or where you are abusive, it is definitely time to get professional help.

In focusing on increased understanding of and comfort with the normal fluctuations in emotional distance that occur in relationships, we have included two skills—self-soothing and coming to peace with disappointment. These are essential for accepting the differences inherent between partners and increasing the chances of meaningful intimacy. But even with understanding, good skills, and a fairly high success rate of translating skill into action, couples often need to intentionally create a climate that offers a good chance for that intimacy to thrive.

## CHAPTER 4

# ❧ Creating a Climate for Intimacy

Chapter Three provided a discussion about the impact of personal boundaries on a person's comfort as she moves closer and farther away from another person. We offered ideas that might help a woman manage her discomfort with those feelings so she can move through the ebb and flow of relationships. In this chapter, we talk about ways couples can build on this knowledge and turn their relationships into vessels of continuing growth for both individuals and the couple. This requires that both women work on the relationship so that intimacy has a chance to flourish. At times, deepening intimacy means risking emotional vulnerability, and at others, it requires a concrete effort such as spending quality time together.

## Trust and Openness

Possibly the hardest part of building intimacy is developing trust and risking openness. Intimacy requires taking risks: revealing our thoughts and feelings and being open to hearing our partner's ideas and emotions. We need to say honestly what we feel and think, and share the range of our thoughts and feelings, not only the positive ones.

*In trying to be open with her partner, Ling was not sure just how honest to be. Should she tell Carina every one of her thoughts and feelings, even the negative ones that might upset them both?*

Ling faces a dilemma. She wants to be honest but she is afraid of hurting Carina's feelings and losing her trust. One guideline that Ling can use in this situation is to ask herself, "How persistent is this thought or feeling?" If it is persistent, she had better express it. To fail to do so could damage the relationship. But the key factor here is persistence. Infrequent, fleeting memories about good times with an old lover do not qualify as persistent. Dissatisfaction with things that Carina cannot change, which only bother Ling on rare occasions, may also not fit the persistence criterion. By using this as a guideline, Ling can be honest without abusing Carina's feelings.

Any sharing or openness that creates even a little vulnerability is a risk. While learning about our partners and helping them understand us, we risk being criticized or not having our positive feelings returned. Particularly if we are sharing a fear, insecurity, or weakness, we may feel extremely vulnerable. It is easier to take these risks if we trust that our partner will not hurt us on purpose, that she will keep our confidences and will try to understand, rather than judge. If we feel judged or punished when we disclose our thoughts and feelings, we will probably withdraw.

*Francie remembered an incident that was the beginning of the end of her relationship with Ellen. When Francie got the teaching job she had always wanted, she was very pleased and excited. However, she soon began to feel frightened and inadequate. When she tried to talk to Ellen about her feelings, Ellen dismissed it all by saying, "You're making a big deal out of nothing. Your fears are childish. You'll do fine at the job." Francie felt so hurt and belittled that she vowed she would never share important feelings with Ellen again. As Francie distanced herself Ellen also withdrew to protect herself from the anxiety stirred up by Francie's withdrawal, and eventually they broke up.*

This story could have had a very different outcome. Ellen could have responded with acceptance and understanding instead of putting down Francie for her feelings. Francie could have confronted Ellen about how hurt she was by Ellen's response and requested different behavior from her. Ellen could have talked to Francie about Francie's pulling back. Either partner could have enhanced their intimacy, rather than damaging it.

Healthy intimacy requires ongoing individual and combined effort, because partners are each growing as individuals even as their relationship matures. Few of us are completely comfortable with ourselves, or with others, without some significant work on ourselves.

As we learn to express ourselves openly and take risks that invite intimacy, a paradoxical process occurs. Obviously, the more we learn to trust each other the closer we can become, but it often stirs up very strong feelings. This is true for many of us as we experiment with being more separate than we were in the initial stages of the relationship. As we move back and forth along the continuum of togetherness and separateness, it can get quite terrifying. Susie Orbach and Luise Eichenbaum, in their book *What Do Women Want,* call this the fear of engulfment and the fear of abandonment.[1] Many problems in intimate relationships are related to these fears.

When partners feel close to each other, we may fear being overwhelmed and losing our identity and sense of self. This may lead us to withdraw. One or both women may also pull back because feeling close activates our fear of being alone. Realizing how close and attached we are can be frightening. We worry about being left, about not surviving without our partner, and about being devastated by rejection and abandonment.

But by definition, intimacy means opening ourselves up, sharing all parts of ourselves, exposing our dreams, feelings, and weaknesses. It implies vulnerability and risk, which can cause different reactions.

*Rosa avoided getting close because she was afraid that a partner would find out who she "really was" and would reject her.*

*Tina held herself back from sharing very much with her lover, Becky, because she didn't trust that Becky wouldn't use it against her sometime.*

*Abby knew intimacy was linked somehow to her sense of control. She was not sure how it worked, but she knew that she felt very uncomfortable and tense in a close relationship. It was as if she were "out of control."*

These vignettes are good examples of situations where self-soothing could help. If the women could calm themselves enough to risk vulnerability, they might discover that their partners really weren't trustworthy, and they could use that information to decide whether to stay in that relationship. At the same time, the three women would also find out that they can survive without the support they were hoping for. On the other hand, they might find that their partners were able to meet them halfway for a deeper connection. This is growth. We take risks, move closer (or farther), and get scared. Then we calm ourselves in order to stay as close as we can even though we are scared. This allows us to discover whether our trust in ourselves and each other is justified. When we realize that we both have survived the vulnerability that we risked, we feel even closer and have found greater intimacy. The cycle then begins again. The joy of relationships is that we can do this forever.

## Balance of Power

Shared intimacy also requires attention to the balance of power in the relationship. If one partner makes all the decisions, controls such important aspects of the relationship as money, conversation, or sex, or is looked up to by the other but does not look up to her partner, the balance of power is not equitable. There are real-world power differences such as skin color, gender, ability, education, financial resources, physical size, and age. There are also interpersonal power differences such as ability to express feelings, comfort with oneself, and verbal quickness. It is vital that couples become aware of and discuss the impact all of these differences have on each of them and on their relationship.

> *Hootoksi and Marcia were having a fight about whether the waiter's inattention to Hootoksi was because she was Indian. Marcia finally realized that this was the same conversation they had been having for months. Hootoksi wanted Marcia to realize that racism is alive and well in lesbian and gay communities. Marcia had been very uncomfortable acknowledging that being white gave her more privilege even among fellow queers. She was beginning to get it.*

When the power balance is not equitable, resentment builds. In addition, the relationship could be ripe for the development of unhealthy dependency. Statements such as "I cannot live without you," "You are my whole life," or "If you ever left, I might as well kill myself" are examples of serious problems. If one partner gives up her own growth because her partner is attending to all the details of living, one of the women may end the relationship.

As is the case with insecure boundaries, power imbalances interfere with the natural flow of intimacy, including the contact, merger, and separateness phases. Lesbians are not usually comfortable maintaining a close connection with someone who is much more, or much less, powerful than they are. In *American Couples* Philip Blumstein and Pepper Schwartz wrote that their research showed lesbian couples to be more concerned about equal power balances than married and cohabiting heterosexual couples and gay couples.[2]

Power balances in relationships are continually changing. One person may be more powerful than the other at various times and for different reasons. This is normal. However, when an imbalance is not acknowledged or not managed in a way that is respectful of both partners, a problem exists.

We mentioned in Chapter Two that John Gottman and his colleagues have found in their research that one of the crucial variables in the health of a relationship is the ability to influence one's partner—a form of power sharing. They found that when a member of a couple cannot influence the other's thoughts and feelings, the relationship is damaged.[3] The foundation necessary to being able to accept your partner's influence is respect. Without mutual respect intimacy is virtually impossible to achieve.

> *Rebecca had just finished ranting about her interaction with the car mechanic. She was getting ready to call the garage when her partner, Callie, had another suggestion. She reminded Rebecca how well it had worked before when Rebecca had taken a few extra hours to think through how to handle an angry situation. Even though Rebecca was furious, she realized that Callie was right. She thanked her and went off to mow the lawn and think. Callie felt good about their interaction and important in her contribution to the outcome.*

## Signs of Caring

Intimacy requires that each partner understand what the other needs and wants to feel valued and appreciated. Then it is easier to provide what is most important. These signs of caring do not have to be expensive or on a large scale, but they do need to be personal and frequent. Feeling close is enhanced by showing we care—often and in a variety of ways.

Sometimes we do not recognize the signs of love and caring given by our partner, because we have a different way of expressing them. And the signals of appreciation and respect we offer may go unnoticed, because they do not fit our partner's ideas of intimacy.

> *Angelina and Peggy both were frustrated. Each felt that she was not getting what she wanted and was not feeling valued and supported. Neither knew quite what was going wrong. When Peggy was upset about something, she wanted Angelina simply to listen to her. Instead, Angelina offered suggestions and gave advice, and Peggy felt criticized and cut off. Typically, she got angry with Angelina for not listening, and then Angelina felt hurt, because her efforts to show Peggy that she cared were unappreciated. The problem was that Angelina's signs of caring were what she would have wanted to receive if*

*she were upset. Angelina liked to get advice and suggestions when she was upset about something. She, in turn, got frustrated with Peggy's response to her. Instead of helping her solve the problem, Peggy worked at getting Angelina to talk about her feelings.*

These two really care about each other, but they go about showing it in exactly the wrong way for their partner. When Peggy gets upset, she wants "feeling talk," so that was what she provided for Angelina. However, Angelina wants "action talk" when she gets upset, and offered that to Peggy. In this example, neither woman got what she wanted, and each felt rebuffed and invalidated in her attempts to show she cared. Eventually they may stop trying to get support from each other. This, of course, will just make things worse, because the less we offer the less we receive.

Peggy and Angelina each made the mistake of assuming that her partner wanted the same thing that she, herself, wanted. Like many of us, they gave what they wished to receive, not what the other wanted. When it comes to showing we care, the golden rule needs to be changed. Rather than treating our partner as we wish to be treated, we need to treat her the way she wants to be treated. If we don't know, we have to ask her. We need to listen respectfully to our partner's requests and to notice which of our behaviors pleases or displeases her. Because our previous lover liked to be left alone when she was angry does not mean that our current partner wants the same. It is essential to share and check out what makes each of us feel loved, cared for, and appreciated. Peggy and Angelina could resolve their frustration by talking with each other about how they want the other to respond to them. If Angelina learned to listen to Peggy's feelings, and if Peggy responded with practical suggestions and advice for Angelina, this issue would no longer be a problem.

The companion behavior to listening to your partner is being clear with her about what *you* want. No one is a mind reader, so you need to figure out what works for you and tell her. Since none of us is perfect at always knowing what we want, especially when we are beginning to learn what that is, we need to give ourselves permission to change our mind about what works for us. Many of us don't know what we want until we get what we *don't* want. When that happens, we can say "oops" to our partner and give her our next best guess. Even the fumbling around creates openings for intimacy to grow.

## Quality Time

Another way to build intimacy is to spend quality time together. Some women complain about being so busy that they have to make appointments to see each other. If this is what is required, then we should do it. We can make these times into "dates" and keep them. We risk losing intimacy by taking the relationship for granted and by putting our energy everywhere else. Work, school, chores, kids, and other demands on our time too often take priority.

Some couples make sure they check in with each other, even briefly, about the events of the day. One way to structure this is for the women to take turns listening to each other without having a dialogue about what the speaker is saying. The listener is there to sympathize and support, not to challenge or educate her partner. In that process the listener learns more about her partner and the speaker feels cared for. (This exercise not only encourages intimacy but also is a very useful tool for minimizing how much the pressures from the world contaminate and stress the couple relationship.[4] We can take turns listening to each other at the beginning of our time together in the evenings or weekends.)

> Charlie felt disappointed and discouraged. Newly launched as a real estate agent, she thought she had sold her first house and had been sure her career change was going to be a success. Then the deal fell through, and all Charlie could think about was going back to selling shoes, nine-to-five. But when she got home that day, she was touched and reassured by her partner Renee's reaction. Renee listened to Charlie talk about her disappointment and fears. She didn't try to fix anything or change the subject, even though she had some ideas that might help in future deals. She just allowed Charlie to talk out her feelings.

Quality time is also needed for relaxation together. This includes time for entertainment and working together on enjoyable projects as well as time for communicating deeper thoughts, feelings, and concerns.

Couples usually need to plan time for sex, too. After the first six months to a year sex is less likely to be spontaneous. Many couples find that the more they keep sex in their lives, even in a scheduled way, the more likely it is for them to have sex, period. Not all of us need or want sex in our lives but if we want it in our relationship, we will probably have to make it a priority. The particular intimacy sex brings to a relationship is best kept alive by practicing it, rather than just thinking about it.

## Shared Goals and Interests

Shared goals and interests can also increase intimacy. They help create the support that gives a sense of continuity and purpose to the relationship.

This extra support enables us to keep the periodic hassles and boredom of daily routines in perspective.

When we know that our efforts are directed toward mutually agreed-upon goals, it is easier to tolerate occasional neglect from a partner.

*Jesse found it easier to bear Andrea's long overtime hours because she knew that the situation would last only until their bills were paid off. It was important to both of them to get out of debt.*

*Alinda and Mary found that having shared vacations to plan and look forward to helped them survive the drudgery of their jobs at the factory.*

*Valerie and Roberta tried to take a class or to be involved in political-action work together each year. Last year they started a support group for women of color. They found that while their separate interests added variety to their relationship, they also needed common activities and interests to enjoy together.*

Shared goals and projects are a sign of commitment. They provide a feeling of stability and a shared future. Each investment of time, money, and energy that benefits both partners is a contribution to the future of "we."

However, too much togetherness can be as destructive to healthy intimacy as too little. A couple can overdose on togetherness and feel smothered. Both partners need to be separate people, with their own interests, lives, and identities. The two women can then come together in their shared goals and interests with energy and excitement about being together.

*Aretha felt much more positive about her relationship with Myra than she had about any of her previous relationships. She was sure that this was because she had forced herself to live alone after her last relationship in order to become more self-sufficient. She always used to feel that she was missing something in herself. She needed someone else to feel complete. Now, having lived on her own, she could feel like an equal in her relationship with Myra. She had become less needy, less dependent, and less controlling. Now when the two of them made decisions about how to invest their money, Aretha took for granted that she had as much say as Myra.*

As you work to build and enhance intimacy in your relationships, some questions to ask yourself are:

- Do I share my thoughts, feelings, and dreams openly and honestly with my partner on a regular basis?
- Do I ask my partner questions, express interest, and encourage her to share her thoughts and feelings?
- Do I update my love map periodically?
- Do I judge or criticize my partner's feelings as unreasonable, overreactions or just plain wrong?
- Do I undermine my partner's trust by lying, revealing her confidences to other people, or using her disclosures against her in a hurtful way?
- Do I disagree out loud in a respectful way that invites conversation about the issue?
- Do I practice self-soothing when I am anxious and would rather get my partner to change her behavior?
- Do I look for ways to foster my own personal growth?
- Do I look for ways to foster our growth as a couple?

There is no easy path to intimacy. It takes attention, intention, and time. We must attend to what is and isn't working in our relationship and find ways to improve our intimate connection and act on them. We also need to make time to be together so our work can produce results. We learn how to be in a long-term relationship by being in one. There is no exam we can study for and pass. We learn how to be intimate by practicing being intimate!

## CHAPTER 5

# Understanding Differences

Novelists, poets, and songwriters do not agree on how intimate relationships get started. Some believe in love at first sight; others, that love follows getting to know each other. Social scientists are as blind as lovers when it comes to knowing why two particular individuals fall in love. One psychological theory is that opposites attract, and another is that similarities do. Perhaps in our partnerships we require enough similarity for some common ground and enough difference for interest and challenge.

Differences can enrich a relationship and the lives of each partner. However, most of us are not always energized by these disparities. During our first few years together, when we are learning about each other and sorting out the solvable from the unsolvable problems, negotiating our dissimilarities may require a lot of energy. When we first get together, frequently our early impression is how alike we are—in interests, communication styles, sex drives, and so on. While there is some truth to that perception, it is far more likely that the differences outweigh the similarities.[1] And as the relationship progresses, even the small differences can expand.

In a relationship certain differences between partners matter more than others. For example, eye color is usually less of an issue than age. Some differences, such as values and spiritual paths, reflect choices we make as we grow up. Others, including age, class, and race, are part of the biological makeup or background of who we are. Still others are specific to the dynamics of being in a relationship—how close or intimate we like to be and how we handle power.

All of these dissimilarities require attention if they are to be assets instead of liabilities. Two concepts underlie how differences can enhance a relationship. First, partners can become more intimate, rather than more distant, as they deal with difference. Second, a growing body of research supports that accepting your partner as she is and not struggling to change her are critical to enhancing intimacy.[2]

It's important to remember that stress plays a crucial role in how couples respond to their differences. Partners can happily tolerate great dissimilarities when they are rested, have good emotional and social support (individually as well as for the couple relationship), and are enjoying their lives. Differences can seem overwhelming when partners are stressed. It is then that couples commonly focus on their disparities as the problem instead of identifying and managing the original stressor.

## Class

In the United States, many people deny that class exists. We emphasize individuality and individual responsibility so much that we largely ignore the influence that class attitudes and values have on a person's behavior. We are all influenced by our class background—the class we came from as well as the one we identify with. We are also affected by the class our parents came from and the one they identified with.

Class refers not only to income and education but also to a world view—whether we believe we have power in the world and in our lives, or not. Being middle or upper class is often associated with a sense of entitlement, a belief in one's rights, and an optimism about the future. This perspective influences attitudes about work, money, taking risks, and setting goals. For example, the upper class often makes money on money—by investing rather than by working. For many middle-class people work is something that, even if it is not lucrative, should be emotionally fulfilling. From a working-class perspective, work is for survival. If you like it, if it is creative or expressive, or if it's what you really want to do, then it isn't really work. Historically, for working-class people, the availability of work and working conditions have been under someone else's control.

*Josie and her partner, Wa-chang, realized finally that some of their worst fights happened because they were from different class backgrounds.*

*Josie's family had been the "poorest family in the parish." Wa-chang came from an upper-middle-class background; she could not remember wanting for anything.*

*One of their ongoing battles had been about Josie's job. Wa-chang wanted her to quit and start her own business. Wa-chang believed in Josie's talents as a clothes designer and had faith that people would beat a path to her door once they found out how good she was. Josie was not convinced. She thought Wa-chang was naive about making a business work and certainly did not understand Josie's feelings.*

When Josie and Wa-chang began to comprehend their class differences, they came to appreciate some of the causes of their conflict. Josie was not being stubborn, difficult, and ungrateful for Wa-chang's support. And Wa-chang was not just a naive, foolhardy risk-taker. Each had been approaching the issue from her own class perspective and failing to appreciate her partner's.

Wa-chang grew up believing that the future was bright and that she deserved having things turn out well. It is relatively easy for her to take risks. For Josie, planning for the future, not to mention taking risks, is somehow asking for trouble. The same risk seems bigger for someone who does not have that confidence, which may be based on class background. "Going for it" is much easier when you are confident that things will turn out well.

Because many working-class families are poor, this affects later attitudes toward money and security. As adults, some people become very frugal, as Josie did. Others figure they might as well enjoy it while they have it and spend their money before it is wiped out by the inevitable future disaster. The idea of choosing to be poor may be regarded as pretentious—or even hypocritical—by the working class. Trying to get along with one coat for environmental reasons, keeping the heat down, and walking around with layers of sweaters on when you can afford to keep the house warm, or buying used clothes when you don't have to may all appear ridiculous from a working-class perspective.

*Possessions had never meant much to Billie. All through her twenties she prided herself on the fact that she could put everything she owned in a foot locker, and there was no problem shutting it, either. Not having a lot of stuff made her feel free. She hated the way advertising duped people into buying things they didn't need. Billie refused to have any credit cards and thought people who did were asking for trouble. She preferred to keep her living style simple and even spare. "Less is beautiful," she was fond of saying.*

*Her partner, Vera, had grown up poor and hated it. She finally had a good job and wanted to indulge her longing for comfort and convenience. She liked having a cell phone, and if she had to take out a large loan to afford the car she wanted, so be it.*

*These two had many heated discussions about how Vera spent money. What always got to Vera was when Billie started lecturing her about materialism and consumerism. Vera figured that she was entitled to a little comfort, and she wished that her partner would "get off her high horse."*

While Billie and Vera may never agree about "things," they can come to understand each other better and to problem-solve specific issues related to class differences. Some of these will be solvable and others may be perpetual. (See Chapter Seven.)

For other couples, issues relate more to growing up with money than without it.

*Diana could have lived comfortably on the income from a trust fund left by her grandmother. She desperately wanted to spend her time writing poetry but felt guilty about it. Why should she be able to write full-time when other women in her writers' support group could not afford to? Diana's partner, Estelle, was understanding, up to a point, But sometimes Estelle grew tired of hearing about it. Estelle was very practical and could not see why Diana was working at a job she hated when she didn't have to. For Estelle it was as simple as that.*

Probably the main problems in cross-class relationships arise when the partners assume that each knows what the other thinks or means. Since class differences may not be obvious, partners may fail to comprehend that their perspectives and behaviors are a result of these differences. They may think that a family feels discomfort with a partner because she is a lesbian, when at least as much of the discomfort is because she is from a different class.

When there are relationship issues in areas such as work, money, taking risks, and making plans, it is worthwhile to check out whether your class backgrounds may be influencing the situation.

## Age

Sometimes couple dissimilarities develop because of significant age disparities. Of course, it is impossible to say how much of a difference is "significant." Ten years or more may not feel significant to the partners when they are in their late twenties to mid-sixties. However, women at either end of the age spectrum report that a decade's difference in their ages significantly impacts their lives as a couple.

As with other couple disparities, age differences can have advantages as well as disadvantages. They can affect goals, aspirations, perspectives, energy level, and shared social histories.

Some partners enjoy hearing their older lover tell stories and reminisce about the "old days." Others feel left out and even discounted because they don't recognize the songs or the names that are so familiar to their partners. The older partner may miss the understanding that she experiences with friends her age. They have lived through the same eras and have a comfortable sense of shared experience that is missing with a younger lover. In this situation, both women may need separate friends to validate their individual experiences.

Many older women have as much or more energy than their younger partners. Where this is not the case, both women may have regrets about not being able to share activities or interests. Sometimes the younger woman worries about her partner's health and possible dependency later. Her partner may be concerned about being a burden or being abandoned. These issues are not limited to partnerships where there is an age difference. As with all such perpetual problems, your concerns and feelings need to be aired and discussed. There may not be any definite solution, but at least you can work toward living peacefully with them.

A younger partner typically brings a fresh look at life. She may take for granted ideas and behaviors that the older partner's generation struggled to achieve, but she offers new ideas and challenges to accepted ways of thinking. An older partner often offers wisdom from her life's experiences. Many couples use this to great advantage. Both women can benefit from the broadening of experience that comes from being in a relationship with someone whose formative years were in different decades. It is important to remember that being younger does not mean immature and that being older does not mean outdated. Both women need to feel competent and respected.

*Cynthia and Marie were not very concerned about their age difference when they first got together. For the most part, the fifteen-year span between them was an advantage. With her schooling far behind her, Cynthia, at fifty-five, had enjoyed watching Marie's progress through her graduate program. She was pleased to offer tips and knew that their relationship would have had more rough spots if she had not understood, more than Marie, what the pressures of graduate school would be. For her part, Marie loved the feeling of being settled and stable that living with Cynthia provided.*

*After Marie graduated, she took a fast-track job with a consulting firm. She was required to work long hours and travel a good deal. At the same time, Cynthia's career was moving in an entirely different direction. She had accomplished most of what she had set out to do in her field. She was ready to work less and spend more time relaxing and pursuing other interests. She would have liked Marie to be more available.*

Cynthia and Marie realize that their work goals and aspirations reflect, at least in part, their age disparity. They are at different stages in their work lives. Their plan is to make sure they listen to each other and discuss how they can satisfy their separate needs as well as nurture their relationship.

## Politics

*Zoe and Gina met at a meeting to plan how to gain acceptance for a domestic-partnership plan for city employees. Gina was a little intimidated by Zoe at first, because she seemed so sure of herself and ready to take on the city council. Gina was a newcomer to political action, and she was a little afraid of personal confrontation, preferring instead a less aggressive, more educational style. Somehow they ended up on the same subcommittee and have been together ever since. But the relationship has not always been smooth. And much of their conflict has been about politics.*

*Gina came from a small Midwestern farm town. The members of her family prided themselves on being broad-minded and liberal. And they were, especially if you compared them to other people in their town. Zoe's family had a multigenerational history of radical politics, including communist grandparents and labor-organizing parents. Gina's background was relatively conservative compared to Zoe's.*

*Gina held back from saying anything about Zoe's political views or activities for far too long. She was afraid that Zoe would accuse her of being politically naive or just plain wrong. She was all too aware that Zoe read more about politics than she did. And Zoe was so articulate that she could dance rings around Gina with her words. So when Gina did express herself she tended to come on very strong and be somewhat defensive.*

Over the years, these two women have fought about a number of issues. They disagreed about the NAFTA Treaty (North America Fair Trade

Agreement) and the impact it would have on workers. They argued about whether to vote in elections where the only candidates in an election were Republican and Democrat. One of their worst fights was over Zoe's wish to go to Mexico and help organize the women workers in the border towns. Gina was very concerned about Zoe's safety and she worried that Zoe's confrontational style would put her at risk. Besides, she knew she would miss Zoe badly.

Although Gina never did completely support the decision, Zoe eventually did go. They discussed it enough so that, although they did not agree, they at least each felt that the other had heard her concerns. Both partners wondered how they managed to stay together when they looked at the world so differently. Often they chalked it up to the things they did have in common; increasingly, they credited their good communication. Frequently they acknowledged that their differences brought a richness to their relationship that more than balanced out the conflicts.

## Values

Not all couples have to deal with disparities that are as sharp as those between Zoe and Gina. But most couples find out sooner or later that their values are somewhat unalike. Some common areas of difference are child rearing, family relationships, and spending money. Let's look at some examples of dissimilar values and how couples can work with them.

Conflict about how to raise children can arise in any kind of family. Stepfamilies, in which one woman is the legal mother and the partner comes along later, seem particularly vulnerable. Such was the case for Doreen and Masie.

*Doreen moved in with Masie and her three children after they had been in a relationship for a year. Doreen had always thought that Masie was too lenient with the children, although she tried to keep out of it. She liked the children and seemed to get along fine with them until the move. When she was actually living in the same house, she found that some of their behavior was intolerable. Doreen wanted Masie to "shape the kids up" about keeping things neat. She hated that they paid little attention to her when she tried to get them to clean up after themselves. Masie wanted Doreen to be happy, but she did not want to nag the kids about things she didn't think were important. She felt torn.*

This kind of situation is difficult because it can get complicated very quickly. And strong feelings are involved where children are concerned. It can help to clarify with each other that your struggles are about your values regarding raising children, not about what is "right" or "wrong." Talk about how you each were brought up. It can show where your values developed and place the current situation in a broader context. It's also crucial to clarify to everyone what roles the two adults have. Is Doreen to be a housemate, to whom the children owe basic consideration? Is she empowered to enforce rules Masie puts in place? Does she have any financial responsibility for the children? Remember that it takes time for the "old" family to incorporate a new member.

> *Tobie and Carrie were arguing about what to do with the dog they had seen in the alley. Carrie felt compelled to try to save abandoned or hurt animals. While she couldn't do anything to stop the horrors that humans inflicted on each other, she could help individual creatures that humans had injured. She had plans to give most of her money to a clinic that neutered dogs and cats for free. Tobie also loved animals—they had four dogs and six cats at home—but she was more interested in working on environmental issues. She was especially excited about cleaning up the stream in their neighborhood. These disagreements often ended with Carrie telling Tobie that she was cold-hearted and mean, and Tobie telling Carrie that she didn't care about preserving the planet for the next generations.*

One reason that value differences are so difficult in relationships is that they are very important to us—often part of our identity. And we truly believe that our values are best. If we thought that other values were better, we would change the ones we have. So it is hard to accept that someone we love and respect actually has values that differ from ours. How can she be so misguided? Stubborn? Or wrong? When our values are challenged because our partner does not agree, we may forget that these differences are part of what attracted us to each other in the first place. We need to understand each other's values, their history, and their meaning. And we need to believe that we can be different from each other and both be okay.

John Gottman recommends taking time to tell each other about what specific values mean to you.[3] Spend ten to twenty minutes telling your partner what is important to you about family (or other values). For instance, how do you show your love and respect to your family? Do not anticipate that your partner will disagree; instead, tell her about your feelings and thoughts. The partner who is listening should speak only to ask for clarification. She should listen to her partner's underlying values. Then switch roles. The goal of this exercise is to deepen your understanding of each other's values and their historical roots, which can lessen the impact of any right versus wrong debate that you may have.

## Spiritual Paths

Some couples find that they have differences stemming from religious traditions or spiritual paths.

*Corrine grew up in a Southern Baptist Black church and sang in the choir. Her church activities were crucial as a part of her support network in her extended family. Sashiko was a Buddhist and committed to its spiritual disciplines. They each attended spiritual functions alone and together.*

*From an Orthodox Jewish family, Leah intensely disliked the Christmas season. Her partner, Missy, grew up as a practicing Roman Catholic. They compromised on how they celebrated the holidays. They exchanged presents with each other on the solstice and Hanukkah, and Missy usually spent Christmas Eve or part of Christmas Day with friends.*

*When Van and Lindsey began their relationship, neither of them was involved with anything they would have described as spiritual. In the last few years, Van had begun attending the neighborhood Lutheran church and was considering getting baptized.*

Lindsey and Van illustrate a situation where partners start off with similar values, and then one partner changes. Can the relationship accommodate changes when one partner moves in a different direction? There is no hard and fast rule. It depends on many factors. How good is your communication? How much history do you have together that provides a foundation when these changes are happening? How critical are the differences to your everyday life together? How much room do you give each other to be separate? Partners need to be able to be themselves and feel comfortable. Each of you has to answer for yourself how dissimilar you can be from your partner and the degree of change that you can handle. But these answers usually cannot be predicted ahead of time. It may be that you once thought you could never live with someone who calls herself a Christian, but when your lover of fifteen years invites you to her baptism, you realize that she is still the person with whom you want to live.

## Differences in Closeness and Power

In their book, *Reconcilable Differences,* Andrew Christensen and Neil Jacobson propose two primary arenas where couples have potentially problematic differences: closeness or intimacy, and power,[4] i.e., the "distribution of authority, dominance and control."[5] Even though their research is on heterosexual couples, our experience suggests that these dynamics are also true for lesbian couples.

When couples struggle with issues of intimacy or power, each woman may feel betrayed, wounded, or powerless. It is important for the couple to acknowledge that these problems arise from differences; each woman needs to talk about and accept the whole "package" that is her partner.

Comfort with closeness and balance of power are relative to individual relationships. In one relationship you may be asking to spend time with your partner, while in the next you may be trying to get more space. Neither closeness nor power is absolute. Your experience of where you are on those continuums not only can change from relationship to relationship but can also shift during the lifetime of one relationship.

### Closeness

In Chapter One we mentioned the back-and-forth flow between separateness, contact, and merger in healthy couple relationships. All couples must find the unique balance between these that meets their needs. Lesbian couples often have a different slant on this task than gay or heterosexual couples because usually both women have been conditioned to focus on togetherness. Consequently, they both may be sensitive to any separateness that the other partner wants—or seems to want.[6] When the romance stage winds down and the individual women re-engage in their previous activities and friendships, couples often discover that they are out of balance on the separateness-closeness continuum.

*Tori and Liz loved each other dearly, but lately they were trying to figure out what had gone wrong. Tori wanted to spend all their free time together, just as they had the first year of their relationship, but Liz really wanted to spend more time alone. Tori felt as though Liz was backing away from her, and Liz felt like Tori was suffocating her. They had just started couples therapy, and their therapist suggested that they try to look at these different degrees of togetherness as something they needed to negotiate, not a sign of imminent breakup. But it was hard.*

*The therapist suggested that each woman notice her thoughts about spending time together or apart. Tori should pay particular attention to even tiny twinges of wanting to spend time without Liz, such as taking a bath or reading a book. Liz should attend particularly to any inklings of desire to spend time together, such as going to a movie or taking a walk.*

*The therapist also had them pick a three-hour period of time once a week, usually on a weekend day, when they spent time doing things on their own, with or without someone else. They also had the assignment of spending a three-hour period on a date with each other sometime during the week. She told them to pay attention to their feelings and to practice self-soothing if they got anxious during any of these activities.*

As both women became aware of wanting time together and apart, they were on firmer ground to talk about their different wants and needs. They both were able to calm themselves when they moved closer together or farther apart. Gradually, it became easier for Tori and Liz to negotiate time both together and apart.

## Power

Housework and child care are two very common areas of potential difference with which couples may struggle.

*Mira and Keisha were exhausted. Their two-year-old whirlwind had just gone to bed at eleven o'clock, and they were still in the middle of their nightly fight about who should have done what to ease their burden of caring for their child. Mira kept referring to their original agreement of three years ago that made Keisha responsible for evening child care. Mira would sometimes hear herself calling Keisha lazy. Keisha kept reminding Mira that with her part-time job the agreement had to be changed.*

*Kyla and Ingrid were fighting again over whose turn it was to clean the cat litter box. They were both exhausted from the seemingly constant bickering over household chores. Neither of them liked housework, but Ingrid found herself doing most of it because it bugged her sooner than it did Kyla. It didn't seem to matter what agreements they made: Kyla did not do her jobs soon enough for Ingrid, and so the fighting began. Ingrid had taken to calling Kyla a slob, and Kyla thought Ingrid had become neurotic.*

Ingrid and Kyla are fighting over responsibility. Ingrid thinks the apartment needs to be kept at one level of cleanliness and Kyla at another. Six months earlier both women thought the other was the perfect lover and roommate. Have they changed that much? Not likely. Kyla and Ingrid are sorting out how to manage responsibility and standards in the housekeeping arena.

Christensen and Jacobson point out that people tend to treat differences contemptuously, and therefore destructively, in one of three ways.[7] The first is to see the difference as a sign of "badness" in the other person: "You're just lazy." The second is to view it as a deficiency in emotional adjustment: "You are completely neurotic." The third is to see the other person as incompetent: "You don't know how to communicate well." We know from John Gottman and his colleagues' research that contempt is one of the signs of serious relationship trouble.[8] We also know from experience that telling your partner that she is a slob does not make things better. In Kyla and Ingrid's situation they need to find a way to make housecleaning—not each other—the problem.

A variation of the housework struggle occurs around the theme of play versus work. Often couples polarize, with one woman making sure the "work" gets done and the other ensuring that "play" happens. When things are going well with a couple, this difference may ultimately lead to both women taking on both attributes, but when there is tension or pain in the relationship, the polarization can lead to even more pain.

*Bridget and LaShawn were frustrated with each other about whether they should stay home and get ready for their party the next night or go to the opening of their friend's painting exhibit. Bridget was very worried about leaving the preparation until Saturday because she knew she would get stuck with it since LaShawn had karate practice. Even though she knew they had to cook and clean, LaShawn hated the idea of giving up the fun of going to the opening and supporting their friend. Bridget "knew" that once they got to the gallery she would have trouble getting LaShawn home before eleven.*

In this example, the problem is the pull between the party preparations and the gallery opening, not the different wants of the women. LaShawn and Bridget were able to cut short their usual "You only think about play" versus "You want us to miss out on all the fun" argument and problem-solve the real issue. In the end, LaShawn agreed to leave the party by nine and to do some of the food prep when they got home. Bridget agreed to go to the opening and to wait until LaShawn got home from karate to finish the cleaning. They felt excited about this problem-solving approach and particularly pleased that by listening to each other's priorities they got to do both activities.

It can be very difficult to accept any differences in your partner, especially if the disparity touches a vulnerability in one or both of you.[9]

*Kay had grown up in an emotionally distant family. Her family never hugged or said they loved each other. Her partner, Erica, came from a family that was very loud and obvious about their caring for one another. Whenever Erica's father was angry at anyone, however, he withdrew for days. So, when Kay forgot to give Erica a hug or was quiet after a hard day at work, Erica thought Kay was angry.*

Erica has a vulnerability around expression of affection. Since the two women care a lot for each other, they need to accept this difference as perpetual and then to find a way to manage it. Once they can do this they may end up feeling very close.

*Erica told Kay how scared she was that Kay had not hugged her for two days. Kay realized she had been very preoccupied by work and had gone internal, like she often did. She also realized that Erica got scared when this happened. Kay reached out and took Erica's hand, kissed it, and gave her a hug.*

Couples can be strengthened and enriched by the differences that each partner brings to the relationship, as well as by those that reflect individual growth and change while they are together. Good communication and acceptance about these differences goes a long way toward deepening a couple's pleasure and intimacy.

## Dyke Differences

There are some differences that are more common in pairings of women. Under the heading Dyke Differences we include the issues of sexual orientation and gender. Every generation of women who love women has pushed against the boundaries of what society takes for granted about gender and sexual orientation. And lesbians continue to wrestle with these questions of identity in new ways. As we explore some of the new thinking we pay close attention to how these changes can affect lesbian couples.

Queer theory,[10] which has emerged in the last decade or so, challenges people to think of sexual orientation, gender, race, and class as fluid concepts that interact to produce a person's experience of herself at any given time. A woman in a relationship with another woman in the 1970s might call herself a lesbian, but were she in a similar relationship in the 1870s, she would likely not have had a name for herself but only the experience of loving her friend. Women who dressed and lived their lives as men a hundred years ago did not refer to themselves as transgendered, they just lived their lives.[11] Queer theory proponents argue that identity changes over time and should not be rigidly labeled.

### Sexual Orientation

*Ruth was seventy-eight years old. She had come out to herself in 1943 when she worked in a steel factory in Pittsburgh. Three of Ruth's coworkers were also "that way" and the four of them became lifelong friends. Ruth considered herself to be gay and proud of it. However, she could not get over her greatniece, Emily, identifying as "queer." Ruth thought queer was insulting and not at all descriptive of her gay friends. She didn't even like the term lesbian, which a lot of women she knew used, because it smacked of those politically correct women who didn't much like men. Ruth didn't want to sleep with men, but she had many long-time gay male friends. The one thing Ruth did know was that she and Emily both thought that women were very attractive and once even found themselves watching the same fifty-year-old friend of the family. Ruth figured that no matter what each woman called herself they both liked girls.*

Not all women in relationships with other women define themselves as lesbian. Some women don't like the "L" word and prefer dyke, gay, bisexual, or queer. Others refuse to adopt any "label." There are some couples for whom the relationship is an extension of friendship, and they see it as a unique relationship; these women may self-identify as heterosexual or straight.

Often what women call themselves is related to current politics, age, when they came out, and where they live. Women in their late fifties and older may prefer "gay" or "friend." Women in their forties and fifties typically use "lesbian." Women in their twenties and thirties often use "dyke" or "queer." Those who live in small towns or rural areas may use different language than their counterparts in large urban areas.

As we talked with lesbians across the age spectrum it became obvious that the difference in labels is more than a name preference. Some younger women like the inclusive tone of "dyke" and "queer" because these words do not imply that they are attracted only to women. "Queer" also takes some of the emphasis off sex and describes a lifestyle that is outside of the mainstream. For them, "lesbian" is associated with "lesbian separatist" and is seen as rigid and exclusionary of some women and all men. Women who were influenced by the women's movement often choose to use "lesbian," because they like language that does not subsume women under a male-dominated category, like "he" being used for both women and men. For them, the term "lesbian" represents a hard-won victory over exclusionary language. Women in later life often choose "gay" because it more closely describes their experience as a vulnerable, hidden minority made up of men and women. For these women, "lesbian" may be too confrontational.

There is no problem when members of a couple see themselves as similar or are not threatened by their partner's self-identity. There is also not a problem if one of them changes her identity over time and her partner is comfortable with it. However, problems may arise when partners' self-definitions clash and the couple cannot manage the difference.

*Nan had gotten involved with Darcy while Darcy was married to her husband of fifteen years. Nan had been quietly out to a few friends and her sister for about ten years. They met at work and instantly fell in love, or at least that what they said looking back on it. Darcy left her husband and moved in with Nan. Everything was fine until Darcy wanted to be more out than Nan was comfortable with. Darcy went from calling herself "bisexual" to "lesbian" to "dyke" to "queer." The last was too much for Nan, who hated that word and the images it conjured up for her. Darcy also wanted to go to San Francisco and march in the gay pride parade. Nan was not comfortable with the direction Darcy was moving, and she flat-out disliked some of the "dykes" Darcy was beginning to hang out with. She asked Darcy to move out.*

Another situation that can be challenging is that of partners who have, from the beginning of their relationship, differed in the way they define themselves.

*As a child, Gretchen knew she was different; later, she learned that the word for her was "lesbian." For the last two years Gretchen had been involved with Trae. Trae had been married for twelve years and began to relate to women romantically after her divorce. Unlike Gretchen, Trae had always been attracted to men. When Gretchen pushed her on it, she described herself as bisexual, but she disliked using any label that limited her.*

These two women define their identity very differently. An additional complication here is that Gretchen believes some stereotypes about bisexual women. She doesn't like to admit it, even to herself, but she feels threatened when Trae mentions that a particular man is attractive. One of her fears is that Trae is not really committed to the relationship because she is attracted to women *and* men. Gretchen needs to learn about bisexuality and overcome her prejudices; she needs to soothe herself and learn that Trae's bisexuality does not mean she is less committed to the relationship.

It is important to remember that the same label has various meanings for different people. One woman who calls herself bisexual or queer may be attracted to men but is no longer interested in relating sexually to them. Another woman may want to relate to both men and women. The same descriptive label may also serve various purposes at different times for the same person. For example, Trae may describe herself as bisexual as she explores a lesbian identity—leaving her options open. Later she may identify as a lesbian. At another period in her life she may return to defining herself as bisexual to include her attraction to a particular man. In lesbian relationships each woman needs to be as clear as she can about how she identifies herself and what the implications of the identity are for the relationship.

### Gender

Lesbians and gay men were first described in the late 1800s as being "inverts," women and men who wanted to be like the other gender. Research has since proven that theory wrong, but it is true that lesbians and gay men have played with and challenged the stereotypical behavior, dress, and attitudes that society has ascribed to the female and male. Over the years this has taken the forms of butch/femme, drag queens, and kings and cross-gender roles—for example, women being mechanics for their own cars. It should come as no surprise, then, that lesbians are still pushing the gender envelope.

What is gender? Gender has long been thought of as a stable, enduring chromosomal characteristic. The 1934 edition of *Webster's Dictionary* defines gender as "Sex, male or female."[12] In some circles, gender is no longer assumed to be fixed. Felice Newman, in *The Whole Lesbian Sex Book,* defines gender as "how you relate to your biological sex." She describes the interplay between sex, gender, and sexual orientation in this way: "Think of your sex as your physical equipment, your gender as what you do with it, and your sexual orientation as the territory of your desire."[13]

Many, if not most, women who love women still self-identify as lesbian, gay, or bisexual women. But there is a growing trend, especially among younger women, to self-identify in more fluid terms. Transgendered is an inclusive term that includes people who do not feel that their outward sex characteristics match the gender with which they identify. Among these groups are female-to-male (F to M) and male-to-female (M to F) transsexuals, transvestites, drag queens and kings, and butches/femmes whose experience of being female differs from the dominant view of society.[14]

Transsexuals are men and women who prefer to, and often do, live their lives as a gender other than the one they lived as children. This may or may not involve the use of hormones or surgery. Transvestites are usually heterosexual men who like to dress in women's clothing as a sexual turn-on. Drag queens and kings dress in the clothing of the other gender. There is often much playfulness in their interactions and an exaggeration of the sex-role characteristics they are taking on, like a man wearing a tight dress with falsies and very high-heeled shoes or a woman wearing men's clothing and a dildo in her pants (packing). Butch and femme can be a game women play with roles and clothing, or it can be a deeply held sense of oneself as different from the mainstream definition of the female gender.

Thus, a woman in a lesbian relationship might self-identify as dyke, bi, trans, or boy (boy because she feels masculine but doesn't want to take on the heterosexist trappings of the word "man"). Another might identify as an M to F, bisexual femme. Still another might call herself a lesbian woman. And they can all change those identifiers over time. We like Felice Newman's comment on this newfound fluidity: "Your gender identity can shift and change over the course of a lifetime. Or, your gender identity may remain constant—but your acceptance of yourself, your capacity to be on the outside exactly who you are on the inside, may grow over the years."[15]

In some places in the United States, groups and organizations that in years past identified as gay and lesbian—or gay, lesbian, and bisexual—are now using the title gay, lesbian, bi, transgendered, and questioning (GLBTQ). This signals support for people of all identifications and increasingly for a mixture of identities. This is the reality that queer theory is reflecting: a fluid mix of gender and sexual orientation that can and does change over time. Queer theory "focuses on mismatches between sex, gender and desire."[16]

How this affects a lesbian couple—if we can call it that after the last few paragraphs—is that a woman may begin a relationship assuming she is female and attracted to women and evolve to a place where she considers herself male and attracted to women, men, or both. If only one woman in a couple changes her sense of her identity, her partner may find that she is attracted to a woman who now considers herself to be a man and who may wish to undergo medical treatment to be anatomically male. It can seriously challenge the "lesbian's" view of herself. Can she still be a lesbian if her beloved is a man?

> *Lisa and Erin had been lovers for three years when Erin decided that she really was trans. While Lisa had known that Erin was very butch and had occasionally wondered if she were transgendered, it was still new territory when Erin started identifying as trans. They saw a therapist, talked to their friends, and spent hours discussing how Erin's trans identity would affect their relationship and place in the dyke community. Even though both women were nervous, they were committed to trying to work through this transition.*

While a partner's changes in gender identity may seem threatening to some women's lesbian identity, it is helpful to view this change as a difference to be negotiated. If a couple can stay engaged with each other through the difficult times, a trans partner's comfort with her chosen gender may bring new openness and depth to a relationship.

Lesbians who came out in the '70s and earlier can disagree vehemently or be overwhelmed and confused by the current options of who to be. Dykes of the '90s cannot imagine the rigidity of even the recent past. If we could ask women who loved women in the 1700s, they would not identify with any of the currently available labels. The connecting link is that all of us have dared to step outside mainstream society's rules in order to be our authentic selves. Being pioneers, whatever the generation, can be challenging for couples. There are few road maps to guide us. One suggestion is to remember that a difference is a difference is a difference. Respect your partner and keep the focus on the difference, not her, as the issue.

## CHAPTER 6

# ♪ Communicating

We communicate whether we intend to or not. Communication is inherent in our daily behavior, and it's an unavoidable part of being in a relationship. Communication is complex. It includes not only the words but also the music and the dance—our voice tones, eye contact, body posture, and gestures. Our actions, or lack of actions, are often more powerful than our words.

> Jo insisted that she really did want to spend time with her partner Hortensia's family, but whenever the family invited them over for a visit, Jo was always too busy to go. Hortensia believed what Jo did, not what she said; she concluded that Jo didn't like her family and wondered why. Was it because her father tended to drink too much on family occasions? Were her sisters not friendly enough? Was it too noisy with all the kids around?

> Gloria got very frustrated when she asked her partner, Kay, what was wrong, and Kay responded, "Oh, nothing," with a big sigh. Gloria didn't believe the words when the music didn't fit. Kay's slumped posture and her tone of voice suggested that she was upset about something.

We communicate for many purposes: to ask for help, to pass the time, to negotiate getting something we want, and, especially in intimate relationships, to get approval from our partners. Often we are not aware that part of the reason for our communicating is to get approval—until we don't get it. Then we feel unappreciated and hurt.

> *Lucille told her lover, Sandra, "I bought some great towels today at the January white sale at Sears." When Sandra responded with, "Do you think we really need them?" Lucille felt criticized and unappreciated.*

On the surface, Lucille was simply conveying information to Sandra about the towel purchase. But beyond conveying information, she also wanted approval and recognition. She wanted Sandra to acknowledge her for being clever and thinking ahead, for being thrifty by buying on sale, and for being considerate because Sandra mentioned months ago that it would be nice to have some new towels.

Lucille's self-esteem—in the sense of how she sees herself—was a major part of this discussion of towels. This is often the case: We talk about towels, household tasks, or how we were raised, when something else is the real topic. When we don't get the approval, recognition, or agreement we want, we may feel slighted or rejected. We may get very upset and respond as if our core identity or the future of the relationship is on the line over what seems to be a trivial matter.

## Why Is Good Communication So Important?

Couples often go into counseling feeling distanced from each other, and they explain their situation as "a problem with communication." This description may turn out to be an understatement, but it does acknowledge something that couples recognize: Communication is about connection.

To communicate well you must be able to convey your thoughts, emotions, wants, and needs to your partner and, in turn, to listen to what she has to say. It sounds simple enough, but as Eric Marcus points out in *Together Forever,* good communication is "a complicated, messy, wonderful, terrifying, comforting, disturbing, reassuring and profoundly individual thing. It can be as simple and sweet as nightly kisses before going to bed or as painful as a recurring argument over a long-past infidelity. Some couples go about it gingerly and with great reserve; others go at it with unbridled passion. Some are adept at it; others have struggled for years to learn how to understand each other."[1]

On the mundane level, even brief exchanges, including those about humdrum topics like the grocery list or the neighbor's new fence, represent a turning toward our partner, which builds emotional connection.[2]

On a more profound level, intimacy grows with the deepening levels of open and honest communication. Disclosing information about yourself and "being known" allows your partner access to what is going on inside you. This can be scary because it requires you to be willing to put your fears aside, to relinquish some control and self-protection, to trust—yourself and her—beyond what feels comfortable. It can seem very risky. (See Chapter Four.) The other side of this process is maintaining an ongoing interest in knowing your partner better. According to Betty Berzon, if you treat your partner not only as an object of your love but also as an object of your interest and curiosity, you are saying, "I care about who you are, who you have been, who you want to be. I open myself to you to listen and learn about you. I cherish you, not just my fantasy of who you are, not just who I need you to be, but who you really are. . . ."[3] Being interested in knowing your partner and being willing to be known creates and reinforces the relationship bond and enhances intimacy.

## Different Communication Styles

So knowing and being known builds intimacy. And that's a good thing. But what if you are more reserved than talkative? What if you tend to keep your thoughts and feelings private rather than expressing them freely? In his study of forty happy lesbian and gay couples, Eric Marcus noted that lack of communication was especially distressing to those partners who liked to talk things out but found themselves in relationships with partners whose first instinct was silence.[4] According to Otto Kroeger and Janet Thuesen in their book *Type Talk*, the psychiatrist Carl Jung suggested that differences between individuals were based on preferences—which emerge early in life and form the foundation of our personalities.[5] These preferences are neither right nor wrong—just differences. But they can lead to misunderstandings and even become perpetual problems in a couple's communication if partners don't understand themselves or each other (see Chapter Seven).

One of these preferences has to do with introversion versus extraversion. According to Jung, this preference is the most important distinction between people because it describes the source, direction, and focus of a person's energy. Extraverts are energized by what goes on in the external world, while introverts are energized by what goes on in their internal world. All the activities that the extravert finds exhilarating, uplifting, and exciting drain the introvert. And the reverse is equally true: The reflection, introspection, and solitude that produce energy, focus, and attention for the introvert are a drain on the extravert's energy. While these preferences are a matter of degree, extraverts are more likely described as sociable, expressive, and gregarious.

They are energized by action, especially interaction with others, and have a tendency to speak first and then think. Introverts, on the other hand, tend to be quiet, private, reflective, and internal. They prefer to talk one on one, and think carefully before speaking.[6] Here are some common scenarios where an introvert and extravert are paired up.

*Galen takes so long to answer questions from her partner, Jane, that Jane wonders sometimes if Galen is "brain-dead." When Jane pushes for a response, Galen inevitably says, "I'm thinking about it."*

*When she needed to make a decision about selling her business, Renel thought things through on her own and then told her partner, Ali, that she had decided to sell. Ali was shocked and angry that she was left out of the process. Renel was sure that she had told Ali something about it, but Ali was equally confident that Renel had not.*

*It took Karen and Heather years to figure out how to manage their different needs for "space." Karen needed a lot of "down time" to recuperate from working with people all day. On the weekends she liked to work on house projects and spend time alone with Heather or with one of their couple friends. Heather was much more sociable and wanted to go out and have fun on the weekends. She enjoyed parties, going places, and doing things. They struggled because each wanted the other to share, and enjoy, her preferred activities.*

If these couples can come to understand that they are dealing with personal styles that represent fundamental differences in personality, they are less likely to take their partner's behavior personally. The couple can identify whether these differences really are perpetual problems, so they can explore, understand, and manage them better.

If these scenarios resonate with you, or you believe that you and your partner might benefit from assessing your style difference further, you could explore the topic of personality types.

## Different Perspectives

In addition to fundamental personality differences, we also need to appreciate that other people—including our partner—see things differently than we do. And their view is as true for them as ours is for us. They are not simply trying to contradict us.

One way to think about this is to understand the difference between "hard" and "soft" meanings.[7] Hard meanings apply to concrete items that can be measured objectively such as a table or a tree, or to very clear concepts like grandmother or student. Soft meanings are much more difficult to define because they involve personal, subjective judgments. Words such as "trust," "respect," and "control" often mean various things to different people, depending on their values, attitudes, and experiences.

*Sofia agreed to go to her ex-partner's third Alcoholics Anonymous birthday celebration. In doing this Sofia saw herself as mature and unselfish because she was setting aside her old pain and resentment to recognize her ex's change and accomplishment. She assumed that her new lover, Martha, would see it the same way. Not so. Martha felt that Sofia was being inconsiderate of her feelings and disloyal to their relationship.*

Both Sofia and Martha believe that their perceptions are accurate. However, it is not an objective *fact* that Sofia is being either mature or inconsiderate. These are words with soft meanings which involve opinions and value judgments. If this couple confuses fact and opinion, it will be impossible for them to understand each other's point of view. Just as they could bicker endlessly without understanding each other in this situation, so a couple can argue about what somebody *really* said.

In any communication there are two real messages. There is what the expressor thinks she said, or intended to say, and what the listener thinks she heard. Whether these interpretations are the same depends on the context. The message always occurs in a context that includes the history of the relationship, the current emotional states of the people, nonverbal behavior, and the overall situation.

Vivien: *"I wish we could go to Hawaii this winter."*
Shae: *"Hawaii's too expensive, and besides, I can't take time off work."*
Vivien: *"Well, Ginny and Doris manage to go."*
Shae: *"Well, maybe you'd better find yourself a partner who makes more money than I do."*
Vivien: *"Well, maybe I should."*

This conversation led to a major fight, which left both Vivien and Shae feeling hurt, rejected, angry, and wondering what happened.

To understand this situation, we need to know something about the context of their discussion.

*Background.* Shae thought that Vivien disapproved of her working at the child-care center because of the low pay and long hours. Vivien felt unhappy that Shae never seemed to want to spend time with just the two of them.

*Current Situation.* They had just seen Vivien's former lover, Ginny, and her partner, Doris, who were leaving for Hawaii in two weeks.

Vivien thinks: *"Maybe if we went on a vacation together we'd feel closer."*
She says: *"I wish we could go to Hawaii this winter."*

Shae thinks: *"Why is she always suggesting things we can't afford? Next she'll be on my case about getting a different job."*
She says: *"Hawaii's too expensive, and besides, I can't take time off work."*

Vivien thinks: *"There she goes with that work stuff again. I know she thinks I'm lazy, and she has always resented that my grandmother left me that money."*
She says: *"Well, Ginny and Doris manage to go."*

Shae thinks: *"Now she's comparing me to Ginny again. Can I help it if I'm not rich? She has no respect for me."*
She says: *"Well, maybe you'd better find yourself a partner who makes more money than I do. "*

Vivien thinks: *"She doesn't really care if I stay or go."*
She says: *"Well, maybe I should. "*

We notice how the topic moves quickly from vacation to finding a new partner. The discussion was really about the relationship all along, but neither woman knew that until they were both too angry to talk about it.

Just as we can learn other skills, each of us can improve our communication skills. Whatever our perspective and whether we are a woman of few words or a "chatty Cathy," we can be true to ourselves and still use specific techniques that make it more likely that the messages we send are the ones received.

## Improving Your Communication Skills

Good communication requires listening and expressing skills. As an expressor you try to be clear and precise and to state exactly what you're thinking, feeling, or wanting. You do not assume that your partner is a mind reader or that she will not understand. Good communication means having the impact you intended to have. When you are successful, your intention equals your impact upon the listener.

As a listener you try to understand what the expressor intends. When you really listen, your intention is to do one of four things: understand someone, learn something, enjoy someone, or provide help or solace as needed.

### Listening

Sometimes we confuse listening with hearing. Our partner asks, "Were you listening to me?" and we pull ourselves away from cooking dinner or watching television long enough to say, "Sure, I heard every word." Maybe we *can* even remember some or all of the words we heard, but we aren't really listening when our attention is divided.

Good listening is a commitment and a compliment. When you truly listen to your partner, you make a commitment to try to understand how she feels and how she sees things. You avoid filling in the gaps with assumptions or immediately leaping to give advice. As much as possible, you put aside your own judgments, assumptions, attitudes, and feelings—your filters—while you try to look at things from her perspective. Listening is a compliment; it is like saying to your partner, "You are important to me. I care about your feelings and your experiences."

Good listening is active, not passive. You have to resist the tendencies to mind read, to judge without asking for more information, or to rehearse your next response rather than focus on understanding what your partner has said. The only way to find out if you understood what your partner meant is to ask. This means you have to ask questions and give feedback.

You first gather information by asking questions about what your partner is saying. Then you need to check out your interpretations by giving feedback to see if what you thought you heard is what she intended to communicate. In this give-and-take of the communication process, you get a fuller appreciation of what is being said.

We'll now give some examples of what happens when neither partner is using good listening skills.

Caren: *"What a day I've had."*
Wande: *"It couldn't have been worse than mine. First the truck kept stalling, so I was late getting to that new painting job. And then the woman was so bossy, she stood over my shoulder all day and complained about everything."*

Caren: "*The truck always does that. It's no big deal. The profs are piling on so much work that I don't know how much more I can stand. And then I got back my English paper and I got a C.*"
Wande: "*I was ready to blow up at this woman and quit the job, but I didn't want to lose the money.*"
Caren: "*You can bet I'm worried about money, too. Those loans are just piling up, and if I flunk out I'll have to start paying them back and won't even have a degree to show for it.*"
Wande: "*Can't you think about anything besides school? Don't you care anything about me?*"
Caren: "*That's just great! My profs think I'm a lousy student, and you think I'm a rotten partner. I might as well give up.*"

In this example, Caren and Wande were so caught up in their own situations that they didn't listen to each other. They were competing to be heard, and the conversation quickly deteriorated. Both ended up feeling misunderstood and badly treated.

Good listening techniques by either Caren or Wande could have averted this disaster. Here is one way that Wande might have responded differently.

Caren: "*What a day I've had!*"
Wande: "*I figured something was up when you looked so exhausted. What happened?*"
Caren: "*The profs are piling it on. And I got a C on that English paper I worked so hard on.*"
Wande: "*You sound really discouraged.*"
Caren: "*I am. I'm not even caught up yet, and they just keep adding more tests and assignments. I'm afraid of what might happen.*"
Wande: "*Are you afraid you'll fail?*"
Caren: "*Yes, sometimes I am. And then I'll end up with all these loans and nothing to show for it.*"

In this situation, Wande set aside her own frustrations while she listened to Caren. She asked questions: "What happened? Are you afraid you'll fail?" By doing this, she got more information about how Caren was feeling, and why. She also gave feedback: "You sound really discouraged." This feedback allowed Wande to check out whether her perception of Caren's feelings was correct. And it was. By asking questions and giving feedback, Wande developed a fairly good understanding of Caren's concerns—and Caren felt understood. After

Caren had a chance to be listened to, it was then Wande's turn to talk about her day, and Caren's turn to listen actively.

The initial conversation could just as easily have been changed by Caren as by Wande. Here is how Caren could have used good listening skills.

Caren: *"What a day I've had!"*
Wande: *"You think you had a bad day! I had problems with the truck, and that painting job was horrible."*
Caren: *"It sounds like we'll have a lot to talk about tonight. Why don't you start by telling me about your day?"*
Wande: *"Well, first the truck kept stalling out so I was late getting to the job. And then the woman kept following me around all day, complaining about everything."*
Caren: *"That sounds awful. What exactly did she do?"*
Wande: *"She decided she didn't really like the trim color she had chosen, so she had me change it. Then she kept telling me how to paint. And the final straw was when she blamed me for paint spatters on her sidewalk that I never made."*
Caren: *"It sounds like you couldn't do anything right."*
Wande: *"Exactly."*

Here Caren took the role of asking questions—"Why don't you start by telling me about your day? What exactly did she do?"—and giving feedback and support—"That sounds awful. It sounds like you couldn't do anything right." Caren's questions and feedback helped her be sure that the message she received was the one her partner sent—or intended to send. In each of these examples, both partners asked two questions near the beginning of the conversation. They followed the "two-question rule."[8] According to this rule, when your partner responds to your first question, you follow up with a second one based on her answer to the first. The two-question rule helps you to stay focused on the expressor rather than slipping back into your own concerns. When you show your partner that you care about her thoughts and feelings by truly listening, she is more likely to do the same for you. And at the same time, you are strengthening your relationship by nurturing your fondness and appreciation for her. (See Healthy Relationship Strategy #2 in Chapter Two.)

Often the situations where it's hardest to use good listening skills are those where you need them the most. One of these situations is when you are being criticized or when your partner is upset with you.

*Lindarae and Reba had just come home from a party. Lindarae did not feel well before they went. At the party she felt hurt and angry because Reba spent so much time talking and dancing with others and so little time with her. In addition, she had wanted to leave much earlier than they did.*

Lindarae: *"I never want to go to a party with you again."*
Reba: *"I didn't realize you were so upset. What's going on?"*
Lindarae: *"You just ignored me all night while you danced with every woman there. And then I couldn't get you to come home. You can be so insensitive!"*
Reba: *"So, when I danced so much and wanted to stay, you felt bad?"*
Lindarae: *"Who wouldn't?"*
Reba: *"It's true that I was having fun dancing, and that I wanted to stay longer than you did. Was the party really awful for you?"*
Lindarae: *"Well, I really didn't feel good even though I tried not to show it. And then I didn't know as many people as you did. I hoped that you would spend more time hanging out with me. It seemed like you didn't even care how I was doing."*
Reba: *"I can understand why you felt bad. If I saw it that way, I would have been upset too. I'm sure I could have paid more attention to how you were doing. Maybe we need to work out some signals or have some plans for checking in with each other at parties."*
Lindarae: *"That sounds like a good idea."*

In this situation, Reba did not assume she knew why Lindarae was upset. She asked, "What's going on?" When she got some information from Lindarae, she gave her feedback to make sure she understood: "So . . . you felt bad?" Rather than getting defensive and counterattacking, Reba acknowledged that her partner was correct about some things: Reba had enjoyed dancing and wanted to stay at the party longer. Then she followed the two-question rule and asked for even more information from Lindarae: "Was the party really awful for you?" When Reba understood more clearly what was going on for her partner, she appreciated Lindarae's feelings and said so. This gave Lindarae support and reassurance. Then they could both move to learning from this experience and to problem-solving for the future.

### Blocks to Listening

We are more likely to listen poorly and interpret incorrectly when we are stressed or when the topic is a sensitive one.

*Marlee had moved into Francine's house because neither of them wanted to uproot Francine's children from their familiar school and neighborhood. But Marlee had never quite felt it was her home. For one thing, she was used to living in the city, and Francine's house was in the suburbs. Marlee had put most of her furniture in storage, except for her desk and her comfortable old reading chair. One day, Francine asked Marlee if she had ever thought about redoing the upholstery on the chair.*

*Thinking she heard disapproval and irritation in Francine's voice, Marlee blew up. She felt angry and defensive that Francine should criticize and want to change the one thing that had helped Marlee feel she belonged in the house.*

Regardless of our stress level or the sensitivity of the topic, there are twelve blocks to listening. We all use some of these blocks sometimes; a few may be favorites that we use often. The goal is to become more aware of our patterns so we have the option of changing them if we choose to. We mentioned some of these blocks earlier in this chapter: mind reading, judging, rehearsing a response, and giving advice prematurely. The others are sparring (including putdowns and discounting), needing to be right, comparing (where we are busy seeing if we measure up), daydreaming, derailing (changing the subject or joking it off), taking over (where we launch into our own story about the topic before the other person finishes hers), filtering, and making assumptions. These last two can be especially challenging in couple relationships.

Out of necessity, we all filter information. It is impossible for us to attend to everything that is going on at any one time. For example, if we are absorbed in reading a book, we filter out the traffic noise and may not even hear someone calling us. But when we filter out some details and fill in others without checking them out, we operate on incomplete and biased information.

A complication of filtering occurs when we classify our impressions into familiar categories and then fill in the details. We pay attention long enough to decide if the present experience is similar to one we have had in the past. As soon as we classify the experience, person, or situation as similar to a previous one, we may act as if they actually are the same—whether they are or not. This is one way we help the past repeat itself.

Another way the past may complicate the present is when the "ghosts" of the past turn up in our present relationship. Each of us brings a history about relationships with us. We have both the experience of growing up in our own family and a history in previous relationships. Consequently, we each have our own way of filtering and responding to situations. When our reaction to something our partner says or does is based more on some unfinished business with a parent or a previous lover, it usually leads to misunderstanding and hurt or angry feelings.

*Clare grew up in a home with alcoholic parents where parties always ended up being drunken brawls. If any social gathering got noisy at all, Clare couldn't stand it. On many occasions she left parties early and insisted that her partner, Melissa, come with her.*

*After the first year together, Manou found herself becoming very angry and critical of almost everything her partner, Perry, did. Manou was very upset because, as she put it, "I sound just like my mother!"*

*Hilda's last lover left her very suddenly to be with another woman. When her new partner, Lucia, commented that a new coworker at her office was very attractive, Hilda felt panicky. She was afraid to ask Lucia any more about the woman.*

It's not always easy to know what part of our reaction is solidly based in the present and what is a hangover from the past. Reflecting back and talking with your partner about how it was in your family and in previous relationships, and then making connections between then and now, can help illuminate current events. This looking to the past for clues about inexplicable reactions or overreactions is not about blaming. It is about understanding yourself, about solving those "little mysteries of who you are . . . and who she is" and why the behavior of either one of you may be baffling—perhaps to you both.[9] The goal of this exercise is to increase your awareness and identify any leftover business from the past that might be influencing and complicating the present.

Making assumptions is the twelfth block to listening. This can take many forms. For example, it can be easy to think of your partner as an extension of you, especially when you have lived together for a number of years. Familiarity is one of the great perks of long-term relationships, but it has its downside. We all want to be understood and appreciated for our individuality and complexity, and that includes the possibility that we might change our minds about what we like or want in our lives.[10] You may assume that you know what your partner means, likes, or feels, but the only way to know for sure is to ask her. An additional benefit of these reality checks is that you can update your love map. (See Healthy Relationship Strategy #1 in Chapter Two.)

### Expressing Skills

Expressing ourselves clearly and precisely requires awareness and disclosure, as well as body language that is consistent with our words. We express ourselves about four aspects of our experience: our observations, our thoughts, our feelings, and our wants or needs.[11]

#### Observations

When we express our observations we are reporting "just the facts"—no inferences, opinions, and conclusions. We stick to what we have seen, heard, or personally experienced.

- *I did the laundry this morning.*
- *It was so hot at work in the summer of '93 that they sent us home early five days in a row.*
- *I heard that Danelle is moving to Detroit.*

#### Thoughts

Our thoughts depart from the facts and involve coming to conclusions: developing opinions, beliefs, and theories.

- Go Fish *is a wonderful movie.* (Opinion)
- *You were right to quit that job.* (Value judgment)
- *Sex at least once a week is necessary for a good relationship.* (Belief)
- *She must be mad at me, because she hasn't called in weeks.* (Theory)

We frequently express these thoughts as if they were facts, rather than our opinions or our theories. It is important to remember that our thoughts are our thoughts—not the absolute truth.

#### Feelings

For many of us, expressing our feelings *is* difficult. The first challenge is knowing what we feel. This takes practice. We have to get to know ourselves and become aware of our physical responses, which signal us when we are having a reaction. We also need to become aware of the thoughts that go along with our feelings.

One way to get clearer is to improve your vocabulary of feelings. The chart below may be useful.[12] When you wonder how to describe what you feel, check this chart to help you choose the best description. Don't be surprised if you need more than one word, because we often experience a cluster of feelings at the same time. If you are feeling disappointed, for example, are you also feeling angry? Hurt? Where do you feel that in your body? Is your jaw tense? Is your stomach in knots? Is it hard to talk? Is it hard to keep quiet? Are your teeth clenched? Are your eyes stinging? What are you thinking? It may help to keep notes or a feelings journal to help clarify what different feelings are like for you.

*Feelings List*

| calm | secure | relaxed | busy | close |
|---|---|---|---|---|
| tender | safe | sexy | happy | warm |
| irritated | loving | confident | strong | threatened |
| restless | peaceful | enthusiastic | content | pressured |
| proud | attractive | sad | depressed | stupid |
| touched | tired | grumpy | hurt | sorry |
| pessimistic | trapped | confused | guilty | thrilled |
| shaky | rebellious | apathetic | ashamed | generous |
| relieved | overwhelmed | bored | foolish | useless |
| angry | anxious | shy | vulnerable | disappointed |
| | excited | desperate | | |

Once you know what you feel, the next challenge is to express it. You may be afraid that your partner won't want to hear about your anger or will think you are stupid to feel scared. But shared feelings are another building block of intimacy. It is often easier to discuss feelings about past events than to share the feelings that you are actually experiencing at the moment. You can try starting with past ones and then work toward expressing feelings as you feel them.

- *I felt very relieved when you started going to Gambler's Anonymous last year.* (Past)
- *I was crushed when my first lover told me she wanted to break up.* (Past)
- *I feel anxious right now about talking with you because I'm afraid you'll be critical of my plans.* (Present)
- *I am so happy to see you, I may just burst with joy.* (Present)

When you express feelings, you are not making observations or judgments or giving opinions. "I feel" is different than "I think." Sometimes we confuse these two.

For example, "I feel hurt" is a feeling. "I feel that you are trying to hurt me" is *not* a feeling. It is an opinion and a judgment about the other person's behavior, not a statement about our own feelings. "I feel resentful" is a feeling, but "I feel as if I am living with a stranger" is not. One way to tell whether a statement clearly expresses a feeling or a thought or a judgment is to look at the word(s) that come after "I feel." "Hurt" and "resentful" each describe a feeling, but "that you are trying to hurt me" and "as if I am living with a stranger" are not feelings. They describe the expressor's thoughts. To clearly identify these as thoughts, and not feelings, the statement should be "I think that you are trying to hurt me" or "I think you are behaving strangely." Since we have feelings and thoughts, the complete message might be something like "I think you are trying to hurt me, and I feel angry" or "I think you are behaving strangely, and I feel scared about it." In general, feelings are not being expressed clearly when the word "feel" is followed by:[13]

1. words such as "that," "like," or "as if" (examples above);
2. the pronouns "I," "you," "he," "she," and "it"; for example, "I feel I am walking on eggshells around you";
3. names or nouns referring to people; for example, "I feel Gina has been irresponsible," or "I feel my girlfriend is cheating on me."

It is also helpful to distinguish between what we are feeling and how we think others are behaving. "I feel attacked" says more about my interpretation of what you are doing than about what I'm feeling. This is also often true with words like "abandoned," "betrayed," "manipulated," "put down," "taken for granted," "rejected," or "patronized." Experiment with this yourself. Imagine that you say to you partner, "I feel put down." What are you really saying? Are you describing a feeling of yours, or are you describing some behavior of hers that you don't like? Perhaps a more accurate statement on your part would be, "When you talk on and on about how athletic and smart your former girlfriend was, I think you are comparing me with her, and she comes out ahead. Then I feel hurt and resentful."

English can be a very tricky language in which to express feelings. Care and attention to how you express your emotions can go a long way toward avoiding misunderstandings and making connection and intimacy easier.

## Wants and Needs

As we mentioned in Chapter Two, it is often hard for women to ask for what we want. Despite the fact that we are the experts on the topic and no one can read our mind, we may still have difficulty being clear. We may want our partner to figure out what we want so we don't have to discover it ourselves and ask for it directly. If we are afraid to ask, or we believe we shouldn't ask or shouldn't have to ask, we are likely to express our needs in an angry way.

And then there is the question of what is a "want" and what is a "need." We may use the terms interchangeably or describe what we want as a need in order to emphasize just how important an issue is to us. "I *want* you to do this" is not as compelling as "I *need* you to do this." It is helpful to examine, and share with our partner, what we mean. Does our request reflect a preference? "I want you to come with me to visit my daughter." Or is this issue more critical to our well-being? "I need you to go with me to see my daughter." Perhaps you are afraid of her boyfriend or feel desperately in need of moral support as you face her homophobia. If so, it would be useful to provide this information so your partner understands that it really seems like a need to you.

When we try to have an intimate relationship without expressing our wants or needs, it is like driving a car without having a steering wheel. We can go fast, but we can't change directions or steer around potholes in the road. Relationships can best grow and change when each partner clearly expresses her wants and needs.

- *Can you pick up my shoes at the repair shop?*
- *I'm really tired tonight. I'd just like to snuggle on the couch by the fire.*
- *I want for us to set a time to talk about our vacation plans.*
- *Would you hold me for a while?*
- *I need some time to myself this weekend. Can we spend time together Friday night instead of Sunday afternoon?*

In expressing our needs, we are not blaming or finding fault. We are simply describing what would help or please us, and making a request of our partner. It is important to distinguish between *announcing* and *expressing* our wants. When we announce, we leave out making a specific request of our partner. For example, we may say, "I'm cold," hoping that she gets the message that we want her to cuddle. However, she may respond to this announcement by turning up the thermostat, throwing us a blanket, or suggesting that we put on a sweater. And then we may feel hurt that she didn't get the hint. The chances of getting what we want are better if we add the request to the announcement. In this case, "I'm cold. Would you cuddle with me for a while?"

Not every situation requires using all four of the types of expression—observation, thoughts, feelings, and wants or needs. But if we leave out something, or if we mix up the different kinds of expression, our intent probably will not equal the impact on our listener.

> *Susan was hurt. She thought her partner, Allison, was making plans to visit her family and hadn't even asked her if she wanted to be included. Susan's response was to accuse Allison: "I know you want to spend the holidays with your family—without me." Allison had no idea what Susan was talking about—and got defensive.*

Susan left out a lot of information in her accusation of Allison. If she had included all parts of the message, it might have looked something like this:

> *"I heard you talking on the phone with the airlines about flights to D.C.* [Observation] *I figure you're going to visit your family for the holidays and don't want me to go because I'm Jewish.* [Theory] *I feel very hurt* [Feeling], *and I want us to talk about this."* [Want]

Our partners deserve to have complete messages. They are then better able to understand us and to consider changing their behavior to address our wants or needs.

> *Deanna and Gweneth were just about ready to sit down to a gourmet dinner that Deanna had prepared when Gweneth got a phone call. She was on the phone for some time. When she returned, Deanna said, "Our dinner got cold while you were on the phone."*

On the surface, Deanna was making an observation. But she delivered this message with disappointment and anger in her tone of voice and body language. She left out expressing her feelings and her judgment that Gweneth cared more about whomever was on the phone than about her.

When we leave out parts of our message, when we are less than honest, or when the words and music don't match, our partners are likely to become confused or defensive.

### Guidelines for Expressing

*Be aware.* When you decide to express yourself, you need to be clear about the content of your message and your intent in expressing it. Sometimes this requires preparation, maybe even rehearsal. Then, you need to be aware of and consider what kind of state your partner is in. If she has just come home after a difficult mediation session with her ex-husband about child support, she may not be ready to listen to your complaints about dog hair on the rug. Being aware of the other person also means paying attention to her while you are expressing. Is she asking questions? Sitting like a lump on the couch?

It is also important to be aware of the context. Is the environment quiet and private or noisy and full of interruptions? The dinner table with two children under six is not a place to have an important discussion. And while a crowded restaurant may be fine for talking about some things, it is not a place to talk about sex.

*Be clear and straightforward.* These messages can feel risky. You may be afraid of being criticized, hurting your partner's feelings, or not receiving what you ask for. However, indirect or unclear messages usually produce the frustration and anger that you are trying to avoid. You can't get the understanding and intimacy you want unless you are honest about your feelings and thoughts.

Here are some suggestions for clear and direct communication:

- Avoid asking questions when you want to make a statement. Don't ask, "Do you really think we should spend the money?" if what you really mean is, "I'm worried about money, and I don't think we can afford a DVD player right now."

- Use "I" messages when expressing your thoughts, feelings, and needs. "I think you work too much" is clearer and more direct than "All our friends think you work too much." In another example, "I want a hug" is better than "Everybody needs some affection now and then," and "I don't like it when you leave dirty dishes on the counter" is better than "People should clean up after themselves" or "You are a slob."

- Focus on one thing at a time. This means staying with one topic rather than bringing in other issues. Don't start complaining about your partner's eating habits in the middle of a discussion about who is going to take the car to work. If you start to get confused because she (or you) has introduced a new topic, you can say something like, "I'm getting confused. I would like to talk about the car first and get that settled before we move on to another topic."

- Don't go on and on without giving your partner a chance to respond or checking to see if she understands. Communication is a two-way process, not a monologue. Some couples find it helpful to use an egg timer or alarm clock and after each five-minute period (or some agreed-upon amount of time), the expressor and listener switch roles to make sure that both are involved in listening as well as expressing.

*Be honest—albeit with tact and consideration.* Don't say you are anxious about meeting your partner's ex when you are angry about being pushed into the three of you having dinner together. Don't tell your new girlfriend you love the sweater she gave you when you are allergic to wool and know you'll never wear it.

In being honest, it is also important to be considerate and tactful. If partners convey too many *trivial* negative thoughts and feelings, the relationship is likely to suffer. So, how do you decide whether something is too trivial to mention? Just stopping to think may make it clear. If not, in evaluating whether or not to express something, you can ask yourself whether you would want your partner to do so if the situation were reversed.[14] This helps you keep the same standards of honesty for yourself that you ask of your partner.

Good communication should not be confused with having to talk about everything. There are days when you're not going to feel great about your partner. You do not need to share with her your reactive fantasies of finding a new "perfect soul mate." There is no such thing as complete openness or honesty, nor should there be. You have the right to your private thoughts and feelings, and so does your partner. Further, there are times when it is best to keep one's mouth shut. There is simply no substitute for common sense and good judgment in this or any other area. You have to consider the possible consequences of what you say. In most cases you won't have to consider for long because the consequences are not serious. Other issues are potentially more volatile, however, and you should take into account the value, and the timing, of discussing them.[15]

*Be supportive.* Name calling, sarcasm, threats, and unwillingness to listen to or consider our partner's opinions are all ways of communicating disrespect. This negativity introduces contempt into the interaction, and contempt is "relationship poison" because it conveys disgust and inevitably leads to more conflict.[16]

You are being supportive when you acknowledge and respect your partner's opinions whether you agree with them or not. Another way to be supportive is to acknowledge your partner's feelings, even if they don't make sense to you.

*Anaga never fully understood why her partner, Kerry, couldn't stand to throw anything away. Even when Kerry explained, Anaga didn't quite get it. But she knew that Kerry had strong feelings about this, so she was agreeable to setting aside storage space in the basement for Kerry's stuff.*

*Eva knew that Nikki disagreed with her about how to deal with her boss. Nikki was clear that she would handle the situation differently than Eva. But Eva appreciated that Nikki listened to her and respected her decision—even though she disagreed with it.*

In addition to working on listening and expressing skills, good communication requires empathy. Empathy helps us understand our partner's thoughts, feelings, and positions more clearly. One way to increase our empathy is to remember that each of us is simply trying to survive physically and emotionally. From this point of view, everything we do is just a coping strategy to minimize pain and threat, and maximize pleasure and safety.[17]

We cannot eliminate the differences between our partner and ourselves, nor should we try. Instead, our goal is to use these differences as a way of generating closeness. Empathy and compassion generate acceptance where partners feel understood. This sense of understanding builds a more satisfying, secure, and intimate relationship.

## CHAPTER 7

# ⁊ Managing Conflict

For many people, conflict has negative associations. The word itself may conjure up images of an exhausting struggle in which there is a winner and a loser. At best, you may envision an unpleasant clash that is painful or uncomfortable and, therefore, to be avoided. Perhaps your parents fought frequently and unskillfully. You may believe that conflict is a signal that your relationship is in trouble, that you are mismatched or have failed somehow in reaching the goal of having a good relationship.

In fact, conflict is a normal and inevitable part of relationships. Because you and your partner are individuals, with different opinions, wants, experiences, perceptions, and values, you will be in conflict with each other about something at some point in your relationship. You cannot avoid disagreement altogether unless you raise denial to an art form. But how you manage conflict is another story.

*Elaine and Jean have been partners for almost a year and have always spent most of their free time together. Their friends kid them about being Siamese twins. Jean is very devoted to Elaine: She tries to guess what Elaine wants and then do it before she's even asked. She is a good mind reader most of the time. If Elaine feels good, Jean feels good. If Elaine is in a bad mood, Jean soon feels down. Jean can't stand for Elaine to be disappointed or upset with*

*her. She is very uncomfortable if they disagree about anything. The idea of a*
*verbal fight scares Jean to death. It is unthinkable.*

Jean has a hard time knowing what *she* wants. She is very focused on her
relationship and on what Elaine wants. Since she can't stand for Elaine to be
upset with her, she avoids knowing or asking for what she wants, in case it's
not what Elaine wants. She accommodates and sometimes even placates
Elaine, at least on the surface. At the same time, Jean sometimes builds
resentments. Or she may resist doing what Elaine wants, but in an indirect
way. For example, when Jean doesn't want to do things, she often gets a
headache. She frequently gets headaches when she and Elaine have planned
to go dancing. The only place to go dancing in their area is at a local men's
bar. Jean hates that bar, but she has never said this to Elaine. So she gets
headaches. She doesn't do this on purpose, it just happens.

## Asking for What We Want

The conflict between Jean and Elaine highlights issues around "wanting." Because we are women, many of us were taught early in life that wanting is not acceptable; wanting is greedy, selfish, demanding, and not nice.
Good little girls wait until something is offered, share what they have, and
don't ask directly for what they want. Getting what we want means that
someone else will be deprived. Since other people's needs are more important, we learn to put their needs first. Jean is a good example of that training—she only wants Elaine to be happy. Then she will be happy. Deep
down, Jean is afraid that if she asks for what she wants, she won't get it; fur-
thermore, no one will love her. So she resorts to indirect, and even manipulative, tactics to try to get at least some of what she wants. At other times,
Jean convinces herself that she doesn't really want anything, she gets confused about what she wants, or she makes Elaine's desires her own. It's hard
for many women to believe that we have the right to *have* wants and needs.
It is a step further to become aware of what these wants are and to ask for
them clearly and directly.

What does Jean do when she doesn't get what she wants? Though she
may not be sure what she wants and does not ask clearly for it, she does react
when she is not happy with what she is getting. She may feel any or all of the
following: disappointed, hurt, deprived, angry, betrayed, or cheated. These
feelings provide the motivation for conflict. They fuel Jean's struggle to try to
get what she wants from Elaine, to punish Elaine for not giving her what she
wants, or to resist Elaine's pressure to do what Elaine wants. Jean gets

headaches when Elaine wants to go to the bar. Then they spend the evening at home, which is what Jean wanted all along but did not ask for directly. Each time Elaine suggests they go to the bar, they go through this ritual. Each feels frustrated with the other and bad about herself.

This kind of below-the-surface struggle happens because we are fearful of open conflict. There are many reasons for this. Some of us hold to the belief that truly happy couples never fight. Conflict means the relationship is (or soon could be) in trouble. Trained to be peacemakers and soothers, many of us are as uncomfortable with our own anger as we are with our partner's. Anger may have been very controlled and unexpressed in our families. Or we may have grown up with family violence. In any event, many of us may have learned to ignore or swallow our own angry feelings. We give in to our partner and try to smooth over any difficulties.

Whether parents follow the motto of "Never disagree in front of the children" like Jean's parents did, or they engage in brawls, children often do not learn how to deal effectively with conflict. The message they learn is that in intimate relationships there are either no disagreements or that disagreements lead to violence.

When conflicts are not addressed openly and directly, devious power plays and indirect attacks are more likely. Such strategies as "forgetting" something that is important to your partner, "just not being interested" in sex, apathy toward your partner, and exaggerated interest in work and other people by comparison may be signs of smoldering resentments that are not being addressed. Jean's indirect approaches include her headaches. She is also sometimes just too tired to do what Elaine wants. Elaine accuses Jean of pouting, but Jean would never acknowledge that—because she doesn't acknowledge that she's not getting what she wants.

Recognizing and expressing wants is linked to self-esteem and a healthy sense of being separate (see Chapter Three). Jean needs to believe that "It's okay to want; I deserve to have my needs met; I have a right to ask directly for what I want." She also needs to learn that wanting and getting are different. Just because Jean asks does not mean that she will have her request granted. Since she so rarely asks for anything, but waits until it is important that she gets it, she is devastated if things don't go her way. Then she convinces herself that there is no point in asking for anything ever again. "I don't get what I want anyway, so why stick my neck out? I'll just be disappointed."

It is possible for conflict to change from being a "dirty word" for Jean and Elaine. If Jean gets clearer with herself about what she wants, if she expresses these desires to Elaine, and if the couple negotiates about meeting them, Jean's indirect methods will not be necessary.

## Conflict Styles

There are three styles of fighting that describe how most couples try to resolve their differences. Some couples do whatever is required to avoid conflict, other couples fight a lot, and yet others are able to talk through their differences and work our solutions without arguing.

Research indicates that no one style is necessarily better than another.[1] Many relationships can work well even though the couple tends to shove things under the rug. Other couples can have loud arguments and still report being very satisfied in their relationship. The important thing is that the style works for *both* people. Couples run into trouble if partners have different styles. For example, one woman may want to talk through a conflict while the other wants to ignore it.

> *Lois believes in talking disagreements through—she calls it processing. In her previous relationship, she and her ex managed to work out their differences pretty successfully using this approach. She was taken aback when her new partner, Rene, complained that as far as she was concerned they were spending far too much time "processing things to death."*

Difficulties can also occur if the style followed doesn't really work for the couple. For example, partners may both avoid conflict but not truly let the issue go.

> *Jackie and Lorraine both disliked conflict intensely. When they disagreed, they dropped the subject and avoided each other for a while. Eventually they didn't talk to each other about much at all because many topics had become off-limits. They had little real communication, and their sense of closeness was eroded.*

If partners identify their styles and talk about what works and doesn't work for each of them, hopefully they can reach some agreements about how they want to handle their conflicts.

> *Bobbie and Muretta have a problem about how they fight. Bobbie comes from a family of "yellers," and when she gets angry, she raises her voice. This upsets Muretta, who gets very frightened when people yell. Bobbie maintains that*

*she is just expressing her feelings and there is nothing wrong with what she does. Muretta insists she cannot stand it and inevitably they end up arguing about Bobbie yelling rather than about whatever started the disagreement.*

These two have different emotional styles, which are unlikely to change since these styles are part of their personalities. Bobbie is passionate and emotionally expressive; Muretta prefers to talk things over calmly and rationally. When Bobbie yells, Muretta feels overwhelmed and unable to think clearly. They need to realize how their styles are different, be respectful of these differences, and find an approach that feels comfortable, or at least workable, to both. Perhaps Bobbie could time-limit her yelling, lower her voice a few decibels, or face the window rather than yelling directly toward Muretta. For her part, Muretta might take notes while Bobbie vents, make sure there is enough physical space between them to feel less overwhelmed, or only have these interactions outside. Another possibility is that Bobbie could yell for a certain amount of time, then they could take a short break and come back together when Muretta feels she can express herself clearly and Bobbie indicates that she can listen.

## Perpetual Problems

Whatever your styles, there are two kinds of conflicts in relationships—resolvable and perpetual problems.[2] As we mentioned in Chapter Two, almost 70 percent of all couple conflicts fall into the category of perpetual problems—the ones that keep coming up over and over again. These will be an ongoing part of your life in some form or another, because they are fueled by underlying and fundamental differences between you and your partner.

Success in a relationship depends, in part, on figuring out which problems are resolvable and which ones are perpetual. As we pointed out earlier, it is not possible to resolve all of your conflicts, nor is it necessary to do so in order to have a healthy relationship. It is necessary to resolve the problems you can and to learn to cope with those of the perpetual variety. You do this by avoiding situations that worsen them and by developing strategies and routines that help you deal with them.[3]

*Kiri and Ravella have very different ideas about what constitutes an acceptable level of order in the house they share. Kiri could have written the adage, "A place for everything and everything in its place." Ravella always has a number of projects going on, which means piles of papers and materials here*

*and there. She also has a tendency to misplace things. Their frequent bicker-*
*ing about this issue sometimes flares into nasty arguments.*

This couple needs to keep acknowledging their difference and continue talking about it because it is an ongoing and often daily occurrence. A sense of humor and a light touch on Kiri's part will go a long way toward smoothing the rough places with this perpetual problem. Similarly, Ravella's genuine attempts to contain her things and good-naturedly compromise with Kiri will be helpful. Undoubtedly, when one or both of them are stressed, they may have a blowup about something important like Ravella misplacing her wallet and causing them to be late to a party because she has to find it. Hopefully, Kiri can get over her fit of pique, and Ravella can be appropriately contrite, so they can carry on with their evening and have a good time.

## Solvable Problems

Solvable problems are more likely situational, specific, and focused on a particular issue. They are usually less intense than perpetual problems because they are about what they seem to be about. Of course, the arguments may still be unpleasant and even painful. In addition, if solvable conflicts do not get resolved, they can deepen and become perpetual problems.

*When they first started living together, Annie and Jan agreed on a system for household tasks. Grocery shopping is Jan's job. However, she has been working long hours, is under a lot of stress, and has not been keeping up with the food shopping. Annie has tried to be understanding, but it has been weeks now since Jan did a thorough shopping job and they are run-ning out of things. This morning when there was no milk for her cereal, Annie hit the roof.*

*Ever since they brought their newborn baby home from the hospital, Diane has felt like she couldn't do anything right for him. Her partner, Mina, the birth mother, complains that Diane isn't doing enough, but every time she tries to diaper him or soothe his crying, Mina suggests that she do it differ-ently. Diane is beginning to feel incompetent—and resentful.*

Both of these situations began recently and appear solvable, assuming that they are not expressing deeper issues. Jan is under temporary stress, and she and Annie need to work out a different arrangement, at least for the time being. Mina and Diane are also in a stressful situation—happy, but stressful nonetheless. Assuming that Mina's critiquing of Diane's every move is a new behavior, these two need to talk through what is going on for each of them and resolve how they are going to be with each other, and with their baby.

## Do's for Addressing Conflicts

Here are a number of suggestions for dealing with conflict.[4] Many of these are useful for both perpetual and solvable problems.

- DO make sure your partner feels that you understand and accept her. It is hard, maybe even close to impossible, to accept advice or requests for change when we feel misunderstood, rejected, or judged and found lacking.
- DO treat your partner with the same respect you would show to a guest. Would you berate a guest for breaking a glass or blow up at company who arrived late for dinner? We already possess the skills required for behaving civilly and sensitively to guests—we usually don't require special training. We just don't always apply these skills in our intimate relationships.
- DO keep your language in the realm of complaints rather than criticism. Complaints address specific behavior; criticism is global and adds blame and general character assassination. For example, "I get nervous when you drive this fast. I thought we agreed that you would keep to the speed limit when I'm with you" is a complaint. "Here you go again, driving recklessly. You know how scared I get; you don't care about my feelings. And you're going to get us both killed" is a criticism. Since you can turn any complaint into a criticism by adding, "What is wrong with you?" to it, delete this phrase from your vocabulary.
- DO avoid directing contempt, which includes sarcasm and cynicism, toward your partner. Sneering, eye rolling, and name calling are also in the contempt family. Contempt is poisonous to relationships because it conveys disgust and leads to more conflict. It is fueled by long-simmering negative thoughts, which you are more likely to have if your differences are not resolved. Work on resolving or relieving those conflicts, cultivate positive thoughts, and practice the strategy (from Chapter Two) of nurturing fondness and affection for your partner.
- DO try asking yourself, "How did I contribute to this conflict?" as a way of reducing your defensiveness. Defensiveness is really a way to blame your partner, and it merely escalates the conflict. The more you can hold on to yourself, avoid taking everything your partner says too personally,

and take responsibility for your contribution to the problem, the more likely you will keep the discussion on track.

- DO "soften your start-up" when you bring up a complaint. If you go straight for the jugular, you'll get a lot of blood. It won't be a pretty sight and you will likely get a battle or withdrawal from your partner. The start-up is important because research indicates that discussions almost inevitably end on the same note they began.[5] So if it starts off badly, it will probably end up the same way—not to mention the in-between. There are various ways to soften your start-up. The next section, which outlines a structure for negotiating, elaborates on these suggestions: Be descriptive, clear, and specific, use "I" messages, and be polite and appreciative. An example of a harsh start-up is "You never pay any attention to me." You can soften your start-up with rephrasing: "I know that you have been really busy, but I miss having fun times with you. I'm feeling a little lonely."

- DO bring issues up sooner rather than later. Like mushrooms, resentments grow in the dark, and the intensity of negative feeling increases as well. It becomes harder to initiate a discussion with a gentler start-up.

- DO learn to put on the brakes when your discussion starts going badly. Gottman refers to this as "making and receiving repair attempts." He has even developed a long list of scripted phrases that you can use to try to de-escalate tension and keep the discussion from spiraling out of control.[6] Some examples are "I see your point," "Let's find our common ground," "I'm sorry. Please forgive me." "Can we take a break?" "I feel blamed. Can you rephrase that?" and "I need things to be calmer right now."

- DO develop your skills to calm the situation by soothing yourself and each other. Being able to soothe yourself keeps you from experiencing severe emotional distress even if your partner is criticizing you. Instead of feeling flooded, overwhelmed, and shell-shocked, you can listen and respond appropriately. You are also more able to hear your partner's repair attempts. To soothe yourself in the midst of a conversation, you may need to breathe deeply, to "count to ten," or to really focus on listening rather than on rehearsing your own response. If you become over-whelmed and too distressed to think clearly—it's been described as "brain freeze"—you need to take a time-out to calm yourself. Your system has become flooded with adrenaline and it will take twenty minutes for it to physically recover. During this twenty-minute time-out, make sure that you monitor your self-talk. It won't calm you down to spend the time criticizing your partner, or yourself, in your mind. Hopefully you have had a previous conversation with your partner about what you can do to help calm and soothe each other. So when you return to the discussion, you can employ some of those approaches—as can she.

- DO allow yourself to be influenced by your partner (see Chapter Two). While it is important to remain clear about your own wants and needs, you also need to listen to her about hers. This will allow the two of you to negotiate solutions that satisfy you both. By exploring your wants and preferences in a collaborative way, you increase the chances that you will develop creative solutions that truly address the issues and that you can both genuinely support.

- DO tolerate each other's faults. Until you accept your partner—warts and all—you will be on a mission to change her. Resolving conflict is not about one of you doing all of the changing. It is about negotiating, finding common ground, and searching for ways to accommodate each other without giving up yourself.

## A Structure for Dealing with Conflicts

For couples who could benefit from having a structure for working on negotiating solvable problems (and even working on perpetual problems), we offer an eight-step model of the negotiation process. This model has been adapted from *Self Care* by Yetta Bernhard and from *Parent Effectiveness Training* by Thomas Gordon.[7]

Sometimes you or your partner may be clear about what you want. Sometimes one or both of you may have identified a problem behavior or a problem issue, but do not yet have a specific idea about how to resolve the situation. This approach can be used in either case.

### Step One: Warm-Up

This is a solo part, where you need to ask yourself the following kinds of questions: Am I really angry or only mildly irritated? What do I want my partner to do, or not do, that is different from what she is or isn't doing? What specifically do I dislike? What do I want? Do I really want this change, or do I want to hurt my partner? Is this issue really important to me? Are my feelings in proportion?

### Step Two: Set the Time

Ask your partner for a definite time to talk. If you encounter some resistance, be persistent; tell her that the issue is important to you and that it hasn't gone away and won't until you discuss it. Try to set the time for as soon as possible, but also respect your partner's wants. If the topic is a hot one, set a limit on how much time you'll talk. Sometimes it is easier to get agreement on meeting for fifteen minutes or a half hour, rather than leaving the amount of time open-ended. If you do not finish in the time you agreed upon, arrange to extend the current discussion for another set amount of time or to continue at a specific later time.

### Step Three: State the Problem

If the situation is that there is something your partner does, or does not do, that you don't like, clearly describe what that is. Keep it to the point: simple, direct, and short. It is very important to stick to the facts, without blaming and adding your feelings about the behavior. If you have a hard time being clear or keeping your feelings out of it, you may need to practice this step in advance. Rehearse what you are going to say and your tone of voice.

If the situation is a more general issue, such as planning vacations, saving for retirement, or landscaping the back yard, both of you should give your perspective on the issue by stating all the information you have about it. Ask yourself, "What are the facts surrounding the topic of planning vacations?"

### Step Four: State Feelings

Use "I" messages to describe how you feel—"I feel angry, hurt, disappointed, confused." Avoid the blaming quality of "you" messages, such as "You make me feel so mad when you just sit there like a lump." Instead, take responsibility for your reactions and feelings and say, "I feel mad." Include the other feelings you may have underneath, or secondary to the anger, such as "I'm scared about feeling so angry and about talking with you about it. I'm really nervous right now." Resist the temptation to blame your partner for your feelings and to end by saying, "And it's all your fault that I feel the way I do." Blaming will likely make your partner defensive; after all, she has been attacked and blamed by you. Plus, the discussion is harder to keep on a constructive tack.

### Step Five: Make a Specific Request

Ask specifically for what you want. Make your request simple, clear, and direct. You want your partner to do, or not do, what? Avoid asking for changes in "attitudes" because these are not specific. For example, "I want you to be more considerate" is not specific enough. Exactly what is it that you want her to do, or not do, that would show you consideration? Asking her to "clean up her dishes" is also not specific enough. Is she showing the consideration you want if she brings them from the living room into the kitchen?

Do you want her to pile them in the sink? Or wash them and leave them in the rack? Or dry them and put them away?

### Step Six: Respond and Negotiate

This is where the partner who has been on the listening end gets to talk. If this is you, hopefully you will really have been able to listen without getting defensive and will have checked already, or will check at this point, that you clearly understand the problem, your feelings, and the specific request your partner has made. You can make this check by summarizing; for example, "Let me make sure I understand. When I don't call and let you know that I will be late, you worry about what may have happened to me. You want me to call if I will be late, so that you won't worry."

You then respond to the change proposed by your partner—not to your feelings about the problem or to the questions of whether or not it is a real problem. Telling her that she should not feel the way she does, or that the problem is not a real one, is not an acceptable response. Appropriate responses to specific requests usually take one of five forms:

1. "Yes, I'll do it."
2. "Yes, I agree, with the following conditions." The conditions must relate directly to the proposal and not involve some other issue as a trade—the reason being that this introduces another issue, and may take the negotiations off track. The following is an example of appropriate conditions: "I am willing to schedule and take the car in for tune-ups as long as you are willing to pick it up if I am working out of town."
3. "No, I won't do it." This may indicate some hostility or some previously unshared strong feelings or wants.
4. "No, I don't want to do that, but I would be willing to do this." You make a counterproposal.
5. "How about a time-out? Let me think about this until [a specific time in the future]."

When the situation under discussion is an issue rather than one partner's specific request of the other, both of you toss out ideas for possible solutions. In this brainstorm, all ideas are shared—practical or not—without evaluation in order to encourage the fullest and most creative solutions to emerge. Avoid the "that won't work because" mentality. Wait until later to evaluate the ideas. Once all the ideas for a solution are out, you can negotiate the solution or combination of approaches that appeals to you.

### Step Seven: Reach Resolution

If you have come to an agreement, then the conflict is resolved. Set a trial period after which you can meet again to modify or continue the agreement. Agreements for changes to the solutions can be renegotiated whenever they stop serving either partner's needs.

If you have not been able to reach an agreement in the time allotted, set a time for another session and declare this one over.

### Step Eight: Clarify the Agreement

Repeat the agreement aloud, in turn, making sure you both have exactly the same understanding about it. It's a good idea to write the agreement down on paper, because our memories are often imperfect.

## Troubleshooting the Negotiations

*If you get too distressed or angry to continue negotiating or if the process is going off track:*

Use the "time-out" technique. Time-out means just that. It is a break in the action, much as it is used in sports, to give you and your partner a break to regroup, calm down, and plan your strategy. Both must agree to abide by the time-out; i.e., one person must not follow the other through the house trying to re-engage her in discussion before the time-out is over. The person who calls for a time-out needs to specify how long she wants. Take at least twenty minutes (because of the adrenaline issue we mentioned earlier). You can always approach your partner after one time-out and request another, if you need more time. We also recommend that you take no more of a break than twenty-four hours because longer than that usually means you are avoiding the issue and leaving your partner hanging.

*If you have a tendency to blame:*

Practice the "I" message technique. This involves describing your feelings *as* your feelings; i.e., "I feel hurt when you. . . ." It is important not to confuse "feel" with "think." "I feel that you are a jerk" is *not* an "I feel" message. Neither is "I feel that you are trying to manipulate me." These are "I think" statements. To tell the difference, look at the word that follows the word "feel." Is it a feeling or is it the word "that"? If it is "that," you know that "that" is *not* a feeling. (See more on feelings in Chapter Six.)

*If you have trouble listening, or if either of you feels unheard or not listened to:*

You might try repeating your partner's ideas back to her (or even in your own mind) to make sure that you didn't miss or misunderstand anything. The key thing is to check out your comprehension of what she has said before you respond with your ideas or point of view. Keep in mind that she is the expert on what she said, or at least on what she meant. Don't go on until *she* agrees that you heard her accurately and understood what she said. Often a misunderstanding in communication occurs very early in the process and the whole discussion gets off on the wrong foot.

*If you store up old resentments and then throw them into each argument:*
Make a grievance list that contains all the things that you ever resented or were hurt about. Don't leave anything out. Then go through the list. Cross off any grievances that you really can let go. Now look at the others to see which ones might be suitable for conflict resolution. Go through the eight steps outlined to address the items on your list.

*If you are getting nowhere in your attempts to negotiate:*
Consider the possibility that you are working with a perpetual problem (see below). Get some outside help: Go to a workshop, read a book (see the Resources section), see a counselor, or use other interventions that are likely to improve your understanding of yourself and your partner, your skills, and your conflict styles.

## The Most Common Couple Conflicts

It is possible to predict what a couple fights about even without knowing anything about them. The most typical areas of marital conflict are money, sex, work stress, housework, "in-laws"/family (biological and chosen), and children.[8] Look over the list. Do at least some of the hot buttons in your relationship appear?

Even though every relationship is different and a couple may be very happy in their relationship, these issues—and others—are likely candidates for conflict because they touch on the most important tasks involved in any relationship. The following outline of relationship tasks has been adapted from *The Seven Principles for Making Marriage Work*, by John Gottman and Nan Silver, and from *The Good Marriage* by Judith Wallerstein and Sandra Blakeslee.[9]

1. Building togetherness and creating autonomy. As a couple, you need to create a psychological "identity" for your relationship—what you want it to be—and also include a sense of individual autonomy in the "we-ness."

2. Separating from your family of origin (if you haven't already) and redefining your ties with family. Defining yourself as partner first, daughter second. (Done in concert with number one.)
3. Exploring sexual love and intimacy.
4. Making your relationship a haven of peace.
5. Making a safe place for conflict.
6. Coping with crises.
7. Providing emotional nurturance.
8. Sharing laughter and keeping interests alive.
9. Becoming and being parents (if there are children involved).
10. Dealing with money. You have to balance the freedom and empowerment that money represents with the security it also symbolizes.

You and your partner may have different ideas about these issues and tasks, how important they are, and how they should be accomplished.

*Stephanie always wanted to have children and thought that her partner, Ari, did too. At first there were obstacles such as needing to finish school and being able to afford a living space that was big enough. But now that they are in a position to actually go ahead and find a donor, Ari's enthusiasm seems to have faded.*

*Cathy jokes that her Scottish ancestry is responsible for her approach to money. She credits her grandmother, who used to advise her to "Watch the pennies, and the dollars will take care of themselves." Her partner, Denise, is more of a spender who practices "shopping therapy" whenever she can. Every year at tax time they get into arguments about what to do with any refund.*

*Greta is more interested in sex than her partner, Jen. If the frequency or intensity of their sex life slips a bit, Greta is convinced it is the beginning of "lesbian bed death." Jen's attitude is more casual and relaxed—which alarms Greta even more. She is convinced that Jen is not taking the issue seriously enough.*

*Adrian is unhappy with the local public junior high school and wants to send her daughter, Shauna, to private school. The problem is the money. Both she and her partner, Melanie, would need to keep working full-time to afford the tuition. Melanie would have to postpone her dream of working only part-time and pursuing her writing.*

The challenge for each of these couples is to work together as a team to devise a plan that both partners feel good about. (Check the chapters on decision-making, sex, and children for ideas about solutions for different conflicts.)

## Addressing Perpetual Problems: Overcoming Gridlock

In our relationships—just like in traffic—we can be hopelessly stuck and frustrated. If you and your partner seem mired in an endless recycling of the same argument, it may be that you have become stuck in a gridlocked perpetual problem.[10] The goal in relationship gridlock is not to solve the problem but to move from being stuck to having dialogue, so you can learn to live with the problem. You need to do so because if it is a perpetual problem, it will likely be with you for the duration of your relationship.

Signs of gridlock include:

* making no headway in discussions—which can then turn ugly,
* getting more polarized in your positions,
* feeling hurt,
* feeling rejected, and
* emotionally disengaging from your partner.

In order to get beyond feeling stuck, first you must understand the underlying cause of the gridlock. Gridlock is a "sign that you have dreams for your life that are not being addressed or respected by each other. These dreams are the hopes, aspirations, and wishes that are part of your identity and give purpose and meaning to your life."[11]

*Daphne and Mickey have been together for ten years and have three children. One of the issues they argue about is vacations. Daphne wants to spend vacations with her extended family on the East Coast. They have a big house on the water where everybody gathers during the summer. The cousins get to meet each other and have a ball. The adults can visit and take turns cooking, lifeguarding, and lying in the hammock. Mickey would prefer to have some time alone with Daphne where they do something active—a skiing, backpacking, or bicycle trip—and then have some adventure as a family, just the two of them and the kids.*

What dreams might be embedded in this conflict?

*Daphne: Extended family is very important to me. My happiest memories of growing up are of times at my family summer place. I want my children to have those memories too. My dream is for us as a family to have the feeling of closeness and connection that I had with the community of my extended family.*

*Mickey: I have spent a lot of time and energy trying to get over the effects of growing up in a very dysfunctional family. I moved across the country to get some distance from my family—to escape actually. I am very cautious about getting too involved with Daphne's family. I see some dysfunctional patterns there as well and it scares me. My dream is to establish our own traditions with ourselves, our children, and our friends.*

Once the dreams are uncovered, Daphne and Mickey can talk about them. One option is for them to take turns talking honestly about their dreams. One talks for fifteen minutes while the other listens, then they switch. The listener's job is to listen as a friend would, to ask supportive questions, and to understand why this dream is so important. If you try this yourself, remember that the purpose is not to resolve the conflict. It is to encourage a dialogue and to lessen the hurt so the problem becomes less painful.

Hopefully, once you each understand what hidden dreams underlie a perpetual problem, you can support your partner's dream. This does not mean that you will do whatever your partner wants or take on her dream as yours. The goal here is to be supportive. Listening, being interested, and understanding (not necessarily agreeing) is one level of support, and that may be as far as you can go. You may be willing to go further and support the dream in some tangible way—say financially. You may even be willing to join your partner in realizing her dream.

Ending the gridlock requires making peace with the issue. You need to clarify what aspects of the issue are nonnegotiable. These are the ones you cannot give up without violating your basic needs, core values, and sense of integrity. And you need to figure out what aspects you can be more flexible about. Try to make the first list short and the second long. Then share this information with your partner—perhaps using the eight-step negotiation process outlined earlier in this chapter. Work toward a solution that honors and respects both of your dreams.

## When Conflict Turns to Violence

While differences and conflict are inevitable, violence is never necessary. Verbal, emotional, physical, and even sexual abuse is not the exclusive domain of heterosexuals. It can and does happen in lesbian relationships and the dynamics are similar to those in abusive heterosexual relationships.[12]

Domestic violence is a pattern of abusive and coercive behaviors, including physical, sexual, and psychological attacks, as well as economic coercion, that one person uses to control her current or former intimate partner.[13] The woman who is abused loses her sense of personal power, confidence, and control. Which partner is abused does not depend on size, role, or physical abilities. The woman who abuses often has low self-esteem and few anger-management skills, is afraid of losing control over her partner and herself, and believes that violence is permissible. The sequence of eruption and violence is followed by guilt, apologies, and promises of "never again." A honeymoon period of closeness is followed by a repeat of the violence. Alcohol or drugs may be involved, but not necessarily.

Until recently, violence in lesbian relationships has not been well documented. One reason for this is that the women have not identified the behavior as abusive. Women who grow up in families where abuse is "normal" are particularly prone to minimize or fail to label their partner's behavior—or their own—as abusive.

> Phillipa grew up in a violent family. Her mother was physically abusive, and both parents kept up a steady stream of criticism, putdowns, and threats directed toward Phillipa and her younger brother. Phillipa was regularly accused of being "stupid," "worthless," and "a dirty slut." Her parents threatened the children with physical beatings and abandonment if they did not do what their parents wanted them to do. There were enough beatings to make these threats quite believable. This was all "normal" family life.
>
> Phillipa's first partner, Judy, had a "short fuse," as she described it. When Judy lost her temper she usually directed her anger at Phillipa. She blamed Phillipa for whatever had gone wrong—and yelled and screamed a lot. Because Judy had never physically assaulted her, Phillipa did not think of Judy's behavior as abusive. Judy's yelling and the things she said were not as bad as what Phillipa had grown up with. She did get scared when Judy blew up, and her feelings were hurt by Judy's attacks, but she did not realize that she was being abused. After each episode, Phillipa minimized it—"It wasn't so bad," "It didn't really bother me too much," or "That's just how Judy is." She did not name Judy's behavior as abusive—so she just put up with it.

Another reason for the lack of documentation on violence in lesbian relationships is that even when a woman knows that her partner is being abusive, or that she herself is abusive, she keeps it secret. This may happen because she feels afraid or ashamed, or because she lacks the support of the lesbian community.

> *Adrienne was so intimidated by her partner Helen's threats of suicide that she hardly went anywhere anymore except to work. Helen wanted her to stay home—and she did.*

> *Randa and Jordan both felt guilty and ashamed after they would "lose it" in a fight and scream and hit each other. Neither of them would even think of telling anyone. It was too embarrassing.*

> *When Tamara finally admitted to herself that her partner Joy's behavior was abusive, she was mortified She blamed herself for allowing it to happen. Her stance of "I should have known better; I should have stopped it before it got to this point" made it hard for her to tell even her counselor about the situation.*

> *When Dionne summoned up the courage to tell some other lesbians about the beatings by her partner, May, they were shocked and disbelieving. "I just can't believe May would do that" and "You must have done something to provoke her" were typical responses. When Dionne finally made the break from May, she also left the area where she had lived for ten years, because she had felt such a lack of support from the community.*

Although some abusive behaviors are more dangerous than others, most of them are potentially dangerous, and all show a lack of respect and an attempt to intimidate and control the other person. Barbara Hart points out that there are situations in which both partners are abusive; both may be physically violent, or one may be physically abusive and the other verbally abusive. While she opposes all violence, Hart distinguishes between *incidents* of violence and *battering*. The critical ingredients are that the batterer uses violence or abusive behavior to gain *power* and *control* over her partner, and that there is a pattern of using violence to achieve these ends. A woman is battered if she is "controlled or lives in fear of her lover because of actual attacks, or threats or gestures."[14]

How do you know if you are a victim of domestic violence or if your partner's (or your own) behavior is abusive? One way is to think of abuse as being along a continuum from mild to severe. At the severe end are behaviors such as forced sex, choking, beating, and hitting with objects like sticks. At the milder end are behaviors such as name calling, verbal threats, and insults.

*It took Dorothy some time to realize that her partner's behavior was emotionally abusive. Esther's criticism and belittling were often subtle. She constantly said things like, "Let me fix that because you'll probably break it," "Are you sure you're really qualified for that job you are applying for?" and "You look so much better since you lost weight, but now your clothes look awful on you." No particular comment was all that bad, but the sheer number of them and her tone of voice combined to undermine Dorothy's confidence and self-esteem.*

*During the time they were involved with each other, Ginger thought of her partner Lynn's behavior when she got angry as cruel but not as abusive. Lynn never actually hit Ginger, and she never even threatened to. What she did do was break Ginger's things, tear up her writing, or destroy something that was important to Ginger. Afterward, she would apologize and buy Ginger a present, trying to replace what she had ruined.*

One of the problems with abuse is that it escalates so that even behaviors that might be considered mild may be indications of a growing tendency. It gets worse. Another problem is that *both* partners in an abusive relationship tend to minimize the frequency, intensity, seriousness, and impact of the abuse. Abuse is always unhealthy—for the abused and the abuser.

If you think you're being abused, get help. Contact a counselor, a women's shelter, a domestic-violence hotline, Web site, or someone who can give you support and help you find the resources you need to change your situation. The book *Getting Free* by Ginny NiCarthy clearly identifies what abuse is and how to get out of an abusive relationship. *Naming the Violence: Speaking Out About Lesbian Battering*, edited by Kerry Lobel, is written by and for battered lesbians and those who work with them. There are also a number of lesbian and gay antiviolence projects around the country that can help both the abused and the abuser. (See Resources.)

We recommend that therapists working with lesbians and lesbian couples check for domestic violence. Don't assume that abuse and battering don't happen in lesbian relationships.

When addressed in a healthy way, conflict is an inherent and useful aspect of couple relationships. The ability to resolve conflicts involves applying skills—many of which we likely already have—to both solvable and perpetual problems. As with other skills, we get better with practice. If we are empathetic and accepting of our partner, resolving our conflicts can help us feel even closer and more intimate with each other.

## CHAPTER 8

# ᔥ Sex

As a sexual minority, we are regarded by much of our society as sexual out-laws, deviants, or perverts. We know we are "not normal" from society's per-spective but we may wonder if we are normal as compared to other lesbians. We may wonder which sexual behaviors, fantasies, or desires are normal and truly lesbian.[1] Thanks to homophobia, sexism, and cultural taboos on the open sharing of information about sex, we have had too little access to infor-mation about sex between women—until more recently, when there has been a relative explosion. (See Resources.)

There are as many ways to have lesbian sex as there are lesbians—and women who have sex with other women, no matter how they identify.[2] In fact, the more we look for what is "normal" for lesbians, the more we box our-selves into narrow lives and narrow expectations. There is no "normal." There is only the exploration and expression of our own sexuality as we create our own unique sexual lives.

Sex therapist Lenore Teifer believes that "sex is fundamentally a cultural phenomenon. It doesn't exist in a fixed way but is created in relation to whatever is going on in the culture at any given moment."[3] So what was cutting-edge years ago is less so now. The "love that dares not speak its name" has changed. Controversies about SM and butch/femme have given way to a generally lighter—even playful—attitude and the gender-bending of the '90s. The personal ads sport a new crop of initials. Who knows what it will look like in 2050?

In her book *Lesbian Sex: An Oral Tradition,* Susan Johnson makes a similar point from a different direction. "We are all captives of our time in history and thus much of what we know and feel, enjoy and fear is born out of the intersection of our own private life with the public life around us. How we define our lesbian identity, how we express our lesbian sexuality, how we understand our lesbian selves are all importantly influenced by when we were born, when we came out, when we first made love to a woman."[4] Since sex is always changing, the point, according to Teifer, is to be prepared to deal with cultural messages in ways that don't infringe on the enjoyment of sex.

In this chapter we will focus on three sex-related concerns commonly expressed by lesbian couples as well as address the topic of monogamy versus nonmonogamy.

> *Eleanor woke up luxuriously savoring the familiar sounds and smells of a Sunday morning. She and Audrey had been together for nine years and had their own Sunday ritual for the last three. Audrey got up early, made coffee, and read the paper. By the time Eleanor woke up, Audrey had everything ready for a delightful breakfast in bed. Eleanor loved this comfort, but she missed the lovemaking that had been their Sunday-morning fare the first years of their relationship. She remembered how they would make love, take a bath together, and then go out to breakfast. Eleanor wanted sex as much as ever, but now Audrey usually wanted to make love only once every month or so and had stopped initiating at all. Eleanor masturbated a lot and was content most of the time. But today she found herself really missing their sexual connection and wondering if anything was seriously wrong.*

As is the case for most long-term couples, sex has decreased over the course of Eleanor and Audrey's relationship. Another important aspect of this relationship is that Eleanor wants sex more often than Audrey and she wants Audrey to initiate it. This couple illustrates the three main concerns about sex that lesbian couples identify: namely desire, frequency, and initiation. As we look at these concerns, we'll show how they often overlap and arise quite predictably over the course of a couple relationship.

## The Biology of Desire

No one knows the origins of sexual desire. Most likely a variety of factors, both biological and cultural, affect desire. More and more, researchers are focusing attention on the biological components of desire—especially hormones. The strongest correlations between hormones and sexuality emerge when pure, disembodied desire is the object of study. For example, in one study, five hundred women took their basal temperatures every day for several months and also recorded the day in the month when they first noticed the stirrings of sexual desire. The results showed an extraordinary connection between the onset of sexual desire and the time near ovulation.[5]

The provocative core of this new research in behavioral endocrinology and psychophysiology suggests that each of us approaches our erotic encounters already primed by a premixed neurological and hormonal "cocktail," which influences both the strength and the staying power of sexual passion. In short, our sexual desire is orchestrated by our body chemistry.[6] Of course passion is also influenced by many other factors (more about those later). The point is that the biochemistry of the brain influences how often and how much each of us wants sex and it may do so more than we ever imagined.

Another way to think about this is that love is "a natural high."[7] Remember when you first fell in love? Most people report not being able to get enough of each other in those first weeks and months. The most ordinary activity, like going to the laundromat together, is an exciting and deeply rewarding event. Not to mention the sex. It is hot, fun, uninhibited—and "absolutely amazing."

It turns out that the experience of intense passion has a biological base in which the body is literally swamped with amphetamine-like chemicals such as dopamine, norepinephrine, and especially phenylethylamine (PEA). Romantic love may well be a genuinely altered state of consciousness, which would explain why new lovers can "talk until dawn, make love for hours on end, lose weight without trying, and feel so outrageously, unquenchably optimistic."[8] Their brains are soaking in natural uppers. It's as though our erotic thermostats get overwhelmed, so we want scads of sex, get our fill, and then want more. It must be love.

But it doesn't last. The universal truth is that this state of bliss does not last. A number of studies that have measured the duration of infatuation—from the first moment of euphoria to the first feeling of neutrality for one's love object—have found that romantic rapture predictably burns out after eighteen to thirty-six months—at least for heterosexual couples.[9] Lesbian couples are not that different. There seems to be a plunge in sexual frequency after about two years."[10]

*After the first year or so of their relationship, Ally and Lena found they weren't having sex as often, and it wasn't as passionate as before. They were both worried that these were signs of the "lesbian bed death" that they had heard about—and vowed would never happen to them.*

It is also true that other factors contribute to the demise of infatuation. The fact that our lover has priorities other than making us happy is one; her minor flaws or irritating habits, which we overlooked or minimized initially, are others. But perhaps equally important to our decreasing infatuation is our brain physiology. The theory is that our body cannot maintain its revved-up, lust-crazed state of romantic bliss either because we gradually build up a tolerance to the brain's natural stimulants or because levels of PEA and related substances begin to drop. The "natural high" fades and the downshift in sexual desire takes over. Reality intrudes.

According to Janis Abrahms Spring, in the stage of love after infatuation, the brain releases a new set of chemicals called endorphins—natural painkillers that soothe the individual and create a sense of security and calm. These chemicals can help couples move from a heated infatuation to an intimate, sustaining attachment. This description of chemical changes implies that the transition from romantic to a more seasoned love is smooth and effortless as our brain and body chemistry carry us from one phase to another. Not so. In any long-term relationship, partners pass through stages that often include a sustained period of disenchantment.[11] For your relationship to survive, you need to be prepared for, and accept, the vicissitudes of love. One of these vicissitudes—for the postinfatuation couple—is the emergence of a desire gap.

## The Desire Gap

Early in the relationship, when the brains and blood streams of you and your new lover are awash in the aphrodisiac properties of PEA and other brain molecules, any differences in libido are likely to go unnoticed. As the body chemistry changes, and returns to a more usual state, the impact of yet another biological factor emerges—testosterone.

When you think testosterone, you may think "male" and "horny" and not necessarily in a kindly way. The fact is that women, as well as men, produce testosterone and that it has been shown to affect our sexual desire. In 1987, Barbara Sherwin conducted a now-classic study on the effects of hormone-replacement therapy on the sex lives of women who had undergone surgical removal of their ovaries. She found that the women who received the testosterone-estrogen cocktail (rather than estrogen only or a placebo) reported a greater upsurge in sexual arousal, more lustful fantasies, a stronger desire for sex, a greater frequency of sex, and higher rates of orgasm.[12] Subsequent research on women's naturally produced testosterone has yielded similar results. In the absence of infatuation, women with high baseline levels of testosterone—so called "high-T" women—tend to be significantly more sexually interested and responsive than "low-T" women. There is now a substantial body of endocrinological research to substantiate the statement that libido requires a supply of testosterone in women, as well as men.

When the body chemistry of infatuation recedes and the preexisting desire levels emerge, the differences become apparent. The many other factors that affect sexual desire may also reveal themselves at this time.

Sexual desire is a very complex motivation—more complex than biology alone. It's a combination of genetic programming, body chemistry, and life experience. In sex, as in other areas of a relationship, no two of us are alike. Everyone has different attitudes, histories, expectations, vulnerabilities, needs, and hopes. Our passion is also influenced by physical and emotional factors, including menopause, internalized homophobia, depression, anxiety, stress, past sexual trauma, certain medications (such as antidepressants), and a host of medical disorders. Factors such as these, in combination with our body chemistry, determine our sexual desire.

*Signe and Aidan had their very first fight about sex. They discovered that they had very different expectations. Signe wanted lots of sex. For her it was a fun diversion from their financial worries. For Aidan, who was very stressed about not having a job, being sexual felt too vulnerable.*

*Tia was convinced that part of her partner Lee's lack of interest in sex was due to her internalized homophobia. If Lee wasn't sexual she didn't have to deal with her feelings about being a lesbian.*

*After so many years of being together, Ruby knew that when Nadine had one of her bouts with depression, she would not want to be sexual—maybe for months.*

*As she approached menopause, Joanna found that she had less "libido," as she called it. Not only had her sexual desire dropped, but her orgasms were less intense as well. She still enjoyed sex but sometimes missed how she used to be.*

*Kirsten was so concerned about infecting her partner that every time she had an outbreak of herpes she slept in the spare room. Sex was out of the question.*

*Lenore had been sexually abused as a child. Sometimes, when she and her partner, Emily, made love, she had flashbacks to those childhood experiences. This happened less and less as she began to talk about it and to trust Emily more.*

*Semeka had gained some weight in the last year and was very self-conscious about her body. She was less interested in being sexual than usual.*

A drop in sexual desire or a discrepancy in sexual desire between partners can lead to less sex. Disillusionment may take over.

*Over the course of their two-year relationship, Reyna and Alicia went from having sex daily to about once a week or so. Reyna felt disappointed and even betrayed. It just wasn't enough for her. Alicia felt confused by her loss of interest in sex and angry with Reyna for pressuring her. Even if Reyna didn't actually say anything, Alicia knew what she wanted. They were both miserable.*

*And to make matters worse, each of them had been in similar situations before with previous lovers. Each of those relationships had ended after a downward spiral of mutual anger, bad sex, more anger, and still worse sex— or none at all.*

Reyna and Alicia are in a perfect position to benefit from "desire education."[13] Full of anger, shame, fear, and discouragement, they need some hope. Sexual passion is partly rooted in our natural body rhythms; if the thrill is gone, or if it is different for each partner, neither has failed. Nor has their relationship failed. There may be emotional baggage junking up their sexual connection—and their relationship—but that is not the only thing going on.

Whether a couple's desire gap is biologically based or rooted in other causes, they need not feel ashamed and despairing about their dilemma. In order to bridge the desire gap, couples need to stop blaming themselves or each other. Each partner needs to take responsibility for herself and participate in figuring our how to deal with their differences. This can allow them to see their relationship more realistically—and as something perhaps worth sustaining rather than as bankrupt and hopeless.

## Bridging the Desire Gap

Now that we know it is possible for partners to love each other and still have different levels of desire, the question arises: What's a couple to do?

Some couples may be almost perfectly matched in terms of desire. However, even then, it's all relative. One partner will generally be a little higher or lower in desire than the other. And even for these partners with similar libidos, at any particular point in time—like when one wants sex and the other doesn't—there is a high-desire and low-desire partner.

When people comprehend that their partner's experience of passion is both different from their own and entirely valid, they can become more generous in their capacity to stretch and respond to it. For couples who have been sexually estranged, the result is not likely to be immediate sexual fireworks. However, they can begin to build a budding sense of mutual intimacy and trust that begins to energize both their erotic and their emotional connection. Accepting their desire differences as both normal and natural, they can relax and consciously create their sexual intimacy. Pat Love describes this as moving toward a "state of marital grace called mature love."[14]

*After what seemed like years of painful fights about sex, Mel and Netsy decided to see a therapist. At the point they came into therapy, Mel, the low-desire partner, was feeling terribly defective for not wanting sex more, guilty about repeatedly refusing Netsy's fervent desire for her, and angry that Netsy was "putting her in this position." Netsy, the more sexually desirous partner, was also hurting. She was tired of being rejected, of feeling "too demanding," and of being hurt and angry about having the door slammed in her face over and over. From her perspective, she had showed Mel "her real self" only to have Mel not want her.*

*The therapist they saw was able to help them understand the physiology underlying the desire differences between them and how this played out in their behavior. Then it was easier not to take what had gone on between them so personally. However, they recognized that they still had a long way to go to get reconnected. To begin the process, the therapist asked them to share with each other what kind of sexual-emotional activity would feel most loving and satisfying to them. For Netsy it was what they came to call a "release"—a periodic fifteen- to twenty-minute session of sex where Netsy had an orgasm and rested in Mel's arms afterward. For Mel it was a leisurely massage session that might or might not move from sensual to sexual—depending on her wishes. Cautiously at first, Mel and Netsy began to respond to the other's requests for behavior that previously they had avoided or gotten into fights about. The result was a growing sense of emotional connection, caring, and intimacy that had eluded them as their fighting about sex had taken over their relationship.*

In his discussion of committed couple relationships, David Schnarch suggests that the high-desire/low-desire pairing phenomenon is inevitable in relationships. While it is particularly noticeable—and painful—in the sexual arena, he notes that it also exists in other areas as well. For example, one partner may be high-desire about saving money, having children, or taking vacations. He believes that this desire discrepancy is built in to the structure of relationships and can't be "fixed, rebuilt or resolved."[15] We can't avoid it. These desire differences are part of how relationships invite—and even require—us to grow.

However, these disparities can also polarize us and bring our relationship to the brink of disaster. You may be reminded here of the discussion on conflict in Chapter Seven where we talked about "perpetual problems." If sexual desire differences seem to fit into this category, here are some suggestions about what to do.

- Get clear about who you are and what you want: For example, how often do you want sex, and how do you like to be touched?
- Communicate with your partner. Even early in your relationship you will likely find some differences between you which you can explore. You can use the high-desire/low-desire partner concept to help understand the role each of you falls into. For example, the high-desire partner, by virtue of being in that role, will tend to feel like she is more demanding, exposed, and deprived. The low-desire partner will feel more resentful of being demanded of, inadequate (because in our sex-saturated culture, low desire is, by definition, defective), and guilty about depriving her partner. These feelings are perfectly predictable given the nature of the roles. The intensity of feeling may vary depending, in part, upon how discrepant the desires are, how long the couple has been struggling with the issue, and how much emotional baggage has collected. But the basic feelings depend on the role. If the low-desire partner was in another relationship where she was the high-desire partner, she would have the feelings associated with the high-desire role.
- Hold on to yourself—to your knowledge about yourself, your feelings, and your own personal integrity—as you negotiate with your partner about how to address your respective wants and needs. This clarity about

who you are, along with the capacity to calm and soothe yourself (instead of expecting your partner to take responsibility for your feelings), is the hallmark of differentiation, which David Schnarch sees as essential to intimacy.[16] You both need to be able to be separate people in order to truly meet.

- Recognize that differentiation is a lifelong process of taking your own "shape"—of becoming more uniquely yourself by maintaining yourself in relation to those you love. It can be the key to expanding your sexual relationship and rekindling desire and passion.

When a substantial gap exists between you and your partner, your ultimate erotic satisfaction will depend on a steady, vigilant effort to sustain your sexual connection. Even when two people love each other deeply, postinfatuation passion is seldom a free ride. It takes awareness and attention, time and energy.

Later in this chapter we'll turn our attention to more specific how-to's for enhancing and sustaining your sexual connection over the course of your relationship. But first let's look at how the other two common concerns, namely frequency and initiation, overlap with sexual desire.

## Frequency

*Looking back over their twenty-plus years together, Carolyn Sue and Jama describe their two years of celibacy as one of the most difficult periods. However, they are also clear that during that time they learned how to be truly intimate and were able to reestablish their sexual connection on a much richer and deeper level.*

If a lesbian couple is not being sexual, are they still partners? While a married heterosexual couple would likely continue to see themselves as a couple if they went through a period of reduced or no sexual contact, lesbian partners might interpret this same situation as signaling the end of their relationship. At the very least they might worry that something is very wrong.

Data indicate that almost all couples have less sexual contact the older they get and the longer they have lived together. Lesbians in long-term relationships are having less sex (read genital contact and orgasm) than women with men or men with men.[17] Although it hasn't been measured, Laura Brown suggests that lesbians are probably doing a lot of other things like talking, kissing, cuddling, and sensual touch, which don't make it into the frequency count.[18]

Couples typically explain this reduced frequency as due to lack of time, physical energy, or just being used to each other. What they may not realize is how much is mediated by the biology of desire. As we discussed earlier, after the romance and infatuation stage—when the hormones and chemicals have abated—individuals return to their more usual physiological state. At this point, differences in desire may surface.

A discrepancy in sexual desire between partners can lead to less sex. So can a drop in sexual desire due to one of the many physical or emotional factors we mentioned earlier—current stress, past history, depression, medication, and so forth.

Reduced sexual frequency is also common during the conflict stage of relationships. For one thing, many of us do not want to be sexual when we are angry with our partner. Also, not being sexual can sometimes achieve the distance that one or both of us wants at this stage in order to feel separate. However, when a couple tries to avoid the inevitable conflict of this stage by avoiding sex entirely, we see how relationship difficulties can contribute to sexual problems.

> *Randy and Stella both hated to fight. When Randy got angry with Stella about how busy she was and how she was always too tired to have sex, Randy kept her feelings to herself. She didn't want to fight about it. Eventually Randy just lost interest in being sexual.*

Randy and Stella have difficulty with conflict, which complicates their problem with sex. Maybe Stella's lack of interest in sex is situational because she is busy and tired, or perhaps Stella is the low-desire partner no matter how stressed she is. Whatever the reasons, they have an issue about frequency that is compounded by their inability to handle conflict. Couples who have worked out how to deal with their conflicts can more easily talk about and work on sexual wants and needs in the same way as any other area of concern or difference.

A key point in this discussion of frequency—and a critical way that sexual desire and frequency concerns intersect—is the fact that the low-desire partner always controls the frequency of sex. No matter what the high-desire partner does (unless physical force, which we do not advocate, is involved), she cannot make her partner have sex—or want to have sex. This can lead to a sexual pattern that doesn't really work for either partner: The high-desire partner learns to initiate sex more often than she really wants it because she anticipates that she will get refused a lot. The low-desire partner is encouraged to remain passive because she can have all the sex she wants without ever taking the lead. In addition, the low-desire partner usually does not want her lover to lose interest in sex completely and at the same time feels guilty about thwarting her high-desire partner's sexual desire. In fact, the low-desire partner is training her high-desire lover to badger her for sex. She sends the message that the only factors that motivate her to have sex are her guilt about frustrating her high-desire partner or her fear that her high-desire partner will stop wanting her.

> *After going around and around about how often they had sex, Amanda and Gail decided to try an experiment. For one month Amanda agreed to have sex whenever her high-desire partner, Gail, wanted to. At first they were sexual every day, which was what Gail always maintained she wanted. Gail loved it. But then, as the month wore on, Gail found she really wanted to read at night. She realized that she and Amanda had created a false dichotomy where Gail was the lustful, passionate one. While it was true that she was the high-desire partner, the contrast was not as dramatic in real life as it was in her mind. Once they broke their gridlock about frequency, they could both relax about sex.*

## Initiation

There is a joke about two lesbians who are sitting on a couch, the sexual tension between them so thick you could cut it with a knife. Then, at precisely the same moment, both women throw open their arms and exclaim, "Take me, I'm yours."

Biology also seems to play a role in sexual initiation. Hormones don't cause behavior in the same way that turning the steering wheel of a car causes it to veer left or right.[19] However, they do seem to increase the likelihood that—all things being equal—a given behavior will occur. For example, a study of lesbian couples found that the women were about 25 percent more likely to initiate sex and had twice as many orgasms during the midpoint of their cycle than at any other time of the month.[20]

Culture plays a role as well. As a result of feminism, women of recent generations are less hesitant to initiate sexual situations than were their predecessors. However, for some women, issues about initiation may still reflect the legacy of sexism. The tradition of men being the initiators and women needing to wait to be approached may contribute to some women's discomfort taking the lead during sex. And, even if one partner is more skilled and comfortable with initiating, she may resent being responsible for taking the lead all the time. It is likely that the high-desire partner is also the one who initiates more.

Partners who are less comfortable with initiating may want sex to "just happen." The problem is that for most couples, after the romance and infatuation stage, sex does not just happen. So it is important that couples in long-term relationships talk about their wants and feelings in order to address concerns about unbalanced initiation. Perhaps they need to clarify exactly what is and what is not initiating. One partner may look for particular words or behaviors and not recognize things that the other says or does as initiation. If initiation is an issue, there may be ways that one partner can encourage and support the other to lead more often. The partner who tends not to take the lead may also need to become more aware of what interferes with her initiating, and what she might do to overcome these hurdles.

Whether the issues are about frequency, initiation, or desire, two things are most important in a couple's sexual relationship. The first is that each woman explores and honors her own personal sexual wants and needs, instead of imposing someone else's standard on herself. Second, these wants and needs must be shared with each other so that both women can be involved in the ongoing process of achieving mutual sexual satisfaction.

## Why Bother?

If sex in a long-term relationship is this much trouble, why would a couple, and particularly a low-desire partner, be interested in making the effort?

In *The Lesbian Love Companion,* Marny Hall points out that our real love stories are not always the traditional ones. Not only does girl not always meet girl and live happily ever after but sex is not "the sine qua non of close relationships."[21] Each of us wants different levels of sex in our relationship.

Studies of long-term lesbian and gay couples report that virtually all of the couples said that although sex played a less central role in their relationship over time, it was still important and its absence was often a cause for concern.

Even low-desire partners usually don't want sex to disappear entirely and forever from the relationship. Plus, there is the issue of the wants of the high-desire partner. Neither woman in a relationship gets to have it her way all the time. If she does, resentments are likely building in her partner. As David Schnarch says, "You have the right to have your preferences but you don't have the right to make your partner live by them."[22] This holds true for sexual expression as well. Of the infinite varieties of sex, there will be some things you want to do, some you don't, and those you may be willing to do to please your partner. You have a right to have your boundaries as well as to change them if and when you feel differently. So if you want to stay together—and have a mutually satisfying relationship—you need to work it out.

There are also more positive motivations to put energy into enhancing your sexual life. In *The Whole Lesbian Sex Book,* Felice Newman states that we all deserve as much erotic pleasure as life can offer, which she suggests is more than any of us can conceive of.[23] With information and encouragement she believes that we can have the sex life of our dreams. In his discussion of exploring our sexual potential, David Schnarch talks about the possibility of intense sexual experiences that involve "physical and emotional union in the context of consuming mutual desire, heart-stopping intimacy, and deep meaningfulness."[24] On a more practical note, Lenore Teifer points out that sex can be ecstatic or boring but it can also be "something in the middle: a way to comfort others, to find relief from the drudgery of our lives, an affirmation of our ability to please someone else or affirmation of our own desirability."[25]

It is not necessary to wait for sexual desire in order to initiate or respond to sexual contact. What is required is the willingness to be sexual.

## Exploring Your Sexual Potential

The couples interviewed by Eric Marcus for *Together Forever* talked about how their sexual relationships had changed over the years. Although physical affection remained a critical part of their relationships, sex became less so. Worth noting, however, is that while sex became less frequent, it was more intimate and while it was less spontaneous, it was more adventurous.[26]

Could the message be that with sex, like with everything else in life, the more you know and understand about it—in this case about your own sexual response and your partner's—the more you enjoy it?

Those who want to expand their sexual potential are not only looking for more and longer orgasms. Expanding sexual potential is not just about trying new techniques and positions or using different toys, although all of these may be a part of the process. It's about heightening arousal through emotional connection, reducing our anxiety and holding on to our differentiated self during sex, and expanding our capacity to profoundly connect with our partner by deepening our intimacy during sex.

As Sondra Zeidenstein describes it in her article "The Naked Truth," "I don't look back on wild sex with longing—too acrobatic, too endlessly demanding, not for this old body, my poor back, my thinning tissues. I want something a lot more passionate. I want what I have: sex that is the pure and simple physical expression of love between two people who know, because of how their bodies are changing, that they are not going to last forever."[27]

David Schnarch maintains, "Intimacy is not for the faint of heart."[28] Long-term intimacy within a committed relationship hinges on our ability to validate ourselves—to be our own person and be responsible for taking care of ourselves—rather than requiring that our partner be responsible for making us feel safe or good about ourselves or whatever it is we want to feel.

## Ways to Heat Up Your Sex Life

Lesbians in the later stages of long-term relationships talk about boredom with lovemaking routines and a lack of passion. If this sounds like you—and you want to enhance the sexual part of your relationship—be prepared to make it a priority in terms of both time and energy.

This means talking about sex. Good communication is one of the most effective skills you can bring to a sexual relationship. Sexual communication means being able to articulate your desires, fantasies, history, limits, and concerns—and being able to listen without judgment to those of your partner.

It also means developing your sexual capacity. David Schnarch suggests that the brain is our largest sex organ and that neocortical sex has to do with developing our sexual potential—our capacity for profound sexual experiences that are not measured by the nerve spasms or muscle contractions that create the physical experience of orgasm. As Lenore Teifer points out, orgasm is really "just a strong neurological twitch, like a convulsion. It's just a reflex. It's the symbolism that makes it feel so good."[29] However, having your neocortex run your desires doesn't just mean controlling them; it means creating them by fantasizing and thinking up new things to do.

The following list of suggestions to increase passion combines ideas and inspiration from *The Whole Lesbian Sex Book*[30] with those from women in couple's enhancement groups facilitated by one of the authors. (Needless to say, always practice safer sex and inform yourself about how to use sex toys appropriately before you play. See Resources.)

- Exercise your libido by reading erotica, masturbating, watching porn movies—whatever turns you on. And if you're not sure what turns you on, take responsibility for your own sexuality and find out.
- Get away for the weekend—go to a motel, a beach cabin, or housesit at a friend's . . .

- Soak in a hot tub.
- Have sex in different locations—on the living room couch or the kitchen table, or in a car. . . . Use your imagination!
- Break out of your routine and get inspired. Shop together for a new sex toy or check out a steamy video . . . or a live erotic show.
- Take a physical risk together like skydiving, going on a roller coaster, or rock climbing.
- Make a "pass."
- Give each other a massage.
- Tell your partner she is the most special person in your life.
- Go on a "date."
- Take time away from your partner (so you miss her!).
- Indulge in long kisses.
- Do something "romantic," like eating dinner in front of the fire or having flowers delivered to her workplace.
- Read to each other from lesbian novels.
- Meet somewhere and pretend you are strangers.
- Talk about your sexual fantasies and play some of them out.
- Tell stories or fantasies to your partner while you are touching her.
- Try some of the exercises in books: Check out *Lesbian Sex* and *Lesbian Passion* by JoAnn Loulan or *For Yourself* and *For Each Other* by Lonnie Barbach.
- Try using lubrication, if you don't already. Experiment with different flavors and consistencies.
- Talk to your partner—let her know what you want and ask her what she wants. If you are shy about talking about sex, know that you aren't alone, and that most of our inhibitions about talking about sex are cultural. We had to be taught what is okay and not okay to say. So we can retrain ourselves and learn to be more comfortable talking about sex. (See Newman in Resources section.)
- Write your partner a love letter in which you remind her (and yourself) what it felt like to fall in love with her, what characteristics you love about her, why you honor and respect her, what you find attractive about her, and why you cherish your partnership.
- Leave her a note—in her lunch bag, on her pillow, in her appointment book, or on the steering wheel of her car—in which you describe in detail what you would like to do to her.
- Take the risk that whatever you try may not work out perfectly, and try it anyway.

## Monogamy/Nonmonogamy

"One of the hottest potatoes in any relationship is the issue of monogamy."[31] Surrounded by a mainstream culture that subscribes to the tradition of fidelity in marriage, most of us were raised to expect monogamy as part of a committed relationship. Despite the fact that we can't legally marry, most of us say we prefer to be monogamous in our committed relationships.[32] However, the fact that we may distinguish between "just having sex" outside the primary relationship and having "an affair" or even "an emotional affair" illustrates that monogamy means different things to different people.

In our discussion of this topic, we'll use the definitions suggested by Eric Marcus, namely that monogamy means a single emotional and sexual partner, and nonmonogamy describes an arrangement where a couple agrees that sex outside the relationship is allowed.[33] First we look at the advantages and disadvantages of monogamy and nonmonogamy. Then we discuss the reality that people make mistakes, agreements are violated, and affairs happen. However, despite the pain of these events, couples can and do rebuild their relationship after the devastation.

### Pros and Cons

Monogamy can provide a relatively stable situation for a relationship to develop and deepen without the threat of distraction, disruption, and insecurity that nonmonogamy can pose. Partners focus their attention within their relationship so that the creativity generated from that focused attention enhances their relationship. Couples can deepen their intimacy—as a result of confronting difficulties—in a direct way when they do not have the option of using an outside sexual relationship to avoid working out issues. A commitment to monogamy also helps assure that neither partner will bring new sexually transmitted diseases into the relationship.

Monogamy has disadvantages as well. One or both partners may feel restricted or required to go against her nature. Monogamy requires taking the time and energy to nurture the sexual component of a long-term relationship. Sometimes monogamy serves as a cover for one or both partners' terror of being abandoned by her lover. When anxious partners use a monogamy agreement to protect themselves from experiencing their fears, monogamy is not a choice—it is a defense.

Nonmonogamy also has its advantages and disadvantages. It allows the couple more flexibility to manage outside attractions. Most women in nonmonogamous couples say that their sexual desire and the quality of sex in their couple relationship is enhanced. On the other hand, a woman may find it hard, or impossible, to work through her discomfort with sharing her partner. It can also become complicated if the outside sexual partner, or one of the members of the couple, gets emotionally attached. It takes time to negotiate agreements and to coordinate the logistical arrangements for nonmonogamy. It can be used as a way to distance a partner and avoid confronting the emotional and sexual challenges that you are likely to face in a relationship.

### Making the Choice

Each of you needs to take your preferences into account when you are deciding whether to be monogamous or nonmonogamous. It does not matter how many advantages there are to a choice if one or both of you does not feel good about it. If you and your partner want a long-term relationship, you need to honestly and realistically evaluate which arrangement you want and which will nurture and sustain your relationship. In short, will your choice get you what you want?

Many couples don't discuss these options or make a conscious and deliberate choice early in their relationship. Sometimes it's because they don't know if the relationship will develop into something serious or because each woman assumes both of them are abiding by the same guidelines. And often, at least initially, you are having too much sex with each other to even think about having sex with anyone else. However, as we discussed earlier, the biology of desire is such that this will change.

To make a conscious choice, you have to talk with each other about your views, needs, and what you think will work best for you and for the relationship. Your decision will likely be based on some combination of factors, including your previous experiences, health concerns, personal/political/religious beliefs, wants, and the wish to accommodate your partner's wants.

*When her partner, Dulcie, first mentioned the idea of nonmonogamy, Natalie had reservations, but she was willing to discuss the possibility.*

*From the beginning Shareen and Maura agreed that nonmonogamy needed to be a part of their relationship. Both women felt strongly that the option to have sexual relationships with others—women or men—was critical to making their relationship work.*

*Leela liked being monogamous. She described it as a "better fit" with her values and personality.*

Regardless of what choice you make early in your relationship, you need to reevaluate that decision later and modify whatever is not working. Even if neither of you wants to change your current agreement, talk about it periodically. Once every ten years is likely not often enough to have this kind of conversation.

### Making Monogamy or Nonmonogamy Work

Commitment to monogamy with your partner means doing what it takes to honor your commitment. If you know that you are vulnerable to temptation under certain circumstances, then avoid those circumstances or the people who threaten your willpower.

> *Teeka knew from past experience that she was at high risk for getting sexually involved when she combined being out of town with drinking alcohol. As a part of her decision to be monogamous, she realized that she needed to not drink when she was away on business trips.*

And if, despite your precautions, you do meet someone to whom you are attracted, remind yourself of your agreement and the impact on your partner and your relationship if you violate this agreement. If you need to, get support for keeping your agreement—from friends, a counselor, your spiritual practice, or wherever it is available.

Some couples find it helpful to acknowledge and discuss their attractions. After all, the agreement is about monogamy, not about noticing other women. However, both partners need to be comfortable playing this way. If your partner gets jealous if you even look at another woman (more about that later), mentioning women you find attractive would be torture for her, not fun.

As for nonmonogamy, it is usually not easy either. The couples who make nonmonogamy work spend time talking about it and developing guidelines for an arrangement that suits them best as individuals and allows them to achieve a successful long-term relationship together. The point of guidelines is to provide enough structure so that both women feel secure in their relationship and still have the freedom to have outside sexual relationships.

Guidelines might include some of the following ideas.[34] Sex with other partners is allowed but:

- must be kept a secret,
- must be discussed,

- not with mutual friends,
- only in anonymous sexual encounters,
- only when one partner is out of town,
- not at home or in the couple's bedroom,
- only as a threesome, or
- partners always spend the night together when both are in town.

A couple may agree to shift between being monogamous and non-monogamous, depending on how the women feel at any given time. So, for example, if one partner is not feeling secure, she may ask that they be monogamous for the next few months. When she feels stronger they open the relationship again.

### Safer Sex

Needless to say, when engaging in sex with outside partners, follow safer-sex guidelines. An outside lover may not even know her health status—or that of her previous partners. And of course, you have no guarantee that she will tell you the truth. So be "safe not sorry," as the adage goes.

Felice Newman defines safer sex as "the practice of assessing risks and taking precautions that you hope will prevent you from acquiring or transmitting STDs (sexually transmitted diseases)."[35] In order to assess the risks, you need to know what behaviors put you at risk and to what degree. The risk factor is contact with bodily fluids. HIV can be transmitted through contact with blood (including menstrual blood), vaginal fluids, semen, and breast milk. Hepatitis can be transmitted through contact with blood or feces. HPV and herpes can be transmitted through skin-to-skin contact. Newman categorizes sexual activities as high risk (e.g., sharing sex toys without a condom), risky (e.g., unprotected cunnilingus when a woman is not bleeding), low risk (e.g., French kissing), or no risk (e.g., frottage with clothes on).[36] However, even a low-risk activity can become high risk if one partner has a small cut on her hand or a sore in her mouth. Make sure you know which behaviors fall in which category and the specifics of how to make activities safer, regardless of their degree of risk. (See Resources.)

You are not free from safer-sex concerns just because you and your partner have decided to be monogamous. Some STDs can lie dormant for months or even years after exposure. You can transmit an STD you don't even know you have. And, of course, not every woman who makes a commitment to monogamy keeps it. Newman suggests that monogamous couples adopt the strategy of using latex barriers during sex for six months and then get thorough gynecological exams, Pap smears, and blood tests for STDs. If all tests are negative, you may decide to discontinue using latex barriers. However, if one partner has a viral STD, such as herpes, HPV, hepatitis C, or HIV, safer-sex practices are recommended. If one of you has a bacterial STD, such as chlamydia, you can use the latex until treatment is completed.[37] Nonmonogamous couples need to be especially attentive to safer-sex practices. Some nonmonogamous women decide to fluid-bond only within their couple relationship. This means they share bodily fluids only with each other and use latex barriers with everyone else. Should one partner "slip" and not practice safer sex, the commitment is to tell the other partner right away so both can assess the risk and make safer-sex decisions.

## Jealousy

Jealousy is an intense and complex emotion. In *Love Matters. A Book of Lesbian Romance and Relationships,* Linda Sutton describes it as "made up of a number of different emotions combined in a highly combustible way."[38] Jealousy is confusing because we don't know whether we are keenly intuitive or delusionally paranoid. It is also compelling and challenging. When we are in its grip, we are vulnerable to behaving badly.

*The more serious their relationship became, the more jealous Conner became about her partner Nina's relationship with her ex. Why was Nina still allowing her ex to live in her house? And why was Nina so concerned about her ex's feelings? Conner was all for maintaining good relationships with previous lovers to build extended family and all that. But how close is too close?*

*From the beginning Mayumi and Sonja defined their relationship as nonmonogamous. For the first two years they had been so enamored of each other that they had not even noticed anyone else. Recently however, Mayumi noticed that she was attracted to a coworker. When she told Sonja about this, she made it very clear that this attraction did not pose a threat to their relationship. But Mayumi did want to pursue a sexual relationship with this individual. Sonja was surprised at the strength of her reaction. She was torn by the news. On the one hand she really believed in nonmonogamy but on the other she was scared and jealous.*

*Evalina was very disappointed when her lover, Michelle, said she wasn't yet ready to live together. Suspecting that Michelle was seeing someone else, Evalina found herself driving by Michelle's place every morning checking for cars. When she started going by at night as well, she knew her jealousy had gotten out of hand.*

Each of these situations—and many more—can arouse the "green-eyed monster" that lurks in all of us. To be realistic, sex outside the couple relationship is potentially disruptive because it triggers normal insecurities and fears. For example, even though she tries not to, Sonja wonders what this other person is like. Is she smart? Attractive? Athletic? Will s/he be a better lover than Sonja? What if Mayumi decides she would rather be with her (or him)? Jealousy is usually all about comparison, anticipated loss, and abandonment.

Although it has its roots in previous experiences, including childhood experiences, jealousy is a very normal feeling that you can use constructively.[39] You can view it as a signal that something in you, your partner, or the relationship needs attention. Perhaps your (or your partner's) tolerance limit about the other's independent involvement has been reached. Maybe it is a sign that your agreements about sex need to be reevaluated. It may be an indication that you (or your partner) need to talk to a trusted friend or seek professional help to deal with some "unfinished business" from your (or her) past, which is inflaming the current jealous feelings. Regardless, once you acknowledge and name your feelings, you can begin dealing with them.

To make the best use of jealousy as a warning signal that something in the relationship needs attention, you need to distinguish between feeling left out and feeling you are about to lose something that is precious to you. If your partner is paying attention to someone else—whatever form that takes—it is normal to feel "out" while the other person seems to be "in." However, these jealous twinges should fade after the particular event is over. If the jealous feelings persist and you are not able to tolerate the level of "sharing" of your partner that is considered appropriate in your circle—or that you have agreed to—perhaps your feelings relate to an underlying fear of loss, which is the more serious type of jealousy.[40] In addition to any work you may need to do solo about your jealousy, the best bet is to talk to your partner about it. Then you are confronting your jealousy instead of letting it fester. If you can identify specific situations that trigger your jealousy, perhaps you can work out together some ways to reduce your reactions. Assuming that your partner is not purposefully trying to make you jealous, she is not responsible for your feelings. Although her behavior does impact you, she did not create your feelings and she can't fix them. You could try to get her to behave a certain way so you feel better. However, then your behavior becomes controlling, which doesn't make for a healthy relationship. And if she agrees to make these changes, she may eventually get resentful. So instead of thinking that she should modify her behavior so that you never feel jealous, you need to get support to cope with your reactions.

## Affairs

Whatever agreement you and your partner make about sex, recognize that people make mistakes. Statistics—for heterosexual married couples—indicate that in the United States, one in every 2.7 couples is affected by infidelity.[41] We don't have data on lesbian couples, but the likelihood is that we aren't that different. Breaking the rules violates your partner's trust and causes shock, hurt, and disappointment—at the very least. Whether there is a breach of trust depends on what you agreed to, or thought you agreed to. This is why clear agreements are so important.

Partners in lesbian couples have outside sexual relationships for all kinds of reasons. These reasons may be clear at the time, may only be clear later in time, or may never really be clear. You may have an affair because you are angry at your partner, to distract yourself, to boost your ego, to feel separate, or to end a relationship.

*Laura insisted she had no idea why it happened. Most of her friends figured that she slept with Shannon to boost her ego. Laura had been feeling pretty low ever since she was laid off. And to top it off, her partner, Amanda, had just gotten a big promotion and was all caught up with her new job. When Shannon paid so much attention to her, Laura found it hard to resist.*

*After years of sacrificing her own dreams to help her partner, Jamie, get through graduate school, Maya felt taken for granted and even resentful. Rather than deal with these issues with Jamie, Maya turned to her friend Ben for comfort, support, and, eventually, sex.*

*Cindy Lou knew that Jeanine would never really believe that she was serious about ending their relationship unless she got involved with another woman. So she did.*

*Dana was devastated when she discovered that Tori, her partner of five years, had cancer. Looking back now she thinks that her affair with Noelani provided a distraction from the stress and worry she was going through over Tori's illness.*

*When Hannah started to feel closed in by her primary relationship, she typically had a sexual relationship with someone else.*

In her book, *After the Affair,* Janis Abrahms Spring outlines three stages of healing that the "hurt" and the "unfaithful" partner each go through as they react to, grapple with, and recover from an affair.[42] The first stage is a whirlwind of emotion. The woman who has or had an outside sexual relationship—the unfaithful partner—may have feelings such as relief and irritation at being discovered, as well as guilt, self-disgust, and anger. The hurt partner will likely experience a profound sense of loss—of identity, control, sense of specialness, self-respect, and of trust. Both partners may be unsure about what the affair means for the future of their relationship. The first challenge is to name and normalize your feelings.

In the second stage partners confront their ambivalence about whether to stay or leave. Exploring options helps settle your emotions and leads to a considered and deliberate decision, which is based on your individual situation and needs. The issue is whether or not to recommit. Questions to consider include "Can I ever trust her again?" "Can I be faithful in the future?" and "Is she right for me?" Whether an affair is a death knell or a wake-up call depends on the many factors that go into a couple's decision to recommit—or not to.

If the decision is to recommit, the third stage of healing becomes rebuilding your relationship. Spring outlines strategies and tools to restore the lost trust and intimacy.[43] This may take months, or even years, as you sort out the meaning of the affair, rebuild trust, decipher how your earlier life experiences may have contributed to the situation, deepen your communication and intimacy with your partner—including sexual intimacy—manage your differences better, and forgive your partner and yourself.

*Lil and Juanita had been together for seven years in a monogamous relationship when Lil had a brief affair with a woman she met in a nearby city. Juanita was devastated when Lil told her about her fling—as Lil called it. Juanita felt betrayed, angry, and confused. One day she wanted to pack up and leave and the next day she felt scared and followed Lil around the house like a puppy. Lil sometimes felt guilty and sometimes defiant. She felt bad that Juanita was upset but she also knew that she really loved Juanita and that this fling was not a threat to their relationship. However, she was also afraid of losing Juanita. So she kept talking, listening, negotiating, and courting Juanita until they were a couple again.*

Lil's affair created a crisis in her relationship with Juanita. As they talked and fought and cried together, some things about their relationship came to light. Although they cared deeply for each other and were committed to the partnership, there was some work they needed to do. They realized they had fallen into patterns of superficial communication and were taking each other for granted. They used this crisis to clarify what they wanted in their relationship and to reevaluate how they could get more of what they wanted with each other.

Whether a couple chooses monogamy or nonmonogamy, they should identify what each partner needs to feel good about their relationship; they should set up a structure that allows both partners to get these needs met. Sometimes this means that partners don't get all of what they want. One partner could decide to give up the relationship because a monogamous relationship is what she wants and needs, or she could decide to try nonmonogamy because she would rather be with her partner than exercise her preference for monogamy. It is important for couples to discuss their concerns and to periodically reevaluate whichever agreements they make. Even if one or both of the women violates the rules, the couple does not necessarily have to break up. There may be room for further negotiation, which may enhance their intimacy in the long run. The crucial variable is communication and a willingness to redesign and refine what makes them happy.

## CHAPTER 9

# ৶ Making Decisions
## *Living Arrangements*

For some couples, living separately best serves their individual needs and the health of their relationship. However, a favorite act of togetherness for many couples is living together.[1] Making a home is far more complicated than just picking the place to live or deciding where to put the couch. It involves mixing the habits, tastes, and preferences of two different people on topics as varied as how to organize the refrigerator, where to hang pictures, and what laundry detergent to use. Couples have to make countless decisions in the process of determining living arrangements. Each of you needs to be prepared to speak up, to disagree, and maybe even to argue, to take a stand, to give in, to compromise, to negotiate, and to adjust.[2]

> *For the two years they had been together, Rachel seldom was willing to spend the night at her lover Aiko's house. It was true that Rachel's place was bigger, and there was Rachel's dog to consider, but Aiko was getting tired of the commute and of living out of a backpack every weekend.*

> *When they got the news that their rented condo was going to be sold, Jaelin and Katie were distraught. They were planning to look for a house to buy together—but not until the following spring.*

*Lacey wanted to move back to Madison after her partner Bess's mother died. They had moved to Montana to help out for a while and ended up staying for over a year. Now Lacey was ready to get back to the place she considered home, but Bess sounded like she wanted to stay where they were.*

## Decision-Making

Each of these couples needs to make some decisions. Decision-making styles vary. Some of us weigh the options and move relatively quickly to conclusions, while others wait until we have thoroughly explored all of the possibilities. Some make a decision and never—or hardly ever—look back; others continue to examine the alternatives long after a decision has been made and implemented. Some of us make lists of the pros and cons of each alternative, while others of us feel our way through until one option intuitively feels better. And there is always the default approach of delaying a decision until our partner or our circumstances decide for us. Whatever the style or process, we believe that making a conscious and deliberate decision is better than sliding into one—whether it's about a relationship or anything else.

Some decisions involve only you and they can be hard enough to make. Decisions that also involve your partner are easy if you are in agreement. When you are not, it is helpful to be aware of your personal decision-making style so that you can apply your skills most effectively and also let your partner know what's going on with you. To get a better idea of your own style of decision-making, remember a time when you made a decision that you felt good about. Then reconstruct how you went about it and exactly how it played out. Some questions to ask yourself are:

- What was the situation?
- What exactly was the issue you were making a decision about?
- Did you need additional information? Where did you find it?
- Were other people involved? If so, how?
- How would you describe the steps (or the process) you went through?

Then reflect on other decisions that you have made. Was the approach similar or different? Keep looking for a pattern (or patterns) that describe how you make your best decisions, so that you can consciously apply what you know about yourself to future decision-making tasks. If it's helpful, you can also reflect on your less successful decisions and identify pitfalls to avoid. After your analysis is completed, you can let your partner know how you go about making decisions and what you need in the process—more time, more information, fewer options, etc.

## Shared Decisions

To make good decisions as a couple, it is important to be clear with each other about what you want individually. You also need to carefully consider whether the proposed decision will accomplish what you intend and whether it will be good for your relationship

*Rae Ann and Hallie have been dating for over a year. When they stay together, it's mostly at Rae Ann's because her place is bigger and more comfortable. Recently they have begun to talk seriously about living together. Rae Ann wants to spend more time with Hallie and anticipates that will happen if they live together. Hallie is also interested in living together, but for different reasons. She hates living out of a suitcase and having to commute and leave her cats alone. She figures that living with Rae Ann will solve those problems.*

Obviously, Hallie and Rae Ann need to talk more about their goals—for themselves and for their relationship. Otherwise, the decision to live together may create more problems than it solves.

If you are used to living alone and making decisions on your own, it may be difficult, at first, to get used to shared decision-making. But there is no alternative if you want to be in a relationship. Neither of you gets to have it your way—at least not all of the time. You almost guarantee that your partner will build resentments if you make major decisions, or even minor ones, unilaterally. If you buy a new dining-room table or even rearrange the bedroom without consulting her, you are treating her as less than an equal. These decisions affect her, too. She has to live with the new, or rearranged, furniture. Excited as you may be about your new purchase or arrangement, she may see it differently. You may have believed you were doing a wonderful, generous thing. You may feel offended that your partner isn't appreciative of your efforts. But think about how it looks and feels from her perspective. Even if she likes the new table or the rearranged bedroom, she will likely feel disempowered and disrespected if you did not ask in advance or give her the option to have it changed back. She may rightly wonder about where her wants and needs fit into the relationship. Unresolved resentments can undermine a relationship. Avoid them by making decisions jointly and negotiating when you need to.

## Negotiation

Ideally, negotiating with your partner can be a positive experience in which you produce a wise agreement in an efficient manner and improve your relationship at the same time. In their book *Getting to Yes,* Roger Fisher and William Ury outline some basic elements for successful negotiating.[3] The first is to see yourself as working side by side with your partner to solve the problem rather than seeing each other as adversaries. One way to visualize this is to imagine that the two of you are on the same side of the table and the problem to be addressed is on the other side of the table. A second element of successful negotiating—and this is key—is to focus on interests, not positions. This means that you avoid getting attached to your own particular solution to the problem (i.e., your position) and stay open to the various possibilities that could address your needs and what is important to you (i.e., your interests).

In this process, you and your partner need to define the problem and agree to negotiate. Each of you needs to state and explore your wants (your interests), remembering that wants are not demands. Stating what you want does not require your partner to do anything. It is not her responsibility to make sure that you get what you want—or vice versa. At the same time, hopefully, you wish to help each other get what you each want (without sacrificing your own interests). Once your wants have been stated and explored, the next task is to generate a variety of possibilities and options before deciding what to do. Sometimes the solution "pops out" once the wants are clear. Sometimes you need to spend some time brainstorming options.[4]

You will be a more effective negotiator if you are "unconditionally constructive" in your approach. This means that you follow negotiation guidelines that will be good for the relationship and good for you, *even if* your partner does not follow the same guidelines.[5] The suggested guidelines are:

- Balance emotion with reason.
- Try to understand your partner.
- Consult her before deciding on matters that affect her.
- Be reliable.
- Be open to persuasion and try to persuade her.
- Accept her as worthy of your consideration and care and be open to learning from her.

Not every decision needs to be negotiated. Hopefully you and your partner can make the majority of your decisions smoothly and easily. But when you do need to negotiate, keep these ideas in mind.

# Living Arrangements

Some couples assume that living together is part of the natural, inevitable progression of a relationship or that it is a litmus test for commitment. The decision to live together should be just that—a decision. We recognize that sometimes there are practical matters, such as one woman getting an eviction notice, which lend a sense of urgency to the situation. However, even under pressured circumstances, partners can apply decision-making and negotiation skills to ensure that their joint decision about living arrangements is a conscious and deliberate choice.

## Living Separately

Some women live separately in order to satisfy their particular living-style preferences or to have more control over their time and environment. Some women like to live apart from their lovers because they enjoy feeling separate and whole all by themselves. There are many other situations in which couples decide to live apart.

- The illness of a family member or a work assignment may make living together impractical or impossible.
- Either woman (or both) might not want to have to agree on day-to-day matters such as bedtimes and housekeeping standards.
- A nonmonogamous couple may simply find it easier to live separately.
- A woman who has recently ended a live-in relationship may not be ready to move in with anyone as yet, including her new lover.
- One or both women may want or need to hide the relationship, and living apart can offer some cover.

*When Izumi was deciding where to apply for her internship program, she discussed the pros and cons of different ones with her partner, Liza. No matter what, they would be living apart for almost a year. They agreed that the most important factor was which program was the best match for Izumi's interests and career plans; however, the distance factor was a close second. They could see each other more often if they weren't on opposite sides of the country.*

*Mona and Jasmin live less than a mile apart. Mona lives in a big house with two other women, three cats, one dog, and a lot of clutter. Jasmin has a one-bedroom apartment that she keeps as "neat as a pin." A graphic artist, Jasmin likes to work and sleep at odd hours, and she likes it quiet. Mona is an early-to-bed, early-to-rise type who enjoys the bustle of a big household. Their living arrangement respects their individual styles, helps them avoid arguments, and allows them to easily spend time with each other.*

*Years after ending a long-term relationship that had been emotionally abusive, Tania still enjoyed living by herself. She wasn't sure she would ever live with a partner again. Although her new lover, Alison, understood Tania's reasons, it was hard for her not to take Tania's reluctance to live together personally.*

While there are good reasons for those couples who live apart to do so, they usually comment that a disadvantage is the coming and going. The commute can get wearing, and there are additional complications if one or both of you are actually *living* in two places. The food in your refrigerator may go bad, or you may have trouble keeping track of what clothes you need where. You may have to transport your pets, or come home to feed them and perhaps feel guilty about not paying as much attention to them as you would like because you are over at your girlfriend's so much.

### Long-Distance Relationships

The members of a couple may live farther away from each other than across town.

*Kim and Marsha had been lovers for twelve years; they had lived most of that time in New York. Kim was fluent in Korean, Japanese, and English and worked as a United Nations translator. After years as a computer programmer, Marsha went back to school for a PhD in mathematics. When she was offered a university teaching job, Marsha moved to the Midwest, and the two began living apart. They had huge phone bills, as they called each other almost every night. They both knew that some day they would need to figure out something better than indefinite separation. Meanwhile, they arranged to visit each other as often as they could.*

Sometimes living far apart is the first choice of a couple and sometimes it is a make-do solution. It can be exhausting to spend a lot of time traveling back and forth, trying to maintain enough contact to keep a relationship alive. The expense is prohibitive for some couples, and the wear and tear may drain and eventually destroy the relationship.

However, there can also be benefits to this arrangement. Kim and Marsha were pleased with the side effect of a renewed sex life. Now that they saw each other infrequently, their lovemaking had increased in intensity and quality. Marsha also noticed that they fought very rarely, and it was usually over not getting enough of each other. Another advantage to living apart is the quality of time spent together. Both Marsha and Kim think of their time together as vacations, so they plan their visits carefully to make sure that they get as much free time together as possible. Kim buys new clothes, gets as much work out of the way as she can, and plans exciting activities for the two of them to do in New York. Marsha finds new restaurants, looks up women's events, and buys lots of flowers when Kim comes to visit her. It is easy to see how this might feel like courtship all over again.

Marsha and Kim are good examples of how a dual-career couple may be faced with living separately, at least for a while. They have to trade off taking the job or educational opportunity with living together. This situation does not arise only in the case of an academic career.

- A woman may live with her lover in Seattle eight months out of the year and be fishing in Alaska for the other four months.
- Two women in the military may be posted to different places.
- A musician may be on the road for a good part of the year.
- A woman who is laid off may need to relocate to find work. If her partner has a steady job, she may stay where she is for the financial security it provides for both of them.
- A woman may need to move to pursue a particular educational opportunity. For example, she may get accepted to a physical therapy program in another state or enroll in a computer course too far away to comfortably commute.

When only one member in a couple has a job, they are freer to move together when work forces relocation. However, both women in a lesbian couple usually work to support the household(s). This increases the possibility that they may have to live apart at some time in their relationship. If you and your partner have to live apart for any reason, you need to have supportive communities that both honor your relationship and nurture you as an individual. When you see your partner infrequently, it is a good idea to develop a circle of friends and family who can provide companionship and be understanding if you drop out of sight for a while when your partner comes to town.

Some partners live very far apart, even in different countries. This kind of relationship demands patience and the willingness not to see a lover for long periods of time. There has to be enough connection to keep the relationship alive during the time apart.

> *Maggie and Fanchette had known each other for four years when they became lovers. Fanchette lives in France, and Maggie in the United States. Neither woman wants to move or to be monogamous, but each wants the other as her primary relationship. Both are published writers and need to live alone in order to work best. Their intimacy is very intense and exciting the entire time they are together—usually three to four weeks, twice a year. In between, they write to each other several times a week and talk on the phone once a month. During visits, each is treated like an honored guest in the other house. Typically, they get into spats after a couple of weeks together, but they always manage to talk things out. Overall, they are pleased with their arrangement and hope it will last forever.*

Fanchette and Maggie have agreed that both are free to have other ongoing sexual relationships—and they both do. Fanchette has a lover she sees weekly for dinner, theater, and sex. Maggie has a friend she sleeps with twice a week; sometimes they are sexual, sometimes not. The arrangement gives Maggie someone to cuddle, because she gets lonely. Both feel secure in the arrangement, but they run the risk of one of their secondary relationships becoming increasingly important. The lover Maggie has in California is much more available to her than is Fanchette; if Maggie needs to talk and the time-zone differences complicate communicating with Fanchette, the balance in the relationship could shift in favor of a lover closer to home.

Couples do not have to live together to be happy. Sometimes living separately is a temporary solution; at other times, it is the preferred choice. Communication can be more awkward and difficult when you have to rely on email, letters, and phone calls. Travel time, money, exhaustion from going back and forth, and the periods of separation are all potential liabilities of living apart. Intense time together, prolonged romance in the relationship, the sense of being on vacation when with each other, and the opportunity to pursue chosen work are all potential advantages. The main point is that couples do not have to live together to be a couple. The two women concerned must decide what living arrangement suits them best.

### Living with Others

There is another way in which some couples have broken the traditional mold of living together. They live with other people who are not part of their biological or legal families. They may call their household a collective, a commune, an extended family, or a convenient arrangement. These households can include just lesbians, heterosexual women, children, men and women, or any combination that the lesbian couple chooses.

> *BJ and Iramus live in a large old Victorian house they bought with five friends three years ago. While there is one other couple in the household, the emphasis is on each woman's individuality. All seven housemates agree that they do not want to fall into the habit of assuming that couples always want the same thing.*

In this kind of situation, the couple may not be easily identified by outsiders. Partners may or may not share a bedroom, for example. This kind of setup usually saves money for the couple, and allows the partners to have day-to-day intimacy (not necessarily sexual) with more than one person. There are more people with whom to share talk, activities, and tasks. Many couples have lived happily for years with friends and feel that group living has added a richness to their relationship that would be missing if they lived alone as a couple.

### Living Together

Most of us have heard the joke, "What does a lesbian bring on the second date?" The answer, of course, is "a U-Haul." So far as we know, there is no research data that demonstrate conclusively that lesbians start living together sooner than other couples do. But most of us laugh at the joke, so perhaps there is some truth to it. The speculation about why this may be the case varies. One idea is that as women, we tend to link love, sex, and marriage. Since we can't legally marry, living together becomes the substitute commitment.

Often a couple moves in together in the romance stage of the relationship. Eventually, the magic of the partially known gives way to the almost-taken-for-granted. Then any problems that earlier may have been obscured by the romantic glow come into clearer focus. Especially if the two women have been friends before they fall in love, they may be very surprised when the inevitable conflicts arise. Issues about money, commitment, monogamy, time together, and household responsibilities will likely emerge sooner when living space is shared.

On the other hand, living together is what many—if not most of us—have in mind when we imagine ourselves "coupled." Not only is it practical and convenient to live with our lover/partner/best friend, it can also be delightful, fulfilling, and relationship enhancing. For most of us, it is also a statement about the relationship and about our willingness to make a commitment to it. Perhaps living together takes on more significance because we are not able to be legally married. For most everyone, home is a place we can be ourselves, but for lesbian couples, the safety of our home goes way beyond that. It is often a sanctuary. Home may be the only place where we are openly affectionate, where we kiss and cuddle and call each other "honey."

Here are some issues to think about and discuss when you and your partner are deciding whether or not to live together.

### How Out You Are

How out each of you are affects your partner more than if you live separately.

*Leanne was very closeted at work. She was afraid her life would be much more difficult if her coworkers found out she was a lesbian. Carrie, her partner, was as out at work as you can get; she was one of the bartenders at a lesbian bar. When they moved in together, Leanne insisted on getting a two-bedroom apartment so people at her work would think they were roommates, not lovers. She also refused to have any explicitly lesbian literature in view at their home. Carrie was upset with this charade but kept it to herself.*

Leanne and Carrie could have serious problems about this issue unless they can come to terms with their differences. They can maintain disparate degrees of outness for years without too much trouble, but if each partner expects the other one to change how out she is, then they could have difficulty. This couple could misinterpret any friction over how out to be as not loving each other or not respecting each other's limitations.

Before you move in together, talk to your partner about your expectations of each other's outness. How out can each of you realistically be? What are your fears about being more out of (or in) the closet? Are these fears realistic? Keep talking about this as a problem of outness, not of love.

### Friends and Family

You are likely to see more of each other's friends and family. This means you need to clarify what your expectations are of each other in these situations. For example, do you love to have people stop by or do you experience this as an intrusion and prefer that visitors call first? What are your partner's preferences? How does your partner feel about your long conversations on the phone with your ex? Are there people in your life that your partner doesn't like? What are your expectations about how much effort your partner should make to get to know your friends, to spend time with your family, to participate in the social activities with your coworkers that you plan to have at the house?

### Children

When one or both of you has children, it is important to clarify the non-parent's role with them and any parenting-style differences between the two of you. Do you want your partner to be a parent? Does she want to be just a housemate? Are your values about child rearing compatible? How similar are your expectations of how children should behave and what to do when they don't? These are a few of the many questions you will need to consider. (See Chapter Eleven.)

### Cleaning Standards

You will have to deal with each other's standards of cleanliness and neatness.

*Magda did not think that bathrooms needed cleaning more than twice a month; Char thought every week was minimal. Char actually liked cleaning bathrooms and decided that Magda should do the living room/dining room as her share of the chores. Magda thought these areas needed even less attention than the bathroom, which was a source of extreme frustration for Char.*

What to do? After they move in together, couples often discover that they have different ideas about how clean their home should be kept, how much clutter is acceptable, or how long to wait before doing the dishes. The solution is to talk about it. It may be difficult, but it is next to impossible to change anything without talking about it.

Char and Magda could address their dilemma by listing all the chores, choosing the ones each wants, and dividing up the rest evenly according to time requirements or some other equalizing element. Once they divide up the chores, they have to learn not to interfere, even if Char thinks she has a better way for Magda to do it. If Char doesn't stay out of it, she may find herself doing a lot more of the chores than she bargained for. Char and Magda also need to negotiate minimum cleaning standards acceptable to them both. Each will likely have to give a little. Or they can agree that the bathroom will be cleaned to Char's standards and other rooms to Magda's. Char may wish to reserve the right to put some time into extra cleaning before they have company. Another approach entirely would be to have someone come in to do the heavy cleaning periodically and divide the rest of the tasks between them. Whatever their agreement, they need to evaluate their system from time to time.

## Legal Matters

Couples living together face a variety of legal matters. These differ depending on whether you are renting or buying, or whether one of you is moving into a place that is either rented or owned by your partner.

The reasons couples live where they do, choose the type of housing they do, and decide to rent or buy may be simple or complex. Factors in the decision often include what the couple can afford, current living situations, jobs, climate, good schools, features like good light or a garden spot, enough room for each partner to have her own space, proximity to family and friends, and how welcome they feel in the area.

Basically there are three choices: your place, her place, or a new place. Moving into your lover's place is fine, so long as it becomes home to both of you. This may involve repainting, changing furniture, or whatever else it takes to make the new occupant feel at home.

Whether a rented place is new to one or both of you, you now have a contractual relationship with each other. If you are renting, this contract will likely be in the form of a lease that constitutes a legal relationship between each of you and your landlord. You may also have a formal or informal side agreement between the two of you, such as who pays what (if it's not fifty-fifty) and what happens if one of you wants to move out.

If the home you will occupy together is owned by one of you, there are other decisions to be made. Is your lover a renter? Will she be buying in to the house? What will the terms be? How will you hold the title? There are endless options. The question is what will work best in your particular situation. Determining this requires discussion and clear understanding about each person's preferences, wants, rights, and responsibilities.

*Leticia had no interest in owning a home—ever. She was more than happy to pay rent to her partner, Penny, and not worry about repairing the roof or dealing with yard work.*

*After three years, Mai and Katje decided to own their home together. It had been Katje's house for a year before Mai moved in. Now the relationship felt secure, and Mai had finished school and was financially able to handle part of the mortgage. They worked out a percentage ownership agreement and financial arrangement that felt fair to them both.*

Buying a home together is usually more than just a financial arrangement. It is often an important and symbolic step in the relationship. But whether you rent or buy, inform yourself about the options and the legal implications of your decisions. There are excellent resources available both for information and for referrals to gay-friendly attorneys. (See Resources.)

### Merging Households

You will have to make decisions about the myriad details involved in merging households: whose furniture will go where, what to purchase, decorating alternatives, how to manage the household finances, and general day-to-day operations, like cooking and shopping.

Couples sometimes move in together with very few possessions and enjoy buying things together. However, women who have been on their own have furniture, dishes, and so on. If this is your situation, you will have to decide whose things you will use, whose go into storage (or the yard sale), and what additional items you will purchase. If you buy jointly, you should have an agreement about how to divide your possessions if you break up. If you buy separately, you need to decide whether both of you have equal access to or use of what each other purchases. If you already have more than you need, you should negotiate carefully whose couch goes in the living room, whose dishes go into the cupboards, and what happens to the extras.

*Lisbeth had dishes, silverware, and some furniture from her previous marriage. Ardis hated using Lisbeth's "straight" dishes, but Lisbeth loved the dishes and was unwilling to give them up. They talked and finally decided that because Ardis's discomfort was so strong, Lisbeth would store her dishes and they would pick out a new set together. Ardis would buy them and if they ever broke up, she would keep the dishes she purchased.*

Possessions can be a tricky issue for couples. You may be more attached to specific "things" than you realize, and if you give them up too readily for your partner's sake, you may have regrets or resentments later. Or, you may agree to live with something you don't really like because you are so in love with the woman who does like it. Where possible, keep as many of your individual possessions as you can, until you have lived together for a time. After a couple of years, you can reevaluate whether you want to hold on to your stuff. If you don't, you can have the yard sale then.

Other classic couple decisions have to do with shopping, cooking, and cleaning up. Some couples agree that if one cooks the other cleans up. Some do the opposite—whoever cooks also cleans up—claiming that it encourages relatively neat cooking habits. Some food shop together, others alternate weeks, and still others trade off food shopping for some other task they would rather do. What matters is that the system suits and feels fair to both women. It is also wise to revisit agreements periodically to make sure they are still working well.

There are no guarantees, of course, but the more you know about each other and your living habits before you share a common household, the more likely you are to enjoy living with each other. It's much better to solve problems in the relationship before you move in together. The success of the venture depends on being clear and honest about what you want, and on having discussions, negotiations, and agreements prior to moving in, as well as afterward. Look closely at what each of you wants and needs and then design—and redesign—the arrangement that is most satisfactory.

Some couples craft "living-together agreements," which help them clarify their intentions and lessen future disagreements and misunderstandings. These contracts are particularly important when a couple mixes assets, shares expenses, or has children. And if the couple does happen to split up, these agreements can help facilitate the ending process and avoid arguments or litigation.[6]

*After eight years together, Brenda and Karli decided that they wanted to write up a contract. Good friends of theirs recently broke up and fought bitterly over property. It was ugly. Brenda and Karli decided to get things clear—not that they had any plans to break up. They read about how to write a living-together contract and decided that they wanted only to address their finances and possessions. They didn't need to spell out details of their living together, like who cleans the litter box. But they did need to address how they would share the animals if they were no longer together. Although it seemed a little odd at first, they eventually got into it and actually enjoyed the process.*

No matter what decision you and your partner make about living arrangements, clear communication and ongoing negotiations help ensure the success of your shared decision-making.

## CHAPTER 10

# ᕝ More Decisions
## *Work, Money, Time, and Play*

Living arrangements are among many areas where couples have to make lots of decisions. In this chapter, we'll look at decisions about work, money, time, and play—from whether to go into business together and how to plan vacations to whether to merge finances and how to make time for each other.

## Work

Most lesbians have to work to survive. No husband is going to take care of us, and typically, we have not been socialized to take on a traditional provider role ourselves. Since on average women earn less than men, it is usually a financial necessity for both partners in a lesbian couple to work. In addition, the majority of lesbians believe that both women in a couple should work, the rationale being fairness and the strong desire to be independent.[1] For all these reasons, we usually arrange our relationship so that neither partner is the sole provider except under special circumstances, such as a partner's being ill, returning to school, losing a job, or bearing a child.

### Division of Labor

Given these attitudes, it is not surprising that lesbian couples usually also try to create an equitable sharing of household tasks. Indeed, these high ideals of fairness and equity for home and work can be a source of friction.

*Helene had always been hard-working and career-oriented. To Beth, work had just been a necessity; she much preferred to put her energy into her relationships. For the first four years they were together, Helene worked long hours, insisting that it was essential to her career plans and their shared future. During this time, Beth did more than 50 percent of the housework, and she was always available to listen and help Helene unwind from her highly stressful day.*

*Then Beth took on a new and challenging job. For the first time in her life she was very excited about her work. However, this new development raised some problems. Beth now got home later than Helene and when she did arrive home, she didn't feel like cooking. Beth's cooking had been a hobby for her and a treat for Helene, but now she had much less energy in general. She was less available to listen to Helene talk about her "hard day at the office." In fact, she wanted Helene to listen to the report of her workday— something new for Beth. What was Helene's reaction? She was grumpy and unhappy about all these changes. Beth was resentful that she was not getting her turn and felt unsupported She even began to wonder if Helene was threatened by the possibility that Beth might eventually make more money than she did.*

As this situation illustrates, our decisions about work have an impact on our relationships. We need to discuss them well in advance in order to make the necessary adjustments at home. And even then, there may be some unanticipated effects.

For example, Helene and Beth were quite aware that Beth was the more relationship-oriented partner: She took more responsibility for running the household, organizing their social life, and maintaining their emotional connection. It is quite common for one partner to focus more energy on the relationship and the other to be more involved with work. However, now this couple is facing a major transition. Beth is changing from a "job," where she worked out of need for money, to a "career," where her work is meaningful and enjoyable to her. While a job may be enjoyable or unpleasant, a career likely means getting paid to do work you love to do. It would be ideal if we could get paid more for a career than for a job, but this is not always the case. For example, a musician may decide to spend her time performing rather than working at a job that pays more. A lawyer may decide to continue working at that job, rather than take a pay cut to go into a career she would prefer. Clearly these decisions can significantly impact our relationships.

Early in their relationship, Helene had a career and Beth a job. With Beth's change to a career, the balance in the relationship was upset. No longer was Beth directing as much energy into the relationship and this shift was hard for Helene to accept. Although they had talked about Beth's work change and both felt that the decision was a shared one, neither realized what its impact on their relationship would be.

At this point, these partners need to renegotiate their expectations and responsibilities. Helene could shift to doing more care-taking of Beth and of the relationship, or they could both agree to be satisfied with both being more focused on work. Helene is, in fact, very supportive of Beth's new career, but she misses the attention she used to get. She needs to share her feelings with Beth, or Beth may continue to be suspicious that Helene is competitive over earnings.

## Work-Related Separations

Negotiations are in order when couples confront work-related separations. One type of challenge arises when one partner has to decide about a job transfer, a voluntary relocation, or a new opportunity—somewhere else. Depending on the other partner's work situation, the decision may be more or less complicated. In any event, most employers do not offer the same understanding or employment assistance to the partner in a same-sex couples as would be forthcoming for a heterosexual couple. If you are closeted, the employer doesn't even know there is a partner to be considered.

## How Out to Be at Work

Whether to be out at work or how out to be may become more of an issue when you are in a long-term relationship than when you were single. Keeping your relationship a secret may feel very painful. After all, your relationship is an achievement about which you can rightfully feel proud. Not being able to talk about it can feel unfair.

For most of us, the workplace requires that we manage information about our lives, our lifestyle, and our difference: to display or not to display; to tell or not to tell; to let on or not to let on; to lie or not to lie—and in each case, to whom, when, how, and where. Basically we have three choices. We can be completely out, selectively out, or completely closeted.[2]

The main advantage of being completely out is being able to be yourself and talk openly about your life. However, there can be risks. The worst-case scenarios may include losing your job, getting passed over for a promotion, having your boss or supervisees think less of you, being ostracized, or dealing with the hostility of straight coworkers or of gays or lesbians who are in the closet. Some of these negative scenarios do happen, but it depends on your situation. What kind of job do you have? What are your company's antidiscrimination policies? Where are you located? If you are a youth counselor at a locally funded agency in a small town in the South, you are in a far different situation than if you have the same type of job in a large agency located in San Francisco. While our fears are sometimes unrealistic, there are simply some jobs and some locations where it is not a viable option to be out.

Another option is to be selectively out and choose whom you talk to about your partner and your life.

*Dava considered herself out to the lawyers and other staff members in the firm where she worked. She took what she described as a very matter-of-fact approach. Her theory was that if you talk about your life and your partner just as openly as everyone else does, people will or will not figure it out. In any event, they'll take their cue and be matter-of-fact in response. With her clients, however, she was much more guarded. There were some, she was sure, who would not want her to represent them if they knew she was a lesbian.*

If you opt to be completely closeted, there are costs. You have no guarantee that you won't be discovered. You have to live with the constant fear of being found out and the discomfort of lying and of denying who you are. It takes a lot of energy to censor all your conversations and usually you don't develop very close relationships with coworkers. However, this may seem a small price to pay compared with the alternative.

Not surprisingly, partners do not always agree on how out to be at work or how out their partner ought to be.

*Every summer Benita's company hosted a huge barbecue. Every summer she and her partner, Ailsa, had a big fight about going. Benita was out at work and proud of it. Ailsa wanted to go with her to the barbecue but was afraid that she would run into someone there from the school district where she worked.*

*Fern's partner, Vera, was very closeted at work. Vera's supervisor stopped by the house occasionally to drop off paperwork. Before he arrived, Vera always asked Fern if she would mind leaving the house for a while. Fern looked "too much like a dyke," and Vera did not want her supervisor to suspect anything. Fern was upset with herself that she felt so hurt about it, but she did.*

When partners have or want different degrees of outness at work, various scenarios may unfold. If you are the more out partner, you may pressure your lover to be more public in order to validate the relationship or to make a political statement to the larger world. You may not be sure whether your lover's closetedness is really necessary. Perhaps you think it's an indication of her shame about being a lesbian. In this case, you might encourage her to see a counselor so she can cope with her internalized homophobia. You may imagine that her hesitancy has something to do with the relationship and wonder if there is something she is not telling you. If you are the more closeted partner, you may see your caution as essential to your job, work relationships, and ambitions. Both partners may feel misunderstood and unsupported.

If one of you is more out than the other, it is important to identify the issue as being one of differing degrees of outness rather than differing levels of commitment to the relationship. Thoughts such as "If you really loved me, you wouldn't care what your coworkers thought" or "If you really loved me, you would be more affectionate in public" confuse the issue. In our examples, Ailsa does not love Benita less because she doesn't go to the barbecue. She may go and choose not to be openly affectionate toward Benita at the event. This also does not mean she loves her partner less; some women are uncomfortable about any public displays of affection. Their discomfort may increase, of course, if they are afraid that someone from the workplace might see them.

It's sometimes difficult for lesbians to accurately assess the negative consequences of being openly lesbian. If Vera or Ailsa did not hide their sexual orientation, would they lose their jobs or their credibility with coworkers? Some fears may be unrealistic or based on internalized homophobia; others may be quite realistic. Most of us grew up in environments that promoted negative attitudes about lesbians and lesbianism (though this is changing in some parts of the country). Getting rid of negative attitudes about oneself is a lifelong process. As one woman said, "Just when you think that you are *done* with coming out, you meet someone new or the issue arises in yet another way."

It's no wonder that we may feel that it's hard enough to handle homophobia in the workplace, much less to confront the issue at home. It would be nice if we could all have something like a decompression chamber in the entryway of our homes. Then we could simply walk through this chamber and quickly change from the closeted or armored lesbian we may have to be at work to the sensitive, loving, and comfortable-with-her-lesbian-identity woman we want to be at home.[3] Unfortunately, we—or our partner—may expect that we instantly change the moment we walk through the door.

Some women leave their jobs or change careers in part because of the strain that being closeted at work puts on their relationship. Others stay because they love their work or cannot afford to quit. When partners differ in how out they are on the job, they need to approach any problems this creates with compassion for each other's concerns and feelings. Even when they do not agree with the other's choice about how out to be, each woman can try to understand and respect her partner's perspective and decision.

When both partners are out to the same degree at work, they may have less tension over this issue. Similarly, when each woman in a couple has a comparable income, they may have fewer conflicts about money.

## Money

In our society, money is often equated with ability, status, talent, and worth. When money is tight, or when one partner makes considerably more than the other, finances can be a source of disagreement and misunderstanding for couples. Partners may feel competitive about income. Conflicts may arise over what constitutes a necessary rather than an optional expense, how much of a savings cushion is essential, or what is a fair amount for child support.

Couples address differences in earning power and spending habits in a variety of ways. Some partners pool their resources completely, others divide household expenses proportionally to their income, and still others pay equal shares regardless of income.

### To Merge or Not to Merge

Even when both women in a couple have approximately the same amount of money and income, they still have to determine whether or how to merge their finances.

While some couples decide to keep their money totally separate for years, others open a joint bank account after a few months. Because there are so few symbols to validate lesbian relationships, having two names on checks may take on a symbolic meaning. Joint credit cards or cosigned loans may provide a similar sense of union. However, having joint plastic, joint accounts, and cosigned loans can be risky.

If both of you are good money managers, communicate well, and are happy in the relationship, the chances for problems are minimal. But if one of you is an impulse buyer, forgets to note checks written, or has very different spending habits than your partner, conflicts are likely. Another problem is that you can get burned financially when a relationship ends.

*Hilary and Paula fought every time they tried to balance their joint checkbook. Hilary often forgot to write down checks, and Paula wanted the balance accurate to the penny.*

*Tobi discovered one day that her partner, Jen, had almost emptied their joint savings account to place a bet on a horse that "couldn't lose"—but did.*

*Mary Kay ended up paying for a number of purchases that her ex-lover, Barbara, made on a joint credit card after they split up. Mary Kay was stuck with the bills because the card was in her name and she had neglected to close the account.*

We don't want to discourage having joint accounts and merging finances, but it's important for couples to be realistic about the issues that may arise.

## Managing Expenses

There are various strategies for managing household expenses, but don't be surprised if it takes you months—or years—to work out a system. Even then, be prepared to modify it based on altered financial circumstances or other situations.

Basically you have three ways to manage your household expenses: You can keep your finances totally separate, merge them completely, or do something in between. In their book *Second Marriage*, Richard Stuart and Barbara Jacobson talk about the one-pot, two-pot, and three-pot arrangements.[4] The one-pot model assumes complete interdependence. The couple pools all of their money and decides together how to spend it. In the two-pot model both partners control their own resources. They may decide to share some expenses either equally or proportionally, but the money is kept strictly separate. The three-pot model assumes that partners have both shared and separate monies, so there are three pots: hers, hers, and ours. Each partner has total control over her own pot, and the couple decides together the use of money in the common pot. There are two major variations of the three-pot model:

1.  Couples decide on a fixed amount of money or percentage of income for the separate pots. They then pool the rest, making sure that there is enough to cover shared expenses.

2.  Couples decide on a fixed amount or a percentage of earnings for the common pot. The two partners keep the rest in their separate pots.

No single approach is necessarily better than the others; it depends on your financial situation, your personal needs and values, how well each of you manages money, how long you've been together, and how much you trust each other around money issues. What is important is that the agreement between you is clear, understood, and acceptable to you both—and works.

A couple may choose the one-pot approach because their resources are limited and they need to pool all they have just to meet expenses. They may decide to merge finances as a symbol of their commitment and intention to remain together, or they may simply value mutual support. For many couples, pooling money is a way to strengthen the bond that helps hold their relationship together. Couples who have been together for a long time often find they move toward merging their resources completely, but it may not happen for many years.

Couples who choose the two-pot approach do so for a variety of reasons. One partner may have children from a previous marriage and need to track expenses for legal reasons. Some women make this choice to avoid conflict, to feel independent and separate, or because of a negative experience in a previous relationship. Many couples opt for keeping finances separate and splitting joint expenses fifty-fifty—or according to some other formula—as the least complicated and safest approach to take in a new relationship.

Partners who want both separate and shared money choose the three-pot approach. For many couples, it's the best bet because they each have their own money that they can make decisions about and they also have a joint fund for sharing expenses and buying things together. This approach can also be useful when there is a large difference between partners' incomes.

*When they decided to live together, Marcie and Crystal agreed to split joint household expenses fifty-fifty. Marcie made a great deal more money than Crystal, which caused various problems. For example, Marcie liked clothes, but she felt guilty buying something for herself that Crystal couldn't afford so she didn't buy things she wanted. Crystal insisted on paying her own way whenever they went out to eat. This meant that they didn't go out as often as Marcie would have liked, and their choice of restaurants was limited. Marcie had proposed pooling their money, but Crystal was hesitant because she was afraid of feeling dependent on Marcie. Though she didn't like the phrase "poor but proud," that's how she felt.*

One way Marcie and Crystal could ease their money tensions would be to adopt a three-pot system. If they renegotiated the fifty-fifty split, each could contribute an agreed-upon amount to a joint account that would cover household expenses and entertainment. Each would keep the rest of her earnings. It would broaden their choice of restaurants, and Marcie could still indulge her passion for clothes. Crystal could feel secure, knowing that all expenses were covered, and she could even save some of her separate funds.

If you decide to merge your funds, either partially or completely, make sure that you are really merging. Putting money in a joint account is not actually merging unless you both see that money as joint and the decision-making about it as truly shared. It should now be "our" money. If one or both of you still acts as if your finances are separate, or if the one with more income feels entitled to make all the decisions, you have "cosmetic merging."[5] This situation leads to problems because you both likely have different expectations about what merging your finances really means.

Whatever decisions a couple makes about finances, it is essential to have a clear agreement. It's helpful to write it down, because our memories are often poor about what we talked about a year, or even a month, ago. The purpose of this written agreement or contract is to clarify the arrangements and prevent future problems. Couples who already live together, or who are planning to, definitely need to discuss and agree upon how they will share the rent and household expenses. Some of these issues we discussed in Chapter Nine, which addresses living arrangements. For example, if your partner owns the house in which you will live, are you paying rent or buying in? What about items you purchase together? What about things each of you owned before you moved in together?

There are other questions with financial implications that go beyond living arrangements. Does she expect that you will support her when she goes back to school in two years? Do you expect that she will contribute financially to the support of your children from your previous marriage? To avoid misunderstandings, arguments, and resentments, you need to discuss and resolve these kinds of issues.

## Managing the Paperwork

Once you have decided how many pots you will use—and which expenses you consider joint ones—the next challenge is the paperwork. Even if you keep your finances totally separate, there will probably be expenses you share; you'll have to decide how to track them and devise a system to ensure the bills get paid. There are many methods for tracking shared expenses once you have decided to do that.[6]

## Post a List

Put a list on the refrigerator or some other convenient spot. Divide the paper in half so that each of you can note, in your column, the amount you spent on each item. At the end of the month total these amounts and settle up.

## A Receipt Jar

When you make a household purchase, write your name and the date on the receipt, or on a note, and put it in a receipt jar. Settle up at the end of the month.

## A Money Jar

Put an agreed-upon amount of money in a jar for household expenses. You may want to do this weekly, semimonthly, or monthly. If you run out, put in an additional agreed-upon amount. Or you could arrange an envelope system instead of a jar so you have envelopes for different budgeted expenses. You might have one envelope for food money, one for entertainment, etc. Each envelope contains the monthly budgeted amount. If you run out of funds in one envelope, you can allocate from another and still stay within your budget.

## Trading Off

One of you can pay for groceries this week, the other next week. This method is less organized and less exacting. If either of you likes to keep things even, this is not the best approach to use. One of the more structured systems will avoid disagreements about who paid for what and whether it's even or not.

Making sure the bills actually get paid first requires that there is enough money. If there isn't, then more careful budgeting or regrouping is in order. Assuming there is enough money, the easiest way is often for one of you to take responsibility for paying the joint bills and keeping track of the joint account, if you have one. If neither of you enjoys keeping the books, or if you are equally bad at it, you may want to alternate the task every month, quarter, or year. You can divide things up other ways: One of you could pay the bills and the other balance the checkbook, or one partner could handle the bills and the joint checkbook and the other keep the financial files in order. This latter task could involve organizing and filing receipts, bank information, and other records (an accordion-type folder works well), or it could mean entering the data into a computer program, or both. Then when you need information for taxes, wonder how well you are doing on your budget, or need the receipt for the HDTV you purchased three years ago, you have it.

## Value Differences

Attitudes and values about money vary widely. Some of us believe that we all need to "live simply that others may live." Others propose that, as women, we need to claim and display our economic power: to charge fees comparable to male colleagues, to live in upscale sections of town, to wear fashionable clothing, to contribute to causes we believe in. Whatever our personal and community standards, we are frequently pulled by opposing sides in deciding how to earn and spend our money.

For some couples, value differences based on class background can complicate the financial process.

*Sally grew up in a working-class family. Her mother saved everything she could and went without in order to put aside money for Sally's college education. Assata, on the other hand, was raised in an upper-middle-class family where she had everything she wanted. Both of Assata's parents had inherited money, and her father was a senior officer in a large corporation. Assata and Sally soon had conflicts over money. Whenever Assata wanted to buy something they did not absolutely need, Sally balked and always came up with a reason not to spend the money. For Sally, spending money was like throwing away a life preserver.*

Until they caught on, Assata and Sally fought over making purchases without realizing that the problem reflected their childhood values—not their current realities. When they finally talked about what was happening, they were able to take into consideration Sally's anxiety about spending money. Sally figured out just what monthly amount they needed to put into savings in order for her to feel secure. Assata worked out a budget showing how much they needed to pay their expenses each month. Then they allowed themselves to spend a portion of the remainder for fun and joint purchases.

Differences in earning power between partners can be problematic. Sometimes partners feel competitive about their incomes or fall into the trap of equating income level with worth or power in the relationship.

*When Marcelle and Letty looked at their income levels they found that Letty had a higher, more consistent income. Marcelle made a livable wage as a waitress, but tips fluctuated. And there was always the threat of the bar's closing. They had a frank discussion about money during which Marcelle acknowledged that she had been deferring to Letty's wishes about vacation plans because Letty contributed more money to the vacation fund.*

Even if each woman in a couple has the same amount of money and income, there may be problems related to differences in earning power. The couple still has to address any differences in spending and saving patterns.

*Alva enjoyed clothes and music and considered money spent on these items well spent. Her partner, Page, regarded very few material items as essential. Clothes and CDs were not on her list of necessities.*

Again, different values need not keep the couple apart, but the women need to be honest with each other and find a way to live together without feeling threatened by each other's decisions about money. These couples probably should not merge finances, but instead use the three-pot method so they cover their joint living expenses and allow both of them to use the rest of their money as they individually prefer.

Money is rarely a simple issue for couples because it taps underlying themes. These themes include trust, independence, commitment, and the question of permanence that the pooling of funds raises, as well as all the tension of societal roles, power, class, and self-worth. Difficult as it may be, we have a better chance to forge truly egalitarian couple relationships by facing these issues directly and working through them.

### Financial Planning

The longer you are together the more likely you are to merge finances, usually partly out of convenience and mostly out of commitment to the relationship and plans to spend the rest of your lives together. In this situation, the merging likely involves financial planning for the future, including buying real estate, purchasing insurance, making investments, and developing retirement plans. Although you can do all this on your own, a financial adviser may be helpful.

As in all financial matters, you need to pay careful attention to how you structure your financial arrangements so they reflect your goals and protect your individual and combined interests. Because lesbians cannot legally marry, there are no built-in legal protections, such as community property laws, if one of us dies or the relationship ends. This is where thoughtful arrangements, agreements, and careful estate planning are critical.

## Contracts and Agreements

There are a lot of details and decisions involved in sharing one's life with a partner. To act as if love is all we need is to ignore some practical realities. And to do so is to miss a wonderful opportunity to create an agreement and contract that celebrates the specialness of the relationship.

The authors of *A Legal Guide for Gay and Lesbian Couples* recommend written agreements as a way to avoid misunderstandings and conflict. However, they also point out that these are no substitute for trust and communication.[7]

Some of us have difficulty talking openly about money, budgets, credit cards, sharing expenses, and future expectations and obligations—much less having a written contract. We may feel it indicates a lack of trust to suggest writing agreements down. Some of us assume contracts are useful only in case of a breakup.

Agreements are also advantageous during the course of a relationship. They signify that issues have been discussed and resolved and that plans are made. Contracts can always be changed. Evaluating a contract annually can be an opportunity to think through, appreciate, and renew a relationship commitment.

*Janis and Sarah drew up a contract in which they agreed on how they would share the expenses of living together. They also specified how they wanted to divide up the tasks of daily living for the next year while Sarah was in school. They included their decision to be monogamous and a number of lighter items, such as:*

*"Janis vows to retain a sense of humor about having so many animals in return for Sarah's promise to clean up any dog shit in the yard."*

*"Sarah promises to respect Janis's passion for her TV soaps."*

*"Janis promises to leave dirty dishes in the sink, not on the kitchen counter."*

Thus contracts can acknowledge day-to-day living issues and the depth and richness in a relationship while providing guidelines for the "what ifs" every couple faces. Once done, these guidelines can contribute to the bonds that hold us together as they provide a sense of structure and commitment.

## Time

Many couples complain that there is not enough time—for work, school, separate activities, being together alone and with the kids, and for keeping up the house or apartment.

For women the issues of time, work, and money are intricately related. The statistics about women making less than men and the concepts of comparable worth and equal pay for equal work underscore this problem. A woman may work long hours and still not make enough money to live on or to support her children. She may sacrifice her free time so that she can make more money, or she may prioritize having free time over money and settle for a less comfortable lifestyle.

*Ariel decided to take a part-time job so that her contribution to the savings account would be equal to her partner Yvonne's. They were saving for a down payment on a house, and Ariel wanted her share to be a true fifty-fifty. Yvonne didn't like Ariel working more, because they hardly saw each other, but she understood and respected her partner's strong feelings.*

*Kenyatta had figured that she and Jewelle would have more time with each other if they lived together. She had anticipated that the time they used to spend commuting would be available for couple activities. Instead, they seemed to have less time together after the move. For one thing, Jewelle spent more time with her separate friends than she had before. Kenyatta decided that they definitely needed to talk about it. She regretted that they had not discussed their expectations more fully before moving in together.*

*Mary Beth and Jermaine worked different shift schedules. This meant that some weeks they barely saw each other and some weeks they could spend most of their free time together. One way they managed to stay connected during the periods when they were on different shifts was to leave love notes for each other—on their pillows, in lunch bags, in the refrigerator.*

Sometimes the problem is not so much that there is not time, but that a couple is dissatisfied with how they are spending their time.

*Aline and Veronica felt that they didn't have any quality time with each other. Their weekends were fitted with chores and business, even though they both insisted that what they really wanted on the weekends was to relax. It just never happened that way. Once they figured out that they actually needed to schedule in time for doing fun activities together, their weekends became much more satisfying. They worked out doing the chores and errands during the week, so they could have outdoor adventures on weekends.*

## Being in Business Together

The issues of work, money, and time are each complex in and of themselves, and they often overlap. For instance, when partners are in business together these three issues are very intertwined.

*Sung-Lin and Dori operated a mail-order business together. They also worked regular nine-to-five jobs. Their big complaint was that the only time they had together was spent working on the business; there was never any time for fun. Eventually the business began to generate enough income so that one of them could quit her day job and focus on the joint business. This left much more time for them to just hang out together.*

*Carlotta and Meg went into business together after being lovers for two years. They had both always dreamed of owning a restaurant. Now, three years later, they were out of the red and felt they could begin to relax a little. As they looked back, they reflected that the hardest part of those early years had been keeping their business relationship separate from their love relationship. Until they figured out how to do that, they had many a fight, supposedly over how to run the restaurant, but really about their relationship. Once, they had an intense disagreement over the redesign of the restaurant menu, when the underlying issue was Carlotta's unhappiness with their sex life. That kind of argument seldom happened anymore.*

One strategy that helped Carlotta and Meg keep clear was their agreement not to talk about business matters at home and not to talk about private matters at work. As much as possible, they left the restaurant behind when they came home and their personal relationship at home when they went to work.

Whether couples work together or not, the relationship suffers when one or both partners is not able to leave her work behind when she comes home. Some suggestions and techniques to ease the transition from work to home are:[8]

- Slow down and begin to unwind at the end of the day by saving easier tasks for then.

- Listen to relaxing tapes or music on the drive or bus ride home or when you arrive home.
- Arrange with your partner (and children) to have some time alone immediately after you come home—particularly if you have had a bad day.
- Have a stress-reducing conversation with your partner as a ritual of reconnecting after work.[9] This involves taking turns—about ten to fifteen minutes each—just listening to each other talk about your day. When you are the listener, your job is to be a cheerleader: Show genuine interest, take your partner's side (even if you think she is being unreasonable), communicate your understanding and support, don't give advice (unless she asks for it), express affection, and validate her feelings. Not only does this help you both decompress after your day but it helps build your bank account of emotional connection.

## Play

Some of us are at play when we remodel the kitchen or compete in a game of chess. For others, play means reading a book, playing basketball, cooking dinner for friends, or going dancing. With all the choices—and possible individual preferences—there is plenty of opportunity for couples to have conflict about how to play.

Good communication is essential. You both need to be clear about what you like and want and what your expectations are of each other. Every couple has to work out a balance between time together and time alone, not to mention time with friends—yours, hers, and your joint friends.

*Kelly had lots of friends and liked to go out to a movie or dinner with them sometimes—by herself. She feels that having her separate friends is good in case she needs to talk with someone about her relationship, and so she doesn't rely only on her partner, Del, for support. Del would prefer to spend her free time just with Kelly. Over the years they have come to realize that this is just how it is. While Del isn't thrilled about it, she accepts that it is important for Kelly to spend time with her friends.*

*JonAnn wanted Wynona to spend time getting to know JonAnn's friends. These people were important to JonAnn, and she wanted to share her partner with her friends and vice versa. However, Wynona needed a lot of alone time, and she didn't have much in common with most of JonAnn's friends.*

The truth is that your partner will probably not like your friends as much as you do, nor will you like hers as much as she does. Just as you won't share all of the same interests as your lover, you won't share the same interest in each other's friends. One way to preserve friendships with people your partner doesn't care for is to spend time with those friends without her. This also gives her space to spend time with her friends by herself or to have time alone.

## Vacations

Partners often have different ideas about what a vacation should be. Vacations—particularly ones where you go away—require so many decisions that it's not always a good idea to go on one when you are not getting along. Some couples find that they do vacations well, even when they are having a lot of conflicts in their everyday life. However, most of us find that our conflicts become magnified when we have to deal with all the decisions involved in a vacation: "Where do we go?" "What will we do today?" and "When shall we have lunch?"

*Kimi and Bozena were both self-employed. They each set their own work schedules and took very little time off. Their vacations were few and far between and typically were more frustrating than fun. Kimi liked to plan ahead and be packed a week in advance; Bozena left everything to the last minute. Partly as a result of this style difference, even talking about a vacation usually turned into an argument. The few vacations that they did manage to take ended up being compromises that neither was very happy about.*

Obviously, in order to solve this problem, Kimi and Bozena need to talk to each other. They each need to clarify what they want and then problem-solve. Possible solutions might include separate vacations, long weekends, regular time together on certain weekends, and taking turns organizing vacations according to different wants—somewhat like taking each other on an extended date.

Another complication to be aware of is homophobia. Of course, you can play "straight" but this is not necessarily easy nor what you want to be doing on your vacation. A solution may be to travel with friends so you form your own "group." The reality is that unless you go on a lesbian cruise, travel to a lesbian resort, or visit a known lesbian-friendly place, you have to address two questions: "Will we be welcome?" and "Will we be comfortable?"[10] To find the answers to these questions you can do the research yourselves or enlist the help of a lesbian or lesbian-friendly travel agent. (See Resources.)

Each of these issues—work, money, time, and play—is complex in and of itself but they overlap as well. As lesbians, we have a unique opportunity to develop couple relationships that emphasize equality and a balance of power between partners. How we handle the issues of work, money, time, and play determines, in large measure, how close we come to an equitable sharing of power and responsibility in our relationship.

## CHAPTER 11

# ໒ Lesbian Couples with Children

Lesbian mothers in earlier decades were almost completely invisible. Lesbians with children in the 1970s and '80s were pioneers who could not take for granted their right to bear or keep their children. Now in the beginning of the twenty-first century, many young lesbian women assume that parenting is an option; meanwhile, lesbian grandmothers go on Olivia Cruises together. Things have changed!

Thanks to feminist work in the 1960s we, as well as heterosexual women, now have more choices about whether (and how) to have and rear children. Many lesbians do not have children, and we in no way want to imply that every lesbian should or even should want to. But as more lesbians choose to mother children it is important to discuss what it means to single mothers, couples, and the children themselves.

Commonly accepted language is in short supply when we talk about lesbian mothers and their children. Mainstream culture uses "mother" to describe the female parent. As lesbians, we have been creative in our ways of naming two female parents; for example, biological or adoptive mother, other mother, second mother, co-parent, co-mother, Mama for one and Mom for the other, and sometimes the mothers' first names. It gets even more complicated when we add new partners. In this chapter we use "mother" or "biological" or "adoptive mother" to describe a woman who is a legal parent. We use those terms in addition to "nonbiological" or "adoptive" or "other mother" to describe a mother who has been in the family since the child arrived and functions as a parent to the child, regardless of her legal status. We refer to partners who join already existing families as "stepmothers." "Co-parent" is our term for a man or woman who has a parenting role and is not a current romantic partner of the mother. Most important of all, however, is that each family find names that speak to them meaningfully.

## Coming Out/Being Out

In spite of the personal and political gains for lesbians and gay men since the Stonewall Rebellion in 1969, coming out and being out are still major decisions for many of us. When lesbians are parents, coming out takes on additional risks because of the potential negative impact on the children and their relationship with their mother(s). Lesbian mothers and their partners must decide whether or not to come out to their children, when and how to do so, and how much to be out as a family to the rest of the world. Many parents who come out to their children take years to do so. Others tell their children in many ways from the day the child is born or arrives in the household.

Mothers who had their children in heterosexual relationships, and later self-defined as lesbian, experience coming out and being out differently than mothers who came out as lesbian before having children. These differences center around the presence of a potentially homophobic or supportive father, the positive or negative exposure the children have had to lesbianism before the parents split up, and how out the mother is.

When a mother comes out to herself as lesbian, she usually separates (or already has separated) from the father of her children. The mother and children have gone through a separation process that is often wrenching and at worst brutal. When the mother leaves her male partner to join a woman, the new relationship is associated with the demise of the children's home and family, which is hard on everybody involved. Many women fear that their ex-husbands will want sole custody of the children if their lesbianism becomes known. This worry may continue long after the divorce is final.

*Both Donna and Irene had been recently divorced. They had four children between them. When they decided to move in together, they explained their combining households to the kids as a plan to cut expenses. Irene had wanted to come out to the children and work on being a family, but did not do so out of respect for Donna's situation: Donna knew that her ex-husband would be likely to sue for custody of the children if he found out about her relationship with Irene.*

Even when losing the children is not at stake, many women fear that their children will reject them, be upset, or be harmed by the knowledge that their mother is a lesbian.

*When Dee and Janice first became lovers, Dee had been clear that she did not want to parent Janice's ten-year-old son, Erik. Janice also had wanted to wait until Erik had his own sexual identity established before she came out to him. She was afraid of somehow influencing him. Partly for these reasons, Janice and Dee did not live together. Time marched on. Erik turned fifteen and they had not yet discussed their relationship with him.*

*After her husband died, Hester acted for the first time on her feelings for women. She was sixty-eight years old. Her five children were grown, and three of them had families of their own. She decided not to say anything to them about her relationship because she was afraid that they would be negative and unaccepting of her partner if they knew. As it was, her children included her partner, Mattie, as part of the family. Both she and Mattie doted on the grandchildren. The possibility that they would be denied contact with them was another reason not to come out.*

*Three years ago, Ramona was convinced that her two young daughters would have been freaked out if they knew about her lifestyle. At eleven and nine, they had been upset enough about the divorce. She decided it would be best if they lived with their father, and he had agreed. But she had always planned to have them live with her eventually. Now that she was settled, she was ready for them to be with her; however, she still had not come out to them. She couldn't imagine their living with her and her partner and not knowing, but she was afraid they wouldn't want to move in if they knew.*

As parents, these women face a double dose of the coming-out dilemma. They have to cope with society's homophobic attitudes, which may have influenced their children, and they also have to fight their own antilesbian conditioning. Hester faces the possible homophobia of two generations—her adult children and her grandchildren. Between them, Janice and Ramona confront children of different ages, sexes, and in different living situations.

As you consider coming out to your child, we recommend asking yourself the following questions in order to be realistic in your assessment of potential problems. If you determine that there is real risk, use your answers to anticipate difficulties and problem-solve them as necessary.

- What is the worst thing that could happen if I came out to my child?
- What are the other possible negative consequences, and can I accept them?
- How can I reduce or minimize the negative consequences?
- Can I turn the consequences into positives?
- What is the best thing that could happen?[1]

### How Do Children React?

What do we know about how kids react to a parent's coming out? According to Joy Schulenburg, author of *Gay Parenting*, children are amazingly flexible, and most of those she interviewed responded positively.[2] Our own experience supports her findings. While some children reject their parents immediately, but not necessarily forever, most children are more concerned about their own relationships with their parents than about their parents' sexual orientation. "Just so she's still my mom, I don't care about that other stuff" is a very common reaction.

Of course, children's reactions vary by age, by beliefs they have about lesbian and gay people, and by the timing and approach their mother takes in coming out. Most children and parents seem to think it is better to tell a child when he or she is young. This avoids the risk that the youngster will find out from someone else or in an undesirable way.

*"The kids at school are teasing me. They say you are a lezzie. Is that true?"*

*"Dad says that you and Misty are queer. What is he talking about?"*

Another advantage of talking to children early is that they are less likely to have adopted society's negative attitudes toward homosexuality. Schulenburg suggests that this negative conditioning is pretty well established by age eleven or twelve, and that boys seem to be more susceptible than girls. In addition, children's feelings about a mother's lesbianism may change over time. Just because a child is uncomfortable or accepting at one age or at one point in time does not mean that she or he will remain that way. Continuing to talk is important.

*Guidelines for Coming Out to Children*

- *Sort out your own feelings about being a lesbian first.* The most positive coming-out experiences are reported by parents who were comfortable with themselves.
- *Plan ahead.* It is best to plan ahead not only about the time and place and tone you want to establish, but also about possible reactions and how to handle them.
- *Reassure your children.* Tell them that your being a lesbian does not change your relationship with them or your feelings for them.
- *Be prepared to answer questions.* Young children may have little curiosity and no questions—yet. But older children may want to know, for example, why you can't just find a man to fall in love with and marry, or why people don't like lesbians.
- *Be prepared for your child to withdraw for a while.* Withdrawal is more common with preadolescents, adolescents, and even adult offspring. They may not want any additional information and may resist talking about their feelings. Give them time and check in periodically. You need to recognize that adolescents' main concern is likely to be for themselves—how will this affect them? The assurance that you will be sensitive to their feelings and will not embarrass them in front of their friends may be helpful. Another typical concern of adolescents is their own sexuality—are they going to be gay because their mother is? Although they may not ask this question directly, parents are wise to address it. Having a lesbian parent does not mean your child is or will be gay, too.
- *Stay calm.* Just as it often takes time for a parent to accept having a lesbian daughter or gay son, so it can take time for a child to accept having a lesbian mother.
- *Use resources.* In some areas, most often urban ones, support groups or activity groups for lesbian families may be available. Books, films, and videotapes about lesbian families can also be helpful. (See the Resources section.)
- *Keep talking with your child.* We cannot emphasize enough that coming out is ongoing for you and your child.[3] Make your explanations simple and straightforward, and gear them to the age and level of understanding of your child. It is also important to leave the door open for further discussion. Children adapt better when there is ongoing dialogue about these issues. Sometimes friends, partners, or other resources can be helpful in talking with children about their questions.

Coming out to children does mean taking a calculated risk. The risks, such as temporary or longer-term rejection by your children, custody problems, or overt hostility toward your partner by your kids, need to be taken seriously. On the other hand, there are some clear advantages to you in coming out and being out with your children. Secrets and avoidance interfere with intimacy—between the adults, between the children and the adults, and between the children. If you are out, you and your partner are both more able to be yourselves and to nurture your relationship than if you are closeted, especially if the children live with you. And all of you can then work on defining and clarifying a definition of family that suits your particular wants and situation. Being out with your children has advantages for them as well. They grow up with a parent who is modeling positive self-esteem and taking a stance of integrity even though it may conflict with society's expectations. Growing up in a family where openness is valued leads to more honest relationships in general.

Being out also gives parents a better opportunity to protect children from the damage of homophobia. Children are helped by learning that homophobia is a form of bigotry within other people and not a problem their mother(s) or family has.[4] Mothers need to instruct their children in how to recognize and deal with it in other people. Janet Wright's research on lesbian "stepfamilies" also supports this view. She found that children find support in knowing other children with lesbian mothers. Children realize that their family is not the only one that is different and that there are other children with lesbian and gay parents.[5] Acceptance and support from anyone in the children's lives, and particularly from grandparents and extended family, contribute greatly toward children's growing up with positive self-esteem and the ability to see themselves and their families as healthy and strong.

## How Are We Doing as Parents?

Since the late 1970s researchers have been examining children of lesbian mothers and gay fathers. They have found that our children are psychologically and emotionally very similar to children who have heterosexual parents.[6] There are even a few findings in the research that suggest that being raised by lesbians produces some positive differences. Charlotte Patterson reported that her sample of children of lesbians indicated that they experienced more reactions to stress, such as fear, and at the same time a greater sense of well-being.[7] She suggests these seemingly contradictory results could mean either that children with lesbian mothers experienced more stress than the children they were compared to or that children reared by lesbians may be more willing to experience and express more feelings in general. This latter interpretation better fits our experience.

Ailsa Steckel found in her study comparing children reared by lesbian and heterosexual couples that the boys in heterosexual-parented families were slightly more likely to be more aggressive than the boys in lesbian-parented families.[8] These results invite continued exploration into the different effects various family types have on children, with an eye toward improving family life for everyone.

There is ongoing controversy over whether children, and especially boys, need to live with a father or male role model in order to develop a healthy sense of self and gender-appropriate self-identity. Louise Silverstein and Carl Auerbach examined the research about fathers. They concluded that children need "at least one responsible, caretaking adult who has a positive emotional connection to them and with whom they have a consistent relationship" and that the gender of a parent is not as important.[9] They also cite research that finds that boys do not need a heterosexual male parent to develop and maintain a masculine gender identity.[10] Whether or not children need a mother or father in the home for healthy development, it is very important that they maintain positive relationships with their own particular parents and adults of both genders. We encourage you to support your children's relationships with their other parents, and not let your struggle with an ex-partner or ex-husband interfere with the best interests of your child.

## Family Forms

Language that accurately portrays the experience of lesbian-parented families and also carries the weight and familiarity of traditional language has not been easy to find. For instance, we use "stepfamily" even though that word has always meant the legal entity created when a man and woman marry and one of them already has children. We use "lesbian-" and "heterosexual-parented family" (instead of "lesbian family" or "heterosexual family") to remind all of us that the children of the family may not share their parents' sexual orientation. We choose not to use "nuclear family" because lesbian-parented families often are imbedded in an extended family of biological, legal, and chosen relationships; instead we use "family of origin" to describe the families in which people grow up. Finally, we use "complex family" to describe stepfamilies that add another child or children by birth or adoption. We encourage you to use our terms or craft your own with the goal of finding language that works for you and your family.

### Stepfamilies

Stepfamilies are created when a mother partners with another woman who may or may not have children. While most of these stepfamilies are created in the wake of the ending of a heterosexual-parented family, there are increasing numbers of stepfamilies that develop after lesbian divorces as well. The dynamics of forming a stepfamily are similar regardless of the genders and sexual orientation of the parents.

*Mamie had four children and two uninvolved ex-husbands before she met Grace. Mamie wanted her partner to be another parent. Initially the children resented Grace, but eventually they were glad to have someone else in their lives whom they could count on besides Mamie.*

*Madelaine had a five-year-old son, Tony, from her lesbian relationship of ten years. When she became involved with Theresa, they decided that they wanted to live together but not have Theresa take an active parenting role. Everyone liked this arrangement, especially Tony, who found that he had gained a good friend.*

When one or both women bring children into their lesbian relationship, it creates a family structure much like heterosexual-parented stepfamilies. One of the main differences, however, is that there is no legal status that describes how people are connected to each other. The mother's lover is not a legally sanctioned stepmother, nor are the children her legal stepchildren. If the couple is not out to the children, the other woman may be "just a friend" or "my mom's roommate." Even if they are out, there may be no better language. There is no commonly accepted word. Some children call the partner "my mom's lover" or "my mom's partner," but this is only half the truth, since it ignores the possible relationship between the partner and the child. We have chosen to use the language of stepmother and stepchildren, when the partner lives with the mother and children, to emphasize both that there is an important relationship and that it is not the same as the one with a child's original mother(s).

Having two responsible, caring adults in their lives is a bonus to children.[11] However, a new adult moving too quickly into a parenting role can be problematic for everyone concerned. We encourage mothers to date and get to know a prospective partner over time before considering having her move in with the family. Especially if you have had a series of live-in partners, it can be very hard on your children to bond with and then lose a number of significant adults. Better to wait a little longer and be surer.

When you do decide to add your partner to the household, there are three tasks that the new family has to accomplish. The biological or adoptive mother has to make room for the stepmother. The stepmother has to determine how to take children into her life. And the children have to figure out how to take the stepmother into their lives.[12] Add these tasks to the necessity of nurturing a new couple relationship and it can feel overwhelming. Here are some generalized guidelines as you consider adding a new adult to a preexisting family.

- Younger children tend to adapt more easily to having a new adult in the family.
- Adolescent boys tend to be more accepting of new lesbian partners than adolescent girls.
- Children who have lost significant adults, through divorce or breakup of the mother's relationship with a lesbian partner, are less inclined to bond readily with her new partner.
- When children have to compete with their mother's new partner for attention, they are not likely to welcome her into the family.
- If the new partner's parenting style and values are consistent with what the children are used to, it is easier for them to relate and for the new partner to fit into the established family life.[13]

## Mother

If you are a mother, you need to decide how much parenting help you want and how best to meet the needs of your children. Most mothers initially are a little reluctant to give up responsibility or the "mom" niche. And usually, your children do not want you to give it up, or even share it! In the beginning (and maybe for the entire time the children are living at home), it is a good idea for you to create and enforce the rules. Again, the age of your child is a crucial variable. Obviously, if a child is two years old, you will want your new partner to set some limits or take the initiative and tell your son that he cannot go outside without his coat.

It is very common for your children and their stepmother to "recruit" you to their sides. Thus, it is important to be clear about who is responsible for what in terms of discipline, chores around the house, homework, transporting children, and all the other thousands of jobs required for running a household. It is easy for the stepmother to become the limit-setter and you to be the "good mommy," or vice versa. You need to be very clear with your children that your lover is not the "bad one." Another pattern is for you to become more of a disciplinarian than you would really like and for your partner to be seen as an insurgent who will help the children get around you. It does help the new adult and children bond, but in the long run it sets up a nasty situation in which you are the one adult and your partner becomes one of the kids. One way to avoid these traps is to make sure that each of you takes the children's side sometimes. Another is to be clear with each other about what you want to communicate to the children, so that you and your partner do not get caught enforcing different decisions.

As a mother you are in the middle of a tug of war for attention between your new lover and your children. Children usually need to come first and may even need more attention than usual, especially if there has been a recent divorce. However, a new relationship also needs time and attention to flourish. This is a hard balance to maintain! But difficult as it is, the beginning of your new family's life together is a vital time to set expectations. You need to make sure to reassure your children that you are there for them. And give your partner enough time alone with you to refresh your memories of why you wanted to be lovers.

### Stepmother

Some women who partner with a mother really want to be involved with children. Others may like children, and accept that her lover and her children are a package deal, but do not particularly want to parent. In a few situations the new partner does not care much for children, does not like these particular children, or does not really want to share a partner with children. If you are in the third category and are considering moving in with your partner, we encourage the two of you to assess seriously the viability of a long-term, live-in relationship. A counselor may be helpful to you in making your decisions. You will not last long in that family if you plan to ignore the children, try to come between your partner and her children, or think that you will be first on her priority list.

> *Hope's lover, Candy, had three children who in Hope's eyes were demanding, ungrateful, and rude. Hope also realized that she was not just a little jealous of the time Candy gave to the children. Candy went to school plays and sports events, helped with homework, drove the kids where they wanted to go, and generally was a mother first—and a lover second. Hope was having second thoughts about the plan to live together.*

If you are willing to share your relationship with children, you need to ask and observe how much time and energy the mother spends on her children.

Look at the mother's parenting style—how does it fit with your values? Carefully consider the long-term implications of being involved in a relationship where there is ongoing stress about priorities.

Since the mother and her children were a family before the addition of a partner, it is very important for you, the newcomer, not to jump into a parenting role too quickly, if ever. The children's ages play a large part in this. Younger children are likely to want and need more parenting earlier on, while older children may resent even their biological or adoptive mother's parenting—let alone yours. Most stepparents have some criticism of the way their partner parents. It might be about how the children speak to their mother or about the mother's lack of follow-through in important tasks. Whatever you feel critical about, sit on it for a while. Get to know the context and the issues before trying to change the family dynamics that were established before you arrived.

One study of heterosexual-parented stepfamilies found much support for stepparents' moving slowly into the preexisting family, and also discovered how wonderful it was for the children to have another stable adult in their lives.[14] Many stepmothers find that they develop good relationships with their stepchildren based on shared interests or rituals they develop together. Some of the activities include fishing, bowling, shopping, cooking, reading mysteries, watching scary movies (that the mother would not consider watching), or getting hot chocolate together after a hard day at school. While love may never develop, stepmothers can have mutually respectful and caring relationships with their stepchildren.

In her interviews with stepfamilies, Patricia Kelley heard repeatedly that family meetings with all the family members present were very helpful in establishing guidelines, adjusting them when necessary, and keeping communication open.[15]

*Derek and Paul were having a house meeting with their mother, Nancy, and her partner, Carey, who was moving in the following month. Both boys, aged eight and twelve, were adamant that they did not need another mother. They told Carey that she could not tell them what to do or make up new rules. She asked them if it was all right to give them a snack after school since she was there when they got home while their mom was at work. They said yes and agreed that it was okay if she reminded them that homework had to be done before computer games or TV. That was their mom's rule. As they sorted out all the possible permutations, all four agreed that Carey could help out in accordance with preexisting agreements, and that the boys would treat her with the respect they would give an adult and housemate.*

## Children

A child's main task is to be a child. This usually includes doing whatever it takes to keep her relationship with her mother the way she likes it. It also means playing, going to school, hanging out with friends, and not spending much time worrying about the family dynamics. In the case of divorced parents, children need to know that they will have access to both parents (if possible), that their mother is still there for them, and that the new woman in their lives is not going to take over. Sometimes children are thrilled to get a stepmother. It often improves their lives because someone else can help with transportation, house jobs, and finances. Having a stepmother often means having someone who is interested in doing things that their mother did not want to do or understand.

> *Steve was so excited he could not stop babbling. His stepmom, Lise, was taking him to a Mets game. Steve's mother, Deanna, hated sports and his dad lived across the country, so he had had no one who wanted to take him to baseball games. When Lise had moved in last year, Steve had hated her. He was sure she was the reason his dad had moved out and he resented having to have a babysitter on Thursday nights so the two women could have a date. But then he discovered that Lise loved baseball as much as he did. They were both die-hard Mets fans and had plans to go to at least five games a year. Steve forgave her for taking his mom away on Thursdays, at least during baseball season.*

Children really do need to come first in stepfamilies. Both partners and other parents need to remember that the adults' job is to maintain the safety net of emotional and financial support and intact relationships with significant adults. Parents need to manage any difficulties they have with each other without putting the children in the middle. Children should not be placed in a position of having to make choices to protect the adults' feelings. Adults need to be adults and children need to be children.

## Fathers

When there is, or has been, a father in the children's lives, the stepfamily may have him or his ghost as part of its life. If he is also homophobic and communicates this to anyone, his presence can be very damaging to the children and hard on the stepfamily. Obviously, when a father and mother co-parent respectfully and well together, everyone benefits. If you are part of a stepfamily where a father is present in the children's lives, it is important to facilitate their relationship and not to put the children in the position of having to defend their father to you. If there are conflicts, the mother needs to work them out with him separately, not in front of the children.

Unfortunately, it may be that coming out to him would risk a custody battle over the children. When this is the case, remember that staying closeted and keeping this magnitude of a secret from your children is very stressful. However, the alternative of telling your children is often worse. It is unrealistic to expect young children to keep your secret, and older children may feel very uncomfortable keeping it from their father. It is also stressful when you decide to challenge your ex-husband for custody as an out lesbian. You need support as you navigate these challenges. Close friends, family, books, information, and connections via the Internet, support groups, counseling, and a good attorney can all help to ease the stress of protecting yourself and your children from or during a custody battle.

### Other Mothers

If the ex is another woman, the same tensions around co-parenting may still be present. In a custody struggle the legal or biological mother usually gets the court's ruling for custody. If a second-parent adoption has been approved, you both are typically on equal ground in the eyes of the law.

It is beyond our scope here to cover relationships with the other parent in depth. We encourage you to read books in our resource section or seek professional help for ideas about how to develop a workable co-parent relationship.

### Legalities

In the absence of a legal marriage certificate, lesbian stepmothers typically have no legal status in the eyes of the courts. If you want to protect the stepmother's right to maintain contact with the children in the event of the mother's death, there are a few preventative measures available. Some are "legal" and formal and some are not.

If there is only one legal parent, you may be able to secure a second-parent adoption, in which the stepparent becomes a second legal parent (we discuss this more later). Some states even allow for three legal parents, in order to protect positive, significant adult and child relationships.

Usually, another legal parent or blood relative will have precedence over a lesbian stepmother if a case goes to court. If you want the stepmother to have visitation or custody rights and the extended family and other parent are hostile to this idea, discuss this with an attorney to see what is possible.

The most important way to protect the child's and stepmother's right to have access to each other is to talk to your extended family. Tell the grandparents, father, aunts, and uncles that this relationship is important to the children. Make sure that your partner participates in extended family gatherings so that family members can see the relationship between the stepparent and child.

### Families of Origin

When a lesbian couple adopts or arranges for the conception of a child, even if only one of the women is the biologically related or legally adoptive parent, both women usually consider themselves equal parents. Some couples, however, add a child or children to their family with the intention of having only one woman be the parent, or of having other women or men be primary parents (co-parents) with the biological mother. As with all lesbian-parented families, it is crucial for the couple to figure out what roles they want each woman to take. If it is the intention of both of you to be equal parents, you will have to spend time and energy to be recognized as such by other people. Unfortunately, regardless of how you define your family roles, the world outside your family will usually apply traditional definitions to fit its concept of how families ought to look. Usually, lesbian couples who decide to parent together are out in most parts of their lives. So, while this may make it somewhat easier to engage with the outside world, it does not mean that you will be taken more seriously than more closeted parents. It does mean that you are freer to challenge people and institutions that are hindering your ability to function as a whole family.

If you are considering adding children to your relationship, here are a few questions we encourage you to ask yourselves.

- *Do you want a child, or do you simply like the thought of having children?* Spend time with children and with parents as you consider this question.
- *Do you have enough time, support, and money to have a child?*
- *How will your work be affected by raising a child?*
- *Do you want to bear a child, adopt, or foster parent?* A lesbian couple is the only kind of couple who may have the option of deciding who will bear a baby. Which one of you would want to give birth?
- *If you are interested in adopting or foster parenting, are you patient enough*

*and sure enough of yourselves to endure the likely homophobia and the almost certain daunting red tape of social-service agencies?*

- *Have you thought through how a child will affect your relationship?* No one can predict exactly how children will affect a couple's relationship, but they will. For some women their relationship is their highest priority and they would rather not risk upsetting it.
- *Have you and your partner discussed or worked through potential trouble spots, such as parenting styles, individual needs for control and discipline, and differing cultural and family backgrounds?*
- *Have you thought about how having a child affects your being out in the world as a lesbian?* When you have children, you lose control of who knows you are lesbian, and you may not be in a position to or want to take that risk.
- *Do you have support from your lesbian community for your choice to parent?* Some lesbians may feel you have abandoned the cause if you choose to have a child. If your community feels this way, have you considered how that will affect you?
- *Are you prepared to cope with effects of heterosexism and homophobia on your child?* Homophobia takes on new meaning when it is directed at your child.
- *Have you considered the impact of racism on your family?* While racism affects us all, interracial families face more complex challenges.
- *Have you thought about the pros and cons of raising a son as compared to a daughter?*
- *Do you want men involved in a conscious way with your child?* If so, what are you willing to do to have that happen? Parents cannot control who is in their child's life, but they can make some philosophical decisions and begin the child's life with those in place. As the child grows up, she will gradually take control over who is important to her.
- *If you have a disability, do you automatically assume you should not parent?* If so, we encourage you to think how your disability might affect parenting, rather than reject it outright.
- *Have you thought about raising a child who has a disability?* What strengths do you bring to this, and what issues are likely to be problems for you?
- *Have you considered alternatives to parenting, such as coaching or being "aunts" or godparents to a friend's child?* [16]

## Baby by Birthing

*Ingrid was nine months pregnant with two weeks to go until her due date. She never thought that she would be ready to go through labor, but she found herself hoping daily that she would deliver early. Her partner, Bridget, was so excited she could talk only about their child and how much fun it was going to be to take her or him to the office to meet her coworkers, to her parents for Thanksgiving, to Ingrid's family for Christmas, and on and on. But first they had to get through the birth and settling in, and then it was "Watch out world, here we come!"*

We are assuming that if you want to bear a child, you already know how to find sperm and how to inseminate the prospective biological mother. In the interests of space we have chosen to focus on the impact on couples after they have gotten pregnant or already have a child. If you are interested in learning more about deciding whether and how to get pregnant, we recommend *Considering Parenthood* by Cherie Pies, *The Gay and Lesbian Parenting Handbook* by April Martin, and our book, *The Lesbian Parenting Book*,[17] for more thorough discussions of getting pregnant (and other methods of bringing children into your family).

Bearing a child begins with finding nonhomophobic prenatal care for the biological mother-to-be. Ideally, the midwife or physician should look upon the childbearing woman's partner (or whoever is so indicated) as the child-to-be's other parent. This means including her in any health-care visits, birthing classes, hospital tours, and discussions of how to take care of the baby and the mother after the birth. This kind of health care is more likely to be available in urban areas than in rural ones. You need to discuss in advance how you two want the nonbiological mother involved in the insemination, pregnancy, and birthing processes. If you are not out as a couple to the health-care provider, it is highly likely that the nonbiological mother will be seen as a very supportive friend who plans to help out.

As the due date gets closer, you need to have financial and medical powers of attorney and health-care directives that specifically address the nonbiological mother's being able to authorize emergency care for both her partner and her baby should the need arise. Make sure the biological mother also has a will that clearly indicates her wishes that her partner, not her biological family, get custody of their baby in the event of the birthing mother's death. Ask an attorney for help in formulating all the legal documents to ensure that you have done the best job possible to protect yourselves.

You also need to discuss how you will present yourselves to your extended families and to the world. Birth is only the beginning! Have you prepared both of your families for the arrival of their grandchild, niece, nephew, or cousin? Are you both claiming motherhood and expecting your families to treat you as a two-parent family? Will the nonbiological mother volunteer at the cooperative day-care center, take your baby to your health-care provider, attend teacher conferences, school plays, soccer games, and so on, or will she stay in the background when the family is outside the home? It is obviously not necessary to answer all of these questions before the baby arrives, but we recommend beginning the discussion of your philosophies of parenting and how you want to share your decisions with the world.

## Baby by Adoption

For the most part, couples who adopt face the same issues as bearing parents; however, you also need to decide how to apply for adoption. Will you apply together as a couple? Or will one of you apply alone—with or without the adoption agency's knowledge of your couple status? Most adoption agencies will not consider a lesbian couple, but if they do, you may find yourselves at the bottom of the priority list for healthy infants, if that is what you want. You are more likely to be offered older/disabled/troubled children who have prior histories that make them difficult to place. The same is true when one of you applies to adopt as a single woman. If one partner is the legally adoptive parent, the nonadopting partner is subject to the same issues as the nonbiological mother, which we discussed previously. As with all adopting parents, even when your application is approved, you have to wait an undetermined length of time for the child. This waiting can be extremely stressful.

Some couples have chosen to adopt children from other countries where they may be able to more easily adopt healthy babies. If you are interested in this route, contact an attorney or agency in your area that is well acquainted with the different laws and guidelines for international adoptions.

*Yiku and Leslie were on their way to China! They had waited for eight months to be approved by the Chinese government to be adoptive parents. Well, actually only one of them was approved to be the mother, but Leslie and Yiku were not going to tell anyone who the legal mother was. They wanted everyone to look at them both as full mothers. Then it took four months for a child to appear that fit what they had asked for. Two months ago the adoption agency had sent them a picture of Shao-yen, their daughter. Leslie would be seen as Yiku's friend who was helping, but she didn't care—she'd talk to her therapist later if it got to her. Today she was on the way to meet her daughter.*

## Second-Parent Adoption

A second-parent adoption is the process by which a lesbian may adopt and become a legally recognized parent of her partner's biological or adopted child. Currently a minority of legal jurisdictions extend this legal protection to lesbian- and gay-headed families. Where this option is allowed, it is necessary for the child's father, if known, to terminate legally his paternal rights. If you have used a sperm bank, it may be that the donor is legally considered to have given up all parental rights already.

Second-parent adoptions often require home studies, evaluation of the adopting parent, and confirmation of the couple status of the two women. If you are approved by the courts, you both become legal parents of your child. In some counties and states this may also include reissuing the child's birth certificate with the two mothers' names in the place of mother and father.

Contact an attorney in your county to find out if second-parent adoptions are a legal possibility. We recommend finding an attorney who has experience working with lesbian and gay issues and who may already be aware of whether this option exists. If it is not possible to get a second-parent adoption, have your attorney implement whatever legal options best protect you and your child. These can include a durable power of attorney or a will that appoints the nonlegal mother as the guardian in case of the death or incompetency of the legal mother.

One of the main differences between families of origin and stepfamilies is that both women in the couple start off as parents. Children bond with both mothers, know them both from birth, and should be able to count on both women for financial and emotional support. There is usually much family loyalty and a sense of belonging to "my family." Decisions and responsibilities are shared by the parents and both love the children as their own. Often there are also differences between the two kinds of families in how out the parents are and have been throughout the children's lives. When this is the case, it usually affects the level of acceptance and comfort children feel about being in a lesbian-parented family.

The presence of a father can bring anything from untold pain and damage to wonderful support. Lesbians who have children outside of heterosexual relationships do not have to contend with legal fathers, but on the other hand those families often work to create meaningful relationships between men and their children.

As a result, the stages of development are different for the two kinds of families. We strongly recommend that you work with these differences and not try to force a stepfamily into the mold of an idealized family of origin.

All families have strengths and limitations. Celebrate your family's strengths and work with its limitations with love and compassion.

## Complex Families

When a lesbian-parented stepfamily adds another child by birth or adoption, it has created one of the more unusual family structures in our society. Complicated family structures are becoming more common in the heterosexual community as well, and this is challenging mainstream institutions to adapt their services to meet new family models. However, complex, lesbian-parented families are usually not acknowledged, much less supported.

One potential problem in complex families is that your new child is being reared in a positive lesbian environment, while the older child or children may have been reared originally in a heterosexist and homophobic household. Thus, situations that seem normal for one child may be embarrassing or ludicrous, or may even seem immoral, to another child in the same family. The child from the previous relationship may have other parents and grandparents to visit from whom he or she receives attention, presents, and money. The younger child may feel left out. The older child could be jealous of the new one. The children may view the two lesbians differently. One may be a parent and the other just another adult to the older youngsters, while to the youngest child, both are "mama."

> Georgette and Sam had been lovers for six years. They lived in an old farmhouse with Georgette's son, Tyree, and Sam's daughter, Angel. Sam had just given birth to a loud little boy, James. The two older children, who normally fought constantly, were amazed to find themselves united—against the new arrival. He cried too much, got more than his share of attention, and was the darling of the lesbian community in the area. Tyree had not talked to his mother about it. Georgette was so tired from getting up at night that Tyree figured that she wouldn't listen much anyway. "At least he's a boy," Tyree had thought. "Now I'm not the only one."

The issues can be complicated and tangled. Keeping communication open among family members, asking friends to bring gifts for the older children if they are bringing things for a baby, spending time with other lesbian-parented families, and family counseling can be useful strategies for easing the journey. It is helpful if the stepmother and older children can develop shared interests, friendship, or another kind of positive relationship before the addition of the new child. Whenever a new child comes into a family, older children need to feel special, too. This is even more important in a complex stepfamily where the older child may not be particularly attached to her mother's partner. It is also important to educate the children about the different kinds of families in the world and about homophobia, both when it comes up and in advance of any incidents. This will help remind your children that bigotry and discomfort are the other person's problem, not something wrong with them or you.

> *Marge and Toni had adopted a two-year-old deaf girl. Toni's ten-year-old son, Mark, was very excited. The family had been studying sign language, and Mark was clearly very talented; he was a better signer than either of the women. Until all this happened, Mark had been belligerent toward Marge and angry about the impending arrival of the little girl. Since his sister came home, something in Mark had shifted. He delighted in helping his sister and was even initiating contact with Marge. Toni thought this was due to Marge's praising him so much as they learned American Sign Language (ASL) together. The two women felt that their family was finally going "to happen."*

As do parents in stepfamilies, mothers in complex families have to be very careful about their wills and powers of attorney. The relationships are different within the family, and so are not consistent from one child to another. You need to decide who gets custody of the children in case of one or both of your deaths. Make sure you both have powers of attorney that authorize emergency health care for all of the children in the family. When you know what you need to support and protect your family, you are more likely to be able to use societal legal processes and institutions to meet your family's needs more effectively.

### In the Event of a Breakup

The courts are not prepared to acknowledge, let alone honor, nontraditional family structures. Therefore, difficult as it may sound, it is particularly important for you to discuss custody and visitation arrangements in the event that the relationship dissolves. The nonbiological or nonadoptive mother who is unable to do a second-parent adoption would probably face an uphill court battle, for example, should her partner decide to take their child away. The court systems in some counties with large, politically active lesbian and gay populations are more likely to award visitation and maybe even custody to nonlegal parents, but most judges still find in favor of the legal parent.

We assume that both of you want the other to continue to be involved, even after a breakup, but it is far better to have thought out the arrangements beforehand, under happier conditions. While they will not be legally binding, these agreements will show prior intent and can give you a starting point if you agree to negotiate. Even if you are both legal parents, there can be nasty struggles over property and children, with the children caught in the middle. This is very hard on them. Research on children whose parents divorced shows that the way parents treat each other can ameliorate the *negative impact* of divorce. If parents fight or use the children and/or custody to try to get back at the other parent, they can do immense damage to the children.[18] We recommend that you use a therapist or a mediator, when possible, to negotiate a visitation or custody agreement. In that way, your family may be able to stay out of potentially hostile court arenas while ensuring that your child has continued access to both of you.

## The Family in the Broader Society

Lesbian families exist within a broader social context, too. At times, the interaction between lesbians and society involves legal relationships, such as wills and custody agreements, but for the most part these interactions involve the human relationships that populate our everyday lives.

### Lesbian Community

*Justine was finally pregnant! The odd thing was that some of her friends were just not excited. They had actually become more distant and less available in the last two months.*

*Jenn hung up the phone. She had just spent two hours talking to her best friend, Suzie, who was worried that Jenn would no longer have time for her, would become totally baby-focused, and probably wouldn't want to go to the bars to dance anymore. Jenn wasn't sure either. She had felt out of sync the last few months and really was nervous that she was changing into a mother instead of a dyke. And she didn't know very many queer mothers with whom she could talk about her feelings.*

*Paige had just moved in with her partner, Serena, and Serena's two teenaged girls. Paige, Serena, and the girls got along well; the problem was with Paige's friends. Some of them didn't seem to want to have much to do with the four of them as a family. Other friends, though, especially other parenting couples, were very excited. Paige wondered if her friendship circle would change drastically.*

While the lesbian community may be supportive in general about lesbians having children, sometimes the translation is ragged. Some women like children, but have little idea of how to incorporate them into their world. Others are uncomfortable with the changes that come with children, so they avoid their friends who are pregnant or have children. Some lesbians have chosen not to have children and prefer not to have them in their lives. Parents need to respect these differing feelings and make time to be with their friends in various ways that are mutually nurturing. The friends, in turn, need to realize that mothers often have less free time than women who do not have children, and to have patience when they get less time than they would like with these friends. The issue really isn't whether there will be changes, because there will be; the issue is how we can adjust to the changes and have friends and children in our lives.

Even though many lesbians now assume that we can rear children if we choose, the lesbian community is not as child-oriented as the heterosexual community. We have fewer children living with us and know fewer couples adopting and giving birth. We need to figure out ways to incorporate lesbian-parented families into our communities, and parenting couples need to figure out what kind of help they want from their friends.

*Jenn asked her good friend Suzie to be present at the birth. Suzie was thrilled and asked Jenn and her partner's permission to take pictures to document the event.*

*Paige and Serena made a point of spending time alone with some close friends who really did not want to be with their teenaged girls.*

Couples can ask for concrete things like company during the day, help cleaning the house, babysitting, or being a check-in person for the teenager. You can also ask for more abstract things, like being a sounding board while you vent your frustrations about your thirteen-year-old son. On a community note, child care needs to be offered at lesbian events if the broader lesbian community wants mothers involved. And all of us need to acknowledge that lesbian mothers need support to remember what is special about being a lesbian while bridging the mainstream family culture and the lesbian/queer/dyke community they inhabit.

## Parents' Families of Origin

Generally speaking it is less comfortable for lesbian-parented families to relate to the broader world than it is for them to relate to the lesbian community. One of the most important parts of the broader world is the parents' own parents.

*Kit's parents were dumbstruck when she told them she was pregnant. They hung up the phone and stared at each other. What would they tell their friends?*

*Tomiko's family didn't take her parenthood seriously when they found out that her partner was pregnant. They assumed that Tomiko would be "like an aunt or something." It wasn't until they saw her with her son, Kim, that they realized that she was really a mother.*

Our families are almost always surprised when we tell them we want to have, will have, or do have children in our lesbian families. They want to know "How? Won't it hurt the children?" and "How does it affect us?" They can have a devastating effect on us, or they can add to our happiness immeasurably. It is our experience that sometimes the arrival of a grandchild brings a previously distant parent back into contact with her lesbian daughter. (Few parents can resist at least some contact with a new grandchild.) Thus, you may have the challenge of having to reconnect with a parent you had already grieved losing because of his or her homophobia.

Remember that they may not move as quickly as we would like, or embrace our concept of family as unquestioningly as we want them to. It does not mean that they won't get there, in the end. It does mean that we need patience and often we have to educate them.

Our having children is often the catalyst that pushes our families of origin into coming out about us, and they need support just like we do.

Thankfully, the 1990s were the decade of lesbian- and gay-headed families becoming news. Many more residents of North America and Europe have become aware of the existence and viability of these families. This means that more of our parents know, or know of, other lesbian-parented families. There are books, videos, and articles you can give your parents and extended family. P-FLAG (Parents and Friends of Lesbians and Gays) has many chapters around the United States, where your parents can meet others who have faced coming out as parents and grandparents of lesbian family members.

It can be harmful to maintain contact with a family that is openly hostile or likely to stage a custody battle. It is not necessary to put up with abuse.

You need to take care of yourselves and your children. Sorting our where to draw the line is the hard part. Some lesbians have told their parents that they will not visit them unless the whole family can come. Others have ended phone conversations or visits when parents have begun to say hurtful or abusive things. Some women report that it has taken years for a parent to come around to a supportive position, while others never do and lose the possibility of being part of their children's and grandchildren's lives.

### The Rest of the World

Children bring us into contact with people and institutions we might never touch otherwise. Lesbian parents need to be very clear about how they want to be in the world to increase the probability that they will be taken as seriously as other parents. Our experience in the large, urban areas of the country is that the vast majority of teachers, other parents, coaches, ministers, rabbis, and health-care practitioners are respectful and glad to deal with an engaged parent.

*Martina went to pick up her son Sean at his father's house for their regular weekend visit. Martina took Kevin with her. He was her three-year-old son from her relationship with Monica. Sean's stepmother knew that Monica was Kevin's biological mother. When they knocked on the door, she asked him, "Where's your mother?" He looked at her as if she were stupid. She said again, "Where's your mother?" Finally, Kevin said disdainfully, "Right here," and pointed at Martina. Martina said, "He considers both of us his mothers." "Oh," said the woman, "Kevin, where is your other mother?" He replied, "She's at work."*

Kevin did the educating here and the other woman corrected her assumption. Lesbian parents usually have to push harder than heterosexual parents for recognition. Be prepared to cope with uncomprehending stares.

*Barclay was white as was his biological mother, Sheila. His other mother, Gladys, was black. When Gladys went to get Barclay after baseball practice and he said, "Gotta go, my mom's here," the coach stared, shook his head, and muttered his incomprehension.*

*When Tanya got into trouble at school, her principal asked for a parent conference. Tanya's biological mother, Thea, wanted her lover, Estelle, to go with her. Estelle was a professor of education at a local community college. Thea figured she could use the support, and besides, Estelle was very knowledgeable about children, and about Tanya in particular. The principal could not figure out which woman to talk to—the "mother" or the "expert."*

When you get ready to include children in your lives, you need to decide what roles each of you wants to play—in your family and in your contact with the outside world. A particular challenge is how to include the nonbiological or adoptive parent, when most institutions simply do not acknowledge her. At first, your discussion will be theoretical; then, as your child ages, more and more of his world becomes a part of your family's world and the decisions become increasingly concrete. As we have said earlier, the more planning you do, the easier this contact with the world will be. This is especially true with legalities, such as adoptions, wills, and powers of attorney in case of emergencies. How out you are will also affect how you portray yourselves and your family to the world. A more out couple may decide to talk to everyone ahead of time to minimize the shock when contact is necessary, such as with physicians when the children get sick.

We have little control over our children's contact with the world. Our children simply do what is natural for them, as they come into their own. Sometimes contact with the world outside the family is hard and painful; often it is wonderful and heartening.

*Janet was chewing her nails again. Today, her daughter Kelsey was bringing home a friend from school. No big deal, except that this friend knew nothing about Kelsey's two mothers—Janet and Mabel. All of Kelsey's friends up until now were children of her mothers' friends and were supportive of the lesbian mothers. Some of the children even had two mothers themselves. But now— in five minutes—Kelsey was bringing home a little girl she had met in the first grade when school started a month ago. Janet wondered what Kelsey would say, what her friend would say, and what the friend's parents would do. All of a sudden, Kelsey and her new friend walked in and said hello. Janet held her breath as they walked past her to Kelsey's room. As the two girls disappeared around the corner, Janet heard Kelsey's new friend say, "How lucky to have two moms. Do you get more cookies?"*

It is difficult in this culture to be part of an alternative family. We need all the services other parents need, but we need to screen them carefully to receive as nonhomophobic treatment as possible. The extra work is draining and can exhaust a couple who is already tired from work and child rearing. Fortunately, the effort is worth it. Lesbians and the children we have so carefully thought about and worked to have and keep can be happy, loving families. The networks we create to survive in a hostile world are, once they are established, a source of love and support that many other families never know exist.

We have chosen to highlight a few major themes in the evolution of the lives of lesbian couples who parent. Obviously, we cannot adequately cover the range of parenting issues, so we recommend reading and choosing from the dozens of books and articles about heterosexual-parented families and the few about lesbian-parented families. We are particularly partial to our book for lesbian parents, *The Lesbian Parenting Book*. We encourage you to learn about parenting philosophies and the predictable stages families go through as children age. Look at the specialty books that deal with specific challenges and use ones that speak to your particular situations. Give yourself as much support as you can find from friends, experienced parents, family, and professionals, if needed. Most of all enjoy yourself and your children.

## CHAPTER 12

# ᛦ Friends, Family, and Sense of Community

In this chapter we examine what friends, family, and a sense of community mean for lesbian couples. What we find is that each of these can be both a source of support for and a strain on the couple relationship. At the end of the chapter we discuss some ways couples have used celebrations and rituals to acknowledge and strengthen their relationships, and how public ceremonies can enrich a couple's relationship with its friends, families, and communities.

## Coming Out

This chapter assumes that you have come out to at least some friends and family. While coming out as a lesbian or bisexual woman is a multiphase process, we address coming out to friends and family as part of being a lesbian couple. If you are wrestling with whether you are lesbian or bisexual, we recommend attending support groups, reading books, or talking to a counselor or therapist. (See the Resources.)

Once you have decided that you are in a couple relationship, and you want to tell members of your family or friendship circles, there are some issues to take into consideration. If you are simultaneously announcing that you are a lesbian and that this is your new lover, some of your friends and family members may initially be less than thrilled. Many parents take years to adjust to their daughter's identity as a lesbian or bisexual woman. Some, of course, never become supportive; others are very quickly accepting and affirming.

Remember, while you may have known that you are lesbian or bisexual for some time, other people need time to assimilate this information. For them, it may be new news. After parents have done their grieving for the daughter they thought they had and for their dreams of the future—which may have included a wedding, husband, and traditional family—they are freer to accept and embrace your new identity and your partner.

If family and friends do not eventually accept and support your decision, you will have to find ways to protect your relationship if people are hostile toward you. There are many ways to do this.

*Lauree told her best friend, Janyce, that she was not welcome to stay at their house if Janyce could not be civil to Lauree's lover.*

*Marsha had been a faithful member of a small Christian church in her neighborhood for five years. When she brought her new partner to church one Sunday and introduced her to the pastor, it was clear that Marsha was now seen as sinful. Marsha was absolutely clear that she was Christian, pastor or no pastor. So she started looking around for another church that welcomed both her prayers and her sexual orientation.*

*Misha's brother was very supportive of her relationship with Kobi but their mother was furious that her daughter was a lesbian. So whenever the family's rotating annual gathering was at his house, Misha and Kobi were both in attendance. Then Misha's mother had to decide whether to come or not.*

If you do not come out to friends and family about your relationship it will be very difficult for them to affirm you and your partner openly.

*Bertie and Connie had become lovers after Bertie's thirty-year heterosexual marriage ended. Bertie worried that coming out to her children would be too much for them to handle, so she never told them that she and Connie were lovers and intended to be together for the rest of their lives. Both women went to some family gatherings but it wasn't clear what their relationship was. Things came to a head when Bertie's daughter, Linda, did not include Connie on an invitation to a grandchild's birthday party. Bertie was hurt and angry and told Linda so. Linda used the opportunity to tell her mother that since Bertie had never said anything directly to the family, she did not want to assume that Connie should be included in family-only events.*

Sometimes women decide that it is too risky to come out to particular friends or family members. Child-custody issues, fear of being kicked out of the house, or extreme homophobia are common concerns. If you are not out, make sure you clearly state how you and your partner want to be treated by your community. If you want your partner invited home for Thanksgiving, tell your family that you want to bring your roommate or friend. If you want to include your "housemate" on outings with friends, say so. Otherwise people will not know to include your lover. Also, remember that not coming out will mean that you and your partner may have to be apart at some family-only events. It's not about love, this is about not being out—they are different issues. Sometimes when you are upset about not being included, you can confuse the two and doubt your relationship. Keep talking with your partner about your feelings.

Even if you are already out to your family and friends, there still may be some discomfort when you introduce your new partner.

*Pammy had gone home for the first time with her new lover, Arlene. Pammy's mother was very accepting of her daughter's relationship and really enjoyed time with Arlene. However, it was time for her and Pammy's annual shopping day and lunch out. Should she include Arlene? She had never included Pammy's husband when they were married, but she didn't want to seem unsupportive of her daughter's lesbianism.*

*Myrna was getting ready for her fortieth reunion and trying to decide whether to take her partner of three years. The problem was that Myrna had gone to a women's college, and at all the other reunions the women had gathered at a friend's house, and their husbands had stayed at another place, talking and hanging out together. Myrna was torn. Her partner knew no one. It would be difficult for her to be the only nonalumna in a gathering of very long-term friends, but the idea of being the only female spouse with the guys was also daunting. Myrna did want her old friends to meet her lover but wasn't sure how to deal with the situation.*

Sometimes there are not easy answers for these new situations. It does not always mean rejection when someone struggles with new circumstances.

Those who love you may be trying to make new relationship configurations fir into the familiar routine of family or friends.

## Friends

In contrast to lesbian couples, heterosexual couples more often keep romance separate from each partner's leisure activities. Men tend to spend at least some leisure time with their male friends and women with their female friends. While lesbians may also spend time with separate friends, they often share leisure interests with their partner. Thus, there is the temptation to focus romance, friendship, and camaraderie all on one person. Concentrating so much energy on the relationship sometimes means that lesbian couples have few outside friends.

> *Destra and Simone had been best friends for three years before they became lovers. They worked in the same office, ate lunch together every day, and even took most of their coffee breaks at the same time. On weekends they liked to go hiking or skiing. Sometimes they went with another couple or a friend, but mostly they did everything with each other or alone when one of them was unavailable.*

Neither Destra nor Simone had separate friends, because they were so focused on their relationship and each other. There are other reasons that a couple may have few friends. Many of us lead very busy lives. We are so involved with working, going to school, keeping up a household, raising children, and maintaining our relationship that we may never find time to spend with friends. Some of us are geographically isolated; others are closeted. In addition, one or both partners may be unsure about how to balance the time and energy we put into our friendships and our couple relationship.

Maintaining friendships can be difficult when partners have different expectations and patterns of relating to friends. Some women describe themselves as loners. Others prefer to have one best friend or a very small circle of close friends. Still others have a wide circle of friends and even more acquaintances. The fact that women have different styles of making and maintaining friendships may not be clear early in the relationship. In the romance stage many women neglect their friends entirely as they focus on their new lover. When a couple emerges from this stage, the women may discover that they have different wants and styles regarding friends. One woman may want to spend most of her spare time with her partner, who is also her one best friend—if our partner is our best friend, who needs other friends? Her partner, on the other hand, may insist on having a lot of time with her separate friends.

It is a good idea for couples to have a healthy balance between individual time alone, couple time, and time with separate and mutual friends. Even though it is hard to do this, it is important not to neglect any of these elements for too long.

### Friendship Networks

Friends support us. They stimulate interests and perspectives that we may not access in our primary relationship. On a practical note, separate friends are folks we can eat pizza with when our partner is on a diet, go skiing with when our partner hates the cold, complain to when our lover "does it again," talk with about old times when our partner is new, and help us feel good about ourselves because we know they love us.

It would be ideal for each of us to have a number of people who would drop everything and come running if we called for help. At any particular time one may be out of town, another sick, and a third out hiking. So having a number of close people in our lives keeps us from putting all our eggs in one basket. We increase the probability of getting our needs met.

In their book *Brief Encounters,* Emily Coleman and Betty Edwards[1] strongly urge each of us to maintain a supportive network of three friendship circles. They visualize each of these circles surrounding the person who is in the center. The friendship circle that is closest to the center (and closest to the individual) is called the "Tender Circle." These are the people we mentioned earlier who would drop everything and come running if we needed them. Whether our connections with the people in our Tender Circle are blood connections, legal ones, or historical ones, they are strong and deep. Straight, gay, or lesbian, these people are dependable, available, and in frequent contact with us. They love us the way we are.

The second circle is bigger and a little further out from the individual in the center. This group of "Congenial Comrades" is composed of people who are important to us in some way. These friends provide companionship and we see them regularly but not necessarily frequently.

The third circle is called the "Outer Rim." Although contact with them is not frequent, these people may provide stimulation and serve as resource people on whom we can call for specific needs, such as getting a recommendation for an electrician or advice about a project.

Coleman and Edwards maintain that couple relationships are enhanced, not harmed, by the presence of supportive friendship networks. We agree.

As we mentioned earlier, partners likely have different patterns of relating to friends. Not everyone has, or even wants to have, each of these three friendship circles filled up. The important thing is to have a friendship network that provides the caring and stimulation that you need.

It can be useful for each partner to inventory her network periodically. Does either of you have shortages in any of the circles? When good friends move away, or become involved in new jobs or new relationships, it can leave a large empty space in the network. Many of us believe we are not good at meeting people or at making friends and, even if we are, it takes time and energy.

A traditional place for lesbians to meet each other has been at bars. However, many women are not comfortable in this atmosphere or don't connect with the people they meet there. Bars are one place, but certainly not the only place, to meet people. Ginny NiCarthy, in her book *Getting Free,* has a number of suggestions for reaching out.[2] If you already have acquaintances, she suggests starting there. Make a list of these people and see which ones you might like to spend more time with. These are possible friends. While you can make friends anywhere, some of the best places to meet people are support groups, classes, volunteer organizations, school, social groups, co-op preschools, churches, synagogues, and work. Joining a hiking club or a political group or volunteering some time at a lesbian or gay organization are other ways to meet new people who share your interests.

### Jealousy

It is not always easy to find friends, much less maintain the balance between time alone, couple time, and time with separate and mutual friends. Jealousy may become an issue. You may be jealous, simply of the time your lover spends with separate friends. You might want more time together.

Sometimes this jealousy about time is complicated by the fact that the separate friend is a former lover. Often a lesbian's closest friends are previous partners. There are at least three reasons for this. First, the lesbian community is usually relatively small in size. Second, many lesbians are involved in a number of relationships over time. And third, lesbians value these relationships and try to keep them from ending completely. We work very hard to make the transition from lover to friend.[3] For all these reasons, former lovers may be very much a part of our lives.

Understandably, a new lover may be jealous of the ex-partner's closeness, threatened by the friends' shared history, or suspicious of their discussions about her. The former partner may also be jealous. She may get concerned about being neglected or displaced somehow. These dynamics can result in difficult situations and hurt feelings.

*Lonnie felt left out when she and her partner, Jael, spent time with Jael's best friend/ex-lover, Marge. Marge and Jael seemed to talk endlessly about old times, old friends, and in-jokes.*

*Gloria was furious about the birthday present her partner, Consuela, received from her previous partner. The gift in question was what Gloria described as a "sexy negligee." Consuela thought that Gloria was making a big deal out of nothing.*

*Chastity was hurt when her old partner and best friend, Fran, started spending time with Jess. Fran became almost totally unavailable because she was always with Jess. The situation was complicated by the fact that Chastity and Jess had barely spoken to each other in years because of an unresolved dispute about money.*

In these situations, and in the many others that can arise with former and new lovers, open communication is the key. It is not too much to hope that new lovers (and ex-lovers) can recognize their feelings of jealousy, hurt, or fear. Ideally they will express these feelings to their partner (or friend). For a while, the new lover and ex-lover may communicate mostly through the woman who is their common link. The woman who is trying to manage a new relationship and a friendship with her ex-lover may be in the middle. If she is honest with each of the other two, being in the middle can be more tolerable, and eventually she can remove herself and let her new lover and ex-lover work things out. If these women have direct contact with each other, they often become more human and less of a threat to each other.

With time, jealousy usually fades as the new partner and the old friend are reassured about their respective positions and importance. When this does not happen, the woman in the middle needs to look long and hard at her role in the situation. If this is your situation, are you helping to reduce tensions or are you contributing to them? Is there some payoff to you in keeping the rivalry going? For example, do you enjoy being the center of attention? Or are you avoiding making a commitment to your new partnership and holding on to your ex-partner in an unhealthy way? Lack of clarity fuels jealousy. As the woman in the middle, you need to be clear with each of the other two. And your actions need to match your words. If you want your former partner to believe that the friendship is important, you need to put energy into it. If you want your new partner to believe that the couple relationship comes first, you need to make it a priority. Each woman in this triangle—new partner, ex-lover, and woman in the middle—needs to examine honestly her own feelings, motivations, and behavior.

In Chapter Two we discussed the need for new couples to separate from their families of origin. Since old lovers are a form of extended family, this task applies to them as well. It is crucial that the woman in the middle clarifies who her first priority is. We realize that some women are not always sure that their current love relationship will outlast the friendship with an ex-partner. This can make prioritizing very tricky. We recommend waiting until you have reached the commitment stage before declaring yourself as partner first, ex-lover or friend second. Then you are in a better position to communicate more openly and honestly with the others and are not forced to draw lines you are not really sure of.

Sometimes it is not an old relationship, but rather a new one that needs clarification.

*Jena and Megan were both in committed relationships when they met at a martial arts training session in Chicago. They liked each other right off and were excited to learn that they were both moving to Boston within a year. As their friendship grew, Jena became aware that she was attracted to Megan. She wasn't sure how Megan felt. When she finally raised the subject she discovered that Megan was attracted to her as well. Neither of them wanted to risk hurting their love relationships, and yet they wanted to maintain their friendship. They decided to acknowledge the feelings of attraction but not to act on them. Both women felt fortunate that their decision was mutual.*

For many lesbians, emotional attachment precedes sexual attraction. So, in many lesbian friendships, one or both women may find that they are sexually attracted to their friend. Sometimes a woman will become aware of these feelings only after her partner confronts her with the fact that she is flirting with her friend. The partner may feel jealous about the flirting and want clarification about whether or not the friends will be sexual with each other. Sometimes the friends talk about it openly and make a joint decision, like Jena and Megan. For other friends, the decision is made without discussion—the intense feelings of attraction pass. Sometimes it may be better not to discuss your attraction with the other woman. Talking about the attraction can fan the flames and make it much more difficult not to become sexually involved. One guideline is to talk when you are sure you want to set limits not to be involved, as Jena and Megan did, and not to talk if you are wavering. Whatever you decide, you need to keep the communication lines open and the trust quotient high with respective partners. (See also Chapter Eight.)

### Couple Friends

Not only do we encourage partners to have separate friends, but also to have couples as friends. In fact, many couples find that they gradually spend more time with other couples and less with single friends. There is a place for both kinds of friendships.

Just as individual friends validate your individual identity, so couple friends validate your identity as a couple. Some of the ways they do this are by treating you as a couple, assuming that you will continue to be together and comparing notes with you about relationship issues.

Couple friends can broaden your experiences and expand your models of couple relationships. Hearing about how another couple divides up household tasks may give you new options. When you are fighting a lot, the discovery that other couples have had periods of intense conflict can reassure you that your relationship has a chance of surviving. Talking with couple friends can normalize your experience. What you are feeling, thinking, or going through becomes more "normal." Other people have had similar experiences—you don't have to feel crazy or weird, and you may even get some positive suggestions for how to handle your situation.

Some couples hesitate to talk about problems in their relationship. They believe that friends, particularly couple friends, do not want to hear about difficulties. In some cases this may be true. Other couples may be so hungry for confirmation that a lesbian couple relationship can work that they do not want to hear about problems. Long-term partners may feel the pressure to be a "perfect couple" most acutely. However, if you are unwilling to hear about the inevitable difficulties that your couple friends face, you cut them off from using you as a resource. And couple friends can be an extremely valuable resource for each other. But like any other friendships, these relationships require open and honest communication to provide effective support. Friends cannot help when they do not know what is going on.

Couple friends can also help create an atmosphere of safety and support in the world. Not only is it hard to be a lesbian in a homophobic culture, it is also hard to be a lesbian couple. Couple friends, just because they are also a couple, validate our relationship. In addition, they may be fun to be with, to say nothing of providing good advice and supportive hugs.

Some women have couple friends who are vacation buddies. They have more fun because they feel safer and more comfortable being a lesbian couple when they are with other couples. This can be true for a number of forays into the heterosexual world. Everything from going to a fancy restaurant to attending a PTA meeting can be more comfortable with a group.

*Theo and Selena had just been out on their first date with Selena's friend from work, Mae, and her partner, Liz. Both couples were mixed racially— one woman in each couple was African American and the other one was white. Theo and Selena were thrilled to meet another couple who had been together as long as they had and who knew what it meant to be of different races. They were relieved to realize that they both liked both women and that the two couples had a lot in common. It looked like they might be making their first real friends since leaving Cincinnati.*

Of course, this does not mean that friendships with other couples are always easy. Committed couples say it is sometimes hard to meet other couples to socialize with. Finding couples in which all four women are compatible can be a challenge. Sometimes two friends get together with their respective partners only to discover that the partners do not enjoy each other's company. The friendship then remains a separate one, rather than developing into a couple friendship as well. Or a couple friendship may end because a partner in one couple has a falling-out with one of the women in the other couple. There may also be competition. Sometimes one woman feels that their couple friends like her partner better than they like her. This situation can happen, for example, when one partner is more outgoing than the other.

A special complication in lesbian couple friendships has to do with the threat of sexual attraction developing, and what the women decide to do if that happens. There are more possible romantic combinations with lesbian couple friends than with heterosexual couples, because each of the women in one couple could be attracted to one or both of the partners in the other couple. The problems and strategies discussed in the previous section on jealousy apply to situations with couple friends, too. Good communication and listening skills, and clear agreements between partners, go a long way to prevent, as well as resolve, these situations. Sometimes couples find it useful to discuss openly their feelings with the other couple, as well as with their respective partners.

Lesbian couple friends have much to offer each other. There is the wonderful experience both of being seen and of looking out and seeing yourself in the world; not every couple is straight! Couple friends can also offer support in very concrete ways, like helping out when one of you is sick or asking you to dinner when you are going through bumpy times as a couple. Couples can cheer each other on, knowing how hard it is and knowing that no one is perfect. Long-term couples in particular may benefit from having other women in their lives who have been together for many years. There can be a relaxed camaraderie with friends who also know the pleasures of making their relationship work.

## Family

Family can mean several different things to a lesbian couple. It may mean the birth or biological or adoptive family of each partner. It could refer to the couple-with-children unit. For many lesbians, it might consist of chosen family rather than birth or adoptive family. It is primarily because of homophobia that a lesbian may have a chosen family. Some lesbians have been rejected by their biological or adoptive families; others are not out to them, for fear of rejection. Still others want a "family" nearby for support when their family of origin is far away.

### Birth/Biological/Adoptive Family

Partners often differ in how out they are to their respective families. This can cause strain in the couple relationship.

*Tara dreaded the Christmas season. Every year for the last four years, her partner, Ruth, had gone to visit her parents in another state for most of the holidays. Tara wanted to spend this Christmas with Ruth and her own family. She did not want to pressure Ruth to come out to her own folks, but she was tired of never spending holidays together.*

In this situation, Tara and Ruth have very different relationships with their families. Tara's parents treat Ruth like a daughter-in-law. They had not responded that way to all of Tara's partners. They were very cold to Tara's first lover when Tara came out to them. They blamed Tara's partner for "leading Tara into this deviant lifestyle." Tara had always been close to her parents, and their rejection of her lover was very painful. In fact, she now thinks that her parents' attitudes were a big factor in the breakup of that relationship.

Eventually Tara's parents began to accept that her lifestyle was not a passing phase. Now they have adjusted and seem comfortable with it most of the time. They are very fond of Ruth and supportive of the relationship.

Ruth has never been particularly close to her parents but feels obligated to spend Christmas with them. There is a traditional family reunion over the holidays, and she knows it is important to them that she be there. Ruth feels torn between her loyalty to her parents and her love for Tara. Since her parents are in their late seventies, she cannot see the point of coming out and upsetting them at this stage. She resents what she interprets as pressure from Tara.

Clearly, Tara and Ruth illustrate two very different patterns and ways of relating to parents about coming out. These disparities affect their relationship. As we said earlier, coming out is an individual process and a personal decision; however, if partners spend traditional family holidays separately, one or both partners may believe that the other is not taking the relationship seriously, or that their togetherness is not a priority, and this pain can diminish the relationship.

For some lesbians, the biological family was and is a protection against an oppressive and hostile society. This may be particularly true for many immigrant women and women of color. Coming out to family may mean risking the loss of this support and sense of identity and community. Many women decide that it is better to keep their lesbian relationship in the closet, rather than risk such an enormous loss. Unless their partners are in similar situations, it's not always easy for them to appreciate what is at stake. This is a perpetual problem that the couple needs to manage rather than assuming it is a flaw in one or both of the women or in their relationship. The women can deal with the difference as a disappointment and support each other when the less than optimal situation creates tension for them.

Even if both partners are out to their parents and relatives, all problems do not magically disappear. Obviously, the family may reject the partner, or they may be more subtle in their exclusion. Refusing to recognize and acknowledge a lesbian partner as part of the family is exclusion—for example, sending birthday cards to heterosexual partners but not to lesbian partners, or inviting the heterosexual son-in-law of two years to be in the family picture but not the lesbian partner of fifteen years.

Sometimes it is difficult for a couple to tell just why parents do not accept the relationship. It can be more complicated for couples of different races or class backgrounds. Are you being rejected or excluded because you are Asian, white, working class, Jewish, lesbian, or what?

### Chosen Family

For couples who are not out or are not close to their blood-related families, chosen families may have special significance in supporting their lesbian identity and couple relationship. Parents, siblings, children, and other relatives may, of course, be part of a chosen family. The point is that family membership is by selection, not by birth or legal status alone.

Many couples do not think of their partners and friends as a chosen or extended family. This may be the case even when they have clear arrangements and agreements about spending holidays together, co-parenting and godparenting responsibilities, or communal living. For couples who do want a chosen family, children, partners, ex-lovers, family, and friends—lesbian, gay, bisexual, and heterosexual—are all prime candidates for inclusion. This network of people validates and supports our couple relationships. They are there to share the joys and sorrows. They may not always agree with us but we know they respect, accept, and love us for who we are. Chosen families illustrate the building of a community on a personal scale.

### Couple with Children Families

The chosen family of a couple may include children. As we discussed in Chapter Eleven, some children come into the couple relationship through a decision by the couple to add children to their family. Children in these families are very much chosen. Other children come to the couple from previous relationships. How much a couple can participate in a chosen family may depend in part on whether they are out to the children.

Many lesbians are afraid of custody battles with ex-husbands or rejection by their children, so they remain closeted. When a mother is not clearly out to her children, they may sense that something is going on but be confused about what it is. Lesbianism becomes a family secret.

Coming out to children raises many issues. When children have this information about a parent, they have to manage the information just as their mother does. They have to decide whom to tell or whether to tell. They may have to deal with teasing from peers, as well as with their own values and attitudes about sexual orientation. Younger children often take the news in stride. They may even come out for the couple by telling friends or teachers—a surprise for many couples. Adolescents may have more difficulty. In the middle of coping with their own emerging sexuality, dealing with their mother's lesbianism may be an unwanted burden.

Historically, lesbianism has been no more acceptable to the adolescent peer culture than to the adult world. Probably less. However, there is more access to positive information about gay and lesbian people, and more people have come out in the recent past than ever before. All of this contributes to changing attitudes about gays and lesbians in many cities. Do not assume that your child will be miserable and taunted, but do not assume that it will be easy either.

Difficulties can be increased if a youngster is unhappy about the parents' divorce. The child may blame the lesbian partner and try to break up the couple or punish the partner. All the problems of divorce and stepfamilies can apply, but with the additional burden of sexual orientation.

The partner of a lesbian mother does not have an automatically defined role with the children. She is neither a stepmother nor a stepfather. The child (or children) may wonder, "Just who is she anyway?" "Who is she to us?" and "What does her living with me and Mom mean?" In addition, the legal mother may have mixed feelings about how much parental involvement she wants her partner to have. This role confusion can increase if the relationship is a secret. The partner may feel unsure about her role, feel like a third wheel, and hold back from connecting with the child as much as she would like. The pros and cons of coming out to children to improve the family dynamics versus the possibility of a custody battle need to be weighed carefully. And it would be unfair to imply that a lesbian partner cannot have a good relationship with her partner's children unless the couple is open about their relationship with each other.

We do believe that the most full and mutually satisfying chosen family experiences occur when a lesbian couple is open and honest about their relationship. However, it may not be possible for all couples. The family can still be loving and supportive.

## A Sense of Community

"Community" means very different things to various lesbian couples. In smaller towns, all the lesbians—all ten of them—probably know each other. In midsize population centers, the women may at least have heard of or recognize other lesbians by sight. In larger cities, there are any number of different communities. Many of these communities are really friendship circles with no overlap or connection with each other at all. We've heard women say, "I've lived in Seattle for nearly ten years, and I think I know a lot of lesbians. Then I go to a concert and there are hundreds of women, most of whom I've never seen before. Where do they all come from?"

Many of the smaller lesbian communities are isolated from each other. Groups of women who have been friends for years are one example. These women may be in long-term relationships. They find a strong support network for themselves and their relationships in their friendship circle. Social life may be focused around gathering at each other's homes. This may be particularly true for lesbians who came out prior to the late 1960s. They had to survive a hostile societal environment and, hence, have maintained these friendship circles in part for the protection they offer. Others maintain these social patterns because of the difficulties involved when a couple opens itself to the larger lesbian community.

For example, respecting "couple boundaries" is sometimes a problem in the lesbian community. Because lesbian couples may not marry, their relationship rules are not always clear. People outside the relationship may wonder, "Are they monogamous? Do they intend this to be a long-term relationship? Is it okay to spend time with them separately or only as a couple?"

Even when the couple's agreements are clear, sometimes friends are not supportive or respectful of the relationship. The prevailing attitude may be that "couples are short-lived, so if you are interested in a woman who is in a relationship already, you just have to wait a bit, because she soon will be available." This attitude is certainly not supportive of the current relationship. Indeed, the greeting from someone a lesbian has not seen for some time may be, "Are you and _____ still together?" The expectation is clear that you won't be. If the answer is, "Yes, we are," the questioner may be surprised. Instead, we need to take the risk that the relationship has thrived and ask, "How is _____?"

### Social Support for Relationships

Most of us who are in committed relationships want social approval and what gay minister Larry Uhrig, in his book *The Two of Us,* calls "affirmation of the bonding."[4] We want the significant people in our lives to affirm our relationship with our partner. In the United States, this affirmation process typically involves arranging for our partner to be introduced to our friends, coworkers, parents, and relatives. We want these important people to accept our partner, approve our choice, and provide support and encouragement as the relationship develops. Lesbian and gay couples experience more barriers to getting this social affirmation from the broader society than heterosexual couples do. As a result many couples look primarily within the lesbian and gay communities for affirmation.

*Kirsten and Ellie realized one day that they spent all of their social time with other queer couples in their age group, early thirties. Not one couple was straight and there was even one M to F couple as well. Both women had straight friends but they never seemed to feel comfortable with heterosexual couples the way they did with their crowd.*

While some lesbian couples feel a part of the lesbian community, other couples are isolated from the lesbian community and identify *themselves* as belonging to other communities.

*Arlene and Mary were both in their late fifties. They had lived together for thirty-two years. Arlene was a teacher at an elementary school, and Mary was the secretary at the Methodist church downtown. They had several close friends, all of whom were lesbian couples in similar situations. Arlene was sure she would never come out, for two reasons. One was that she loved teaching and would do nothing to risk her job, and the other was that she had read about the lesbian lifestyle and was sure she wanted nothing to do with it.*

*Gitte and Marilyn lived on Gitte's farm in southern Minnesota for almost all of their fourteen years together. These women felt accepted and supported by the other members of their small farming community. However, once in a while they went to Minneapolis to a bar or a restaurant just to see "others like us," as Marilyn put it.*

Each of these couples is isolated from the lesbian community, the first by apprehension and disinclination, and the second by geography. However, each couple has found other communities to identify with, belong to, and get support from. Without some form of community, isolation can force a couple in on itself so much that the partners become absolutely sick of each other. They may then end the relationship, which might have stayed healthy had they been less isolated.

Lesbians who are lovers with a woman and married to a man are typically even more isolated than other lesbian couples. They rely on each other and sometimes a very small group of other people, who are usually women and very often closeted lesbians. Because married lesbians are vulnerable to the criticism that they are holding on to their "heterosexual privilege," they may avoid other lesbians and deny themselves a potential source of support.

*Adele and Harriet had been lovers for eleven years. Adele had made a promise to herself that when her husband died she would start going to gay pride marches and women's events. He had been dead for a year and she had been having a wonderful time. Harriet, however, was absolutely terrified that Adele would become one of "those" kinds of lesbians.*

New or increased visibility within the lesbian community also exposes the couple to other women who are potential lovers. Adele might meet someone else. Being more out may also expose Harriet to more social pressure to end her living arrangement with her husband. Thus, contact with the broader lesbian community may be a mixed blessing in that it offers affirmation and support for their lesbianism but may threaten the couple's balance, and hence, existence.

Lesbians are already an isolated group. Regardless of how much we consider ourselves a part of a lesbian or other community, we are separate from the mainstream heterosexual society. When we are isolated from a sense of community, we do not have role models for our choices or friends to balance us in our relationships. This can be limiting. Ideally, lesbian couples should be able to meet other lesbians to freely play, work, and grow from these interactions in the same way that heterosexual couples can. Until that time comes, we need to understand the extra pressures on our relationships and take care of ourselves the best way we can. This may mean evaluating how necessary it is to isolate ourselves from other lesbians. If it is crucial, then we need to find ways to nurture ourselves as individuals and as couples through involvement with other communities of people. If it is not necessary, we can direct energy toward building a community for ourselves that includes lesbians and lesbian couples as well as the other supportive friends in our lives.

## Celebrations and Rituals in Our Lives

Most societies and religions have rituals and ceremonies that acknowledge major transitions throughout the human life span. These vary from baptisms to bar and bat mitzvahs to marriages and funerals. These rituals not only mark specific milestones, but they also provide support to individuals and their families and continue community traditions.

When our relationships are not seen as legitimate, our participation in these rituals can be inauthentic, painful, and even prohibited. If a lesbian couple decides they want to have a bar mitzvah for their son, for instance, they need to make sure they will be supported by the congregation and rabbi as the child's parents.

*Ardith and Kitty wanted to have their daughter baptized at the Lutheran church they attended. The pastor was very politically active and most of the congregation had a strong sense of the spiritual and political being intertwined. This really had become their spiritual home.*

*Judith wanted to have a bat mitzvah for her daughter at the synagogue she attended. Her partner, Dina, wasn't Jewish but supported Judith's wishes. In fact, Judith, Dina, and their daughter frequently went to family gatherings with other members of the congregation, and they were considered important parts of the community.*

End-of-life rituals provide surviving partners a way to say good-bye and to honor the passing of a life and a relationship. If your partner has been active in a religious tradition it is usually a relatively easy decision to have a spiritually based funeral or memorial service. If, however, you are not involved in an organized religion or do not have an active spiritual life, you may want to create a ceremony or activity to mark your partner's death. (In Chapter Seventeen we stress the importance of having wills and powers of attorney on file so that a woman's parents cannot step in and override the survivor's choice of funeral arrangements.) The important thing is to choose a way of saying good-bye that also supports you, the survivor.

*Molly and Cindy had attended the Quaker meeting in town for twelve years. When Cindy died from cancer, the meeting held a Memorial Meeting for Worship a month after Cindy's death. Her family came, as did many of the members of the meeting. Someone read a brief biography of Cindy, and everyone then settled into quiet worship. Out of the silence the people who wanted to stood and spoke of Cindy, prayed, sang, or read something that moved them. After an hour the worship closed with people shaking hands. Molly felt better that so many facets of Cindy's personality and life had been talked about. It was as if Cindy was free to go, having been seen by those gathered in all her good and not-so-good ways and yet loved for the whole of who she had been. Molly also felt wonderfully supported in her grief and in moving into her life without Cindy.*

*Patsy and ten of her and Frankie's friends took Frankie's ashes out to the desert. Patsy opened the box and spread the ashes on the ground. The group toasted Frankie with root beer, her favorite drink, and remembered her with stones, tears, and laughter.*

## Celebrations of Commitment

It is in the ritual of marriage where lesbians have encountered the most discrimination. Being outside mainstream cultural and religious observances, we have often had to go without or create our own rituals.

If you have decided you want to have a commitment ceremony, there are several things to consider. Do you want a private or public event? A religious or secular ceremony? Are you interested in a traditional ritual, a unique one that you create, or a combination of the two?

### Private or Public

A private ceremony is a couple's statement that they see their relationship in a new light or as permanent or special. It may be simply an honoring of their choice to be a couple. This can mark the beginning of their commitment or an anniversary in the continuance of their relationship.

*Lily and Alice wrote up their own poems expressing their love and commitment to each other. One weekend when they were at the ocean, they read the poems aloud to each other.*

*Tanya and Micki had been partners for two years and living together for one. They decided that they wanted to have a ceremony, just the two of them, to exchange rings and say vows to each other. Each woman decided on what she wanted to say to the other, and they picked out matching rings. One night in February they stood in front of the window looking out on the snow and trees and read their vows to each other. They put the rings on each other's fingers and kissed. They then sat down to a wonderful meal they had cooked together and toasted each other with sparkling cider.*

*Bernie and Matty decided to take a long weekend away together as a honeymoon. They had decided to move in together and wanted to mark their decision in some semiformal way. They made reservations at a lesbian-owned bed-and-breakfast, took Friday off from work, and told no one what they were doing. They came home on Sunday feeling married and ready to begin the next part of their life together.*

Traditionally, ceremonies involving friends and family provide opportunities to deepen the connections between a couple and its community. Public ceremonies offer affirmation, support, and the sharing of joy. Couples, especially same-gender couples, need all the community support we can get, so we encourage you to seriously consider having a gathering to honor your commitment.

*Ani and Shayna decided that they wanted a big wedding with their families and friends in attendance. They rented the community center in their neighborhood and arranged for a band and a catered reception. They had been to a Quaker wedding recently and really liked how people sat quietly without any organized program. The guests at the wedding would stand and say something to the couple about their feelings about the union or advice about marriage. People might speak about one or both of the women in funny and often serious ways. Ani and Shayna printed up cards explaining this tradition and put them on all the chairs that they arranged in concentric circles around their chairs. Many of their friends had never been to a queer wedding before and some were skeptical of the whole thing. By the end of an hour, everyone had been touched by the depth of sharing that Ani and Shayna had inspired. By the end of the day the couple was amazed at how "married" they felt.*

Limited financial resources or distance from loved ones can also affect your choices.

*Perry and Kat wanted a big wedding but they were broke. So they asked their neighbor who had a big yard if they could have the wedding there in the summer. They then asked everyone in Perry's theater group and Kat's graduate program to bring their favorite foods. What a grand party!*

*Betsy and T.R. decided to invite their best friends, two other couples that they vacationed with every year, to join them on a cruise to Alaska. During the cruise Betsy and T.R. would tell the other four women of their decision to be lifelong partners and ask for a champagne toast. This would be their "elopement."*

*Cassy and Darcy both grew up on the West Coast and now lived in Maine. Their parents were in their eighties and not able to travel. So when the two women decided to have a celebration of commitment, they videotaped it, added comments from their friends, and sent it to their parents.*

We have noticed that when two women (or men) have a celebration of commitment or marriage, those attending seem to be very moved, perhaps even more so than at traditional heterosexual weddings. Our guess is that taking an old ritual—marriage—and reworking it to more accurately fit a particular couple reminds us what the ritual is really about. When the gender of the partners is the same it also sharpens our appreciation for the statement the couple is making. We are no longer numbed by the same-old, same-old. (This can also happen with nontraditional weddings for heterosexual couples.)

## Secular or Religious

Until the clergy of the Metropolitan Community Church (MCC) began to conduct rites of blessing and holy unions in 1968, the formal affirmation of holy union or celebration of commitment was not available to gays and lesbians from organized religion. Now, various other Christian congregations and houses of worship—American Baptist, Buddhist, Episcopal, Friends Meetings (Quaker), Reform and Reconstructionist Judaism, Unitarian, United Church of Christ, and United Methodist among others—have affirmed lesbian and gay unions.[5] Now that these established religions are recognizing lesbian couple relationships, those couples who wish to celebrate their commitment in their own religious tradition, with the support of their community, have more options to do so.

*Miranda and Karla had met after church one day two years ago. They had started dating and eventually moved in together. Throughout this time their involvement in the church had been a central theme in their relationship. One day the minister asked them if they had considered getting married, now that their congregation had approved marrying same-gender couples. The two women were pleased to be asked and went home to discuss it. After a few months of conversation they decided to ask the minister to marry them. As was the custom in their church, everyone in the congregation was invited. Karla and Miranda also invited their other friends and those members of their families who were supportive of their relationship.*

*Gitanjali and Shehernavaz were both second-generation Indian women living in New York. When they decided to have a celebration of commitment, Gitanjali's mother suggested that they use a variation on the Hindu ceremony that she and Gitanjali's father had had in Bombay. In addition to shortening the actual event by several hours, the two women took out the references to having children, since they did not plan to have any. But they dressed in traditional saris and retained the wonderful, earthy rituals referring to sex, physical pleasure, commitment, and life together as a married couple. The ceremony was conducted by Gitanjali's uncle and attended by both women's families and friends.*

As mainstream religions increasingly welcome lesbians and gay men, more of us are exploring or returning to traditional denominations. There are also lesbians who have joined groups that celebrate spirituality from a nature-based or Goddess perspective and not from a transcendent God tradition. When you are deciding what kind of ritual you want, you will have to decide whether to follow a religious or secularly based ceremony. If you are either antireligion or heavily involved in a particular spiritual practice, the decision is easy. If you are somewhere in the middle, you may have to do some research to make your decision.

> Betty and Tish had both been raised Methodist. Neither was involved with the church anymore, but when they decided to have a celebration of commitment they realized they wanted some sort of church service. So, they went church shopping. They had heard of a pastor at a nearby Unity church who was willing to marry people if they did pastoral counseling with her. The sessions took two months. During that time Tish and Betty started attending services at the pastor's church. The ceremony they had was similar to the traditional Unity service but altered by the couple with help from the pastor.

> Kyla and Nan both hated the religions of their childhoods, but they wanted some ceremony to mark their tenth anniversary. They settled on a gathering in the woods with flowers, singing, and good food, facilitated by a Wiccan friend.

### Traditional, Unique, or a Little of Both

Some couples know that they want to have a celebration that follows a tradition they value. Others want to handcraft a unique ceremony that is theirs alone. If we use a traditional ceremony, the chances are we will change some portion of it, even it is only the language from "husband and wife" to "partners."

> Miriam and Vicky were getting married at the synagogue. Miriam's parents were coming, but Vicky's father would not because of his belief that their relationship was wrong. The rabbi had talked to both women about marriage and had satisfied himself that they were ready and understood the commitment they were making. The congregation was very excited, and some of the other women had taken over running the reception for Miriam and Vicky. There would be the traditional chuppa, a cloth suspended above the couple, but Miriam and Becky had decided against the breaking of the glass. Some traditions just didn't translate as well as others.

*Sal and Peg wanted a combination ceremony and party to mark their moving in together and hyphenating their names. They spent hours writing vows and cooking favorite foods. When the big day came, fifty friends joined them at a gay and lesbian bed-and-breakfast for the exchange of vows and a huge feast. Everything—from the hand-painted placemats to the multicolored streamers over the two women as they spoke—was Sal and Peg's hallmark. They were artists who wanted their event to be as visually beautiful as it was meaningful.*

### Anniversary Celebrations

Often, lesbian couples do not want a commitment ceremony. Some do not like "copying" heterosexual marriage, and others don't care whether they have an official event. However, many couples do like celebrating their anniversary, especially when they have been together for many years.

*Deirdre and Audre designed their commitment ceremony for their fifth anniversary celebration party. They included the tradition of "jumping the broom" in their ceremony. It was important to Audre, as an African-American woman, to include this tradition. It goes back to the time of slavery in the United States, when slaves were not allowed to marry legally. They were married in the eyes of the community through this ritual, literally jumping over a broom together.*

*Viv and Penny had been lovers for forty years. They had lived most of this time deep in the closet because of Penny's teaching career. Now that Penny was retired and all of their parents were dead, they had begun to come out to other family and friends. On their thirty-ninth anniversary some young friends suggested that they should have a big party to celebrate their fortieth anniversary. At first Viv and Penny were totally skeptical but after laughing about it they decided it might actually be fun. They settled on renting the senior center hall and inviting their sisters, brothers, nieces, nephews, and all the friends they were still in touch with. They asked everyone to bring poems, pictures, or stories to put in an album that covered the forty years the women had been together.*

It is a pleasure for lesbians to honor long-term couples in their communities. Anniversary parties give individuals and couples a chance to celebrate an accomplishment, particularly in the face of the myths that lesbian couples do not last and cannot be happy. What fun it is to join hands with our friends, family, and communities to celebrate our love.

## CHAPTER 13

# ॐ Cross-Cultural/ Cross-Racial Couples

Cross-racial and cross-cultural relationships have been the subject of strong and heated debate for hundreds of years. They evoke opinions varying from complete acceptance to rigid intolerance. Hopefully, prejudice and racism are less prevalent among lesbians than in the general society. As lesbians, we continually experience sexism and homophobia so we may be more willing to challenge our own prejudices. However, even if this is true, cross-racial or cross-cultural couples still have to deal with the broader society, their individual families of origin, and each other.

This chapter addresses some of the ways issues such as acculturation and racism impact lesbian couples, and offers suggestions to help couples clarify and work through these issues.

## Acculturation

In a multiethnic and multicultural society such as ours, children from marginalized cultures are often exposed to more than one culture: At home their parents and elders may espouse their culture of origin, while at school and in the rest of their world, they are exposed to mainstream American culture.

This chapter is based on a manuscript by Vicki L. Sears.

Family relationships play a crucial role in the formation of our individual psychology and set the stage for our future social relationships. For ethnic groups in particular, family relationships serve as an important context for developing a sense of ethnic affiliation and identification.[1] When traditional values vary significantly from those of the mainstream culture, it can be very challenging for individuals to negotiate these differences.

Acculturation means change occurring as a result of contact between cultural groups. Although acculturation may affect each of the cultural groups who are in contact with one another, it generally refers to the change within an immigrant or ethnic group that takes on the values and behaviors of the dominant culture. The more acculturated a person is, the more that person has adopted the values and norms of mainstream American culture.[2] However, acculturation can be specific; a person may be very acculturated in one area of her life but not in others. For example, just because a Korean American is very active in bicultural activities does not mean that she has any close non-Korean friends. A Jewish-American woman may have close non-Jewish friends but prefer to date only Jewish women.

Cultural differences can provide richness to a relationship; they may also bring challenges. Some couples are quite aware of both of these.

*Lara sometimes resented the influence her partner Sherrie's family had over her. Sherrie had explained to Lara the importance of family in Chinese culture, and Lara had even done some reading about it. But she still felt slighted when Sherrie seemed to value her parents' opinions over hers.*

Other couples may not realize that some of their misunderstandings and conflicts are based on cultural differences.

*It drove Storm crazy that when something went wrong, her partner, Kathleen, focused on determining who was to blame. It never occurred to either of them that this could be a cultural difference until they brought the issue up in a couples' counseling session.*

How can you tell if there is a cultural basis for issues between you and your partner? The first step is simply to consider it. Then ask your partner (or she could ask herself), "Who else exhibits this behavior?" If everyone she grew up with does it (not just her immediate family), you likely have a cultural difference. Then you can explore what the meaning of the behavior is to her. Some questions that can help guide this exploration include:

- What is the tradition?
- What is the cultural context?
- What are the values involved?
- What is the function of the behavior?[3]

To return to the situation with Storm and Kathleen as an example, it turned out that Kathleen's focus on blame was related to her Irish-American, Roman Catholic background. When asked, "Who else did this behavior?" she responded that not only her own family but also everyone she knew—having grown up in a predominantly Irish-American neighborhood—did the same thing. While there was a lot more to this behavior than its function, the bottom line for Kathleen was that if she were to blame, she needed to change; if she weren't to blame, then she didn't. Exploring the cultural basis of their conflict eased the tension and helped both of them get more perspective. Kathleen could see that it was a cultural difference and that not everyone saw the world the way she did. For her part, Storm was able to not take it so personally. She could see it more in the context of her partner's cultural upbringing.

Later in this chapter we will return to acculturation when we examine adaptations and the impact of family and community expectations on a couple. But before that, let us turn to racism, which is often an additional issue for partners from different cultures.

## Racism

There is no way to grow up in the United States, or in many other countries, without being affected by racism. It is a pervasive and persistent social poison that affects us all.

We realize it is difficult to discuss racial, cultural, ethnic, class, and religious traditions separately. Even using phrases such as "women of color" and "white women" runs the risk of reducing people to their pigmentation and failing to acknowledge their diversity. We know that we are able to highlight only some areas of a very complex topic. Racism affects self-esteem, job opportunities, and an individual's personal comfort and safety in walking around in the world, to name just a few areas. And racism affects all lesbian couples, whether partners are both women of color, of different races, or both white, because when prejudice and discrimination are allowed to exist in any form, that toleration gives tacit approval to all other forms.

To understand how racism affects lesbian couples, we need to look at what racism involves and how it impacts the individual women in the couple as well as the dynamics between them.

## Defining Our Terms

Prejudice refers to preconceived ideas and attitudes that are based on a person's being of a particular race, ethnic background, religion, occupation, or other group membership. We demonstrate prejudice when we make judgments about others in a generalized way without sufficient reason or information. Most of us learn our prejudices as we grow up and accept the opinions and values of our own group. We may act out our prejudices, or we may keep them to ourselves. Discrimination—action based on prejudice—is mistreatment. It diminishes both the giver and receiver.

Racism involves prejudice toward and discrimination against people of a different race and it also requires the power to impose and societally reinforce the discrimination. Racism is prejudice with power. It can be expressed—openly or covertly—individually, culturally, and institutionally. When a Native-American female senior attorney at a large firm is passed over by a white client in favor of a less experienced white male attorney, we have an example of individual racism (and sexism). Cultural racism operates when the only recognized experts on Inuit customs are white. When a workplace employs no people of color at all, or no people of color in management positions, and that practice is never questioned, institutional racism is at work.

Systematic oppression is the mistreatment of a group of people that is embedded in the values, beliefs, laws, code of ethics, social norms, traditions, institutions, or organizational structures of a society; in other words, the mistreatment is socially sanctioned and maintains an imbalance of power between the group targeted for discrimination and the perpetrators of the oppression. In the United States, lesbians and gays are systematically oppressed based on sexual orientation, and people of color are systematically oppressed based on race. And although people of color in this country may show prejudice toward white people or people of races other than their own, they lack the societal power to systematically oppress those groups.

## How Racism Affects Individuals

Which groups of people are affected by racism and how drastic those effects are depend on the social and economic power structure of the society. Typically, and unfortunately, the dominant culture creates a hierarchy based on race. The lower a group is in the hierarchy, the more severe the discrimination and the more negative the stereotypes about that group are likely to be. This contributes to competition within and between racial groups for scarce resources, such as jobs and educational opportunities. Historically, in

European-dominated cultures, the lighter your skin color, the better. If a woman of color has internalized this belief, she may put herself down for being dark, discriminate against those with dark skin like herself, and prefer to associate with light-skinned individuals. Internalized racism is in some ways like internalized homophobia: The oppressed individual believes the myths of the dominant culture.

There are additional pressures for people of color in a racist society. They may be regarded by others as tokens to be utilized when needed for racial representation. They may be seen as the vessels of some special knowledge and experience that is wanted, but not always respected, by others. And many people of color also feel great pressure to be accepted, since they are seen as representatives of their group rather than as individuals. Many have to perform much better than European Americans, just to be seen as equally competent. Even then, they may not receive recognition for their accomplishments.

### Dealing with Racism

> Frances and Greta had been walking peacefully down the street when a small group of white teenaged boys started following them and making racist remarks about Black lezzies and "nigger" lovers. Greta instinctively crossed the street to get away from them, then realized that Frances wasn't with her. Greta crossed back and began shouting at the boys, thinking herself very brave. The boys eventually retreated. Meanwhile, Frances had just kept walking. When Greta caught up with her and asked why she hadn't either run away or fought back, Frances just shrugged. "Life's too short to spend worrying about a bunch of white boys."

As people of color experience racism over time and witness its effects on those around them, a phenomenon Vickie Sears calls "armoring" occurs.[4] A woman of color builds a shell, or armor, around herself as protection from the onslaught of racism. She learns to watch every new situation and person for potential racist comments or dangers and to pace her responses accordingly. A white woman, on the other hand, has not had to build up this armor. These defenses can lead to difficulties in cross-racial relationships in which one partner is a woman of color and the other is white.

The white partner of a woman of color is less likely to be prepared for racial incidents. She may not notice the overtones in comments people make to interracial couples: "It must have been a blow to your family" or "Couldn't you find a sister?" or "How in the world did you meet?" If she does notice, she may not know how to manage the situation effectively.

*Sue had always thought of her family as accepting and liberal. They had never made a fuss about her sexual orientation or her political involvement in Central-American issues. Therefore, Sue was unprepared when she brought home her new lover, Dolores, a Salvadoran refugee and activist. Her parents and brothers said all the wrong things, from confusing El Salvador with Nicaragua to telling Dolores that the United States wasn't really a racist country and that they had a black friend.*

*Sue could hardly wait to get Dolores home to apologize for her family's behavior. She was amazed when Dolores told her flat out that Sue had acted as badly as any of them. As far as Dolores was concerned, Sue had put her in a very awkward position by defending her and promoting her instead of letting her be herself.*

*It took a lot of angry words and tears before Dolores and Sue were able to set up some ground rules for how they would address the next racist situation they found themselves in. For Dolores it was an unpleasant fact of life in North America; for Sue it was the beginning of learning that her good intentions did not automatically put her in the right.*

In her essay "Across the Glittering Sea," Jewelle Gomez shares one approach she has developed to overcome the negative impact of family influences on interracial couples. From her experience as a black woman in relationships with white women, she decided not to hold anything the "in-laws" do to her against her partner: "After all they raised her, she didn't raise them." This allows her to put her partner's family—and their racism—in perspective.[5]

Family situations are not the only ones in which cross-racial couples come across racism. Many women of color encounter and anticipate such things as slow service in public places or the condescending use of first names by service providers. White partners typically do not. They may not notice the discourtesies or understand that the reason for them is racism. They may try to explain the situation away with something like, "The waitress is probably just busy; that's why it is taking her so long to serve us," thus reinforcing the racism. Or they may be totally thrown by the situation.

*Neisha and Van went on a winter vacation to a ski resort in the Rockies. The first morning, Neisha returned from a trip to the gym and spa very out of sorts. The attendant had been testy when Neisha had requested extra towels for the sauna. She was convinced it was because she was African American. At first Van offered alternative explanations—that the attendant was just having a had day, or perhaps Neisha misinterpreted the woman's reaction. This resulted in a fight on the first day of what was supposed to be a relaxing vacation.*

After they calmed down, Neisha and Van decided to do an experiment. Van would make the same request of the attendant as Neisha had made and see if, as an Anglo-American woman, she got the same treatment. This strategy of conducting an experiment can be a way for couples to reduce conflicts about "what is really happening."[6] Taking this approach prevents the partner of color from having to convince her white partner about the reality of racism or of perceived racism. The white partner can avoid being in the position of challenging her lover's reality or defending "white people." Together they can gather data. Even if the experiment is not totally conclusive, it creates an opportunity for both partners to discuss situations and check them out collaboratively.

Just because women have worked on their racism does not mean it disappears from couple relationships. Dealing with racial incidents typically requires the white partner in an interracial couple to become more aware of the privileges of her skin color. She also needs to develop coping strategies, and maybe even armor, because she is partnered with a woman of color. However, no matter how much anger, pain, and fear a white partner feels, it is her partner who is the target of the racism.

The partner of color will have to work through her resentment both of white privilege and of having to teach her partner how to deal with racism. Because the partner of color is more experienced, her knowledge and skills can help the couple figure out how to handle these situations. One way to do that is to replay each incident verbally and explore how each partner felt. Ultimately, both will feel less vulnerable.

Couples other than interracial ones can also use this replaying strategy to address racism. For example, it is a racial incident when racist remarks are made in an all-white group. As lesbians, it can be heartening to remember that to confront racism is to stand up against oppression based on membership in a particular group, which also includes homophobia and sexism.

### Confronting Racist Comments

If your goal is to educate and create allies, you need to be nonjudgmental and compassionate yet firm when you confront racist comments. It helps if you assume that the person is speaking out of ignorance, not malice. Then you can listen, ask questions, and provide more or new information rather than argue with her or make her feel humiliated or ashamed.

The following ideas and suggestions of what to say when someone makes a racist comment can, of course, also be used when someone makes a homophobic comment.[7]

- "I'm sure you didn't mean to offend me, but you did. Let me tell you why. . . ."
- "Did you know that (members of the group) find that hurtful?"
- "What do you mean when you say . . . ?" (For example, "The Asians are getting all the good jobs.")
- "I don't think that you meant it the way it sounded, but this is how I felt when you said it. . . ."
- "What you just said could be heard as racially biased."
- "Do you really believe that?"
- "I am going to interrupt you because you have just offended me."
- "I can't believe you said that!"
- "OUCH!" (to get their attention)
- "I don't like that."
- "What did you mean by that?" followed by, "Why do you feel that way?"

These approaches can be used with people you don't know very well or even with those you are close to. The last suggestion may be particularly appropriate when the person who makes the comment is a loved one, such as a parent.

*Elyse and her father were driving to the airport to pick up Elyse's partner, Hisae. Elyse's father knew that Hisae had just gotten her PhD in economics. Somewhere in the conversation he made the offhand comment, "It was easy for her because she is Japanese." Elyse couldn't believe he had actually said that, specifically because she had told him what a grueling process Hisae's doctoral committee had put her through. As soon as she could breathe again, Elyse asked her father what he meant. In the subsequent conversation it came out that he resented what he thought was preferential treatment of "rich Asian college students." It was a difficult conversation, but Elyse did manage to get her father to understand that Hisae had not been given special treatment nor had an easy time getting her doctorate.*

## Work and Money

Because of racism, people of color do not have equal access to housing, educational and training opportunities, and well-paying jobs. Some interracial couples have to deal with the effects of this inequality.

> *Carol Ann had a good job as a computer programmer at an insurance company where she met Oliva. Oliva had gone to business school to learn data-entry skills but had not been able to afford additional education. As a Puertorriqueña she also felt pressure to help her family financially. In the tradition of the white middle class, Carol Ann's family did not expect her to contribute to the family. Because she earned almost twice as much as Oliva, Carol Ann wanted to pay two-thirds of the household bills. They finally agreed to a fifty-fifty split, since Oliva felt she would be in a hopelessly imbalanced situation otherwise. Oliva continued to provide help for her family, and money was tight for her. After struggling for two years, Oliva negotiated a loan, with Carol Ann as a cosigner, so she could go to school for further training.*

Not all couples are able to work things out as well as Carol Ann and Oliva. The point is that when there are economic power differences between partners, they need to be negotiated (see Chapter Seven) so that both can live amicably with differences in such areas as job prestige and earning power.

Of course, the white partner is not always the one with more education or a higher income.

> *Alisa had a degree from Columbia and worked as a lawyer; her income was much higher than that of her partner, Kyla, who was an artist. However, Alisa always felt awkward going to art-gallery openings in the small Northwest city where she and Kyla lived. Frequently, Alisa was the only African-American person there, and she felt torn. She had grown up going to the Museum of Modern Art and the Metropolitan Museum of Art and had a strong appreciation for art. On the other hand, she felt extremely visible and not completely comfortable in this particular art-gallery scene.*

It was only after some painful discussions that Alisa and Kyla were able to acknowledge that some of their assumptions, fears, and expectations about each other were based on their being of different races. They decided that it would help both their careers and their personal lives to move to a larger city that had a more racially mixed community. They knew that the move wouldn't solve all of the problems. However, they realized that a different city could offer them more opportunities to experience and create racially integrated environments.

## Adaptations and Expectations

There are several other situations that require good communication between partners. One of these is related to the fact that many women of color have learned from an early age to be adaptive in their lifestyle. They have had to learn to "behave" according to white values and expectations when that was needed and to be themselves within their own group. For example, black women constantly shift between two different behavioral expectations. It takes skill and courage to be able to do this. Frequently a white woman does not notice when her partner adapts her behavior among whites. But, she may notice a great deal and feel uncomfortable when her partner behaves according to African-American values and norms when she is with her African-American friends. When partners are of different races or from different cultures, one may feel left out if she does not speak the other's language or understand her style of humor. She may feel threatened by, rather than appreciative of, her lover's cultural adaptability.

*Ruthie had been clamoring for years to meet some of Denise's relatives in Tokyo, but when they finally got there, Denise was sorry she'd brought Ruthie along. There was a lot of family history Denise wanted to learn, and she didn't feel comfortable speaking Japanese around her lover. Outside the United States, Ruthie's manners seemed brusque and her voice loud and abrasive. Until they had a long, frank discussion about it, Denise had been increasingly embarrassed for her lover and had found herself pretending that they weren't lovers, only very distant friends. Eventually, they decided that Ruthie would travel around the country on her own for a while and take responsibility for learning something about Japanese culture, while Denise stayed with her relatives. When they met again a week later, Ruthie had a better understanding of the culture and was content to enjoy her visit without trying to make everyone like her. Denise realized that she needed to talk more about her feelings instead of distancing herself from Ruthie. Afterward, they both agreed the trip had been demanding, but they had learned from it.*

In addition to pressures from the outside, a woman of color may face expectations and pressure from her family or peers to find a lover within her own group. A woman of color who chooses a partner of a different race may be seen as disloyal. She may be rejected by members of her own group as well as her partner's group. She may feel anger and shame for even having feelings for someone of another race. Added to this can be the effects of internalized racism. For example, a woman of color involved with a white partner may be asking, "What's wrong with me that I can't find one of my own kind?" as well as "What's wrong with her?" Paradoxically, her white partner may be asked these questions, too, by her family or friends. Either partner can also grow lonely and become defensive if she is separated from members of her own group. Unless she has a strong cultural/ethnic identity herself, a white partner may find it hard to understand that her partner wants to spend time with people of her own racial or ethnic group.

> Teresa wasn't sure how she would have survived without her women-of-color support group. Being with other women like herself provided validation, support, and a haven—a respite from being in the watchful eye of the majority culture. Every other Thursday night she knew she could relax and leave certain things unsaid because these women understood. Teresa's new partner, Maxine, who was white, tried to be supportive, but Teresa knew Maxine felt excluded and maybe even a little threatened.

Many white partners can relate to their lover's need to be with other women of color because they may have a parallel desire to be with other lesbians for similar reasons—feeling comfortable, supported, validated, and understood. Even so, like Maxine, most white partners will need to handle feelings of exclusion and loss. It is understandable for the excluded partner to have these feelings and to express them. However, it doesn't mean that the woman of color has to stop meeting her own needs because her white lover feels left out. An appreciation of each other's needs and feelings along with open communication are important in dealing with this issue.

## Family and Community Expectations

In growing up, many women of color see themselves as a part of a group where interdependency and cooperative effort promote individual growth within the community. In this situation, the group norms and expectations are very important. White children typically are taught or take for granted an ethic of "rugged individualism." They do not grow up as much with the idea that they are part of a group. This varies, of course, depending on class and ethnic group, but overall, whites tend to have a more individualistic attitude. An example of cultural difference is that a sign of maturity in Asia is interdependence with extended family, while in mainstream American culture maturity means independence from the family of origin. Although Asian ethnic groups vary in their cultural practices and beliefs, striking commonalities have been identified.[8] From the Asian perspective, a child is expected to consider the wishes of parents and elders in such matters as the choice of a profession or spouse—and to place their preferences above her own. By contrast, European-American families tend to be nuclear, and parents encourage separation and independence from the family of origin in order for the child to pursue her own interests.[9]

When a woman of color comes from an extended family system where everyone is interwoven and interdependent, problems are often handled inside that system. There may be no precedence for talking and problem-solving outside the family structure. To lose that family system can be devastating, whether the loss is based on having a partner of another race, or of the same sex, or both. It means the loss of a crucial support network.

Because of differences in the expectations flowing from the communities or families of origin of women of color, issues of coming out may vary significantly from those of white women. Often there are pressures against being very different and calling attention, especially negative attention, to the racial minority group. Being a lesbian of color may do both.

Thus, the coming-out experience can be very difficult for a woman of color who is strongly identified with her group. Many decide to remain closeted. A white partner, in particular, may not fully understand the risks involved for her partner. She may misinterpret her lover's decision to mean that she does not love her enough to come out. It is important for white partners in cross-racial and cross-cultural couples to know the enormity of the pressures their lovers may feel and for both partners to be aware and respectful of these differences.

Over the past thirty years many families and communities of color have become more accepting of their lesbian daughters. For example, in the 1970s, Filipina lesbians may have experienced minimal to no acceptance by their families and community. The current generation of Filipinas—here and in the Philippines—get much more family, community, and societal support and describe themselves as being part of a global pan-Asian queer movement.[10]

An additional pressure on many lesbians of color is to continue their group by having children. Issues of genocide, high infant mortality rates, high early death rates, and racism can be prevalent in their thoughts. In the Native-American world, for example, children are seen as being the future.

Having children and raising them to be healthy, responsible community members is very important. In this situation, for a woman to choose not to have children means that there will be heavy community pressure. And if she does choose to have children in a cross-racial relationship, there are other issues.

*When Trey and Regina decided to have a family it was very important to Regina that the sperm donor be white so their child would be representative of both mothers' races. As the nonbiological parent, Trey was worried about how her parents would respond to a biracial grandchild. She also wondered if their child identified as a person of color, would that mean that she would somehow be rejecting Trey?*

One of the racist legacies in this country is called "hypodescent." This refers to the assumption that a biracial or multiracial person who is partly of European heritage will want to identify with that heritage but will be assigned to the racial group of the parent with the lowest racial status. In other words, a biracial or multiracial person who is partly white will be seen only as a person of color.

As is the case for all interracial couples, Regina and Trey will need to communicate and cope with a number of race-related topics before and during their parenting career. Their child's racial identity is one of these issues. He or she might want to identify as biracial, white, or as a person of color. Biracial children need to know that they have the right "not to keep the races separate within" themselves.[11] As cross-cultural and interracial couples become more prevalent and accepted, biracial, and multiracial children are becoming more numerous. While they still face prejudice, there are more resources available to them. (See Resources.)

## Falling into Traps

Another issue for cross-racial couples is dealing with their stereotypes and expectations based on race. A woman of color may wonder if she is attracted to her lover because—as a fair-complected, blue-eyed blond—"She is everything I'm not." Some white people may wonder if women of color want to be with them to enhance their status in the world and gain access to the benefits that come from white privilege. Actually, this is a good illustration of a racist belief. In fact, being with a white woman may not enhance her partner's status at all. In the African-American community, for example, it would depend on such factors as class background and education.

Women of color may worry about "ethnic chasers": white people who are always eager to be lovers of or partners with a person of color. They may actively seek out women of color because they feel guilty about being white at some very deep level, or they want to acquire color by proximity, thereby proving how liberal they are. A woman of color may experience wariness and even fear about a white woman who has expressed an interest in her. Given the history of cultural appropriation, a woman of color may also be wondering what she has about her, culturally, that attracts the other and could be stolen from her. No one chooses to have these thoughts rumbling through her mind when she finds herself attracted to a woman, but they may be there.

*After a passionate, long evening of lovemaking, Johanna said to Aki, "I always heard that Asian women were quiet and passive, but you asked for everything you wanted." The pain that simple admission caused Aki led to a series of discussions about what stereotypes each woman had about the other group.*

These issues can destroy a relationship; working through them can bring a couple closer. Even if they surface immediately, it may take months before they are discussed. However, the cost of ignoring them is a loss in understanding, trust, and intimacy.

*Rhonda, a white woman, and Clarice, a Native American, had been lovers for only seven months. They were both students. They had been talking about the manifest destiny movement, with Clarice giving her perspective on history from a Native American's viewpoint. She suddenly asked Rhonda if she were going to "steal ponies" (take something special without honoring or acknowledging the debt) and use Clarice's ideas in a paper she was writing. Rhonda got very hurt and angry. It took Clarice a while before she understood that she had treated Rhonda in a prejudiced way by accusing her of doing what "white people do"—steal from people of color. In the end they were able to sort it out and laugh, because both of them had thought that the first conflict about racial differences would be initiated by Rhonda.*

All relationships challenge partners to confront assumptions, beliefs, and values that can lead to misunderstandings, hurt, and anger. Some women may decide that to enter a cross-cultural or cross-racial relationship is too fraught with perils. Perhaps they've already tried it and decided it was too much work. Perhaps the pressure from their group is too great. Sometimes, no matter how much the women want their relationship to work, they are not able to resolve the racial issues at that point in their lives.

When partners are of different races or cultures, there's a lot of learning about new things, which can cement a relationship and stimulate the partners to grow. As is the case when any lesbians decide to share their lives, there are hazards and joys. Don't let difference keep you from falling in love. Rather, embrace difference for the gifts it can bring to the relationship.

As we said at the beginning of this chapter, racial, cultural, ethnic, and religious traditions are often inseparable. Values and attitudes about such matters as family obligations, child rearing, ancestors, food, spiritual practices, and homosexuality vary from one group to another. Couples need to be aware of these differences, to acknowledge their importance, and to negotiate incorporating them into the couple's life.

CHAPTER 14

# ℘ Recovery and Healing

It's been said that it takes the first twenty or thirty years of our lives to accumulate the experiences and develop the patterns of thinking, feeling, and behaving that we spend the next thirty years trying to understand, unravel, and in some instances, change.

Recovery has been traditionally associated with addiction. However, if we think of recovery as a healing process, then we are all recovering from something. We may be recovering from not getting what we needed as a child to grow up confident and sure of our specialness and worth; from an addiction to food, alcohol, or drugs; from a physical illness; from a devastating breakup; from the effects of sexual or physical abuse; or from anxiety or depression.

It is also true that some of us have more to recover from than others. Some of us may have experienced severe trauma; the trauma may have continued for a long time and a number of stressful events may have happened at the same time. Whatever your situation, it is important to acknowledge your particular circumstances and the impact these events had on you. Comparing yourself with others is not helpful: You can always find someone who had it worse (or better, for that matter) than you. That's not the point. Pain is pain. Healing works best when you have compassion for yourself and listen to what you need for your own recovery.

You may find help in the recovery process via counseling and therapy, inpatient hospital treatment, reading, meditation, spiritual practice, twelve-step programs such as Alcoholics Anonymous (AA) and Overeaters Anonymous (OA), acupuncture, body work such as Feldenkrais or massage, medication, homeopathy, exercise, or support groups. If you identify as being in recovery, we encourage you to seek out whatever resources—people, programs, Web sites, and so forth—that work for you. Remember: Asking for help is a sign of strength.

Sometimes recovery looks and feels like healing, and sometimes it's more like coping—and barely coping at that. All of this affects our couple relationship. While every person and recovery process is unique, as is every couple relationship, there are common patterns. Some of these patterns involve confusing or hurtful behavior; others are constructive and facilitate healing.

When you are in recovery you are focused on your own healing and may be quite self-absorbed. You may not have much attention or energy left over for your partner. In addition, you may want a lot of support and understanding from her. Your partner may be torn between wanting to be supportive, and at the same time, feeling resentful about your demands for her time, energy, and emotional attention. What about *her* life and *her* needs? If each of you is focused on your own healing, it increases the chances that you will both feel needy at the same time. When this happens, neither of you may feel adequately nurtured and cared for.

The recovery process puts less strain on the relationship when you and your partner can be clear with each other about what you are thinking, feeling, and wanting. (See Chapter Six.) Self-awareness and good communication don't guarantee that your situation will be easy, only that it will be *easier*. Some of the suggestions in Chapter Fifteen for able-bodied and disabled partners may also he helpful at this stage. For example, if you know very little about your partner's experience and the recovery process, you will need to educate yourself. Don't rely on your partner to do it for you. She may have her hands full juggling her own issues. Besides, it is an act of nurturance and support to be interested and to take responsibility for your own learning. You may find it useful to go to a support-group meeting, such as Al-Anon or a group for partners of incest survivors, and to talk to others who have gone through this experience. With her permission, you could consult with your partner's health-care providers, as well as your own. You could read and seek out information and support that will help you to understand and deal better with her recovery process.

In the rest of this chapter, we will look at how recovery from specific traumas and experiences may affect the couple relationship, and offer some suggestions for healing.

## Incest and Sexual Abuse

The statistics about sexual abuse are staggering. Even the most conservative estimate is that at least 20 percent of women have experienced some form of sexual abuse as children.[1] A more realistic picture, based on research studies, indicates that the percentage of females in this country who are sexually molested before the age of eighteen is somewhere between 38 and 45 percent. In a substantial proportion of these situations, the perpetrators are relatives.[2]

A survey of 1,566 lesbians found comparable results; 38 percent of the women reported childhood sexual abuse.[3] Sometimes the perpetrator is a stranger, but it's more likely to be at least an acquaintance. For many girls, sexual abuse occurs in the family. The abuser may be a father, mother, grandparent, uncle, brother, stepfather, a trusted family friend, neighbor, or babysitter. Sexual abuse may be a single incident or it may continue for years. It may or may not be combined with physical or emotional abuse.

The impact of sexual abuse in childhood varies, depending on factors including the child or young woman's age when it happened, how long it went on, who the abuser was, whether physical violence was involved, and, especially, how adults responded if she reported the abuse.

Whatever the circumstances, sexual abuse is never the child's fault. The adult is fully responsible. We cannot emphasize this enough. Unfortunately, children typically blame themselves for the abuse and perpetrators of child abuse often play upon this tendency by blaming the child: "It's your fault; you tempted me" or "I know you like this." Secrecy exaggerates the confusion, guilt, and shame. Usually the child is told not to tell: "It's our little secret." She may be threatened emotionally: "Mommy would be angry." Or physically: "I'll cut you up in little pieces."

Beyond blame and secrecy, being used as a sexual object by a trusted adult inevitably produces feelings of guilt, confusion, shame, and fear in a child. The child has no "safe place." She is not safe in her family, her home, or even her own body. The experience is so traumatic that some adult women report not remembering the abuse until they are well into their twenties, thirties, or older. Known as the "repressed memories" response, it has generated a great deal of controversy.

Abuse can have a number of implications for lesbian couples. First, the odds of at least one member of the couple having a history of sexual abuse are greater than with heterosexual or gay couples. Second, the impact of sexual abuse is not limited solely to a couple's sexual relationship—it is also an emotional violation. Incest survivors, in particular, often have difficulty trusting and feeling emotionally safe with their lovers. This is certainly understandable since, in their experience, intimate relationships are associated with violation, betrayal, and abandonment. An abused child is forced to ignore what she knows and wants in order to simply survive. As a result, the adult woman often does not know how to set limits based on what she does and doesn't want. This may be the case in sex as well as in other areas of her life.

As for sexuality, survivors may place great importance on sex in their adult lives, or they may de-emphasize it. They may do each at different times. For example, many women decide not to be sexual while they are working on the abuse issue in therapy. This decision can be especially painful and confusing to their partners, who want to be supportive, but who also want to be intimate sexually. Partners may understand but still feel disappointed or rejected. If this is your situation, it can help to understand that your personal attractiveness is not the issue.

If you are the survivor, you can reassure your partner that this decision is about you, not about her. Be clear with her about what is okay with you and what is not and when. The two of you can explore some alternative ways of being intimate, such as romantic dinners, nonsexual physical contact (foot tubs or massage), long talks, and love notes.

Healing from incest and sexual abuse is a difficult process for both the survivor and her partner. The good news is that awareness about this widespread problem has yielded more information, understanding, and resources for healing as well as support for partners of survivors. (See Resources.)

## Adult Children of Alcoholics

Many people, including many lesbians, grew up in families with an alcoholic or drug-dependent parent. The impact of this experience on children depends on a number of factors. How much did the substance abuse impair the adult's capacity to parent? How much was the other parent, extended family, or community able to buffer the children from the behavior? Were both parents addicted? We now know a good deal more than we did about the impact of parental substance abuse on kids. A number of coping patterns have been identified as characteristic of adult children of alcoholics (ACOAs). The relevance of these patterns depends on the particular set of circumstances. However, many people identify with four general patterns of adapting to life with alcoholic or drug-addicted parents.[4]

1. The oldest child often adopts a "caretaker" role. Caretaker children are super-responsible, serious, capable, and old beyond their years.

   *When you are six years old, your mother is so drunk she can't make dinner, and she won't let you in the kitchen, you have to get good at figuring out how to get something to eat.*

2. Other kids become "pleasers." They try to keep the peace and keep everyone happy. They try to meet their own needs for love by trying to meet the needs of others.

   *I thought if I was just good enough, smart enough, or pretty enough, that my dad would stop drinking and be a dad again.*

3. Some children tune out. "The adjusters" soak up the tension and emotion, but show nothing. Later, they may not even remember much of the violence or dramatic childhood incidents, because they were engrossed in watching TV or listening to music through it all.

   *I have very few clear memories of my childhood. It all seems just a blur.*

4. And some children become addicted to alcohol or drugs themselves, while others may act out in other ways, such as becoming sexually active at a very young age.

The implications for couples can be broad and far-reaching. Growing up with an alcoholic or drug-addicted parent will affect a child's life. At best it means that a mother or father is not as attentive and emotionally available to the child; at worst it results in a childhood littered with secrets and broken promises, incidents of domestic violence or threats, crisis after crisis, or just plain neglect, inattention, and unavailability. Recovering ACOAs are often involved, to some degree, in learning how to speak, feel, and trust. These are all things they may have learned not to do growing up, as a price of making things work better or of basic survival.

Many adult children of other kinds of dysfunctional families identify strongly with ACOA characteristics. One explanation for this is that dysfunctional families share common features. They may fit one or more of the following descriptions: neglectful, mistreating, inconsistent, chaotic at times, unpredictable, arbitrary, denying, disallowing feelings and other needs, having secrets, or being rigid.[5] Often, the children in these family environments were made to feel bad, defective, incomplete, rotten, inadequate, or like failures—at their very core.[6] A woman who does not come from a seriously dysfunctional family background may find it sometimes hard to understand her partner's behavior.

> *Liliana traveled a lot with her job. Every time her partner, Delia, offered to pick her up at the airport, Liliana thanked her and then outlined a backup plan in case Delia couldn't make it. Delia was offended by Liliana's response and accused Liliana of not trusting her.*

Liliana was operating out of the old habit she developed from growing up in a family where she couldn't count on anyone. As a child, something often "came up," and her alcoholic parent failed her. For her part, Delia took Liliana's behavior personally. She assumed that Liliana's response was related to her and to her trustworthiness. In fact, Liliana was responding to a "ghost" from the past.

When children grow up in alcoholic or other poorly functioning families, they may have little idea about what a positive relationship between adults looks like. Craziness was so "normal" in their family that they do not know what is reasonable to expect from others. They often miss out on learning many basics because nobody told them, taught them, or modeled appropriate behavior for them.

> *Diane was never sure whether her behavior was really appropriate, especially in social situations. Her mother was alcoholic, and her father had been severely depressed as far back as she could remember. She described her mother as having been "off the wall" most of the time and says that her father "never did much at all. "*
>
> *Because she never felt sure about what was and wasn't acceptable behavior, Diane took her cue from others. She based her behavior on whatever her friends, boss, or lover thought was the best thing to do. In her relationship, she went along with almost everything her partner, Barb, wanted. And Barb was none the wiser. She just assumed that Diane was in agreement with her. Four years after they began living together, Diane went into therapy because she was so depressed. Eventually she became clearer about what she thought, felt, and wanted—and more confident about expressing herself. This meant big changes in her relationship with Barb. There were times when they wondered if their relationship would make it, but they*

*weathered the rough spots. In fact, their relationship improved, and they now describe those hard times as having been worth it.*

Not everyone chooses to go into therapy as Diane did. Different people may find other resources helpful in working toward their goals for themselves and for their relationships. The increased awareness of the impact of traumas, including childhood abuse and neglect, has resulted in more available options to assist the healing process. (See Resources.)

## Variations and Combinations

Some lesbians come from a family where they had it all: One or even both parents were alcoholic or drug-addicted, and the children were sexually, physically, or emotionally abused or neglected. Other women have parents or guardians who demonstrated some, but not all, of these behaviors to a greater or lesser degree.

Abuse can be verbal, physical, and emotional, as well as sexual. It may also vary in severity. Physical abuse includes being hit, punched, slapped, beaten, or punished to the point of injury. Emotional abuse refers to psychological injury resulting from such practices as belittling, name calling, and making threats of punishment or abandonment. Neglect may also be either physical or emotional. A physically neglected child does not receive the basics, such as food, clothing, and medical attention. Emotionally neglectful parents ignore their children; they don't talk to them, hold them, or show an interest in them. They are not emotionally available.

Regardless of the type or combinations of abuse, adults who were abused as children carry the aftereffects of the trauma. There are five needs that are often disrupted by trauma: safety, trust, control, self-esteem, and intimacy.[7] If you have a traumatic experience as an adult, you may have a significant change in your thinking, such that you may no longer feel safe or able to trust. You may also feel powerless, worthless, or alone. This change may be transitory or may last for a long time. If you were abused and traumatized as a child, your needs were disrupted early enough that you may always have felt unsafe, distrustful of yourself and others, powerless, worthless, and isolated.

Abused children rarely understand that their parents have a problem, not them. They grow up thinking they are bad, unworthy and unlovable, and have nothing worthwhile to offer. In the recovery process, an abuse survivor may seesaw. First she may want a lot of reassurance that she is okay, to the point of clinginess, and then she may abruptly switch and push her partner away, insisting that she neither needs nor wants anyone.

## Effects of Abuse on the Partner and the Relationship

Abuse, of course, affects the partner who was not abused. What kinds of feelings and reactions does she have?

*After Ami went into therapy, Marie learned more than she ever wanted to know about how seriously Ami had been abused as a child. Marie felt so bad for her partner that she was determined to provide a totally warm and supportive environment. She bit her tongue when Ami talked about attending her family reunion. Marie was so angry with Ami's parents, particularly her father, that she could have cheerfully strangled him. She couldn't understand why Ami did not feel the same way. But Ami did not, and Marie felt alone and stuck in her anger and helplessness.*

Marie had responses that many partners have. If your partner is an abuse survivor, you may want to protect her and make up for the past abuse. You also may be very angry with the abuser(s) or the parent(s) who did not protect your partner when she was young. Another frequent reaction for partners is impatience with the recovery process. You usually want the recovery to be over, so that you can focus as a couple on the present and your life together. Then you may feel guilty about your impatience.

Trauma survivors need to get the help they require to recover and take whatever amount of time that recovery demands. Ami needs to know that her internal timetable may not be the same as Marie's timetable for her; she needs to go at her own pace.

Partners of abuse survivors also have needs; they become victims of incest, too, by association. They cannot change the past and must cope with the consequences of the abuse in the present, on a daily basis. If Marie is to grow and change in this process, she needs to give herself permission to have feelings and to talk about her reactions. If it is not appropriate or possible to do this with Ami, Marie needs to seek support elsewhere. For example, Marie has every right to have her own feelings and reactions about Ami's father. However, Ami may be so involved in working out her own feelings that she has little energy for Marie's.

Partners need to practice self-care and patience. You are most helpful to your survivor partner when you validate the reality of the abuse and keep the responsibility for it on the perpetrator. If you are a survivor, you are most helpful to your partner when you try to understand your partner's experience and be responsive to it. Each of you needs to listen to the other's feelings and respect them even though you may not see things the same way. You may have many occasions where you each have to practice being differentiated and soothing yourself. (See Chapter Three.)

Survivors and partners alike need to avoid burdening each other and the relationship to the point of burnout. It is critical to utilize other resources: Talk with friends or a counselor, join a support group, write in a journal, read about child abuse, exercise, or work with an abuse-prevention group or organization.

## Chemical Dependencies

It is well documented that alcohol and drug abuse have been a problem in the lesbian and gay community. In one study, 30 percent of lesbians were addicted to drugs or alcohol.[8] In another survey 29 percent of the lesbians considered themselves to be in recovery from alcohol or drug addiction.[9] It is easy to understand why addiction is such a problem. For a long time the primary social outlet for gays and lesbians was bars. And homophobic behavior from society as well as our own internalized homophobia are hurtful. Drugs and alcohol have long been used to ease the pain. Hopefully, addiction rates will decrease as the resources for gay/lesbian/bisexual/transgendered people expand and as diverse sexualities are more accepted.

Lesbians recovering from chemical dependency are growing a lot. They have to. In many ways they stopped growing when they began using whatever drug came to control their lives. Becoming clean and sober means not only a physical recovery process, but also an emotional, social, and spiritual one. People who use alcohol and drugs to cope with life don't develop other coping skills. Many women report being afraid to do sober the things that they used to do when they were high, such as dancing in public, being sexual, and talking to new people. They have to learn or relearn how to manage the feelings that they used to drown, or at least dilute, with drugs or alcohol. This means developing new coping strategies for handling anger, pain, loneliness, and anxiety, as well as the more pleasant aspects of life.

While a relationship can hardly be expected to flourish when chemicals are at its center, the recovery process puts additional stress on the relationship. The addicted partner struggles to stay clean and sober, and her partner may have developed codependent behavior patterns that she needs to change. Caring, nurturing behavior sometimes moves past healthy into codependency. If one partner "rescues" her lover and unwittingly enables her to continue drinking or drugging, she is engaging in codependent behavior. If the nonaddicted partner protects the addict from the consequences of her behavior, that is codependency. These behavior roles—supermother, martyr, and manager—are highly encouraged for all women.[10] It does not make them healthy, but it may make them more seductive.

> *Cassandra didn't drink every day. Sometimes it would be months in between "episodes." But when she drank, she got drunk—and stayed drunk—for a few days. When that happened, her partner, Laurelin, took over. She covered for Cassandra by calling in sick for her to work, intercepting calls from family, and making excuses to friends. Finally, when the episodes became more frequent, Cassandra made a promise to herself and to Laurelin that if she drank again, she would enter an inpatient treatment program. Cassandra did drink again and she did follow through on her promise to enter treatment. While Cassandra was in the program, Laurelin attended the sessions for family members. There she learned about codependent behavior and realized that Cassandra was not the only one who needed to change. When Cassandra graduated from the program, they were both optimistic. Cassandra was determined to do what she needed to do to stay clean and sober. Laurelin was motivated to cease her codependent behaviors. They knew that rebuilding their relationship would not be easy but they were excited about the possibilities.*

Once the roles of addict and codependent are established in a couple, change requires great patience and a lot of hard work. Both partners have to want to change. Even with desire and effort, changing this pattern is particularly hard because both women are exhausted from what they have been through. Also, much anger, hurt, and resentment have usually been built up on both sides. These feelings need to be addressed at the same time that both women are learning how to live chemical-free lives. That is a lot to have on the table at the same time.

Resources for supporting changes include AA, Al-Anon, and Narcotics Anonymous (NA). These organizations have gay and lesbian meetings in many geographical areas. There are also some treatment programs specifically for lesbians and gays, and many counselors specialize in working with people recovering from alcohol and drug addiction. (See Resources.)

It can be very useful for couples to try to identify the issues and problems in their relationship that are and are not related to the recovery process. While it's not easy to do, it is very helpful to know that those related to recovery will pass.

This is not to say that all couple relationships survive the recovery process. Sometimes the experiences of the recovering woman and the reactions of her partner stress the relationship beyond the breaking point. Sometimes the pace of the changes is too fast, too slow, or too much for the other partner to manage.

Inevitably the couple relationship will change when one or both partners are involved in recovery. It may emerge as a fuller and more satisfying couple relationship, or it may become a friendship. Partners need to realize that the pain and struggles of recovery will pass, but the healing that follows can help correct imbalances that may have existed and expand the potential for intimacy in the relationship.

## CHAPTER 15

# ⑧ Disability and Chronic Illness

When we hear the term "disabled," most of us think about people with the most obvious disabilities. We may picture a person who uses a cane or a wheelchair, for example. We frequently do not include people who have dyslexia, cerebral palsy, or schizophrenia. We may not think about people who are losing their hearing or vision, or who have disabilities that do not have obvious symptoms. Disabled people are often treated as if they are sick. Just because a person has a disability does not mean she is ill. Many individuals who are deaf or use wheelchairs, for example, are as healthy as their able-bodied peers. Likewise, people with a chronic illness are not necessarily disabled. However, someone with a chronic illness, such as multiple sclerosis, chronic fatigue and immune dysfunction syndrome (CFIDS), or diabetes may become disabled by that illness. Disability and illness are different and may affect couples in disparate ways; it is important to distinguish between them.

The community of disabled or chronically ill people is the one group that everyone can potentially be a part of—even against her will. This is why many people with disabilities refer to able-bodied people as temporarily able-bodied (TAB). An accident can disable a person in a moment. Meningitis can cause

---

This chapter is based on a manuscript by Vicki L. Sears.

brain damage, and other infections can cause hearing or sight loss. Many older women and men develop hearing loss, which can seriously affect their ability to interact with others, and aging, damaged knees and hips may create mobility disabilities. This may explain why so many people are extremely uncomfortable in the presence of someone with an obvious disability or illness. "There but for the grace of God, go I" is likely on their minds. We need to go the other way in our thinking, embrace the reality of disability (especially if we are currently able-bodied and have not looked at how people with disabilities are discriminated against), and alter our communities to be accessible for everyone. That way, if we become disabled, we can count on our communities to help us remain contributing members of the world.

## What Is a Disability? What Is a Chronic Illness?

The Americans with Disabilities Act of 1990 (ADA) was a turning point for people with disabilities. Building on the Rehabilitation Act of 1973 and other laws already on the books, the government defined disability as "(1) a physical or mental impairment that substantially limits one or more major life activities of such an individual; (2) a record of such an impairment; (3) being regarded as having such an impairment."[1] It defines physical or mental impairment as

*(1) Any physiological disorder or condition, cosmetic disfigurement, or anatomical loss affecting one or more of the following body systems: neurological, musculoskeletal, special sense organs, respiratory (including speech organs), cardiovascular, reproductive, digestive, genito-urinary, hemic and lymphatic, skin, and endocrine; or (2) Any mental or psychological disorder, such as mental retardation, organic brain syndrome, emotional or mental illness, and specific learning disabilities.[2]*

The ADA defines major life activities as "Caring for oneself, performing manual tasks, walking, seeing, hearing, speaking, breathing, learning, and working."[3] The act also outlines what the government considers reasonable accommodations an employer is expected to make in order to create an accessible work environment. Titles III and IV of the act made discrimination illegal in public accommodations and in commercial facilities and mandated the establishment of telecommunications relay services.[4] For the first time, people with disabilities were given the legal right to expect fair treatment in employment and suitable public facilities and to seek redress if they did not get them.

In her book *We Are Not Alone,* Sefra Kobrin Pitzele reported that one-third of adults in the United States suffers from chronic illnesses.[5] By definition, these illnesses are permanent and cause substantial modification of a person's lifestyle, goals, vocational choices and opportunities, recreational activities, and interpersonal relationships, whether or not they meet the legal criteria for disability. Depending on the illness, it may be relatively easy or very difficult to diagnose; it may progress rapidly or very slowly. There may be periods of remission that are relatively symptom-free as well as periods of acute illness.

Because people who have chronic illnesses typically also have temporary or long-term disabilities, they have problems similar to those in the disabled communities. Accessibility to buildings and to transportation are two such problems. However, there are differences between these groups, too. For example, many members of the disabled communities have adjusted to their disabilities. Perhaps they were born with a disability, or acquired it early in life as a result of an acute illness or accident. Chronic illness, on the other hand, often occurs in adulthood, and the adjustment process may be ongoing, because illnesses are often progressive.

### What's in a Name?

There are many terms that are used to "name" the world of people with disabilities. There is debate in the disabled and able-bodied communities about which words to use. Some people would say "physically challenged." Others prefer "other abled," "differently abled," "handicapped," or "disabled." We have chosen to use "person with a disability" because it not only seems the most accurate description, but it also is increasingly being used by people with disabilities.

### Stereotypes

"Ableism" describes prejudices toward people with disabilities. Some common stereotypes are:

- They are not pretty to look at.
- They are not healthy.
- They are not capable of being employed in meaningful work.
- They are nonsexual.
- If they are sexual, they ought not to have children.
- They are dependent and make their children dependent.
- They are brave in coping with adversity.

- They do not like to talk about "it."
- They like to be asked about "it."
- They need help with everything they do.
- They "suffer in silence."

While the lesbian community may like to think of itself as more sensitive than the rest of society, we are not free of ableistic stereotypes and attitudes. These attitudes affect how lesbians with disabilities and their partners are treated.

Being seen as dependent can result in well-meaning friends, or even partners, providing unnecessary help. Unasked, they may push a wheelchair or explain to a store clerk that we are deaf. At the other extreme, they may put us on a pedestal for being "brave" and "long-suffering." This can mean that we have no room to complain on days when we just feel crabby and out of sorts. Being regarded as a "super-cripple" can put pressure on the person with the disability to keep up this image; she may not feel free to ask for help when she needs it.

It is not uncommon for able-bodied partners to be thought of as strange because their lover is a woman with a disability. At other times they may be glorified as "noble" or "good" for choosing a partner who has a disability. When these couples are out in the world together, they may encounter incidents of rude or dismissive behavior.

*Odessa and Lorna were in the bar one night when a friend of Lorna's came over to their table. Odessa had met Lila only briefly, on one previous occasion. Although Lila clearly meant to include both Odessa and Lorna, she made eye contact with Lorna and directed all the conversation toward Lorna. She invited them to a party and asked Lorna if they could come, and whether Odessa could get up the stairs. Odessa answered that indeed she could.*

Because she used crutches, Odessa was treated as "less than": less than present and less than competent to speak for herself. Her partner was the spokeswoman, the one to talk to, the one who could make decisions. Odessa understood what was happening. She realized that part of Lila's rudeness was due to her discomfort at being so close to someone who had a disability. Lorna also knew what was happening and wisely let Odessa speak for herself. It is not the responsibility of the woman with the disability to adjust to the discomfort of the able-bodied. It is the responsibility of individuals, society, and the lesbian community to acknowledge and correct our own prejudices and acts of discrimination.

> *Petra was furious. She had driven in her friend Helena's car and had realized immediately that Helena had had the car "detailed" with chemicals. Petra had told Helena repeatedly that she was very allergic to chemical cleaning agents and could get very sick. Helena refused to believe Petra and told her that "It's all in your head." Helena was sure that if Petra wasn't told that chemicals had been used, she would never know.*

It's not unusual for people to disbelieve that environmental illness or multiple chemical allergies exist. We are so used to accepting mainstream medicine's pronouncements about what is or is not a real illness or disability that we often fail to listen to our friends who live with these illnesses, such as CFIDS. These illnesses are not fully understood by health-care providers and are often not accurately diagnosed in a timely fashion or are not seen as real illnesses.[6] One of the net results of this communitywide disbelief is that we fail to provide safe, nontoxic environments for people who need them.

Sometimes individuals with CFIDS, environmental illness, or other illnesses or disabilities that are not obvious spend a lot of energy hiding their vulnerabilities. This may be an attempt to protect other people from becoming uncomfortable with a "sick" person, or it may be due to a person's difficulty in coming to terms with her illness. Whatever the reason, when someone cannot be open about an illness, she risks making herself sicker. It is important that we listen to and respect an individual's statement about her health and stamina. It is her body, after all. If we do not respect her limits, we risk doing her serious harm. We would not think of telling a lesbian that she is wrong about her sexual orientation, so we should not even think about telling her that she is wrong about her health.

Dealing with these incidents, stereotypes, and misconceptions requires partners to communicate with each other. They need to express their thoughts and feelings and listen to each other so as to evaluate how they handled a prior situation and determine how they can handle future incidents.

## The Impact of Disability and Chronic Illness on the Couple Relationship

There are a variety of circumstances that influence the ways that disability and chronic illness can affect a lesbian couple. What kind and degree of disability or illness is it? What is the history of the couple relationship? How visible is the disability? How well are the partners able to communicate and deal openly with the issues that arise?

There is another critical factor. Was the disability or illness present before the women became involved or did it occur during the course of the relationship?

*Susanne had been hard-of-hearing as a child and was deaf by the time she was ten years old. She was in her mid-thirties and prepared to be in a relationship when she met Katrina. Through the years, Susanne had worked through many of her feelings about being deaf. She had also dealt with the reactions of lovers, both hearing and deaf. For her part, Katrina was excited about her progress in learning to sign. She was much less excited about discovering her ableistic assumptions and insensitivities, but she was working on them.*

Maintaining a power balance in their relationship was one of the most difficult challenges that Katrina and Susanne faced. For example, Katrina interpreted some telephone calls for Susanne. The tradeoff was that Susanne did more housework. It was an ongoing process to sort out which issues called for tradeoff negotiations and which were conflicts that had nothing to do with Susanne's being deaf.

Susanne's experience in managing her own and previous lovers' reactions to her deafness did not mean that issues never arose. However, it benefited the couple relationship, and Katrina, to have Susanne's past experience to draw from. It is a very different situation when a partner has an accident or is diagnosed as having an illness, and thus newly incurs a disability, during the course of a relationship.

## Adjusting to Chronic Illness and Disability as a Couple

*Erica had been concerned about feeling weak and tired, having blurred vision, pain in her left eye, and sometimes falling or feeling as though her limbs would not hold her. These symptoms had come and gone for a period of months. When she lost control of her bladder on two separate occasions, Erica summoned her courage and went to the doctor. After an exhaustive series of tests, she was told that she had multiple sclerosis (MS). In some ways she was relieved to get a diagnosis; she now had a name for what she had been experiencing. But she was afraid to tell Jay. They had been lovers for five years and had shared many difficult and joyous times. But Erica was uncertain how Jay, who was something of a "jock," would take the news that eventually Erica might have to use a wheelchair or die prematurely from the disease.*

Regardless of how Jay or Erica reacts to the news of the diagnosis, they will go through stages in their adjustment to Erica's diagnosis. These stages include disbelief, developing awareness, reorganization, resolution, and identity change.[7] Not everyone experiences all of these stages, nor do they follow in a predictable, orderly fashion. But it can be helpful to know that the feelings associated with these stages are the normal reactions to grieving a loss and moving on to a life that incorporates the illness. Whether we are coping with the death of a partner or the loss of our sight or mobility (or our partner's loss), we make the adjustment in steps. In relapsing or episodic chronic illnesses,[8] like multiple sclerosis or chronic fatigue syndrome, the need for grieving can be more easily ignored or denied because there can be periods of remission when the person feels fine. But when she does relapse, she may be overwhelmed with despair. For people with chronic illnesses it takes time to really know how much is lost and what losses need to be grieved. Like denial and anger, hope comes and goes. Losses may be grieved at different phases of a disease. A person in the early stages of diabetes, for example, will not yet grieve the loss of sensation in her fingers or toes because these symptoms occur in the later stages of the illness. Grieving often progresses from numbness, to disbelief, to pain and anger, to self-absorption about the loss, to acceptance, and then to reinvolvement with living. People move at various paces through the grieving process.

## Disbelief Stage

At first, both Erica and Jay were in shock. They weren't sure what to do or who to tell about the news. Even when they went through the motions of going to work or reading about MS, neither felt totally "there." Erica described it as her numb period. She was still numb when Jay entered her denial phase. Jay tried to convince herself, and Erica, that the test results had been a mistake. Then she decided that even if Erica did have MS, the course of her illness was not going to be the same as that of other people. Erica would definitely never even need a wheelchair. Erica's journey through the disbelief stage was somewhat different. She avoided talking with anyone about it. She tried to ignore her symptoms and pushed her physical limits even when she didn't need to.

## Developing Awareness Stage

As her denial gave way, Erica ranted and raved about her doctors and her rotten luck. "Why me?" she would shout over and over again. She was angry at everything and everybody. She was furious with her body for betraying her, with healthy people for being healthy, with friends who didn't mention the MS, and with those who asked about it. She alternated between being sarcastic with Jay and feeling guilty for taking her anger out on her partner.

Jay had a much easier time with Erica's anger than she did with the depression that came later in this stage. She understood Erica's frustration and rage. Now that she knew more about what this illness meant, her feelings were mixed. Like Erica, she was angry. "It's not fair" was her main theme. She was relieved that she was healthy and then felt guilty about feeling relieved. Mostly she was afraid of what the illness would mean for them both and for the relationship. Both Jay and Erica wisely sought out a number of support people. They recognized that they each needed to express their feelings but that they also needed to respect each other's limits. They did not want to burn each other out. In addition, Jay started jogging and Erica began to keep a journal.

It was Erica's depression that put the most stress on their relationship. Erica sought out a counselor in part because Jay was no help to her at all. Jay was critical of what she saw as Erica's "giving up on life." She responded to her partner's sadness by trying to cheer her up. In the process, she gave Erica the message that her feelings were not valid. When Erica was not cheered, Jay got irritated with her. The counselor helped Erica understand that her depression was a reaction to real events, to the losses and life changes she was going through. Erica was able to express her feelings and plan ways to cope with her depression. It took a while before Jay trusted Erica's counselor. She was glad that Erica had this outlet, but she felt that she had failed Erica somehow. If she had been a better partner, Erica wouldn't need a counselor. Eventually Jay was invited to attend some sessions with Erica. She was able then to acknowledge her feelings. They talked more openly about what they could and could not do for each other.

During these hard times, it was almost impossible to imagine that it would ever be any different. It took great effort for them both to keep from losing hope completely and from dwelling in the past, wishing things had not changed.

## Reorganization Stage

As Erica allowed herself to feel her anger and depression, she began to accept her limitations and to relate to her partner in ways that took this acceptance into account.

For Erica, the movement toward a state of acceptance was one of listening to herself and her feelings. This meant staying, for a time, with both her physical and emotional pain, and then sharing it with her partner if she wanted. Erica took responsibility for her own self-care as much as possible. She did what she could do and asked for help when she needed it. Erica and Jay learned all they could about MS. They began to find room for humor and celebration again in their lives.

Jay responded to the shift in Erica in this stage. She began to trust Erica to tell her when there was something she could do to help. Jay relaxed and allowed herself to take part in more activities that Erica could no longer participate in.

### Resolution Stage

By taking stock of what she could do, rather than focusing on what was lost, Erica learned to be realistic about herself and her abilities. She discovered, on the Internet, that there were support groups in her city for people with MS and that there were resources that might be helpful to her. She began to see herself as a member of the disabled community and even joked about being bicultural: lesbian and disabled. Jay began to see herself as a member of the "fringe" community, as she called it, made up of people who were partnered with women and men with disabilities.

### Identity Change Stage

Erica described her acceptance as allowing her to trust herself again. It filled her life, pushing out bitterness, anger, and defensiveness. She saw herself as valuable. She made the changes necessary to live her life and yet did not allow the MS to take over. She recognized that her illness was not her identity, but only a part of who she was.

Once she reached the identity change stage, Erica was more able to manage the anger and depression that she periodically felt. And it did not mean that she never had negative feelings or bad days. She often needed to remind herself, and Jay, that acceptance was not a capitulation to her disease and disability. For her, it was taking it in as a part of her life and learning to manage it. She refused to be condemned or useless.

Eventually, ten years after she had been diagnosed with MS, Erica needed to use a wheelchair. She and Jay both went through a miniversion of each of the adjustment stages over again. After some denial, they saw a few new problems that they had not counted on. They realized that they would have to move from their home or do some very costly renovation. The front door would have to be enlarged. The bathroom was inaccessible and so were the kitchen cupboards. The basement was impossible. They went through being angry and depressed about the cost and about how the world is set up for able-bodied people. Sometimes they were in the same phase, both angry or both depressed. Sometimes not. When they surfaced from their upset, they decided to stay put. The best plan seemed to be to apply for a bank loan to make their current home as accessible as possible.

## Pain

Many women who have disabilities are not ill and are not in pain. However, one of the realities of many chronic illnesses is physical pain. Pain is not easy to live with. It is exhausting, especially if it is a daily experience. Tolerance for pain varies by individual and emotional states, but it is easier to respond to if it is predictable.

For example, if Erica knows that her arm is going to hurt when she extends it fully, she will be prepared. She may not experience the pain as intensely if she can anticipate it. She has the choice of using her pain in an angry and manipulative way—by getting upset and trying to make her partner and friends feel bad or responsible. Another option is to use her pain as a teacher to reveal her limits. Some of these limits she may try to push past; some she may not. Erica may also choose to work with visualization and meditation or distract herself from the pain with movies, music, or books. What is crucial is that she acknowledge the pain and learn to live with it. It is also important that Jay knows what Erica's limits are and respects them.

For many people, the sense of helplessness in the face of their partner's pain and deterioration is very hard. Like many partners, Jay had to cope with the fact that she had no control over what was happening to Erica. She could not fix Erica, and she could not make the pain go away. Jay found it difficult to see Erica in pain. She knew she could not make the pain go away, and it was very hard for her to accept that. For Jay, acceptance of her own helplessness was the toughest thing to manage.

## Self-Esteem and Internalized Oppression

People born with disabilities who learned that they were all right and could do anything, and who always saw themselves as different but equal and healthy, are likely to have high self-esteem. Similarly, those who have a positive sense of themselves may more easily regain their self-esteem in the event that they acquire a disability or disabling chronic illness in later life. It can be more difficult for people with low self-esteem.

If you have a disability, you may need to become a warrior in order to build or regain your self-esteem. You may have to fight to be seen as sexual and able to have and raise children. You'll battle societal images of what is beautiful. You'll probably have to combat the fears of others about your dependency. You may have to fight for your right to work and be autonomous. And you may have to wage war with yourself to continue to love yourself and live a full life.

Accepting a stereotype held by those in the able-bodied world—whether it be the pitiful, complaining, and dependent "cripple" or the extraordinary brave and ever-smiling "super-crip" image—leads to internalized oppression. Either image denies your unique feelings and reactions. Adopting any "role" separates you from yourself and your loved ones. It is important to remember and remind other people that even though your body does not always work the way an able-bodied person's does, you are still your unique self. This attitude helps the illness or disability from turning into an identity. This balance gives both of you in a couple room to share, stretch, and grow with each other.

## Children, Work, and Independence

Historically, women with disabilities have been discouraged from having or rearing children. Although there maybe nothing to prevent this, there are some things to consider, such as other people's prejudices, physical aspects of pregnancy, the nature and cost of environmental adaptations to be able to care for a baby, and modifications in child-discipline strategies. For example, children of women with disabilities often have to learn to be responsive to verbal instructions. You may not be able to get to the child as quickly as an able-bodied mother could. Children develop an awareness of their parent's capabilities. If you are an able-bodied partner you may not need to rely on verbal instructions as much, but you do need to positively reinforce the child's response to them.

Like their heterosexual counterparts, lesbians who have disabilities must function in a society that has refused, for the most part, to acknowledge their presence and particular needs. As a result of both physical and psychological barriers, they are often unable to communicate, move around, or work to their fullest capacity or satisfaction.

The passage of the ADA, recent technological advances, and changing attitudes provide more work opportunities for people with disabilities. Many people find themselves fully accepted and in well-paying jobs that they enjoy. However, others experience the barriers of employers' reluctance to hire them, or they become the "token" after being hired. If one partner is no longer able to work, some of the problems a couple may face are financial: lost income and increased medical expenses. And some of the problem is emotional: the loss of identity associated with working and with the job. In addition, the application for retraining programs or for government assistance may be frustrating and discouraging. The working partner may feel burdened and overwhelmed, too. These kinds of problems require the same approach as many of those we have already discussed. Share feelings and listen to each other and find a support group of women with disabilities and their partners or create one from among friends.

There are more tools now than ever before to help people with disabilities maintain their independence. For the deaf there are special devices called TTYs, which allow communication over the telephone, more sign language interpretation at concerts and captioning on television, flashing lights that signal the doorbell, and trained dogs who "hear" for their owners. Specially designed light boards can help individuals who have severe mobility and communication disabilities communicate. Ramps, elevators, and wheelchair-accessible public transportation aid people with mobility disabilities. People with psychological disabilities, such as depression, are increasingly helped by improved therapies—pharmacological and otherwise.

Computers, email, and the Internet have increased the options for people with a variety of disabilities. Online "chatting" and email are naturals for people with hearing disabilities. Computers displaying very large type or with vocal modems are useful for the visually impaired. Dictation software is invaluable to people with quadriplegia or other disabilities that affect their ability to use their hands.

Improved accessibility allows women with disabilities and their partners to attend the same social and cultural events as everyone else. However, even as accessibility and attitudes improve, it behooves all of us, especially the able-bodied, to be sensitive to our own ableism and to challenge our legal and community systems to continue to make the necessary changes to eliminate the barriers that people with disabilities face.

## Support Systems

No one person can meet all the needs of another, whether or not the partner is ill or disabled. Both partners in a couple relationship need a variety of support systems. When an able-bodied woman becomes partners with a woman with a disability, her friendship patterns may change. It depends on the kind and the degree of the disability, but some of her friends may be uncomfortable with her partner, and the friendships may die out. New individual and couple friendships with able-bodied women may not seem to develop as expected. And for the partner with a disability, there is the reaction of her friends in the disabled community to her new partner. In spite of the complexities, these couples need friends, individuals and couples, as part of their lives.

Lesbians with disabilities or chronic illnesses need access to lesbian, gay, bi, and trans communities, as well as to communities of people with similar illnesses or disabilities. It is usually through our participation in these communities that we develop healthy self-esteem, which helps counteract the mainstream's negative stereotypes. When a woman is isolated from these supportive communities by others' attitudes, physical barriers, or her own inability to join gatherings, she is vulnerable to forgetting that she is a valuable, interesting, sexual, and vital person. She runs the risk of focusing on the negatives about herself, for example, what she cannot do, and of pulling further away from people. In some cases this can lead to depression or anxiety.

Lesbians with disabilities and chronic illnesses may have an additional hurdle to clear as they look for support. Disabled communities may be homophobic, and lesbian and gay communities may be ableist. In some large cities there are lesbian and gay disabled communities that offer lesbians with disabilities and their partners respectful support groups. If you do not have such an option, remember that others' prejudices are not about you, and very likely there are members of both communities who want to unlearn prejudice and be more available to you.

Couples where one, or both, of the women has been diagnosed with a chronic illness may need more intense forms of support. One of the gifts of the AIDS epidemic has been the development of mechanisms for supporting individuals with AIDS and their partners. In *Circles of Care,* Peggy Monroe and her colleagues adapted a Quaker tradition of extending care to members of the Quaker meeting community who need support. In this model, a group of people, usually ten to twelve, is part of the careteam. They compile an auxiliary list of the couple's other friends who have indicated a desire to help. The careteam meets regularly with the couple, giving support and helping with more concrete tasks such as getting meals or cleaning the house. Depending on how acute the couple's needs are, the careteam might meet as infrequently as every few months to share a meal and catch up with how the couple is doing. If an illness is in an acute phase, the team may arrange for members on the auxiliary list to bring meals, transport the woman with the illness to doctors' appointments, keep her company in the hospital, take a child to school, or do whatever is needed.[9] Our experience as members of such care-giving teams involves feeling privileged and blessed to be able to help in such a way. Individuals who have had such careteams report receiving enormous amounts of support, love, and much-needed practical help.

## Acute Illness

Family, both biological and chosen, is an important support system for most of us. This can be especially true when a couple discovers that one partner is seriously ill.

*When Max was diagnosed with breast cancer, she was terrified. Her mother had died of breast cancer and even though Max's cancer had been diagnosed as a slow-growing kind, she couldn't shake the sense of being doomed by her genetics. Her relationship with Sondra had never been tested this much in their ten years together and she wondered if Sondra would still want to stay with her if she had a mastectomy. Sondra was mostly worried about keeping up with their bills if Max had to be off work for chemotherapy or radiation. To their dismay, Sondra and Max discovered that some of their friends began to disappear. Even though they knew that some of them couldn't face their fears and their own vulnerability, it still hurt. They also realized that in their focus on Max's illness, they themselves had pulled away from friends.*

This couple decided that they each needed a broad support system. They wanted some of the same people in their individual support systems, but different people, too. They made a game of assigning people to categories. Category one included friends who could hear the full story or update each time they saw them. Category-two people could hear a shortened version of the story. Friends in category three were able to hear only positive news, and category-four folks couldn't hear much past "Everything is fine." They were aware, too, that their support people would shift around and be in different categories at various times. However, this game helped them maintain realistic expectations. It also encouraged them to continue to ask for support from someone, even though she had not been available at one particular time. That person might move into a different category at any time.

Women who have life-threatening illnesses, like their partners, have many of the same needs and challenges as do couples who live with disabilities and chronic illness. This is why we included breast cancer here even though it usually does not fall within our definitions of chronic illness and disability. Breast cancer and other life-threatening illnesses are similar to disabilities and chronic illness because sometimes there is a long period when remission is hanging over people's heads. There are also potentially disabling and chronic conditions related to acute illnesses, such as lymphodema.

Lesbian couples obviously have a higher chance of one of the partners being diagnosed with breast cancer than do other couples. Earlier detection of breast cancer means that more women are living through that diagnosis. Breast cancer is particularly relevant to lesbian couples since we are less likely to get regular mammograms (and Pap smears), which makes us more vulnerable for a later diagnosis at a less treatable stage.[10] We encourage you to get knowledgeable health care for early detection of breast cancer (as well as other illnesses) on a regular basis. If you are diagnosed with cancer, find a support group. Women who participate in support groups tend to live longer and more happily. If you are partnered with a woman with breast cancer, learn what you can about the illness, find a partner of survivors' support group, and find out how you can support her and yourself. We encourage all of you to find good, nonhomophobic health care (if possible), learn what you can about the illness, and use local and Internet sources for support and information.

Psychiatric illnesses may also offer a mixture of acute and chronic problems to manage.

*Stevie's growing-up years were full of trauma. Once Stevie's therapist explained to her about post-traumatic stress disorder (PTSD), Stevie understood why she had such a hard time every November. That month was when the worst childhood abuse had occurred. Some years her flashbacks and distress were so intense that she would admit herself to the psychiatric hospital so she could be in a safe place. As therapy progressed, her flashbacks and other symptoms were less severe and she was less in need of hospitalization.*

*It helped a lot that her partner, River, was so supportive. Before River came along, Stevie had been convinced that she would never be in a relationship. She figured that no one would ever understand, much less be able to live with, the legacy of her childhood. She had resisted getting involved with River but River was a patient woman. Gradually the past was receding for Stevie. River's perspective was simple: "Stevie was worth waiting for."*

Stevie's tenacity and faith in herself were the main reasons she could heal. In this case, she also needed ongoing therapy and the safety of the hospital when her own resources were not enough and her symptoms were especially acute. Obviously, the impact on the couple was enormous, but manageable. Stevie's dedication to healing and River's clarity about Stevie's worth gave them the energy to stay together.

# Sex

For many couples in which one or both partners are disabled or living with a disability or a chronic illness, sex and sexual issues are the same as they are for any other couple. For others, there may be particular considerations or accommodations. But there is no need to buy into the myth that being sexual is impossible. It is true that changing some modes of sexual expression can alter the response cycle, arousal, and sexual feelings, which may be the case for women with a new injury, illness, or disability. Fatigue and pain can alter or diminish sexual feelings. Lifestyle changes in work, money, or play may also affect sex, since sexuality is an expression of the whole person. If you worry about causing your partner pain, you are going to modify your sexual expressions and feelings. The best thing to do is talk to each other about what being sexual means, explore what will heighten your pleasures together, and then enjoy each other.

> *Sylvee was getting turned on. She loved the sensation of getting wet and excited as she waited for her new lover, Anika, to finish work and come over. They had planned a gourmet dinner and a leisurely evening in bed. Sylvee moved her walker around the bed as she set out candles to light the event. Originally, Sylvee had been nervous about being sexual with Anika. She didn't know how Anika would react to a woman with cerebral palsy coming on to her. But she had read Anika correctly—she was as turned on to Sylvee as Sylvee was to her. They had talked about what turned each of them on, or if there was anything either of them did not like, and Sylvee had told Anika that she could not use a dildo in the top position, because her arms weren't strong enough. Anika didn't seem to mind a bit. They had then practiced what they had talked about. Sex was good!*

## Suggestions and Hints

In the following sections we offer suggestions and hints for lesbians with a disability or chronic illness and their able-bodied partners. We include them knowing that they will apply for some but not all couples, depending on the nature of the disability. We encourage you to seek out resources that examine the issues that specifically impact you.

### Suggestions for a Partner with a Disability or Chronic Illness

Adjustment to chronicity in an illness or a disability is 10 percent physical and 90 percent emotional. Loving yourself influences your stress level, your physical/emotional/spiritual self-management, and your behaviors.

Loving yourself, whatever you look or feel like, makes healing more possible. It also makes it more likely to be attentive to other people and to experience loving feelings for them. A chronic condition brings stress, which lowers your ability to cope with the condition and even means that it will take less stress to cause stress. In reaction to stress, your body produces more sugar in your blood, muscles, and brain, which increases your heart rate and blood pressure, dilates your pupils, and releases norepinephrine into your system, producing anxiety. Around and around it goes, circling in on itself.

So, what to do? Try to love yourself! Be gentle and kind to yourself. Talk with your lover about the things that are going on with your body and spirit. Listen to her. Meditate and do deep muscle relaxation. Exercise as much as you can; the weakness created by the lack of exercise breeds on itself. Be aware of your physical and energy limits and tailor your activities to suit your needs. Let your partner do the things she wants to do, without you, if you are not able physically to share the activity. Remember you are a sexual and loving being. Listen to your body and spirit and believe that you are not your illness or disability. Ask for what you need. Remember that you may not always get your needs met, but it is fine and powerful to ask. When your partner cannot meet your needs, get them met by someone else, where possible. Do what you need to do to take care of yourself—including withdrawing, as long as it does not put you in a vacuum. Listen to your lover and her needs, too. She cannot be an extension of you, and she cannot live in a vacuum either. Accept yourself fully and realistically and you will create a positive self-image that you and your partner can share.

### Additional Hints for a Partner with a Disability or Chronic Illness

- Talk about your feelings and fears.
- Teach your partner about your illness or disability, including your potentialities.
- Check out your anger at your partner for not being disabled, if she is able-bodied.
- Maintain your independence but ask for help if you need it.
- If you are angry about the treatment of people with disabilities, consider doing something political about it.
- Make certain you have health directives, durable powers of attorney, and wills if you want your partner to have your possessions or the right to make medical, financial, or burial decisions should you become unable to do so.

- Have some separate friends from whom you can get special support.
- Get counseling if you need it.

### Hints for an Able-Bodied Partner of a Woman with a Disability or Chronic Illness

- Talk about your fears and feelings.
- Be considerate of your partner's energy level, physical and sensory limitations, and emotional resource limits.
- Learn about your partner's illness or disability on your own as well as from her.
- Be aware of your ableism.
- Create your own separate support system and share feelings with your partner.
- Remember that your partner's body is hers. You cannot fix it. You can just be her lover and help her when you can and when it is appropriate.
- Know the attitudes and challenges your partner faces as a woman with disabilities from the medical profession and society.
- If you are angry about the treatment of people with disabilities, consider doing something political about it.
- Remember that your partner's problems are not more important than yours. Ask for what you need.
- Be aware of your own limits in providing support and care for your partner. Ask for help when you need it.
- Get counseling if you need it.

A disability or illness may require a couple to meet challenges that the temporarily able-bodied world neither understands nor appreciates. No one can predict exactly how your relationship will be affected, but you both can learn to anticipate some of the problems and prepare strategies to deal with them. As with all couples, self-awareness and open, caring communication are key.

## CHAPTER 16

# ♪ Later Life

It is no secret that we live in an ageist society. One of the highest compliments we can pay an individual, especially a woman, is to tell her that she doesn't look her age. In Native-American cultures, the term "elder" indicates respect. Western culture has no such positive language for aging, with the possible exception of the movement to reclaim the word "crone" as a term honoring older women. Where other cultures value the wisdom and experience of older people, ours glorifies youth and devalues aging. It is true that there are physical changes with age: Older bodies are less flexible, hair turns gray, reaction time slows, and skin is less elastic. However, a youth-oriented culture regards these natural changes as something to be ashamed of or corrected by plastic surgery rather than seeing the lines on a woman's face as the merit badge of her experience.

The conventional psychology of aging is "almost completely devoted to a study of its discontents: aging as depletion, aging as catastrophe, aging as mortality."[1] There has been little vision and less said about the positive aspects and capacity for growth for people moving into their fifties, sixties, seventies, and beyond. A notable exception has been Betty Friedan's book *Fountain of Age,* which documents the extraordinary possibilities of intimacy and purpose, of "fulfillment beyond career, bonding that transcends youthful dreams of happy-ever-after, and a richer, sweeter intimacy not tied to mechanical measures of sexual activity but to deep and honest sharing."[2] Later life certainly brings new challenges for lesbians and for lesbian couples. But it is far from the dreaded view of age as only a decline from youth. Developmental issues of later life include getting adult children launched and sometimes relaunched into life, caring for aging parents, facing death, coping with loss, managing work and retirement, dealing with mild or even serious health problems, and planning for the future. Of course, these issues are present in different ways depending on age—even a mild health problem may be more limiting at eighty-five than at sixty. Some of the issues are not solely limited to later life, and many are not specific to being lesbian. Deciding how out to be—which continues to be an issue throughout the life span—certainly is specific as are other issues, such as finding housing, developing social support, and providing for spousal rights.

In this chapter we discuss how the challenges of later life—difficult as they may be—can also provide opportunities for new pleasures, personal growth, and freedom. In a recent study of lesbians over fifty-five, the women were generally very satisfied with their lives. They looked back with no regret and, with the exception of those who were seriously ill, looked forward with enthusiasm. They mentioned the deepening of their appreciation for their partner, the joy of becoming a grandmother, the relief of not worrying so much about being out, and the pleasure of having more time with their partner to do the activities they enjoy. Many described later life as a time of tremendous spiritual growth when they found renewed purpose and meaning in their lives.[3]

## How Old Is Older?

*As usual, Estelle handed her membership card to the receptionist at her gym. When she looked at the card, the young woman exclaimed enthusiastically, "Oh, I see you will soon be eligible for the senior discount." Estelle was taken aback; she hadn't realized that turning fifty would include senior discounts.*

*When she received the government pamphlet about Medicare, Norma was insulted to see herself described as one of the "elderly." As far as she was concerned, sixty-five was definitely not elderly. Her mother was in her nineties. Now that was elderly.*

*Ilana's doctor was skeptical about prescribing contact lenses for her because she was in her late seventies. She told him, "Other people my age might be too old for contacts, but I certainly am not." And she got her lenses.*

Perhaps partly because the "baby boomers" are aging, there is more interest, research, and information in the popular press about getting older. This
material is beginning to have a more positive spin than traditionally has been
the case. Articles about menopause, caring for aging parents, and active
retirement abound in magazines and in the media. A few decades ago, women
in their forties might identify themselves as "older." Nowadays many women
in their seventies reserve the term "old" to describe those other than themselves. To a twenty-year-old, forty is "older," while someone sixty thinks of
forty as "young." One woman we know jokingly defines older as being "more
than ten years older than me."

How an individual identifies herself depends on her life situation, health,
and fitness. How a culture defines "older" is much more a matter of conven-
tion—not to mention politics and social policy. For example, sixty-five has
been a marker of "old" because that is when a person is eligible for Social
Security. When the nineteenth-century German Chancellor Otto von
Bismarck established the social security pension system in 1889, he arbitrarily
set the age for retirement at sixty-five. This was an age that very few people of
the time actually reached because the average life expectancy then was about
thirty-seven years.[4] The American Association for Retired Persons (AARP)
allows membership at fifty, and you can participate in Elderhostel programs at
fifty as well. Senior discounts begin to apply anywhere from ages fifty to sixty-
five. In the world of gerontology research, various authors have used different
age criteria to divide later life into categories with descriptors such as "late middle age" and "the young old." And all of these classifications are arbitrary. In this
chapter, we have adopted the definition of later life as being fifty-five and over.

## What's History Got to Do with It?

We are all affected by the tenor of the time in which we live. Our perceptions of ourselves and of our couple relationship as well as how we live our
lives depends, in part, on our age. For lesbians, or gay women—to use the
language many older lesbians prefer—the impact of history depends, in particular, on the era when we identified ourselves or became romantically
involved with other women.

Lesbians in their fifties, sixties, seventies, eighties, and nineties may all
describe themselves as older, but there are tremendous differences in these
women's experiences. Those who came of age—were in their late teens or
early twenties—in the 1920s through the 1960s faced pervasive and unchal-
lenged homophobia in a society that expected women to marry and take a
secondary role to their husbands. Gays and lesbians were viewed as perverse

and diseased. Lesbians were portrayed as loathsome, mannish, corrupting creatures, not fit for normal society.[5]

Not surprisingly, many young women who had glimmerings of their attraction to women either did not act on these feelings, or did and then changed course and married. In the face of such oppressive homophobia, those who continued in the lifestyle had few choices. They could try to assimilate and pass unnoticed, go deeply into the closet, live two lives, or become part of the small "out" gay/lesbian world in such places as New York's Greenwich Village. The choice of invisibility made by many older lesbians must be understood in the context of their history and experience in society.

*When she was nineteen, Jeanne's parents committed her to a psychiatric hospital because she was a lesbian.*

*Evvie always wanted to be a teacher. In her last year of college, she went into the closet because she didn't dare be openly, or even quietly, lesbian in the 1950s—especially in the teaching profession.*

*Bernice remembers how she and her friends would go to the bars; there was also a club in the city where she lived. But as soon as they left, they went right back into the straight life. The people she associated with at the bars were not people she associated with when she wasn't there, and they didn't associate with her either. It was all very separate in the 1950s—it was almost like living two lives.*

*Even though the times are different now, Bernice still keeps her personal life personal. It has become a way of life for her, and she is not comfortable mixing her worlds.*

A number of women married instead of pursuing their attraction to other women. Some thought that marriage would "cure" them, so they denied their attraction to women. Others wanted to have children and the only way to do that was to be married. Still others did not have any inkling about their sexual orientation until much later in life. Women who married and then came out after Stonewall and the advent of the women's movement got involved with other women in the more hospitable and lesbian- and gay-friendly atmosphere of the 1970s and beyond.

*As a teenager Flo and her girlfriend were caught kissing by her girlfriend's mother and there was a big ruckus made about it. After that, she began dating boys and trying to do what she was supposed to do. She went to a psychiatrist to get "cured" and eventually married because the psychiatrist thought it would be a good idea.*

*In 1975, twenty years and three children later, Flo volunteered at a local women's center and fell in love with another woman. That experience led to her coming out.*

*Looking back, Ava acknowledges that there were signs that she was bisexual when she was quite young. However, being from a small town in the Midwest, she followed the expected path and in her early twenties married a man she describes as a "really nice guy." It wasn't until two years after her divorce in 1984 that she recognized her attraction to women. After that, she dated both sexes for a while until she met Silvia. They will soon celebrate their ten-year anniversary.*

The legacy of homophobia is fear, self-hatred, and denial. It is likely that many more women, and couples, would have called themselves gay, lesbian, or bisexual had they come of age when there was less oppression, more support, and the words to describe their feelings and experience.

## How Out to Be

The issue and process of coming out lasts a lifetime. In addition to the evolving cultural climate, there are always new situations, people, and relationships that raise the question for lesbian couples of how out to be. Being out is a continuum; it is not an either-or situation. For example, you can be out only to yourself, out to just your partner, out to close friends and family, out in the workplace, or out publicly in the world.

Coming out is a personal decision for each woman. However, we also believe that there are definite advantages to being more out rather than less. In addition to the political advantages of strength in numbers and the community advantage of having more role models for younger lesbians, there are personal benefits, including a sense of being honest and true to who you are, having less fear and more freedom, and feeling more whole and good about yourself.

Although some older lesbians have been comfortably out from a young age, many more developed a closeted lifestyle that has persisted. Some are uncomfortable with the "L" word and with other labels. Others worry about negative consequences like losing their job, being refused access to their grandchildren, or outing their partner who is still working even if they themselves are retired. Some older lesbians have only recently come out to themselves and do not yet feel inclined to come out to the world. As it becomes easier to be out, however, more older women are telling friends and family and even going public.

*Mary Louise and Celia fell in love when they both were twenty. After she ended their relationship, Celia married and had three children. When her youngest was sixteen, Celia at last rejoined her life with Mary Louise's. For her part, Mary Louise had lived a totally closeted lifestyle, as befitted a teacher starting out in the 1950s. Initially, Celia rented the apartment next door to Mary Louise's as a protective cover, but eventually they bought a house together.*

*Until recently they never went to lesbian events and knew only one other lesbian couple. With retirement, Mary Louise's attitude changed. While she's still not the type to run around telling everybody, "I'm gay," she has relaxed a lot.*

*Ella never really thought about being gay at all. She always found others "like herself," had various liaisons, and then settled down with Jerusha, her partner of sixty-plus years. Both were professional women who enjoyed their careers and they lived openly together but never discussed their lesbianism with anyone, or even with each other. They blended in and considered themselves as normal as the next couple.*

*It wasn't until a former coworker asked if she would be willing to talk about her life with a group that was doing a lesbian-history project that Ella ever acknowledged that she was a lesbian. And that was at the age of ninety-two.*

When an older lesbian couple is not out, the heterosexual community likely assumes that they are two single, divorced, or widowed women who are making the best of their unmarried situation. Although sometimes people try to act as matchmakers for them with eligible men, often they are treated as a couple—albeit an asexual couple. They are invited places together, are asked to host events together at their home, and are usually assumed to be spending time together. This may work out very well for some couples, particularly those in geographical areas where there is less acceptance. However, when a couple is out, there are opportunities for social support not only as individuals but also for the couple relationship itself.

## Social Support

Older lesbians describe their main sources of support as chosen and/or biological family and friends.[6]

*Cora and Marlene had been together for fifty-five years, ever since they met in the navy during World War II. They were not officially out to any of their family members, but were both treated as family by everyone because they had lived together for so long.*

*Jo-Linda and Winn met through mutual friends at an AA meeting. They became lovers on Jo-Linda's seventieth birthday, and six months later they were trying to find ways to justify living together. Winn's daughter, Nan, could not understand why her mother wanted to leave her cozy apartment in Nan's house and move in with a virtual stranger.*

Even though the women in each of these situations have a lot of individual support, they do not have acknowledgment and recognition for their relationship. For those who are out, there is more of a possibility of support for the couple relationship.

*Bess had been with her partner, Jonnie Mae, for five years before she even considered telling anyone in her biological family about their relationship. She first told her four adult children. Even though she knew they really enjoyed Jonnie Mae, she hadn't been sure how they would respond. She was very relieved and pleased that they took it in stride—except for her oldest son, Tom, who was a born-again Christian. While the rest of her children were very supportive, Tom's response was that he would "pray for her." Bess figured that a positive reaction from three out of four of her kids wasn't bad.*

*Lois and Faye were part of a small community of about a dozen gay men and women who lived within twenty miles of each other in a rural part of their state. They initially met through a series of potluck socials hosted by the couple who had been in the area the longest. Out of that grew lots of different activities, including helping each other with building projects. Over time the commitment of the group to look out for each other just naturally grew. For example, when Faye brought Lois home from the hospital after her surgery, they found that their crew of friends had cleaned the house, filled the fridge with food, and stacked the woodpile.*

*It started as an informal couples group. Bobbi and Gayle were each newly out and in their first relationship with a woman. They approached some lesbians at their church who they knew were coupled about getting together to talk about relationships. Eventually a group of four couples clicked, and*

*these couples have been getting together regularly for the past seven years.*
*They plan activities, go on trips together, and most important, they talk*
*about anything and everything.*

Whether with family and friends or through work or other activities,
older gay women frequently identify these connections with others as
extremely important in their lives. Longstanding friendships and relationships are often particularly important.

## Community

Some lesbians find community primarily with their biological or chosen
family and friends; others find it through work or volunteer and political
activities. Gay and lesbian organizations, support groups, twelve-step programs, and church groups often form part of this sense of community.[7]

There are now more organizations and resources for older women—
Older Women's League (OWL) and the Gray Panthers—as well as those
specifically for older lesbians (and gay men). The latter type includes the Gay
and Lesbian Association of Retiring Persons (GLARP) in Los Angeles; Old
Lesbians Organizing for Change (OLOC); Senior Action in a Gay
Environment (SAGE) in New York City; Red Dot Girls/Elder Lesbian
Initiative in Seattle; and Gay and Lesbian Outreach to Elders (GLOE) and
Lesbian and Gay Aging Issues Network in San Francisco.

It is important for the broader lesbian community to see older lesbians as
whole people. Women in later life have interests and ideas that are valuable
in activities and discussions other than those directly related to aging.
Whenever community committees are formed or political action undertaken,
outreach should focus on involving the whole community, including older
people. They bring a perspective no one else has. Qualities that emerge in
later life, namely the ability "to see the picture whole, and its meaning deep
and to tell it true,"[8] provide a wisdom that can serve the community well.

If present trends continue, there will be many more out and older lesbians
who will have an even stronger voice within our communities. In the mean-
time, the lesbians who are now in later life deserve appreciation and respect
for their life experiences, in part because their experience and pioneering
made possible the present-day visibility and vitality of the lesbian community.

Unfortunately, even within the lesbian community, ageism exists. Older
lesbians may still be invisible—they may not be acknowledged, sought after,
or listened to. When ageism is compounded by racism or classism, older lesbians may feel especially alienated from the broader community.

*Both in their late sixties when they moved to a new city, Angela and Maureen went to a lesbian "over forties" group for a while. But most of the women there were in their forties and the discussion topics and activities weren't of much interest to Angela and Maureen. They were one of the few couples in the group and it seemed to them that most of the women were trying to find new partners. They finally hooked up with a group of gay men and lesbians—many of them couples—who were closer to their age and shared more of their interests.*

Some women have started their own support groups specifically for older lesbians if none were available. For those who are comfortable being out beyond a small circle of intimate friends and family, such a group can provide additional support and stimulation.

In addition to connections with age peers, it can be beneficial and even fun for older lesbians to have contact with younger lesbians—and vice versa. Older lesbians often complain that younger women aren't interested in or inclusive of them—and their music is too loud. Younger lesbians complain that older women, when they can be found, discount younger dykes' experiences. The following excerpt from a commentary titled "Baby Dyke" appeared in a newsletter of the Red Dot Girls.[9]

*"Did you call me a baby dyke? Listen up! Just because you've had more time on the planet than me doesn't mean you still don't have a few things to learn. . . . I guess I would just like to know how old I have to be before you give me a little respect, not to mention half a chance on a relationship level. . . . You have to know that when I look at you, I see a sexy woman who was a lesbian before it was even quasi-acceptable. You were the one who made it possible for me to be the strong, proud, outspoken woman that I am today. When did you start caring what everyone else thinks, especially when it concerns your happiness? Hey, just kiss me already! You know I'm right."*

## Sex and Intimacy

Unlike the author of the "Baby Dyke" commentary, many people—not only the young and middle-aged but even older people—assume that sex is over in later life. Some older lesbians may have stopped being sexual because of a disability or a serious illness. Others have simply grown tired of it. They may have had sex routinely with the same partner for years and have compensated for its dullness by developing satisfying nonsexual activities. It is possible to live a happy and satisfying life without sex. You don't need to feel incomplete or inadequate if sex does not play a central role in your couple relationship.

However, you don't have to pretend sex is not important to you if it is. Even if the hormonal changes of menopause affect the level of your sexual comfort and responsiveness, it doesn't need to mean the end of sexual activity and enjoyment.

*Felicia missed sex. She understood all the reasons why she and Zelda were not having sex as often, but she still missed it. Since Zelda had stopped getting very wet when she was turned on, she had not liked genital sex. Zelda described it as losing her markers of when she was excited, plus it hurt when Felicia put her fingers in her. It all added up to too much work and not enough fun. Zelda also did not think about sex as often as Felicia did, so she didn't miss it nearly as much.*

This vignette illustrates a number of changes that can affect sex. While some women report an increase in sexual interest and desire as they grow older, others report a decrease. Changes for women approaching menopause include a decrease in vaginal lubrication and a thinning of the vaginal walls, which may make penetration more difficult, but none of these changes need be the death knell for sex. Sex may just require more time and the assistance of one of the many sensual lubricating products available.

Although there is relatively little data on the sexual interests and experiences of older people, what there is demonstrates that relatively healthy older people who enjoy sex are capable of doing so until very late in life.[10]

*Iris and Charlotte had the giggles again. This often happened when other people made assumptions about them—and their relationship. Today it was about the young intern at their physician's office; he had been a little shocked when he saw Iris's black lace underwear and had stuttered a bit when he asked her to remove it for an examination. They figured he expected baggy cotton briefs with no hint of sexiness. Iris and Charlotte were used to that kind of ignorance. Actually, they rather enjoyed being a little outrageous and shocking people sometimes.*

*Roma and Claudette had been lovers for three years, and they were enthusiastic about sex. Roma came out when she was sixty-two and told everyone she was making up for lost time. Claudette had always enjoyed sensual activities; she now devoted herself to discovering new ways to indulge her senses.*

Sexual pleasure is not an exclusively physical experience, nor is it necessarily an aerobic one. Couples can learn to transcend the limitations of the body—whether the limitation is one of age or disease. In fact, many women report that their sexual lives have grown richer in later life.

*Agnes and Lena had been partners, and lovers, for thirty years. They still loved to touch each other and took pleasure in noticing how their bodies and responses had changed through the years. They did not have genital sex often, but in some ways they enjoyed sex together even more than when they had first met.*

*Before she even had her mastectomy Katrina confided to her partner, Naomi, that she was worried about the effect it would have on their sex life. They discovered, in exploring new ways to touch and respond to each other, that their intimacy deepened.*

The sex of later life is not the same as the sex of youth. Not only is it not physically possible, but also our focus has changed. Life is more and more about being real, and relationships are about intimacy. The heart of intimacy (as we discuss in Chapter Four) is not sexual. Sex can be an avenue to intimacy, and potentially even more deeply so in later life. But intimacy is about opening up to each other; it's about sharing, truly knowing, and being known.

## Work and Retirement

Older women who knew they were lesbians fairly early in life also knew they would need to support themselves financially. Since they did not plan to marry a man who would take care of them, education and work were often at the top of their priority list.

*In 1943, when she was seventeen, Annette's parents kicked her out of the house because she was gay. She lived with a group of women in a boarding house and got a job at a shipyard. After the war, when all the jobs were reserved for the returning men, Annette realized she needed more education and enrolled in nursing school.*

Women who married young and later recognized their sexual orientation were often in very different circumstances. Those in long-term marriages may have worked outside the home, but usually their husband was the primary breadwinner and their work—and income—was secondary. Some who had children stayed with their husbands for the sake of the children or for financial support—or both. Others left anyway, knowing that it could be rough, at least for a while.

*Sunny stayed married to her husband because the longer she stayed married, the more his retirement fund grew, and living in a community property state, she knew she would get half of it. Having worked in the home raising five children, she was well aware that her job options would be limited as an older women with only volunteer experience. As she points out, "There weren't any displaced homemaker programs back then."*

*Eventually Gracie started making decent money at a job she liked. At first it was hard, especially because her husband, Tom, stopped giving her any support for the kids once he found out that she was a lesbian.*

Many, if not most, of us who are fifty-five and older are still working. Some of us plan to work as long as our health allows it, others look forward eagerly to retirement, and still others change course and embark on a new career in later life. As we age, we often become clearer about our interests and skills. Jobs and careers that suited us when we were younger may no longer be a good fit.

*In her thirties, Lana was a Head-Start teacher and worked with disadvantaged families through a hospital-based program. When she was in her late fifties, she realized that she was tired of working for other people. She went back to school to earn a degree in social work and set up a business as a consultant for hospitals and state organizations that worked with poor families. As a happy side effect, her excitement about her new work had a stimulating influence on her partner, Trinity, who was motivated to start her own greeting-card business. This gave an added zest to their relationship.*

The assumption that we will all one day stop working, either by choice or because we are forced to do so, has long been a fact of life in our society. But it has not been that long. The Social Security system and mandatory retirement were first introduced in the United States in 1935, during the Depression, not from humanitarian concerns for older Americans, but because their forced removal from the workforce would create more jobs for the young. Mandatory retirement grew in later years because it was a simple and legal means for employers to rid themselves of their most expensive workers.[11]

Retirement research is not always consistent, but the one element that reliably appears is the importance of choice. Regardless of when retirement takes place or how a job is left, personal, individual control over the situation makes the difference in terms of health and life satisfaction.[12]

*Bernadette had worked for the state for more than twenty years when she began to think seriously about retirement. Through the years she had enjoyed her work, but recently her department had been reorganized yet again and she wasn't sure if her job would be the same. However, she felt that she needed to stay at least five more years to take best advantage of her pension plan. She called it her "golden handcuffs."*

*Phyllis jumped at the chance when her company offered her a generous early-retirement package. Her partner, Lorraine, who was ten years older than she, had retired already. Here was the chance to put their plans of moving closer to their grandchildren into action even earlier than they had dreamed.*

When one member of a couple retires before the other, there are adjustments that need to be made. If your partner retires before you do, you may resent her freedom to sleep in, play golf, and do what she wants when she wants. If she decides to take over the home responsibilities, you may see this as a boon or an encroachment. If she wants to do more things away from home, this, too, can be a source of conflict or pleasure.

For her part, the retiree has a lot more time available and—depending on her interests and ability to create purposeful activities—may get bored.

*Rhoda and Marguerite had been lovers for twenty-six years. When Marguerite retired, they almost broke up. Marguerite had always been the main wage earner, with Rhoda getting a job outside the home every now and again when they wanted to do something special. In general, Rhoda took care of the house. When Marguerite had no job to structure her time, she sat around the house and interfered with Rhoda's routine. They saved their relationship by moving to Arizona and becoming caretakers at a mobile-home park. Marguerite did the maintenance work, while Rhoda collected rents and kept the books.*

Retirement is often a dramatic enough shift to require renegotiating some aspects of the couple relationship. If your retirement income drops significantly, and your partner's income is not enough to absorb the loss, you will have to adjust your lifestyle. Some couples decide to share their living space with others or to buy food in bulk with other households to save money. Some women take on part-time work or do odd jobs for more income.

*When she retired after years in retail sales, Clarissa supplemented her small union pension by selling jewelry at local swap meets. She loved buying, bargaining, meeting interesting people, and being out in the world. Sometimes her partner, Gwen, came with her. Gwen loved to see Clarissa happier than she could ever remember seeing her.*

Because women earn less than men, and older women have had more time to experience this discrimination, many do not have enough money set aside to provide for a comfortable retirement. Unlike Clarissa, they may not be able to find work that they love or may be afraid that they won't be able to. Planning ahead is important to increase the likelihood that retirement is a chance to do what you always wanted to do or what you never had the chance to do. Many people actually become busier when they retire. Some have been so burdened by their jobs that they have really stopped living. When they quit work, they come alive.

*When Mavis retired from nursing, she immediately signed up to provide international disaster relief for the Red Cross. That allowed her to combine her love for nursing with her desire to travel. Her partner, Norine, also a nurse, planned to do the same thing when she retired. They hoped to be able to do some assignments together.*

*Emmie thoroughly enjoyed her volunteer work with people with AIDS. She discovered that the work changed her attitudes and feelings. Not only was she getting more comfortable and confident as she got older, but she was also finding it to be a time of deep spiritual growth.*

## Menopause

Biology dictates that menopause and its sister, menstruation, can only happen to both members of a couple when both are biologically female. While we focus on menopause in this section, we want to acknowledge that it can be humorous and frustrating to have two premenstrual women in the same house. In situations where one or both of you have very intense symptoms, it is important to take seriously each other's discomfort and possible irritability and to find ways to manage the impact on your relationship. This may include seeking help for symptom relief from traditional or alternative health-care providers.

Menopause is an important rite of passage, much like the onset of menses was in our earlier years. This transition can be a relief or a loss if you still want the ability to bear children. Some women have severe symptoms while others hardly notice a change. For many of us, menopause signals the beginning of a new phase of life—when we have accrued some wisdom from our life experience and are usually still healthy enough to enjoy it.

Even before we reach menopause (technically one year menstruation-free), many of us experience a variety of physical changes that highlight the fact that we are going through the aging process. Some of these perimenopausal symptoms are difficult and potentially life changing, while others are humorous.

*Nell had many annoying—and even debilitating—symptoms as she approached menopause. During this difficult time, she found that she needed a "support team" of other perimenopausal women, alternative and traditional health-care providers, and friends to help her sort through the conflicting advice and design—and redesign—a plan tailored to her unique needs.*

*Mimi and Anne were fifty-one and fifty-six. They had been partners for ten years, had made it through stressful family reunions, survived Mimi's shift to vegetarianism, and considered themselves good friends. However, Anne wasn't sure she could handle this latest challenge. They were both having hot flashes and Mimi was more irritable than she had ever been. At least five times a night Mimi would moan and throw off her covers—and Anne's too. Anne would pull them back up, fall asleep, and then she, too, would have a hot flash and throw off the covers. They were not getting enough sleep. On top of that, Mimi's irritability, while not awful, was grating on Anne's nerves because even little disagreements were more unpleasant. Both women were looking forward to being done with this "little" transition.*

Menopause, whether occurring by the natural aging process or prematurely from trauma or hysterectomy, affects each woman's body differently. Some symptoms are more common, such as changes in sleep patterns, poor memory, hot flashes, irregular or very heavy periods, vaginal dryness, and thinning body hair. Migraine headaches, inexplicable panic attacks, and depression are among the rarer symptoms.

Until recently, menopause was not discussed much or well understood. Susan Love, in *Dr. Susan Love's Hormone Book,* does a wonderful job of describing menopause as a natural process rather than a disease. She outlines the signs and symptoms and suggests ways to prevent or manage them.[13] If partners treat menopause as one more difference that needs teamwork, and approach it with respect and humor, they may actually find it a "bonding experience"!

## Health

Like menopause, age does not equate to disease. However, the reality of aging is that it includes the possibility of frailties, disabilities, chronic conditions, or sudden mishaps. We can't deny that aging ends in death. However, most of us will be able to pursue our interests and be involved in activities throughout our lives. Under optimal conditions, serious disability and loss of function due to age are not apparent until shortly before death. While there is no "cure" for aging, we need to focus on maintaining our health, enhancing our vital function, and getting good medical care when we need it.

*Patrice's physician told her that she had to change her eating habits and that she should exercise daily, or she might not live to retire. Makena, her new partner, was a yoga instructor and a nutrition educator. Together they developed a food plan and an exercise routine that gradually moved Patrice toward improved health.*

*An avid skier all her life, Vida was not deterred when she started having trouble with her knees. She took up snowshoeing and even got her partner, who would never consider skiing, to try it.*

Sometimes, managing the challenges of physical illness, an accident, or a limitation can positively affect our emotional and spiritual selves. As we slow down or make alterations, we may focus on aspects of our being that we formerly ignored, thereby allowing ourselves to grow in unexpected ways.

*Marla thought that she knew what living fully, one day at a time, was. After all, she had twenty-five years of sobriety through AA. But when she almost died from a heart attack, it changed her life dramatically. As she told her partner, Davida, "The colors seem brighter, the trees are more beautiful, and life just tastes sweeter now." Her spiritual side blossomed.*

*After she suffered a near-crippling back injury in a car accident when she was in her fifties, Gaia took up weightlifting. For the first two years every workout hurt. But blessed with a good trainer and her own determination, she stuck with it. After a while the lifting not only kept her back pain at bay, but it also gave her a centeredness that carried her for days. And at the age of sixty, she won her first trophy.*

*During her bout with breast cancer, Dorthea became involved in support groups and activities with other women who were battling the disease. She found new friends and a new purpose in her life as she got more involved in lesbian health-care issues. However, she also developed a keen sense of her own mortality as she witnessed women in her support groups die.*

Even if you both are healthy, you may make some decisions based on your physical conditions, capacities, or limitations. You may decide to play more doubles tennis than singles, get a larger-screen television, drive for four hours a day on road trips instead of the former seven or eight, or hire someone to clean the eaves troughs instead of getting up on the roof yourself. When you aren't healthy, or when your partner isn't, you will likely both experience a gamut of emotions from sadness to frustration to gratitude to anger. (See Chapter Fifteen.) As with other issues, the more information you have about your situation and your wants, the easier it is for you and your partner to effectively manage them.

## Spousal Rights

For lesbian couples, as with other couples, one member will almost surely survive the other. A partner's death may be anticipated or may come unexpectedly, leaving little or no time for a couple to prepare or process its meanings and impact. This leaves the survivor to do the grieving process alone. Regardless of the amount of notice, the grieving process can be eased by friends, family, and the survivor's memories of the couple's life together. We talk more about dealing with a partner's death in Chapter Seventeen.

Most coupled older lesbians have given some thought to how to provide for each other when one dies. Some have kept their resources separate so there will be no question or challenge about inheritance. Many report that they have had a will, power of attorney, and power of medical attorney drawn up, naming their partner as the beneficiary and decision-maker. In addition, a health-care directive, which clearly specifies your wishes about what you want and don't want done to prolong your life, is essential to make sure your wishes are respected. This document can give your partner the confidence and reassurance that she will need—and the medical professionals will respect—so the decisions she may have to make are what you would want.

*Alberta was very touched when her partner, Cynthia, announced that she had gone into the personnel office of the institution where she had worked for forty years and made Alberta the beneficiary of her retirement plan.*

*Polly and Lenora had been meaning to get legal papers drawn up but never got around to it. Then when she was seventy-eight, Polly had a stroke that left her partially paralyzed and unable to speak. Since Lenora had no legal status with the health-care providers, all of the decisions about Polly's care were made by Polly's sister and brother. Lenora was grateful that she had a reasonably good relationship with Polly's siblings so they included her in the discussions. Nonetheless, she often felt very frustrated.*

Challenges to a partner's rights can arise when one or both of you are closeted. This is especially true if you have not prepared the appropriate legal documents. If your partner is gravely ill or dies, you may not be accorded the same concern or rights—such as hospital visitation and medical consultation—as a heterosexual spouse or domestic partner would be given. Nor will your grief and loss be treated as seriously as it would be if people know about your relationship. If your partner was not out to her family, you may have a hard time dealing with them and have difficulty maintaining any semblance of spousal rights. Her grown children and grandchildren may not believe, or want to believe, that their aged parent or grandparent had a woman partner.

Being out, by itself, does not offer complete protection, of course. But it does put biological families on alert and provides an opportunity to work through potential problems before they arise. Out or not, every couple needs to have powers of attorney and wills that protect their interests.

*Addie and Gisele met when they were both in their seventies. Within six months they had moved in together. Neither had ever come out to her family, and they were both afraid that in case of death the other's family would intervene and take over all the decisions and property. They decided to see a young woman lawyer whom Addie had heard speak on gay rights. They drew up wills and powers of attorney. Then they came out to their families. Gisele's family was generally supportive, but Addie's children wanted to have her declared incompetent.*

Families may need time to adjust. An older woman may always have been a lesbian, but she may never have come out to her biological family. The news may shock, or at least surprise, them. Family members may react first and come to their senses later, as Addie's did. Or the family may be delighted that their sister, mother, or grandmother has found someone to be with and love. Although families generally seem to mellow over time and become more accepting rather than the reverse, they may never come around. These possibilities need to be weighed when a couple makes the decision to come out.

## The Future

Lesbians in later life look to the future with a mix of hope and concern.[14] The most common concerns include housing, financial security, illness, losing the support of partners and friends through death, and ensuring that they and their partners will continue to have control over their lives.

As we age, it can become more difficult or of less interest to live in the same situation we did when we were younger.

*Much as they loved their acreage, Erlene and Devonne decided to move to a smaller house in town where they had less to maintain and were nearer shopping and services. They had friends who had moved into condos and apartments, but Erlene and Devonne weren't ready to give up gardening quite yet. This new house was all on one floor and relatively barrier-free, so they figured it would still work for them even if one of them eventually needed to use a wheelchair.*

*Edie and Dixie got interested in cohousing. They traveled around the country looking at different cohousing communities and searching for a compatible group. They finally settled on one in a small town—not too far from a city. They figured they could get the smaller feel and slower pace they wanted but still have access to a larger urban center for cultural events.*

Depending on background and individual family styles, lesbians in later life may have the option of moving in with family. While this can work out well, it is important to be very clear about arrangements.

*When Lonnie's daughter and son-in-law built their new house, Lonnie and her partner, MerryLee, helped finance it. In exchange, a mother-in-law apartment was built into the plans. It was a very separate unit, and all involved were very clear about the financial arrangement—and just how much babysitting would be available. Since Lonnie and MerryLee spent about four months of the year at an RV park in the Southwest with a bunch of other lesbians from various parts of the country, Lonnie's daughter would water their plants.*

As we age, we may need help to continue living independently. Many lesbians are estranged from their biological families and do not have children they can look to for assistance. Most older lesbians are hopeful that their support networks—their chosen family—will be available to help them maintain control of their lives.[15] Thankfully, the options for supportive care have expanded from the days when the only choice—if moving in with family was not possible—was to go to a nursing home. Now there are more services to help bridge the gap between totally independent self-care and institutional care, whether on a one-time or ongoing basis. In a number of cities, there are LGBT retirement projects, specifically for lesbian, gay, bisexual, and trans-gendered people.

Although couples who are financially comfortable have more options, there are also ways for women with little money to get the assistance they need to remain in their own homes. Sometimes older couples house-share with a younger person in exchange for help with cleaning, yard work, personal hygiene, or cooking. In many areas there are senior-services programs (some even lesbian-friendly) that can help with information, referral, and solutions to such practical challenges as house maintenance, heating costs, and nutritious meals.

*When she had to go on dialysis, Nila was relieved to find out that it could be done at home. The machine was older and it took longer, but she wouldn't have to travel the long distance to the hospital. Her partner, Ursula, was relieved, too—she didn't want Nila driving so much.*

*Darlene and Juliana moved into an assisted-living facility in Seattle. They chose that city because of its large lesbian community and because the weather was warmer than in their native North Dakota. Before they moved, Juliana wrote to the local lesbian resource center. She learned about the older women's group and talked with the facilitator. When Darlene and Juliana arrived in Seattle, another older lesbian couple met them at the airport and helped them move into their apartment.*

Depending on the level of care a person requires, a nursing home may be necessary at some point. As we know from the media, people are sometimes exploited and even abused in some of these facilities. However, good care facilities do exist. Since alternatives vary depending on locale and cost, some of us will likely have fewer choices about our care. As lesbians, we may also face the lack of acknowledgment or validation of our couple relationship. On the other hand, one couple we know had no problem being assigned a double room together in a nursing home.

There are creative ways to deal with the various situations as we age. Because society does not provide a lot of support for us and our relationships, we often need to be especially clever with our plans, knowledgeable about our rights, and persistent in our self-advocacy.

## CHAPTER 17

# ᕲ Endings

There are two ways a relationship can end: through a breakup or through the death of a partner. In either case, we experience loss and a recovery process that involves grieving that loss and eventually moving on.

## Divorce—Lesbian Style

Women take their couple relationships—and breaking up—very seriously. We have been trained to focus much of our energy on our relationships and even to define ourselves by them. We are Mae's daughter or Toni's sister, Keisha's partner or Janice's old lover. Traditionally, there has been a lot of pressure for a woman to be in a relationship in order to be okay. When relationships end, many women feel less than okay and may even experience a loss of identity: "If I am not in a relationship, I don't exist."

Being in a relationship means various things to different generations of lesbians. To women who came out before the 1970s (or for many who now live in isolated areas) being in a relationship often means having a safe haven in a very hostile world—the only place where she can relax and really be herself. Women who came out in the 1970s and '80s may also see being in a relationship as a strong political statement. Women who came out in the '90s may view a lesbian relationship as one among several options for being in an intimate relationship. Hopefully, the years-old training that "you are not somebody if you are not in a relationship" has begun to weaken its hold on young women, thus, freeing us to choose to be coupled—or not.

The length of a relationship often is the measure of its success, but this does not always hold true. Two women might stay together for forty years and be quite unhappy but unable or unwilling to improve the relationship or just leave. A five-month relationship might nourish the hearts of both women and be remembered as an oasis in a very bleak time in their lives. Which relationship is more successful?

Despite the fact that longer does not necessarily mean better, many lesbians enter relationships hoping that they will last forever. And even though permanence shouldn't be the only goal, it's important to have models of successful, long-term relationships so that couples can know that it is possible and see what multiyear relationships are like.

Throughout this book, we have explored ways to improve the health of lesbian relationships and the happiness of the women in them. It is also important to examine the reasons couples break up in order to learn how to avoid the problems that can lead to divorce as well as how to make the endings, when they do come, as successful as possible.

### Reasons Lesbian Couples Break Up

One study from the early '80s compared lesbian, gay, and heterosexual married and cohabitating couples. In their 1983 book, *American Couples,* Philip Blumstein and Pepper Schwartz found that lesbian couples had a higher rate of breakup than any other kinds of couples in the study.[1] There are at least three factors that may contribute to these results.

The first is that lesbians tend to define our relationships with a capital R very early on. Within two months, or even two weeks, both women may feel that they are a couple in a "Relationship." We talk long-term commitment and often begin living together. Later, some of us may discover that the relationship is based primarily on physical attraction or on the desire to be in a "Relationship." There may be little basis for a long-term partnership. Now what? We have to break up. These endings are often mourned with the same intensity as the divorce of a long-term relationship. Many of these breakups might be more realistically viewed as the end of dating relationships that did not progress beyond the prerelationship stage.

When a relationship ends, partners often feel a sense of failure. Either the failure is in picking the wrong person or in not being a good enough partner. Both women feel bad because their expectations have not been met. The breakup may call into question their ability both to choose good partners and to be successful in a relationship. Since we have these lifetime-partner expectations—often without even realizing it—we are poorly prepared for ending. Lacking the skills and attitudes required for ending relationships, we feel helpless, disappointed, guilty, angry, and panicky.

Slowing down the early stages of a relationship is a good way to increase the chances of creating and maintaining a healthy and satisfying relationship. Taking time to get to know each other leads to a clearer assessment of compatibility and a more realistic prediction for the future of the relationship. Psychologist Laura Brown describes this process as getting and giving "informed consent."[2] You both need to inform yourselves and each other about who you are and what you want and expect in your relationship. You can then consent to be in the relationship based on clear information, rather than on assumptions, hopes, and illusions.

At the same time, you have the opportunity to recognize the disappointments you have in each other. If the disappointments are tolerable, you may decide to proceed to the romance stage; if the disappointments are more than one or both of you want to manage, you can stop dating. If you think about getting to know each other as dating, "informed consent" or the prerelationship stage, you will feel less a sense of failure if you end the relationship. You can realistically say, "I decided that I didn't want to get involved with Amy; we didn't want the same things from our relationship" or "There just wasn't enough in common to share with Tanya." You may even feel proud of yourself for your clarity and integrity.

The second factor is the invisibility of long-term couples. Couples who have been together for fifteen, twenty, or more years are often invisible, even to other lesbians. Some of these couples are closeted because of societal homophobia. Others socialize almost exclusively within small friendship networks made up of other long-time couples. These couples have great stability, but few people know about it. This deprives newer couples of real-life examples of how other women have navigated the inevitable ups and downs of a relationship. Heterosexual couples have examples all around them, and their friends and family members may offer advice when things are not working out. While the specific examples and advice are sometimes not helpful, the support and collective wisdom really can provide genuine benefits.

The third factor comes as a suggestion from Philip Blumstein and Pepper Schwartz in an attempt to understand why lesbians, who place such a high value on relationships, broke up at a higher rate than other couples in their study.[3] Blumstein and Schwartz hypothesized that lesbians are trying to create a new female role as equals within the context of an intimate relationship.

*They have many conflicting desires in their relationships, none of which can be solved by reverting to the traditional female role. Both partners are reject- ing the comfortable supported position that women have been trained for in favor of being a full and equal partner in a relationship. This endangers their desire to place their relationship at the center of their lives and their need for emotional intensity because it means that both women need to be equally ambitious outside the relationship. Moreover, they are at the same time mov- ing away from male traits that they feel provide inequality.*[4]

Changing the status quo, no matter how right it seems to us or turns out to be over time, is very hard on the people who are doing it. This is still true after the turn of the millennium.

Lesbian couples are not always able to withstand the many pressures from within the relationship and the lack of support outside of it. Women expect a lot from their partners. They often feel, "Here at last is what I've always wanted. Because she is a woman, too, she will understand me and meet my emotional needs." These expectations involve a lot of assumptions, and they put pressure on both partners.

Hostility from the broader culture is a given. The lack of societal support, such as legal marriage, as well as outright condemnation, such as sodomy laws, obviously hurt a couple's chances to succeed. There are also ordinary outside pressures that affect all couples—work, children, extended family, school, lack of money or other resources, and volunteer responsibilities. All of these can add to the demands on their time and energy that a couple must manage.

The negative impact that the lesbian community itself may have is less obvious. There are particular pressures, for example, on lesbians who are involved in long-term partnerships. They may be viewed as a "perfect cou- ple." Friends who want to believe that such relationships are possible may not want to hear about any problems the "perfect couple" may be having.

*Else and Beatrice broke up after eight years of what looked to their friends like an ideal relationship. In fact, neither partner had been very satisfied for the last two years. Beatrice was deeply disappointed that Else was not more emotionally supportive. After years of relating to men, Beatrice had expected that in a relationship with another woman she would get all the under- standing and support she felt she had missed.*

*Else was frustrated with what she saw as Beatrice's demands on her time and energy. Else's life had changed dramatically in the last few years. She was laid off, went back to school for job retraining, and began a new job in a nontraditional field. Else liked the work and the pay, but the open homophobia, sexism, and racism on the job caused an incredible strain. A lot of the time she was both physically exhausted from work and emotionally drained from coping with her coworkers. She knew she wasn't putting a lot of energy into the relationship. She kept telling Beatrice—and herself—that things would be better after the job settled down.*

*But it was only when Beatrice began an affair with an old friend, Terry, that her relationship with Else just seemed to blow apart.*

Let's look at this situation. One of the major pressures from inside a relationship is our expectations of our partner or our beliefs of how relationships are supposed to be. Beatrice expected Else to be more emotionally supportive because she was a woman. Outside pressures came into play with Else's stressful job. The more strain she had at work, the more Else wanted her relationship with Beatrice to be a warm cocoon. She expected Beatrice to be more supportive or at least patient.

Their lesbian friends' view of them as a perfect couple was also a pressure. When their friends idealized their relationship, Else and Beatrice were cut off from support. They were not allowed to have, much less talk about, any difficulties.

### But Why?

There are various ways to explain what went wrong in a relationship.

*Pan blamed her partner, Brandy, completely for their relationship's ending. To hear Pan tell the story Brandy was totally a villain and Pan an innocent victim.*

*Jomei described life as being like a lottery. She figured she had just had bad luck so far. She kept hoping she would get a better deal on the next round.*

*Ellen explained that her relationship with Billie ended because of circumstances beyond their control. She had a stressful job and their apartment was so small that they couldn't avoid all those fights. There was really nothing they could have done.*

These three women use different explanations for their relationships's not working out. They all have no sense of control or power in the situation. Bad luck and forces-beyond-our-control explanations, like those of

Jomei and Ellen, do not allow for learning how to make the future work out better. Similarly, when Pan blames Brandy, she feels victimized. Blaming can be used to justify vengeful behavior and even destructiveness. It also makes it hard to let go of the relationship. Pan can't learn how to improve her relationships in the future unless she understands her contribution to what happened.

While Pan takes too little responsibility for the ending of her relationship, Monica takes too much.

> *Monica blamed herself for not being a better partner to her lover. She went through lists of "if onlys," replaying how it could have worked out if only she had said or done something differently.*

The fact is each partner makes a contribution to the relationship's ending. Neither person is fully responsible for the partnership's working—or not working. In order for each partner to understand her contribution, the problems in the relationship need to be separated from the stress of the ending. This is not an easy task.

Else and Beatrice confronted some major stresses in ending their relationship. One of these was Beatrice's involvement with Terry; another was their merged financial affairs; a third was the mix of feelings they both had about the divorce.

Sometimes another involvement is used as a means of ending a relationship. You may believe that you need the support or the distraction that a new relationship provides in order to end the old relationship. You may be dissatisfied or want to leave the relationship but may be unable to deal directly with your dissatisfaction. Another involvement may appear to be the only acceptable justification for the breakup. This process is not always a conscious one; you may recognize it only after some time has passed.

If a relationship ends when one of you becomes involved with someone else, both partners are likely to feel bad. If you initiate the breakup you may feel guilty; if you are the one who is "left," you will likely feel rejection and betrayal. The woman who did not trigger the breakup and who does not have a new lover may feel worse, if pain can be quantified. But both women feel pain.

The guilt that Beatrice felt and the rejection and anger that Else experienced contributed to their difficulties in sorting out their financial separation. Their finances were completely merged. They had never made any plans or even discussed what they would do if the relationship ended.

*After Beatrice moved out, Else was very angry. She refused to talk to her ex-lover regarding arrangements about the car, the house, and the furniture they owned together. Beatrice's inclination was just to let Else have it all, but she was hurting for money. She was paying for an apartment for herself as well as her share of the mortgage on the house where Else still lived. At one point, they had a big fight over the new DVD player they had bought for the house. This purchase had been made on Beatrice's credit card. Else refused to contribute anything toward the monthly payment, to give Beatrice the DVD player, or even to discuss it.*

The third stress this couple faced was managing the mix of sometimes contradictory feelings about the breakup. Else was surprised that in addition to pain, she felt some relief when Beatrice finally moved out. She no longer had to deal with Beatrice's demands and her sulking. She could come and go—and sleep—as she pleased, without worrying that she was not putting enough energy into her relationship with Beatrice. She was angry with her ex-lover, but she also idealized her. She wondered if she would ever find someone as kind and thoughtful as Beatrice had been. Beatrice had been desperate to leave. Once away, she missed Else terribly. She began to doubt her decision to break up, particularly when she remembered the good times. In addition, Beatrice was alarmed to find herself beset by fears. She was afraid of being hurt in her new relationship, of having to take care of herself, of sleeping alone, and just of being on her own—without Else.

### The Ripple Effect of a Divorce

After a long-term couple divorces, each partner often has fears about their friends taking sides. In our example, Beatrice alternates between feeling guilty and justified about her involvement with her new lover, Terry. Since she blames herself for causing Else a lot of pain, she avoids their mutual friends. She knows some of them have taken sides and are angry with her; she sees others as possible supports for Else and wants Else to get the emotional support she needs.

It is true that friends may take sides when a couple breaks up. However, Beatrice almost guarantees that this will happen. In effect, she rejects these former friends by assuming they would be unsupportive. She decides, first, that Else needs support more than she does and, second, that their friends would do better to give Else support. In making these decisions, Beatrice cuts herself off from support and her friends from the information that could balance their view of the situation. She is mind reading what Else needs and what their friends think.

Of course, one or both of you in a breakup may be so hurt or angry that you try to get friends to take your side. Even when this is not the case, mutual friends may take sides anyway. This is very painful, because it means that one or both of you are losing friends, as well as losing your primary relationship. Some strategies may help prevent this. You can talk to your mutual friends together, at least initially, about the divorce. You can each try to be fair to the other when you talk to friends individually. You can ask friends specifically to avoid taking sides. For their part, friends should try to listen to the feelings and distress of each partner with understanding, without harsh judgment, and without taking sides. There are almost always two legitimate stories in a breakup.

Sometimes, however, losing friends is unavoidable. Their values, loyalties, histories, or feelings are so involved that their alliance is solidly with one of you over the other. When this happens, there may be no choice but to accept and grieve the loss. Perhaps with time, the rift can be bridged and the friendship healed.

Dividing up friends is one problem, particularly when the community is a small one. Another issue is meeting your former partner at social events and in public places. This can be particularly touchy if one of you has a new relationship and the other does not. You may decide to divide up the territory or avoid going to certain places knowing the other may be there. You may agree to check in with each other and negotiate who will go to what event. You may avoid going out at all because there is no prior arrangement to avoid confrontation. Some former partners continue to have contact with each other while others take a break because it is too painful, or they are too angry.

*Laura and Anna described their ending as a mutual decision. It was only after Anna got involved in a new relationship that they started having "communication problems."*

*Gertrude and Myrtle broke up after two years of a torrid romance. They had been friends for fifteen years before that and were determined to become friends again. Even though it was incredibly painful, they both stayed in the seniors' aerobics swim class and had lunch together afterward. A year later they were once again comfortable in each other's company and credited their "forced lunches" with keeping them talking.*

*After a very bitter divorce, Parmita and Nina went to a mediator every year to renegotiate their child-support agreement.*

When children are involved, you are almost certain to have contact with your ex-partner. The ideal for your children is for the two of you to respectfully coordinate parenting. But if the most you can tolerate is to arrange how and when to transfer the children between households, then so be it. The important element is to figure out how much contact you need to ensure that your children are well taken care of. If you need help communicating with the other parent in order to take care of your children, contact a therapist or other professional.

There is no one right way to manage contact after a divorce, but often there is a best way for the particular women involved. Ideally, you should communicate with each other to discuss and agree on these practical issues.

### Successful Endings

There is no easy way to break up or to make the ending totally painless. Even mutually agreed-upon separations are likely to have a bittersweet quality. While both women may feel satisfied and even good about the decision to break up, both are likely to experience pain, fear, and ambivalence.

According to Emily Coleman and Betty Edwards in their book, *Brief Encounters: How to Make the Most of Relationships That May Not Last Forever*, to end a relationship with grace and caring requires skills and attitudes that are not common in our society.[5] We must learn to regard endings as a part of the natural flow of life. Endings are also beginnings. They point out that days, meals, vacations, projects, and school programs end, and we adjust to these events. So, too, relationships end—at least in their previous form. Forever is not necessary in order for a relationship to be valuable and worthwhile.

We also need to change our reluctance to discuss the possibility that a relationship may end. Many couples avoid talking about a breakup because it feels like an invitation for disaster. They get upset at the idea of making agreements about what to do "if they break up." In fact, discussions about parting are acts of caring. Some planning can go a long way toward managing conflict if the relationship does end.

Having a clearly spelled-out agreement or contract can ease the difficulty and minimize the messiness of ending your relationship. Learn your legal responsibilities and rights. Legal and emotional agreements about making an ending as easy as possible are important to discuss when you make an exclusive commitment or move in together. When you still love and want what's best for your partner, it is easier to negotiate how you will divide any property held in common. This is also when you should decide whether, or for how long, you will go to counseling or seek clarity from your spiritual community. Breaking up successfully involves many of the same skills that help to develop a satisfying relationship. Good communication, conflict-resolution skills, goodwill, trust, shared goals, and the ability to hold on to yourself when you have different wants from your (ex-)partner are some of the main ingredients. If you are having difficulty negotiating the terms of the breakup, consider engaging a counselor, a mediator, or an attorney. Continuing to fight without resolving anything can build up unnecessary hurt and resentment that may interfere with having another satisfying relationship after the divorce.

You must also decide what kind of relationship, if any, you want to have with each other after the breakup. What kind of commitment is each of you willing to make? If you both agree that you want to be friends, you need to negotiate the terms of your friendship. What are your wants and expectations? How much time are you each willing to spend to work out this transition from lovers to friends? Do you need to consider having a third party help in this process? Does either one of you need some time apart, without contact at all? There is no one right way to end a relationship with a partner. It is up to each of you to take care of yourself and to coordinate that with your partner.

In making the transition from being to not being in a couple relationship, doing something special can be important to bring closure.

*Vanessa set aside a special time to pack up all the pictures, presents, and mementos that reminded her of Sun-Li. She decided not to throw anything out—yet. So she stored the boxes in the basement until she would be ready to sort through them.*

*Monde cleaned the entire apartment and rearranged all the furniture after Louise moved out. This symbolized making the place hers again.*

*Sienna and Becca asked their minister to conduct an ending ceremony with them. They found it affirming to acknowledge the good things about the relationship and each other. It helped them feel more positive about ending their relationship.*

*Ramona decided to take a trip to the desert by herself after Angela announced that she wanted to end their relationship. The desert had always been a place of cleansing and healing for Ramona. While she was there, she designed a healing ritual for herself that allowed her to let go of some of her pain.*

*After the end of her fifteen-year relationship, Georgia's friends gave her a "starting over" shower. They wanted an event to mark the end of her relationship and the beginning of her new identity as a single person.*

## Dealing with Loss

After the loss of a relationship, there are phases in the recovery process and tasks of mourning that need to be accomplished. First we will look at this process after a divorce and then when a partner dies.

William Worden in *Grief Counseling and Grief Therapy* identifies four phases of the grieving process.[6] The first is shock and denial. In the earlier situation with Else and Beatrice, Else was convinced at first that Beatrice's leaving was a bad dream. She was sure that Beatrice would come to her senses, return to their home, and everything would be okay. As she began to realize that Beatrice was not coming back, she accomplished the first task in the grieving process. She began to accept the reality of the loss. Instead of denying that the relationship was really over, she recognized that Beatrice was not coming back. When she fully comprehended that the relationship was over, Else became furious with Beatrice for leaving and angry with herself for "wasting all those years." She felt betrayed and abandoned. Sometimes it seemed that her heart was breaking. She couldn't remember ever feeling so depressed. This period of anger and depression is the second phase of recovery, and the task is to experience the pain of the grief. Else needs to be patient and treat herself gently during this time of healing. The third phase brings with it the challenge of replacing the skills and roles the other person used to provide. Else had to take responsibility for all the jobs Beatrice used to do, such as paying the bills and cleaning the gutters on their house. Eventually, she adjusted to living without her. The last part of grieving is letting go of the old relationship and moving on—reinvesting energy in other relationships. Else could spend her time staying mad at Beatrice, and not have energy for a new relationship, or she could lay her grievances to rest and open herself up to new love.

There is no set amount of time for the grieving process. One sign of progress is being able to think of the person without intense pain. Gradually Else will feel a little less sad, a little less hurt and angry. However, she will probably not feel good as fast as she would like. She may expect to get over the relationship with Beatrice faster than she does. She may desperately want to be done with it, yet not feel finished.

It is tempting to get involved in another relationship to distract yourself from the pain of grieving. Your friends may become uncomfortable with your grief and try to match you up with someone or try to get you to stop feeling your pain. Many therapists and theorists suggest that it takes four full seasons of the year before grief over the loss of a close relationship begins to abate. The Jewish tradition of grieving daily for a loved one also lasts for a year. So, give yourself a full cycle of holidays, seasonal changes, significant anniversaries, and just plain time to integrate the loss of your partner.

If you begin a new relationship before the first year of grieving is over (and many of us do), it may prolong your grieving process, or you may end up grieving years later. Some relationships thrive in spite of the stress that your unfinished grieving adds, but success is dependent on both women's ability to tolerate the mourning when it does surface.

There can be many complications in the mourning process. Often one loss reactivates previous losses.

*As Else grieved for the end of her relationship with Beatrice, she also grieved for the death of her father. When he had died five years previously, she went numb and never did express much feeling, even though she felt close to him. She hardly cried at all.*

This is very common. Sometimes when Else cried about Beatrice, she was aware of how much she missed her father. Some of her tears were about losing him. It seems that we each have a deep reservoir of sadness and pain. Any particular loss can tap into this well of unshed tears. Asking "When is mourning finished?" is like asking "How high is up?" There is no ready answer. This is true for breaking up as well as when a partner dies.

## When a Partner Dies

*Ethel and Rae had been together for thirty years when Rae was killed in a car accident. Two years later Ethel had not yet finished grieving her partner. At first she was in shock. Weeks after the funeral she kept imagining that she saw Rae on the street, or that she heard her car in the driveway. She had to keep reminding herself that Rae was not going to return. For some time Ethel just felt numb; she felt nothing. Then when she started to feel the pain, she threw herself into her work to distract herself. She thought about moving to another city and then decided that the geographical cure probably wasn't much of a cure at all. She wondered "Why me?" and found herself being angry with Rae for dying and at other people because they were alive and Rae was not.*

*Luckily, she had a strong network of friends who were very supportive as she finally allowed herself to feel the depth of the pain, sadness, and rage. Only after she had allowed herself to be aware of her feelings was Ethel able to move on to the final tasks of mourning. She had to adjust to an environment where Rae was missing. Ethel had to learn to take care of things that Rae had attended to for years. Ethel was shocked at how helpless and inadequate she felt in handling everything herself, but she did it. She was late getting the storm windows up, and the lawn was pretty scruffy the next summer, but she managed. During this time, she was amazed at how sad and angry she continued to feel about Rae's death. All their plans for the house and for traveling were shattered after Ethel was left alone.*

Eventually Ethel is likely to pull her attention away from her memories of Rae and reinvest her energy in other relationships. Thus, she will move through the mourning process. She may still miss Rae sometimes, may be sad, and even cry, but it means her life will be focused on the present and the people in it, not on the past.

Ethel's good fortune in having a network of friends to provide support was particularly important because she was closeted at work. One of the potential complications of lesbian relationships is that the couple may not have the support that a heterosexual couple takes for granted during the course of a relationship and in the event of a partner's death. In this case people at work did not learn of Rae's death. If they had, their condolences would not have been based on an understanding of the nature and depth of the relationship. Some might have wondered why Ethel was so upset; after all, they were "just friends."

Other complications in grieving over the death of a partner can be the attitude and behavior of your families. If you have a will that specifies what you want done at your funeral and how you want your property disposed of, you can avoid potential problems. Without such precautions, the surviving partner may be excluded from decisions about funeral arrangements and other issues. Family members of the deceased have been known to swoop in and remove possessions from their daughter's home—including things that belonged to the remaining partner. Having a will ensures the partner some legal protection in the event that her lover's family is antagonistic. The best protection is to have talked to family members while both partners are alive.

Obviously, the more accustomed your family is to your partner, the more likely it is that they will respect and support your wishes after you die.

If we don't like to think about the "what ifs" in breaking up, how much more do we avoid the "what ifs" concerning death? Careful planning, such as having durable powers of attorney and wills, can prevent unnecessary legal and other hassles in the already difficult mourning process. In the absence of a structure of legal and societal agreements established for married people in the heterosexual world, lesbians as individuals and as a community can collude with having our status as couples be ignored—or we can create a structure for ourselves.

*Anita and Sasha had been lovers for three years when Anita was diagnosed with breast cancer. It caught both women completely by surprise since Anita was only thirty-one. The biopsy results confirmed their worst fears—the cancer had metastasized. Two years later Anita was dead.*

*Even though Sasha had had time to prepare, she was still numbed by the experience of watching Anita die. She was grateful that the two of them had drawn up wills and that Anita had been able to give her violin and music to her sister in person. Much of the last six months of Anita's life had been spent with her parents, brother, sisters, and their families. Her whole family lived in the same area where Sasha and Anita lived and everyone wanted as much time with her as possible.*

*One of the things that surprised Sasha the most was how lovingly Anita's family treated her after Anita died They invited her to family gatherings, brought her apples in the fall and flowers in the spring, and even helped her paint the front steps. Nothing could have prepared Sasha for the outpouring of love and support they gave her. She was incredibly glad Anita had been so insistent in coming out to her family when Sasha had been so nervous about it. What would she have done without them?!*

The end of a relationship—whether by divorce or death—is the ultimate separation from our partner and marks the end of a chapter in our life. Sometimes it is useful to understand the ending and other times we have to accept that we will never know "Why?" and "Why now?" We need to grieve our loss and get support to carry us through the unbearable times. And then we need to move on and begin the next part of our lives. Such is the way of healing.

## CHAPTER 18

# ᛦ Beginning Again

Endings are inevitably followed by beginnings. Sunset is followed by sunrise, and winter by spring. Our lives and loves are full of endings and beginnings. Indeed, endings create the space for beginnings, but beginnings do not always happen the way we expect.

After your relationship ends, you will have some sort of beginning down the road. You may not know how far down the road or what it will look like, but guaranteed, you will have another beginning. However, it does not always mean a new relationship. You may begin a life as a Peace Corps volunteer, a grandmother, or a graduate student. Regardless of what new beginning emerges, the question most of us want answered is "How do I get there from here?" In his book about life transitions, William Bridges stresses the need for a "neutral zone," a period when a person takes a break in routine after the old and before the new.[1] It is the time when you allow enough stillness in your mind and soul to permit all the possibilities to bubble up. You may take time off from your regular life for this transition or create pockets of still-time while continuing work, school, or parenting. However you do it, you are allowing long-held dreams and new ideas to grow and be considered. There is no fixed time period for this work. Depending on your circumstances it could take hours, months, or years.

Sasha (from the last chapter) may need months or years to grieve and adjust to a life without her partner, Anita, and she will likely feel very disoriented as she rebuilds her life. Whether Sasha repartners immediately or waits before she starts seeing anyone, at some point she will need a neutral zone to further the "inner reorientation"[2] that allows her to begin again. If she tries to bypass this transition, she may remain stuck or repeat old patterns. For Sasha, being stuck might mean not being able to move her energy from Anita to a new partner. For Else (from the last chapter) getting stuck may mean not being able to let go of her anger toward her ex-partner for getting involved with someone else.

There is no way to predict what your new beginning will consist of. Out of the stillness and confusion of the neutral zone come the seeds of your beginning. If you allow yourself to let go and make the transition, you release the illusion that you can control the precise direction of your journey.

*Jennie's partner, Nanette, had left her for another woman after ten years together. Jennie was devastated. She immediately got involved with a woman in her yoga class and two months later quit seeing her. With nudging from her friends, Jennie attended a two-week meditation retreat to break her cycle of crying and numbness. In the beginning, Jennie found herself meditating on "yuck," as her teacher called it. Then she found an intense emptiness that remained for a week or so. Finally, Jennie felt a lightening and a sense of change. At the end of the retreat she was stunned to find that she had been picturing herself going back to graduate school in biology, something she had once dreamed of doing.*

Whatever you do, your beginning builds on the past and what you have—and have not—learned from it.

## Understanding the Past

An essential ingredient of improving your next relationship is to analyze what went wrong—and right—as you come to terms with the old relationship. When you try to understand why a relationship ended, it is hard to be objective. Even after you overcome your strong emotional attachments, you may still blame your partner, or yourself, for the breakup. It is more helpful to develop a balanced assessment of the relationship.

Write down a short history of the relationship, and attempt to answer these questions:

- What did you like or admire in her when you first met?
- What were the most significant positive experiences in your relationship?
- What did each of you do to make the relationship work?
- What were your greatest sadnesses? Your feelings of failure?
- How did you contribute to these failures? How did she?
- What do you still feel angry about? Guilty? Disappointed? How might you and your partner have contributed to creating these feelings?
- In what ways has the relationship added to your life?
- What did the experience teach you about yourself? About relationships? How will this knowledge help you with your next relationship?

After you finish writing your history, check it for objectivity. If you think it is biased or that it will not guide you toward more successful future relationships, it is worth your time to answer the questions again.

By its very nature, a relationship involves the behavior of two people. Partners work together to produce what is positive in the relationship and share responsibility for what goes wrong. In looking back, you can't do anything about your former partner's mistakes, but you can learn from your own. Look for the *pattern* in your behavior that has interfered with your relationship.

*Loni realized that all three of her lovers had been bad choices if she wanted a monogamous relationship. They all had been in other relationships when they had gotten involved with her. She wondered why she was attracted to already-partnered women.*

*Katarina thought she had outgrown her pattern of having affairs while she was in a monogamous relationship. She was stunned when she finally understood, through couples therapy, that the anonymous online sex she was having was really the same thing.*

*Six months after she and Claudia had broken up, Tess figured out that she had never taken more than four days in a row off work during the two years that they had been together. She always had good reasons for not being able to get away, but now she began to see the validity of Claudia's complaints. No wonder Claudia had left for someone who was more available.*

*As she talked to her therapist about her previous relationship, Queenie realized that her unwillingness to talk about her partner's unhappiness eventually led to the end of their relationship. Queenie always had an excuse for not listening to Dotty's complaints: She was too tired, Dotty didn't say it right, they were Dotty's problems, and so on. But the big picture revealed that Queenie never gave attention to issues that were important to Dotty if they involved criticism of Queenie's behavior. Queenie missed Dotty and wished she could have a second chance.*

We tend to minimize instances in our own behavior that are hurtful to or disrespectful of others. If you can tolerate seeing yourself in a less than positive light (without taking on all of the responsibility), you will be better able to have a balanced and objective view of the history of your relationship. This should help you avoid past mistakes and create a future relationship that is more like what you want.

## Finding a New Partner

Finding a good match in a partner often requires a combination of imagination, planning, thought, willingness to extend yourself, and good luck. While many lesbians become involved with women they already know, you can't count on this or on stumbling onto opportunities—you have to help create them.

*Fiona decided that if she was going to meet any new women, she was going to have to get out into the world more. No one was going to come knocking on her door. So she started by going to the senior center two days a week.*

*Abigail complained to her friend Anna that she only met women who drank too much. When Anna asked where she went to meet women, Abigail laughed and said that she went to the bars.*

*Meja decided that she wanted to meet women who were physically active, so she joined a volleyball team and enrolled in a backpacking class.*

The people you meet are the ones you arrange to find, whether or not you are aware of making the plans. If you are looking for a new relationship, three good steps to follow are defining the kind of women who interest you, figuring out where they are likely to spend their time, and arranging to be there to meet them.

Richard Stuart and Barbara Jacobsen suggest writing a personals ad to clarify what you want in a prospective mate.[3] The idea is not actually to place the ad in a paper, but to use it as a tool to get clearer about how you see yourself and what you expect from a partner. In this ad, describe the kind of person you want under the section, "Who I want to meet." Specify your strong preferences or requirements. These may include age, religion, interests, hobbies, occupation, personal qualities, and anything else you consider important. Then under "What I offer in return," write an honest description of yourself. When you finish your ad, look it over. Underline the most important words in your description of yourself and the partner you are seeking. Have you been accurate about yourself? Have you been too idealistic about your prospective partner? Are the two descriptions compatible? (You can then decide to place the ad if that is one of your strategies for finding dates.)

Once you know what kind of person you want, you can either trust luck to run into her, or you can put some effort into the search. Give parties instead of waiting to be invited; risk the chance of rejection (or success) in dating, rather than avoiding the risk; initiate a conversation with a stranger at a party instead of waiting for her to speak to you; give people a chance rather than quickly eliminating them as unsuitable.

If this last description sounds like you, try this: Decide on three characteristics that are essential in a partner. No, not ten or twenty, just three. So if the essential ingredients are single, over thirty, and bi, eliminate only those women who don't have these three characteristics. Give yourself a chance to get to know any woman who does meet the three essentials. This way you avoid writing women off before you get a chance to know them. Even if they do not turn out to be appropriate partners, they may become (or have) friends.

With the advent of the Internet (and email) the pool of potential partners has expanded exponentially. These tools for meeting women can be great boons, or they can be accidents waiting to happen. The single biggest potential liability is that you don't really know who you are chatting with. A twenty-two-year-old woman in Seattle might really be a fifty-five-year-old man in Chicago. So, how do you get the benefits of the Internet and still protect yourself from unwanted folks? Here are a few suggestions:

- Never give out your name, address, and phone number until you are sure of whom you are talking to—even if she sounds like a very hot dyke.
- If you plan to meet in person, do so in a public setting until you have a good sense of what kind of person she is.
- Don't make promises—to give her money to travel to meet you, to move to her city, or to commit to any kind of a relationship—until you have dated for a while in person.

- Use online chatting and email to add depth to a long-distance relationship with someone you have met in person.

## Deciding Whether to Get Serious

So now that you have met someone who interests you, what next? Keep the following guidelines in mind when deciding whether to move your new relationship into the next stage.

### Someone Who Has What You Want

If there is anything that you very much want in a partner, look for someone who already has it. You cannot trust the power of your love to create what is not there initially.

*Kristin was concerned about ZiZi's excessive time on the computer. ZiZi was a computer junkie and spent hours every day chatting online, surfing the Web, and periodically getting into day trading. Kristin was sure that when they lived together ZiZi would want to spend more time with her and less with her "virtual" community. Kristin was shocked when ZiZi didn't change her habits, and ZiZi was indignant that Kristin would move in with the goal of changing her.*

*It was important to Emily that her partner really did want to live with Emily's pets. She had four dogs and three cats, and that didn't count the canaries. She had learned the hard way that some people just did not want that many animals in their lives. Before she got serious about Chris, she carefully checked out how Chris felt about her pets.*

### Love Is Not Enough

Love is the feeling that your partner is as important to you as you are to yourself. Love is seeing your lover's wonderful attributes—and her not-so-nice qualities—and accepting all of her.

Love is essential for a good couple relationship, but it is not enough in itself. If you two are not compatible in handling the details of daily life or if your goals and values are very different, love may not be enough for a satisfying commitment.

*Heidi loved Kerry very much, but she did not at first realize how determined Kerry was to have children. This was not something that Heidi wanted, so eventually they parted.*

*It was hard for Eleanor to believe that her relationship with Dora didn't work out because they couldn't live together comfortably. But it was true. Their approaches to chores, paying bills, and the details of running a household were very different, and at sixty and sixty-two they were both "set in their ways," as Dora described it. Because they each wanted to be able to live with their partner, the relationship ended.*

*After a year of being with Adrian, Bella saw how different they were. Adrian was focused on security and work, while Bella valued travel and a sense of adventure. She wished she had seen this earlier.*

If love is not enough, infatuation is definitely nowhere near enough! Love is a deeper emotion than infatuation. Though not as intense in the immediate moment, love has a better chance of turning into long-term satisfaction because it is based on accurate knowledge of your partner and genuine and mutual sharing of interests and values.

*Renee was convinced that what she felt for Abby was true love. She was totally ecstatic about Abby, even though she hardly knew her. She got more interested in Abby as Abby showed less interest in her; she was obsessed with thinking about Abby. Everything and everyone else in Renee's life was unimportant by comparison.*

## Similarities and Differences Are Both Important

Difference can bring stimulation and the invitation to expand your life, but it also brings the potential for conflict. Similarity offers comfort and a sense of understanding and being understood, but being too alike can be boring. You need someone who shares your important values and goals, but who is different enough to make life interesting and to broaden your perspectives. Similarities may make life easier, but differences make it exciting. The trick is to find the balance. You both also need skills to stay differentiated in the face of those similarities and differences so that you are not forced to give up the "essential" you to be in this relationship.

*Before they moved in together, Rachael and Sumiko had a session where each outlined to the other what her personal goals were, so that they could compare notes. They discovered that financial security and spending time together were the highest goals for each of them. That made them feel alike—and close—but there were also differences. Physical fitness and exercise were important to*

*Rachael, while a commitment to spiritual meditation was crucial to Sumiko. In this case, they valued these differences. They also decided to have a yearly review of these goals to ensure that there was room for each to change her priorities over time.*

## Apply What You Know

Incorporate your knowledge of yourself from past relationships into the growing understanding of yourself and your lover in this new relationship.

*Annique knew from her past relationships that she had a short fuse around the issue of being late to dates. She also knew that she had worked some of the intensity out of her response in therapy through the last few years. When she told her lover of six months that she was upset when they were late to a surprise birthday party, Annique found herself being pleased with how she said it and with how Erin responded. Erin, who was late to most things in her life, apologized and said she understood that this was important to Annique. She proposed sitting down the next day to make a plan about how to deal with this issue. Annique decided that this relationship looked promising.*

In starting a new relationship, you bring together the past, the present and your hopes for the future. By coming to terms with your past relationships, you can understand yourself better and avoid making the same mistakes again. Being clear in the present about what you want in a partner increases your chances of recognizing her when you find her. And by realistically assessing your compatibility with each other, you are much more likely to build a satisfying relationship.

What you want and what you bring to your relationships will shift with time and experience. What was important to you in your twenties may not even be a consideration in your seventies. Whatever your age, by risking the challenges and stresses of being in a relationship, you are deliberately adding an unknown to your life. The reflection of yourself that you see in a lover's face and the challenge to grow that relationships inevitably provide can add depth and pleasure to this life's journey. Enjoy!

# Endnotes

## Chapter One

1. Philip Blumstein and Pepper Schwartz, *American Couples* (New York: William Morrow and Company, 1983), 316–317.
2. Ibid., 195.
3. Suzanne Pharr, "Two Workshops on Homophobia," in *Naming the Violence: Speaking Out about Lesbian Battering,* ed. K. Lobel (Emeryville: Seal Press, 1986), 203.
4. Judith Wallerstein and Sandra Blakeslee, *The Good Marriage: How and Why Love Lasts* (New York: Warner Books, 1995), 334.

## Chapter Two

1. Susan M. Campbell, *The Couple's Journey: Intimacy as a Path to Wholeness* (San Luis Obispo, CA: Impact Publishers, 1980), 10–15; and David McWhirter and Andrew Mattison, *The Male Couple: How Relationships Develop* (Englewood Cliffs, NJ: Prentice-Hall, 1984), 15–19.
2. John M. Gottman and Nan Silver, *The Seven Principles for Making Marriage Work* (New York: Crown Publishers, 1999), 47–50.
3. Ibid., 61–68.
4. Ibid., 129–130.
5. Ibid., 130–133.
6. Ibid., 102.
7. Ibid., 81.
8. Linda Sutton, *Love Matters: A Book of Lesbian Romance and Relationship* (Binghamton, NY: Harrington Park Press, 1999), 116–119.
9. Campbell, *The Couple's Journey,* 96–99.
10. Wallerstein and Blakeslee, *The Good Marriage,* 27–28.

## Chapter Three

1. Neil Jacobson and Andrew Christensen, *Acceptance and Change in Couple Therapy* (New York: W. W. Norton, 1996), 220.
2. Susan Raah-Cohen, personal communication.
3. David Schnarch, "Constructing the Sexual Crucible" (workshop presented in Seattle, WA, 1997).
4. Jacobson and Christensen, *Acceptance and Change,* 14.

## Chapter Four

1. Luise Eichenbaum and Susie Orbach, *What Do Women Want* (New York: Berkeley, 1983).
2. Blumstein and Schwartz, *American Couples,* 55, 130, 452.
3. Gottman and Silver, *The Seven Principles,* 101.
4. Ibid., 87.

## Chapter Five

1. Ted Huston and Renate Houts, "The Psychological Infrastructure of Courtship and Marriage: The Role of Personality and Compatibility in Romantic Relationships." Cited in Andrew Christensen and Neil Jacobson, *Reconcilable Differences* (New York: Guilford Press, 2000), 35.
2. Jacobson and Christensen, *Acceptance and Change,* 13.
3, Gottman and Silver, *The Seven Principles,* 245.
4. Christensen and Jacobson, *Reconcilable Differences,* 48–62.
5. Ibid., 49.
6. Jacobson and Christensen, *Acceptance and Change,* 220.
7. Christensen and Jacobson, *Reconcilable Differences,* 33–34.
8. Gottman and Silver, *The Seven Principles,* 29.
9. Christensen and Jacobson, *Reconcilable Differences,* 80.
10. Annamarie Jagose, *Queer Theory: An Introduction* (New York: New York University Press, 1996), 99.
11. Jason Cromwell, personal communication, 2000.
12. *Webster's New International Dictionary,* 2nd ed. (Cambridge, MA: The Riverside Press, 1934), 1043.
13. Felice Newman, *The Whole Lesbian Sex Book* (San Francisco: Cleis Press, 1999), 168.
14. Ibid., 170.
15. Ibid., 167.
16. Jagose, *Queer Theory,* 3.

## Chapter Six

1. Eric Marcus, *Together Forever: Gay and Lesbian Couples Share Their Secrets for Lasting Happiness* (New York: Anchor Books, 1999), 93.
2. Gottman and Silver, *The Seven Principles,* 89.
3. Betty Berzon, *The Intimacy Dance: A Guide to Long-Term Success in Gay and Lesbian Relationships* (New York: Plume, 1997), 43.

4.  Marcus, *Together Forever,* 99.
5.  Otto Kroeger and Janet M. Thuesen, *Type Talk: The 16 Personality Types That Determine How We Live, Love and Work* (New York: Delta, 1989), 7–9.
6.  Ibid., 30–31.
7.  Richard B. Stuart and Barbara Jacobsen, *Second Marriage* (New York: W. W. Norton, 1985), 94–95.
8.  Ibid., 103–104.
9.  Berzon, *The Intimacy Dance,* 59.
10. Ibid., 43.
11. Matthew McKay, Martha Davis, and Patrick Fanning, *Messages: The Communication Book* (Oakland, CA: New Harbinger, 1983), 39–42.
12. Marshall B. Rosenberg, *Nonviolent Communication: A Language of Compassion* (Del Mar, CA: PuddleDancer Press, 1999), 37–39.
13. Ibid., 35–36.
14. Stuart and Jacobsen, *Second Marriage,* 110.
15. Eric Marcus, *The Male Couple's Guide,* 3rd ed. (New York: HarperPerennial, 1999), 25.
16. Gottman and Silver, *The Seven Principles,* 29.
17. Matthew McKay, Patrick Fanning, and Kim Paleg, *Couple Skills: Making Your Relationship Work* (Oakland, CA: New Harbinger, 1994), 21.

## Chapter Seven

1.  Gottman and Silver, *The Seven Principles,* 15.
2.  Ibid., 129–155.
3.  Ibid., 131.
4.  Adapted from Gottman and Silver, *The Seven Principles,* 159–185; and Matthew McKay et al., *Couple Skills,* 117–128.
5.  Gottman and Silver, *The Seven Principles,* 27.
6.  Ibid., 170–176.
7.  Yetta M. Bernhard, *Self Care* (Berkeley, CA: Celestial Arts, 1975); and Thomas Gordon, *P.E.T.: Parent Effectiveness Training* (New York: New American Library, 1970), 236–253.
8.  Gottman and Silver, *The Seven Principles,* 187.
9.  Gottman and Silver, *The Seven Principles*; and Wallerstein and Blakeslee, *The Good Marriage,* 27–29.
10. Gottman and Silver, *The Seven Principles,* 132–133.
11. Ibid., 217–218.
12. Barbara Hart, "Lesbian Battering: An Examination," in *Naming the Violence,* 173.
13. Anne L. Ganley, *Understanding Domestic Violence: Preparatory Reading for Trainers* (San Francisco: Family Violence Prevention Fund, 1996), 4.
14. Hart, "Lesbian Battering," 173.

## Chapter Eight

1.  Susan E. Johnson, *Lesbian Sex: An Oral History* (Tallahassee, FL: The Naiad Press, 1996), 8.
2.  Newman, *The Whole Lesbian Sex Book,* 2.

3.  Lenore Teifer, "The Opposite of Sex: A Conversation with Lenore Teifer" interviewed by Moira Brennan, *Ms.* 9(5) (1999), 62.
4.  Johnson, *Lesbian Sex*, 6.
5.  Natalie Angier, *Woman: An Intimate Geography* (New York: Anchor Books, 2000), 218–219.
6.  Pat Love, "What Is This Thing Called Love?" *Family Networker* 23(2) (1999), 36.
7.  Anthony Walsh, *The Science of Love: Understanding Love and Its Effects on Mind and Body,* cited in Janis Abrahms Spring, *After the Affair,* (New York: HarperPerennial, 1997), 71.
8.  Love, "What Is This Thing Called Love?" 37.
9.  Ibid., 39.
10. Marny Hall, "Lesbians, Limerence and Longterm Relationships," in *Lesbian Sex,* ed. JoAnn Loulan (San Francisco: Spinsters Ink, 1987), 141.
11. Spring, *After the Affair,* 71.
12. Love, "What Is This Thing Called Love?" 39.
13. Ibid., 40.
14. Ibid., 42.
15. David Schnarch, *Passionate Marriage: Keeping Love and Intimacy Alive in Committed Relationships* (New York: Henry Holt, 1997), 140.
16. Ibid., 105–108.
17. Blumstein and Schwartz, *American Couples,* 195.
18. Laura S. Brown, "Sexual Issues in the Development of Lesbian Couples" (paper presented at the meetings of the American Psychological Association, Toronto, Canada, 1985).
19. Angier, *Woman,* 279.
20. Ibid., 218.
21. Marny Hall, *The Lesbian Love Companion* (San Francisco: HarperSanFrancisco, 1998), 50–51.
22. Schnarch, "Constructing the Sexual Crucible."
23. Newman, *The Whole Lesbian Sex Book,* 4–9.
24. Schnarch, *Passionate Marriage,* 96.
25. Teifer, "The Opposite of Sex," 65.
26. Marcus, *Together Forever,* 192.
27. Sondra Zeidenstein, "The Naked Truth," *Ms.* 9(5) (1999), 59.
28. Schnarch, *Passionate Marriage,* 100.
29. Teifer, "The Opposite of Sex," 65.
30. Newman, *The Whole Lesbian Sex Book,* 12–13.
31. Paula Martinac, *The Lesbian and Gay Book of Love and Marriage* (New York: Broadway Books, 1998), 181.
32. Ibid., 182.
33. Marcus, *The Male Couple's Guide,* 31.
34. Ibid., 43.
35. Newman, *The Whole Lesbian Sex Book,* 55.
36. Ibid., 57–59.
37. Ibid., 56.

38. Sutton, *Love Matters,* 124.
39. Betty Berzon, *Permanent Partners: Building Gay and Lesbian Relationships That Last* (New York: Plume, 1988), 163.
40. Gordon Clanton and Lynn G. Smith, *Jealousy,* rev. ed. (Lanham, MD: University Press of America, 1986), cited in Berzon, *Permanent Partners,* 162–163.
41. Spring, *After the Affair,* 1.
42. Ibid., 4–6.
43. Ibid.,109–234.

## Chapter Nine

1. Marcus, *The Male Couple's Guide,* 47.
2. Hayden Curry et al., *A Legal Guide for Lesbian and Gay Couples* (Berkeley, CA: Nolo Press, 1996), 2–6.
3. Roger Fisher and William Ury, *Getting to Yes* (New York: Penguin, 1983), 4.
4. Tina B. Tessina and Riley K. Smith, *How to Be a Couple and Still Be Free* (North Hollywood, CA: Newcastle, 1980), 97.
5. Roger Fisher and Scott Brown, *Getting Together: Building a Relationship That Gets to Yes* (Boston: Houghton Mifflin, 1988), 37–39.
6. Curry et al., *A Legal Guide,* 2.

## Chapter Ten

1. Blumstein and Schwartz, *American Couples,* 127, 130.
2. Marcus, *The Male Couple's Guide,* 135–137.
3. JoAnn Loulan (workshop presented in Seattle, WA, 1988).
4. Stuart and Jacobsen, *Second Marriage,* 78–82.
5. Marcus, *The Male Couple's Guide,* 195.
6. Ibid., 199–200.
7. Curry et al., *A Legal Guide,* vii.
8. Barbara Mackoff, *Leaving the Office Behind* (New York: G. P. Putnam's Sons, 1984).
9. Gottman and Silver, *The Seven Principles,* 88–89.
10. Marcus, *The Male Couple's Guide,* 149.

## Chapter Eleven

1. D. M. Clunis and C. D. Green, *The Lesbian Parenting Book* (Emeryville, CA: Seal Press, 1995), 65.
2. Joy Schulenburg, *Gay Parenting* (New York: Anchor Press/Doubleday, 1985), 24–25.
3. Clunis and Green, *The Lesbian Parenting Book,* 68–70.
4. H. McCubbin and C. R Figley, eds., "Stress and the Family, Volume 1: Coping with Normative Transitions," cited in Janet M. Wright, *Lesbian Step Families,* (New York: Haworth Press, 1998), 173.
5. Wright, *Lesbian Step Families,* 158–160.

6. Cheryl A. Parks, "Lesbian Parenthood: A Review of the Literature," *American Journal of Orthopsychiatry* 68(3) (1998), 376–389; Charlotte Patterson, "Children of the Lesbian Baby Boom: Behavioral Adjustment, Self Concepts, and Sex Role Identity," in *Lesbian and Gay Psychology: Theory, Research, and Clinical Applications,* eds. B. Greene and G. M. Herek (Thousand Oaks, CA: Sage, 1994), 1:156–175.

7. Patterson, "Children of the Lesbian Baby Boom," 156–175.

8. Ailsa Steckel, "Psychosocial Development of Children of Lesbian Mothers," in *Gay and Lesbian Parents,* ed. Frederick W. Bozett (New York: Praeger, 1987), 75–85.

9. Louise B. Silverstein and Carl F. Auerbach, "Deconstructing the Essential Father," *American Psychologist* 54(6) (1999), 397–407.

10. H. H. Bity-Pleck, "The Gender Role Strain Paradigm: An Update," cited in Silverstein and Auerbach, "Deconstructing the Essential Father."

11. Silverstein and Auerbach, "Deconstructing the Essential Father," 397–407.

12. Wright, *Lesbian Step Families,* 116.

13. Clunis and Green, *The Lesbian Parenting Book,* 47.

14. Patricia Kelley, *Developing Healthy Stepfamilies: Twenty Families Tell Their Stories* (Binghamton, NY: Harrington Park Press, 1995), 32.

15. Kelley, *Developing Healthy Stepfamilies,* 33.

16. Clunis and Green, *The Lesbian Parenting Book,* 19–21.

17. Cheri Pies, *Considering Parenthood,* 2nd ed. (Minneapolis: Spinsters Ink, 1988); April Martin, *The Lesbian and Gay Parenting Handbook* (New York: Harper Perennial, 1993); and Clunis and Green, *The Lesbian Parenting Book.*

18. Judith Wallerstein and Sandra Blakeslee, *Second Chances: Men, Women and Children a Decade after Divorce* (New York: Ticknor & Fields, 1990), 179–182.

## Chapter Twelve

1. Emily Coleman and Betty Edwards, *Brief Encounters: How to Make the Most of Relationships That May Not Last Forever* (New York: Anchor Books, 1980).

2. Ginny NiCarthy, *Getting Free: You Can End Abuse and Take Back Your Life* (Emeryville, CA: Seal Press, 2004).

3. Carol Becker, *Unbroken Ties: Lesbian Ex-Lovers* (Boston: Alyson Publications, 1988), 211.

4. Larry Uhrig, *The Two of Us: Affirming, Celebrating and Symbolizing Gay and Lesbian Relationships* (Boston: Alyson Publications, 1984).

5. Paula Martinac, *The Lesbian and Gay Book of Love and Marriage* (New York: Broadway Books, 1998), 87.

## Chapter Thirteen

1. Yu-Wen Ying, Mary Coombs, and Peter A. Lee, "Family Intergenerational Relationship of Asian American Adolescents," *Cultural Diversity and Ethnic Minority Psychology* 5(4) (1999), 351.

2. Teresa A. Mok, "Asian American Dating: Important Factors in Partner Choice," *Cultural Diversity and Ethnic Minority Psychology* 5(2) (1999), 105–106.

3.  L. Tien, "Conjoint Work in Cross-Cultural/Cross-Racial Marriage" (workshop presented by the Washington State Psychological Association, Seattle, WA, April, 1999).

4.  Vickie L. Sears, "Cross-Cultural Ethnic Relationships," unpublished manuscript, 1987.

5.  Jewelle Gomez, "Across the Glittering Sea," in *Skin Deep: Black Women and White Women Write about Race,* eds. Marita Golden and Susan Richards Shreve (New York: Anchor Books, 1995), 152.

6.  Tien, "Conjoint Work in Cross-Cultural/Cross-Racial Marriage."

7.  *Tools for Diversity Training* (Portland, Oregon: TACS, 1994). For more information, contact TACS, 1903 Ankeny, Portland, OR 97214.

8.  Ying et al., "Family Intergenerational Relationship of Asian American Adolescents," 351.

9.  H. C. Triandis et al., "Individualism and Collectivism: Cross-Cultural Perspectives on Self-Ingroup Relationships," *Journal of Personality and Social Psychology* 54 (1988), 323–338.

10. Christine T. Lipat, Trinity A. Dodoes, Cianna Pamintuan Stewart, et al., "Tomboy, Dyke, Lezzie, and Bi: Filipina Lesbian and Bisexual Women Speak Out," in *Filipino Americans: Transformation and Identity,* ed. Maria P. P. Root (Newbury Park, CA: Sage, 1997), 244–245.

11. Maria P. P. Root, "Bill of Rights for People with Multiracial Identity," in *The Multicultural Experience: Racial Borders as the New Frontier,* ed. Maria P. P. Root (Newbury Park, CA: Sage, 1996), 8.

**Chapter Fourteen**

1.  David Finkelhor, "Current Information on the Scope and Nature of Sexual Abuse," *Future of Children* 4(2) (1994), 31–53.

2.  Lucy Berliner and Diana M. Elliott, "Sexual Abuse of Children," in *The APSAC Handbook on Child Maltreatment,* eds. John Briere et al. (Thousand Oaks, CA: Sage, 1996), 52.

3.  JoAnn Loulan, *Lesbian Passion: Loving Ourselves and Each Other* (San Francisco: Spinsters Ink/Aunt Lute, 1987), 181.

4.  Claudia Black, *It Will Never Happen to Me* (New York: Ballantine Books, 1981), 49–64.

5.  Charles L. Whitfield, *Healing the Child Within: Discovery and Recovery for Adult Children of Dysfunctional Families* (Pompano Beach, FL: Health Communications, 1987), 41.

6.  Jane Middelton-Moz, *Shame and Guilt: The Masters of Disguise* (Deerfield Beach, FL: Health Communications, 1990), 14–17.

7.  Dena Rosenbloom and Mary Beth Williams, with Barbara Watkins, *Life after Trauma: A Workbook for Healing* (New York: Guilford, 1999), 73.

8.  Eric Rofes. "I Thought People Like That Killed Themselves," in Loulan, *Lesbian Passion,* 134.

9.  Loulan, *Lesbian Passion,* 34.

10. JoAnn Loulan, *Lesbian Sex* (San Francisco: Spinsters Ink, 1984), 188.

## Chapter Fifteen

1. Equal Employment Opportunity Commission (EEOC) and U.S. Department of Justice, *Americans with Disabilities Act Handbook* (Washington, DC: U.S. Government Printing Office, 1991), 1–26.
2. Ibid.
3. Ibid.
4. Romel Mackelprang and Richard Salsgiver, *Disability: A Diversity Model Approach in Human Service Practice* (Pacific Grove, CA: Brooks/Cole Publishing Company, 1999), 48.
5. Sefra Kobrin Pitzele, *We Are Not Alone* (New York: Workman, 1986).
6. Carolyn Gage, "Hidden Disability," in *Restricted Access: Lesbians on Disability*, eds. Victoria Brownworth and Susan Raffo (Emeryville, CA: Seal Press, 1999), 201–211.
7. M. A. Crate, "Adaptation to Chronic Illness," in Mackelprang and Salsgiver, *Disability: A Diversity Model Approach*, 61.
8. J. S. Rolland, "A Conceptual Model of Chronic and Life-Threatening Illness and Its Impact on Families," in *Chronic Illness and Disability*, eds. C. S. Chilman, E. W. Nunnaly, and F. M. Cox (Newbury Park, CA: Sage, 1988).
9. Peggy Monroe et al., *Circles of Care* (Seattle: AIDS Cargiver Support Network, 1998)
10. The Lesbian and Bisexual Women's Study, 1001 Broadway #320, Seattle, WA 98122.

## Chapter Sixteen

1. Jack Levin and William C. Levin, *Ageism, Prejudice and Discrimination Against the Elderly* (Belmont, CA: Wadsworth, 1980), 111.
2. Betty Friedan, *The Fountain of Age* (New York: Simon & Schuster, 1993), 72.
3. Merilee Clunis et al., *The Lives of Lesbian Elders: Looking Back, Looking Forward* (Binghamton, NY: Haworth Press, 2004).
4. Friedan, *The Fountain of Age*, 194.
5. Pat Freeman, personal communication, 1999.
6. Clunis et al., *Looking Back . . . Looking Forward.*
7. Ibid.
8. Friedan, *The Fountain of Age*, 216.
9. Amanda, "Commentary: Baby Dyke," *Red Dot Girls/The Elder Lesbian Initiative* 8 (April, 1999), 2.
10. Robert N. Butler and Myrna I. Lewis, *Love and Sex after Sixty* (New York: Harper and Row, 1988), 1–7.
11. Friedan, *The Fountain of Age*, 202–203.
12. Thomas Blank et al., "Retirement: Timing, Initiation and Satisfaction" (Proceedings of the Gerontological Society of America, Washington, DC, November 19, 1987), cited in Friedan, *The Fountain of Age*, 214.
13. Susan Love with Karen Lindsey, *Dr. Susan Love's Hormone Book* (New York: Random House, 1997).
14. Teresa C. Jones et al., "Looking Back . . . Looking Forward: Addressing the Lives of Lesbians 55 and Older" (paper presented at the Council on Social Work Education Meeting, San Francisco, March, 1999), 8.
15. Ibid., 7.

## Chapter Seventeen

1. Blumstein and Schwartz, *American Couples,* 307.
2. Laura Brown, personal communication, 1984.
3. Blumstein and Schwartz, *American Couples,* 307.
4. Ibid., 329.
5. Coleman and Edwards, *Brief Encounters.*
6. William Worden, *Grief Counseling and Grief Therapy* (New York: Springer, 1982), 11–17.

## Chapter Eighteen

1. William Bridges, *Transitions* (Reading, MA: Addison-Wesley, 1980), 112–131.
2. Ibid., 130.
3. Stuart and Jacobsen, *Second Marriage,* 45–46.

# Resources

## Organizations and Web Sites

### Lesbian Relationships

Partners Task Force for Gay and
Lesbian Couples
Box 9685
Seattle, WA 98109
(206) 935-4206
www.buddybuddy.com

### Parenting/Family

Children of Lesbians and Gays
Everywhere (COLAGE)
3543 18th Street, Suite 17
San Francisco, CA 94110
(415) 861-5437
www.colage.org

Family Pride Coalition (formerly the
Gay and Lesbian Parents Coalition
International)
P.O. Box 34337
San Diego, CA 92163
(619) 296-0199
www.familypride.org

Parents and Friends of Lesbians and
Gays (PFLAG)
1726 M Street NW, Suite 400
Washington, DC 20036
(202) 638-4200
www.pflag.org

*Gay Parent Magazine*
P.O. Box 750852
Forest Hills, NY 11375-0852
(718) 997-0392
www.gayparentmag.com

The Gay, Lesbian, and Straight
Education Network (GLSEN)
121 West 27th Street, Suite 804
New York, NY 10001
(212) 727-0135
www.glsen.org

### Bisexuality

Bisexual Resource Center
P.O. Box 400639
Cambridge, MA 02140
(617) 424-9595
www.biresource.org

BiNet USA
2401 Wilson Boulevard #110-311
Arlington, VA 22203
www.binetusa.org

Bisexual Options
Fritz Klein, M.D.
4545 Park Boulevard #207
San Diego, CA 92116
www.bisexual.org

## Gender/Transgender

International Foundation for Gender
Education
14 Felton Street
Waltham, MA 02453-4117
(781) 899-2212
www.ifge.org

Renaissance Education Association
987 Old Eagle School Road, Suite 719
Wayne, PA 19087
(610) 975-9119
www.ren.org

Ingersoll Gender Center
1812 East Madison Street
Seattle, WA 98122
(206) 329-6651
www.ingersollcenter.org

## Conflict Resolution

Association for Conflict Resolution
1015 18th Street NW, Suite 1150
Washington, DC 20036
(202) 464-9700
www.acrnet.org

## Domestic Violence

The Northwest Network of Bisexual,
Trans, and Lesbian Survivors of Abuse
(formerly Advocates for Abused and
Battered Lesbians)
P.O. Box 20398
Seattle, WA 98102
(206) 568-7777
(206) 517-9670 (TTY)
www.aabl.org

National Domestic Violence Hotline
P.O. Box 161810
Austin, TX 78716
(800) 799-SAFE or (800) 799-7233
(800) 787-3224 (TTY)
www.ndvh.org

## Recovery from Sexual Abuse

The Healing Woman Foundation
P.O. Box 28040-C
San Jose, CA 95159
(800) 477-4111
www.healingwoman.org

Survivors of Incest Anonymous (SIA)
P.O. Box 21817
Baltimore, MD 21222-6817
(410) 282-3400
www.siawso.org

## Recovery from Addiction

Pride Institute Main Headquarters
168 5th Avenue, Suite 4 South
New York, NY 10010
(800) 547-7433
www.pride-institute.com
This organization offers inpatient and
outpatient treatment programs for
alcohol- and drug-dependent gays,
lesbians, and bisexuals. Its toll-free
number is staffed 24 hours a day for
information and advice.

Alcoholics Anonymous
P.O. Box 459, Grand Central Station
New York, NY 10163
(212) 647-1680
www.alcoholicsanonymous.org
Call Alcoholics Anonymous (AA) in
your area for information about AA,
NA, and other 12-step programs—
including gay and/or lesbian meetings.

Al-Anon Family Groups
1600 Corporate Landing Parkway
Virginia Beach, VA 23454-5617
(800) 356-9996
www.al-anon.org

Narcotics Anonymous
World Service Office
P.O. Box 9999
Van Nuys, CA 91409
(818) 773-9999
www.na.org

Overeaters Anonymous
World Service Office
6075 Zenith Court NE
Rio Rancho, NM 87124
(505) 891-2664
www.overeatersanonymous.org

Co-Dependents Anonymous
P.O. Box 33577
Phoenix, AZ 85067
(602) 277-7991
www.codependents.org

## Disability/Chronic Illness

The CFIDS Association of America
P.O. Box 220398
Charlotte, NC 28222-0398
Resource line: (704) 365-2343
Toll-free information line:
(800) 442-3437
www.cfids.org

*Dykes, Disability & Stuff* magazine
P.O. Box 8773
Madison, WI 53708

*Ragged Edge Magazine*
www.raggededgemagazine.com

Deaf Queer Resource Center
www.deafqueer.org

## Cancer

The Mautner Project for Lesbians
with Cancer
1707 L Street NW, Suite 500
Washington, DC 20036
(202) 332-5536
www.mautnerproject.org
This organization provides referrals, peer
support, and information for lesbians
with cancer and their partners. It also
maintains a nationwide listing of
local lesbian cancer projects and
support services.

SusanLoveMD.com
www.susanlovemd.com

## Aging

Gay and Lesbian Association of Retiring
Persons (GLARP)
10940 Wilshire Boulevard, Suite 1600
Los Angeles, CA 90024
(310) 966-1500
www.gaylesbianretiring.org

Old Lesbians Organizing for Change
(OLOC)
P.O. Box 980422
Houston, TX 77098
www.oloc.org

Older Women's League (OWL)
666 11th Street NW, Suite 700
Washington, DC 20001
(202) 783-6686
(800) 825-3695
www.owl-national.org

Pride Senior Network
356 West 8th Street
New York, NY 10011
(212) 271-7288
www.pridesenior.org

Gray Panthers
733 15th Street NW, Suite 437
Washington, DC 20005
(202) 737-6637
(800) 280-5362
www.graypanthers.org

**Menopause**

Susan Love, MD
www.susanlovemd.com

**Legal Resources**

American Civil Liberties Union
Lesbian and Gay Rights Project
125 Broad Street, 18th Floor
New York, NY 10004
(212) 549-2500
www.aclu.org

Lambda Legal Defense and
Education Fund
National Headquarters
120 Wall Street, Suite 1500
New York, NY 10005
(212) 809-8585
www.lambdalegal.org

National Center for Lesbian Rights
(NCLR)
870 Market Street, Suite 570
San Francisco, CA 94102
(415) 392-6257
www.nclrights.org

GLAD
P.O. Box 218
Boston, MA 02112
(617) 426-1350
(800) 455-GLAD or (800) 455-4523
www.glad.org
If you can't find a lawyer through a
recommendation, the local gay/lesbian
publications, or other local resources,
there is another route. The Gay &
Lesbian Advocates & Defenders (GLAD)
in Boston publishes a state-by-state
directory of gay/lesbian and gay/lesbian-
friendly lawyers.

**Finding the Professional You Need**

To find a lesbian or lesbian-affirmative
health-care or mental-health professional, get recommendations from
friends or a respected agency in your
community. You can also search the
Internet or consult your local gay/lesbian
yellow pages or business guide. You can
also contact the organizations below:

Gay and Lesbian Medical Association
459 Fulton Street, Suite 107
San Francisco, CA 94102
(415) 255-4547
www.glma.org

American Psychological Association
750 1st Street NE
Washington, DC 20002-4242
(202) 336-5500
www.apa.org
Ask for the staff person who handles the
Committee on Gay and Lesbian
Concerns, which provides referrals to
psychologists who have interest in
and/or experience working with gays
and lesbians.

American Psychiatric Association
1400 K Street NW
Washington, DC 20005
(202) 682-6000
www.psych.org

Gay & Lesbian National Hotline
(GLNH)
PMB #296
2261 Market Street
San Francisco, CA 94114
(888) 843-4564
www.glnh.org

National Association of Social Workers
750 1st Street NE, Suite 700
Washington, DC 20002
(800) 638-8799
www.socialworkers.org

## Political Organizations

Gay and Lesbian Alliance Against
Defamation (GLAAD)
150 West 26th Street #503
New York, NY 10001
(212) 807-1700
www.glaad.org

Human Rights Campaign
919 18th Street NW, Suite 800
Washington, DC 20006
(202) 628-4160
www.hrc.org

National Gay & Lesbian Task Force
1700 Kalorama Road NW
Washington, DC 20009-2624
(202) 332-6483
(202) 332-6219 (TTY)
www.ngltf.org

# Resources

*Selected Bibliography*

## Lesbian Relationships

Berzon, Betty. *The Intimacy Dance: A Guide to Long-Term Success in Gay and Lesbian Relationships.* New York: Plume, 1997.

————. *Permanent Partners: Building Gay and Lesbian Relationships That Last.* New York: E. P. Dutton, 1988.

Hall, Marny. *The Lesbian Love Companion: How to Survive Everything from Heartthrob to Heartbreak.* San Francisco: HarperSanFrancisco, 1998.

Marcus, Eric. *Together Forever: Gay and Lesbian Couples Share Their Secrets for Lasting Happiness.* New York: Doubleday, 1998.

McDaniel, Judith. *The Lesbian Couples' Guide: Finding the Right Woman and Creating a Life Together.* New York: HarperPerennial, 1995.

Slater, Suzanne. *The Lesbian Family Life Cycle.* Champaign, IL: University of Illinois Press, 1999.

Sutton, Linda. *Love Matters: A Book of Lesbian Romance and Relationship.* Binghamton, NY: Harrington Park Press, 1999.

Tessina, Tina, PhD. *Gay Relationships for Men and Women: How to Find Them, How to Improve Them, How to Make Them Last.* Los Angeles: J. P. Tarcher, 1990.

## Communication, Differences, and Conflict in Relationships

Christensen, Andrew, and Neil Jacobson. *Reconcilable Differences.* New York: Guilford, 2000.

Gottman, John, and Nan Silver, *The Seven Principles for Making Marriage Work.* New York: Crown, 1999.

Kroeger, Otto, and Janet M. Thuesen. *Type Talk: The 16 Personality Types that Determine How We Live, Love and Work.* New York: Delta, 1989.

McKay, Matthew, Patrick Fanning, and Kim Paleg. *Couple Skills: Making Your Relationship Work.* Oakland, CA: New Harbinger, 1994.

Schnarch, David. *Passionate Marriage: Love, Sex, and Intimacy in Emotionally Committed Relationships.* New York: Owl Books, 1998.

Spring, Janis Abrahams. *After the Affair: Healing the Pain and Rebuilding Trust When a Partner Has Been Unfaithful.* New York: HarperPerennial, 1997.

Wallerstein, Judith S., and Sandra Blakeslee. *The Good Marriage: How and Why Love Lasts.* New York: Warner Books, 1995.

Weinstock, Jacqueline S., ed. *Lesbian Ex-Lovers: The Really Long-Term Relationships.* Binghamton, New York: Harrington Park Press, 2004.

## Domestic Violence

Brewster, Susan. *To Be an Anchor in the Storm: A Guide for Families and Friends of Abused Women.* Emeryville, CA: Seal Press, 2000.

NiCarthy, Ginny. *Getting Free: You Can End Abuse and Take Back Your Life.* Emeryville, CA: Seal Press, 2004.

Renzetti, Claire. *Violent Betrayal: Partner Abuse in Lesbian Relationships.* Newbury Park, CA: Sage, 1992.

## Sex

Caster, Wendy. *The Lesbian Sex Book.* Boston: Alyson, 2003.

Dodson, Betty. *Sex for One: The Joy of Selfloving.* New York: Crown, 1996.

Haines, Staci. *The Survivor's Guide to Sex: How to Have an Empowered Sex Life after Child Sexual Abuse.* San Francisco: Cleis Press, 1999.

Johnson, Susan E. *Lesbian Sex: An Oral History.* Tallahassee, FL: Naiad Press, 1996.

Loulan, JoAnn. *Lesbian Sex.* San Francisco: Spinsters Ink, 1984.

Loulan, JoAnn, with Mariah B. Nelson. *Lesbian Passion: Loving Ourselves and Each Other.* San Francisco: Spinsters Ink/Aunt Lute, 1987.

Newman, Felice. *The Whole Lesbian Sex Book: A Passionate Guide for All of Us.* San Francisco: Cleis Press, 1999.

## Gender/ Trans Gender/Butch/Femme

Borich, Barrie Jean. *My Lesbian Husband: Landscapes of a Marriage.* St. Paul, MN: Graywolf, 1999.

Bornstein, Kate. *Gender Outlaw: On Men, Women and the Rest of Us.* New York: Vintage Books, 1995.

Brown, Mildred L., and Chloe Ann Rounsley. *True Selves: Understanding Transexualism for Families, Friends, Coworkers, and Helping Professionals.* San Francisco: Jossey Bass, 1996.

Burch, Beverly. *On Intimate Terms: The Psychology of Difference in Lesbian Relationships.* Urbana, IL: University of Illinois Press, 1993.

Califia, Pat. *Sex Changes: The Politics of Transgenderism.* San Francisco: Cleis Press, 1997.

Cromwell, Jason. *TransMen and FTMs: Identities, Bodies, Genders and Sexualities.* Urbana, IL: University of Illinois Press, 1999.

Feinberg, Leslie. *Transgender Warriors: Making History from Joan of Arc to Dennis Rodman.* Boston: Beacon Press, 1997.

———. *Trans Liberation: Beyond Pink or Blue.* Boston: Beacon Press, 1998.

Loulan, JoAnn. *The Lesbian Erotic Dance: Butch, Femme, Androgeny, and Other Rhythms.* San Francisco: Spinsters, 1990.

McCloskey, Deirdre N. *Crossing: A Memoir.* Chicago: University of Chicago Press, 1999.

O'Keefe, Tracie, and Katrina Fox, eds. *Finding the Real Me: True Tales of Sex and Gender Diversity.* San Francisco: Jossey Bass, 2003.

Weston, Kath. *Render Me, Gender Me: Lesbians Talk Sex, Class, Color, Nation, Studmuffins.* New York: Columbia University Press, 1996.

Wilchins, Riki Anne. *Read My Lips: Sexual Subversion and the End of Gender.* Ithaca, NY: Firebrand, 1997.

## Cross-Cultural/Interracial Couples

Gillespie, Peggy, and Gigi Kaeser. *Of Many Colors: Portraits of Multiracial Families.* Boston: University of Massachusetts Press, 1997.

Root, Maria P. P., ed. *The Multicultural Experience: Racial Borders as the New Frontier.* Newbury, CA: Sage, 1996.

Takaki, Ronald. *A Different Mirror: A History of Multicultural Americans.* Boston: Little, Brown, 1993.

## Parenting

Blau, Melinda. *Families Apart: Ten Keys to Successful Co-Parenting.* New York: G. P. Putnam's Sons, 1994.

Brodzinsky, David M., Marshall D. Schechter, and Robin Marantz Henig. *Being Adopted: The Lifelong Search for Self.* New York: Anchor/Doubleday, 1992.

Clunis, D. Merilee, and C. Dorsey Green. *The Lesbian Parenting Book: A Guide to Creating Families and Raising Children.* Emeryville, CA: Seal Press, 2003.

Gaskins, Pearl Fuyo, ed. *What Are You?: Voices of Mixed-Race Young People.* New York: Henry Holt, 1999.

Hopson, Darlene Powell, and Derek Hopson. *Raising the Rainbow Generation: Teaching Your Children to Be Successful in a Multicultural Society.* New York: Fireside, 1993.

Johnson, Suzanne M., and Elizabeth O'Conner. *Your Guide to Helping Your Family Grow Up Happy, Healthy, and Proud.* New York: Guilford, 2001.

Martin, April. *The Lesbian and Gay Parenting Handbook: Creating and Raising Our Families.* New York: HarperPerennial, 1993.

Nichols, Michael P. *Stop Arguing with Your Kids: How to Win the Battle of Wills by Making Your Children Feel Heard.* New York: Guilford, 2004.

Pies, Cheri. *Considering Parenthood: A Workbook for Lesbians,* 2nd ed. San Francisco, CA: Spinsters Ink/Aunt Lute, 1988.

Rafkin, Louise, ed. *Different Mothers: Sons and Daughters of Lesbians Talk about Their Lives.* Pittsburgh, PA: Cleis Press, 1990.

Ricci, Isolina. *Mom's House, Dad's House: Making Two Homes for Your Child.* 2nd ed. New York: Fireside, 1997.

Saffron, Lisa. *Challenging Conceptions: Pregnancy and Parenting Beyond the Traditional Family.* London: Cassell, 1994.

————. *What about the Children? Sons and Daughters of Lesbian and Gay Parents Talk about Their Lives.* London; Cassell, 1996.

Schulenburg, Joy. *Gay Parenting.* Garden City, NY: Anchor Press/Doubleday, 1985.

Simons, Robin. *After the Tears: Parents Talk about Raising a Guild with a Disability.* San Diego: Harcourt Brace Jovanovich, 1987.

Slater, Suzanne. *The Lesbian Family Life Cycle.* Champaign, IL: University of Illinois Press, 1999.

Snow, Judith E. *How It Feels to Have a Gay or Lesbian Parent: A Book by Kids for Kids of All Ages.* Binghamton, NY: Harrington Park Press, 2004.

Tasker, Fiona L., and Susan Golombok. *Growing Up in a Lesbian Family: Effects on Child Development.* New York: Guilford, 1997.

Wadia-Ells, Susan, ed. *The Adoption Reader: Birth Mothers, Adoptive Mothers and Adopted Daughters Tell Their Stories.* Emeryville, CA: Seal Press, 1995.

Wells, Jess, ed. *Lesbians Raising Sons.* Boston: Alyson, 1997.

Weston, Kath. *Families We Choose: Lesbians, Gays, Kinship.* New York: Columbia University Press, 1991.

Wright, Janet M. *Lesbian Step Families: An Ethnography of Love.* New York: Haworth Press, 1998.

Wright, Marguerite A. *I'm Chocolate, You're Vanilla: Raising Healthy Black and Biracial Children in a Race-Conscious World.* San Francisco: Jossey-Bass, 1998.

## Ceremonies/Unions

Ayers, Tess, and Paul Brown. *The Essential Guide to Lesbian and Gay Weddings.* San Francisco: HarperSanFrancisco, 1994.

Butler, Becky, ed. *Ceremonies of the Heart: Celebrating Lesbian Unions.* Emeryville, CA: Seal Press, 1997.

Marcus, Eric. *Together Forever: Gay and Lesbian Couples Share Their Secrets for Lasting Happiness.* New York: Anchor Books, 1999.

Martinac, Paula. *The Lesbian and Gay Book of Love and Marriage.* New York: Broadway Books, 1998.

Stiers, Gretchen A. *From This Day Forward: Commitment, Marriage and Family in Lesbian and Gay Relationships.* New York: Macmillan, 2000.

## Coming Out

Bernstein, Robert A. *Straight Parents, Gay Children: Keeping Families Together.* New York: Thunder's Mouth Press, 1995.

Clark, Don. *Loving Someone Gay,* rev. ed. Millbrae, CA: Celestial Arts, 1997.

Fairchild, Betty, and Nancy Hayward. *Now That You Know: A Parents' Guide to Understanding Their Gay and Lesbian Children.* San Diego, CA: Harcourt Brace Jovanovich, 1998.

Larkin, Joan, ed. *A Woman Like That: Lesbian and Bisexual Writers Tell Their Coining Out Stories.* New York: Avon Books, 1999.

## Recovery from Abuse

Balsam, Kimberly F., ed. *Trauma, Stress and Resilience among Sexual Minority Women.* Binghamton, NY: Harrington Park Press, 2004.

Bass, Ellen and Laura Davis. *The Courage to Heal: A Guide for Women Survivors of Child Sexual Abuse,* rev. ed. New York: HarperPerennial, 1994.

Crawford, Cristina. *No Safe Place: The Legacy of Family Violence.* New York: Station Hill Press, 1994.

Davis, Laura. *Allies in Healing: When the Person You Love Was Sexually Abused as a Child.* New York: Perennial, 1991.

Haines, Staci. *The Survivor's Guide to Sex: How to Have an Empowered Sex Life after Child Sexual Abuse.* San Francisco: Cleis Press, 1999.

Maltz, Wendy. *The Sexual Healing Journey: A Guide for Survivors of Sexual Abuse.* New York: Perennial, 1991.

Maltz, Wendy, and Beverly Holman. *Incest and Sexuality: A Guide to Understanding and Healing.* Lexington, MA: Lexington Books, 1991.

Matsakis, Aphrodite. *I Can't Get Over It: A Handbook for Trauma Survivors.* Oakland, CA: New Harbinger, 1992.

Robinson, Lori. *I Will Survive: The African-American Guide to Healing from Sexual Abuse and Assault.* Emeryville, CA: Seal Press, 2003.

Rosenbloom, Dena, and Mary Beth Williams with Barbara E. Watkins. *Life after Trauma: A Workbook for Healing.* New York: Guilford, 1999.

Russell, Diana H. *The Secret Trauma: Incest in the Lives of Girls and Women,* rev. ed. New York: Basic Books, 1999.

Wisechild, Louise M. *The Obsidian Mirror: Healing from Childhood Sexual Abuse.* Emeryville, CA: Seal Press, 2003.

## Disability/Chronic Illness

Allen, John D. *Gay, Lesbian, Bisexual, and Transgender People with Developmental Disabilities and Mental Retardation.* Binghamton, NY: Harrington Park Press, 2003.

Brownworth, Victoria, ed. *Coming Out of Cancer. Writings from the Lesbian Cancer Epidemic.* Emeryville, CA: Seal Press, 2000.

Brownworth, Victoria, and Susan Raffo, eds. *Restricted Access: Lesbians on Disability.* Emeryville, CA: Seal Press, 1999.

Donoghue, Paul J., PhD, and Mary E. Siegel, PhD. *Sick and Tired of Feeling Sick and Tired: Living with Invisible Chronic Illness.* New York: W. W. Norton, 1992.

Lechtenberg, Richard, MD. *Multiple Sclerosis Fact Book.* Philadelphia: F. A. Davis, 1995.

Molloy, Susan. *Handling It: You and Your Long-Term Disease.* Melbourne, Australia: Hill of Content, 1995.

Monroe, Peggy, Judy Gough, and Tim Grendon. *Circles of Care: Caring For and Remembering People with AIDS.* Seattle, WA: AIDS Caregiver Support Network, 1998.

## Aging

Adleman, Jeanne, et al. *Lambda Gray: A Practical, Emotional, and Spiritual Guide for Gays and Lesbians Who Are Growing Older.* North Hollywood, CA: Newcastle, 1993.

Adelman, Marcy. *Lesbian Passages: True Stories Told by Lesbians over 40.* Boston: Alyson, 1996.

Cole, Ellen, and Esther Rothblum, eds. *Lesbians at Midlife: The Creative Transition, An Anthology.* San Francisco: Spinsters, 1991.

Doress-Worters, Paula B., and Diana Laskin Siegal, in cooperation with the Boston Women's Health Book Collective. *The New Ourselves, Growing Older.* New York: Touchstone, 1994.

Faderman, Lillian. *Odd Girls and Twilight Lovers: A History of Lesbian Life in Twentieth-Century America.* New York: Penguin Books, 1992.

Gershick, Zsa Zsa. *Gay Old Girls.* Los Angeles: Alyson, 1998.

Gould, Jean, ed. *Dutiful Daughters: Caring for Our Parents as They Grow Old.* Emeryville, CA: Seal Press, 1999.

Jensen, Karol L. *Lesbian Epiphanies: Women Coming Out in Later Life.* Binghamton, NY: Haworth Press, 1999.

Kehoe, Monika. *Lesbians over 60 Speak for Themselves.* Binghamton, NY: Harrington Park Press, 1989.

MacDonald, Barbara, and Cynthia Rich. *Look Me in the Eye: Old Women, Aging, and Ageism,* 2nd ed. San Francisco, CA: Spinsters Ink, 1991.

## Menopause

Landau, Carol, Michele G. Cyr, and Anne W. Moulton. *The Complete Book of Menopause.* New York: G. P. Putnam, 1994.

Love, Susan, with Karen Lindsey. *Dr. Susan Love's Hormone Book: Making Informed Choices about Menopause.* New York: Random House, 1997.

Lynch, Lee, and Akia Woods, eds. *Off the Rag: Lesbians Writing on Menopause.* Norwich, VT: New Victoria Publishers, 1996.

Perry, Susan, and Kate O'Hanlon, MD. *Natural Menopause: The Complete Guide.* Reading, MA: Addison-Wesley, 1997.

Ryneveld, Edna Copeland. *Menopause: A Gentle, Natural Approach.* St. Paul, MN: Llewellyn, 1998.

Sheehy, Gail. *The Silent Passage: Menopause,* rev. ed. New York: Pocket Books, 1998.

## Endings

Ahrons, Constance R. *The Good Divorce.* New York: HarperCollins, 1994.

Bridges, William. *Transitions: Making Sense of Life's Changes.* Reading, MA: Addison-Wesley, 1980.

Cole, Diane. *After Great Pain: A New Life Emerges.* New York: Summit Books, 1992.

Hall, Marny. *The Lesbian Love Companion: How to Survive Everything from Heartthrob to Heartbreak.* San Francisco: HarperSanFrancisco. 1998.

Kirshenbaum, Mira. *Too Good to Leave, Too Bad to Stay: A Step-by-Step Guide to Help You Decide Whether to Stay In or Get Out of Your Relationship.* New York: Plume, 1996.

Pace, Anita L., ed. *Write from the Heart: Lesbians Healing from Heartache.* Beaverton, OR: Baby Steps Press, 1992.

Trafford, Abigail. *Crazy Time: Surviving Divorce and Building a New Life,* rev. ed. New York: HarperPerennial, 1992.

Wallerstein, Judith, and Sandra Blakeslee. *Second Chances: Men, Women and Children a Decade after Divorce.* New York: Ticknor and Fields, 1990.

## Legal Resources

Coles, Matt. *Try This at Home: A Do-It-Yourself Guide to Winning Lesbian and Gay Civil Rights Policy: An ACLU Guidebook.* New York: New Press, 1996.

Curry, Hayden et al., eds. *A Legal Guide for Lesbian and Gay Couples.* Berkeley, CA: Nolo Press, 1999.

Lustig, Harold L. *Four Steps to Financial Security for Lesbian and Gay Couples.* New York: Fawcett, 1999.

# Bibliography

Adelman, Marcy, ed. *Long Time Passing: Lives of Older Lesbians.* Boston: Alyson, 1986.
———. *Lesbian Passages: True Stories Told by Lesbians over 40.* Boston: Alyson, 1996.
Adleman, Jeanne, et al. *Lambda Gray: A Practical, Emotional, and Spiritual Guide for Gays and Lesbians Who Are Growing Older.* North Hollywood, CA: Newcastle, 1993.
Ahrons, Constance R. *The Good Divorce.* New York: HarperCollins, 1994.
Allen, John D. *Gay, Lesbian, Bisexual, and Transgender People with Developmental Disabilities and Mental Retardation.* Binghamton, NY: Harrington Park Press, 2003.
Allen, P. G. "Beloved Women: Lesbians in American Indian Cultures." *Conditions,* 7 (1981): 67–87.
Amanda. "Commentary: Baby Dyke." *RedDotGirls/The Elder Lesbian Initiative* 8 (April, 1999).
Andrusia, David, ed. *Frommer's Gay and Lesbian Europe.* New York: MacMillan, 1999.
Angier, Natalie. *Woman: An Intimate Geography.* New York: Anchor Books, 2000.
Anzaldua, G., ed. *Making Face, Making Soul, Haciendo Caras: Creative and Critical Perspectives by Women of Color.* San Francisco: Aunt Lute Foundation Books, 1990.
Arnup, Katherine, ed. *Lesbian Parenting: Living with Pride and Prejudice.* Charlottetown, P.E.I.: Gynergy Books, 1995.
Ayers, Tess, and Paul Brown. *The Essential Guide to Lesbian and Gay Weddings.* San Francisco: Harper, 1994.
Balsam, Kimberly F., ed. *Trauma, Stress and Resilience among Sexual Minority Women.* Binghamton, NY: Harrington Park Press, 2004.
Banks, Ann. *When Your Parents Get a Divorce: A Kid's Journal.* New York: Puffin/Penguin Group, 1991.
Barbach, Lonnie. *For Each Other: Sharing Sexual Intimacy.* Garden City, NY: Anchor Press/Doubleday, 1982.
———. *For Yourself: The Fulfillment of Female Sexuality.* New York: New American Library, 1975.

Barrett, Susan E. "Children of Lesbian Parents: The What, When and How of Talking about Donor Identity." *Women & Therapy* 20(2) (1997): 43–55.

Barrett, Susan E., and Carol M. Aubin. "Feminist Considerations of Intercountry Adoptions." *Women & Therapy* 10(1–2) (1990): 127–138.

Bass, E., and L. Davis. *The Courage to Heal: A Guide for Women Survivors of Child Sexual Abuse,* rev. ed. New York: HarperPerrenial, 1994.

Bass, E. and L. Thornton. *I Never Told Anyone.* New York: Harper and Row, 1983.

Bates, J. Douglas. *Gift Children: A Story of Race, Family and Adoption in a Divided America.* New York: Ticknor & Fields, 1993.

Becker, Carol. *Unbroken Ties: Lesbian Ex-Lovers.* Boston: Alyson, 1988.

Berkery Jr., Peter M. *Personal Financial Planning for Gays & Lesbians: Our Guide to Prudent Decision Making.* Chicago: Irwin, 1996.

Berliner, Lucy, and Diana M. Elliott. "Sexual Abuse of Children." In *The APSAC Handbook on Child Maltreatment.* Edited by John Briere, Lucy Berliner, Josephine A. Bulkley, Carol Jenny, and Teresa Reid. Thousand Oaks, CA: Sage, 1996: 51–71.

Bernhard, Yetta. *Self Care.* Berkeley, CA: Celestial Arts, 1975.

Bernstein, Robert A. *Straight Parents, Gay Children: Keeping Families Together.* New York: Thunder's Mouth Press, 1995.

Berry, J. W. "Acculturation as Varieties of Adaptation." In *Acculturation: Theory, Models and Some New Findings.* Edited by A. M. Padilla. Boulder, CO: Westview Press, 1980.

Berzon, Betty. *The Intimacy Dance: A Guide to Long-Term Success in Gay and Lesbian Relationships.* New York: Plume, 1997.

————. *Permanent Partners: Building Gay and Lesbian Relationships That Last.* New York: Plume, 1990.

————. "Sharing Your Lesbian Identity with Your Children." *Our Right to Love: A Lesbian Resource Book.* Edited by G. Vida. Englewood Cliffs, NJ: Prentice-Hall, 1978.

Berzon, Betty, and R. Leighton. *Positively Gay.* Millbrae, CA: Celestial Arts, 1979.

Bity-Pleck, H. H. "The Gender Role Strain Paradigm: An Update." [need orig. source and date]. Cited in L. B. Silverstein and C. F. Auerbach, "Deconstructing the Essential Father," *American Psychologist* 54(6) (1999), 397–407.

Black, Claudia. *It Will Never Happen to Me.* New York: Ballantine Books, 1981.

Blank, Thomas, Diane Hyland, et al. "Retirement: Timing, Initiation and Satisfaction." Proceedings of the Gerontological Society of America, Washington, D.C. (November 19, 1987). Cited in Betty Friedan, *The Fountain of Age.* New York: Simon & Schuster, 1993.

Blau, Melinda. *Families Apart: Ten Keys to Successful Co-Parenting.* New York: G. P. Putnam's Sons, 1993.

Blumstein, Philip, and Pepper Schwartz. *American Couples: Money, Work, Sex.* New York: William Morrow, 1983.

Bolte, Angela. "Do Wedding Dresses Come in Lavender? The Prospects and Implications of Same-Sex Marriage." *Social Theory and Practice* 24(1) (1998): 111–131.

Borhek, Mary V. *Coming Out to Parents: A Two-Way Survival Guide for Lesbians and Gay Men and Their Parents.* New York: Pilgrim Press, 1983.

Borich, Barrie Jean. *My Lesbian Husband: Landscapes of a Marriage.* St. Paul, MN: Graywolf, 1999.

Bornstein, Kate. *Gender Outlaw: On Men, Women and the Rest of Us.* New York: Vintage Books, 1995.

Brewster, Susan. *To Be an Anchor in the Storm: A Guide for Families and Friends of Abused Women.* Emeryville, CA: Seal Press, 2000.

Bridges, William. *Transitions: Making Sense of Life's Changes.* Reading, MA: Addison-Wesley, 1980.

Brodzinsky, David M., Marshall D. Schechter, and Robin Marantz Henig. *Being Adopted: The Lifelong Search for Self.* New York: Anchor/Doubleday, 1992.

Brown, Laura S. *Sexual Issues in the Development of Lesbian Couples.* Paper presented at the meetings of the American Psychological Association, Toronto, Canada, 1985.

Brown, Mildred L., and Chloe Ann Rounsley. *True Selves: Understanding Transexualism for Families, Friends, Coworkers, and Helping Professionals.* San Francisco: Jossey Bass, 1996.

Browne, Susan, Debra Connors, and Nanci Stern. *With the Power of Each Breath: A Disabled Women's Anthology.* Pittsburgh, PA: Cleis Press, 1985.

Brownworth, Victoria, ed. *Coming Out of Cancer: Writings from the Lesbian Cancer Epidemic.* Emeryville, CA: Seal Press, 2000.

Brownworth, Victoria, and Susan Raffo, eds. *Restricted Access: Lesbians on Disability.* Emeryville, CA: Seal Press, 1999.

Burch, Beverly. *On Intimate Terms: The Psychology of Difference in Lesbian Relationships.* Urbana, IL: University of Illinois Press, 1993.

Butler, Becky, ed. *Ceremonies of the Heart: Celebrating Lesbian Unions.* Emeryville, CA: Seal Press, 1990.

Butler, P. E. *Talking to Yourself: Learning the Language of Self-Support.* San Francisco: Harper and Row, 1981.

Butler, Robert N., and Myrna I. Lewis. *Love and Sex after Sixty,* rev. ed. New York: Harper and Row, 1988.

Califia, Pat. *Sex Changes: The Politics of Transgenderism.* San Francisco: Cleis Press, 1997.

Campbell, Susan M. *Beyond the Power Struggle.* San Luis Obispo, CA: Impact Publishers, 1984.

———. *The Couple's Journey: Intimacy as a Path to Wholeness.* San Luis Obispo, CA: Impact Publishers, 1980.

Carl, D. *Counseling Same-Sex Couples.* New York: Norton, 1990.

Caster, Wendy. *The Lesbian Sex Book.* Boston: Alyson, 2003.

Charbonneau, C., and P. Lander. "Redefining Sexuality: Women Becoming Lesbian in Midlife." In *Lesbians at Midlife: The Creative Transition.* Edited by B. Sang, J. Warshow, and A. Smith. San Francisco: Spinsters, 1991.

Christensen, Andrew, and Neil Jacobson. *Reconcilable Differences.* New York: Guilford, 2000.

Clanton, Gordon, and Lynn G. Smith. *Jealousy*, rev. ed. Lanham, MD: University Press of America, 1986. Cited in Betty Berzon, *Permanent Partners: Building Gay and Lesbian Relationships That Last*. New York: Plume, 1988.

Clark, Don. *Loving Someone Gay*, rev. ed. Millbrae, CA: Celestial Arts, 1997.

Clarke, Jean I. *Self-Esteem: A Family Affair*. Minneapolis, MN: Winston Press, 1978.

Clunis, D. Merilee, and G. Dorsey Green. *The Lesbian Parenting Book: A Guide to Creating Families and Raising Children*. Emeryville, CA: Seal Press, 1995.

Clunis, D. Merilee, Karen I. Fredricksen-Goldsen, Pat A. Freeman, and Nancy Nystrom. *The Lives of Lesbian Elders: Looking Back, Looking Forward*. Binghamton, New York: Haworth Press, 2004.

Cole, Diane. *After Great Pain: A New Life Emerges*. New York: Summit Books, 1992.

Cole, Ellen, and Esther Rothblum, eds. *Lesbians at Midlife: The Creative Transition, An Anthology*. San Francisco: Spinsters, 1991.

Coleman, Emily, and Betty Edwards. *Brief Encounters: How To Make the Most of Relationships That May Not Last Forever*. Garden City, NY: Anchor Books, 1980.

Coles, Matt. *Try This at Home: A Do-It-Yourself Guide to Winning Lesbian and Gay Rights Policy: An ACLU Guidebook*. New York: New Press, 1996.

Colgrove, M., H. H. Bloomfield, and P. A. McWilliams. *How To Survive the Loss of a Love*. New York: Bantam Books, 1976.

Collins, Andrew. *Fodor's Gay Guide to the USA* (2nd ed.). New York: Fodor's Travel Publications, 1998.

Connolly, Lora. "Long-Term Care and Hospice: The Special Needs of Older Gay Men and Lesbians." In *Health Care for Lesbians and Gay Men: Confronting Homophobia and Heterosexism*. Edited by K. Jean Peterson et al. New York: Harrington Park Press, 1996: 77–91.

Crate, M. A. "Adaptation to Chronic Illness." *American Journal of Nursing* 65 (1965): 73–76. Cited in R. Mackelprang and R. Salsgiver, *Disability: A Diversity Model Approach in Human Service Practice*. Pacific Grove, CA: Brooks/Cole, 1999: 61.

Crawford, Christina. *No Safe Place: The Legacy of Family Violence*. New York: Station Hill Press, 1994.

Cromwell, Jason. *TransMen and FTMs: Identities, Bodies, Genders and Sexualities*. Urbana, IL: University of Illinois Press, 1999.

Curry, Hayden, Denis Clifford, Robin Leonard, and Frederick Hertz. *A Legal Guide for Lesbian and Gay Couples*. Berkeley, CA: Nolo Press, 1999.

Davis, Laura. *Allies in Healing: When the Person You Love Was Sexually Abused as a Child*. New York: Perennial, 1991.

———. *The Courage to Heal Workbook: For Women and Men Survivors of Child Sexual Abuse*. New York: HarperCollins, 1990.

Dispenza, Mary. *Our Families, Our Children: The Lesbian and Gay Child Care Task Force Report on Quality Child Care*. Seattle: The Lesbian and Gay Child Care Task Force, 1999.

Dodson, Betty. *Sex for One: The Joy of Selfloving*. New York: Crown, 1996.

Donoghue, Paul J., PhD, and Mary E. Siegel, PhD. *Sick and Tired of Feeling Sick and Tired: Living with Invisible Chronic Illness*. New York: W. W. Norton, 1992.

Doress, P. B., D. L. Siegal, and the Midlife and Older Women Book Project in cooperation with the Boston Women's Health Book Collective, eds. *Ourselves, Growing Older: Women Aging with Knowledge and Power.* Boston: Simon and Schuster/Touchstone, 1987.

Doress-Worters, Paula B., and Diana Laskin Siegal, in cooperation with the Boston Women's Health Book Collective. *The New Ourselves, Growing Older.* New York: Touchstone, 1994.

Driggs, J. H., and S. E. Finn. *Intimacy Between Men: How to Find and Keep Gay Love Relationships.* New York: Dutton, 1990.

Duberman, Martin B., ed. *A Queer World: The Center for Lesbian and Gay Studies Reader.* New York: New York University Press, 1997.

Eichenbaum, L., and S. Orbach. *What Do Women Want: Exploding the Myth of Dependency.* New York: Berkeley, 1983.

Eldridge, Natalie S., and Lucia A. Gilbert. "Correlates of Relationship Satisfaction in Lesbian Couples." *Psychology of Women Quarterly* 14(1) (1990): 43–62.

Equal Employment Opportunity Commission (EEOC) and U.S. Department of Justice. *Americans with Disabilities Act Handbook.* Washington, DC: U.S. Government Printing Office, 1991.

Erlichman, K. L. "Lesbian Mothers: Ethical Issues in Social Work Practice." *Women & Therapy* 8(1–2) (1988): 207–221.

Faber, Adele, and Elaine Mazlish. *How To Talk So Kids Will Listen and Listen So Kids Will Talk.* New York: Avon, 1982.

Faderman, Lillian. *Odd Girls and Twilight Lovers: A History of Lesbian Life in Twentieth-Century America.* New York: Penguin Books, 1992.

Fairchild, Betty, and Nancy Hayward. *Now That You Know: A Parents' Guide to Understanding Their Gay and Lesbian Children.* New York: Harcourt Brace Jovanovich, 1998.

Falco, Kristine. *Psychotherapy with Lesbian Clients: Theory into Practice.* New York: Harcourt Brace Jovanovich, 1989.

Falk, Patricia. "Lesbian Mothers: Psychosocial Assumptions in Family Law." *American Psychologist* 44(6) (1989): 941–947.

Feinberg, Leslie. *Trans Liberation: Beyond Pink or Blue.* Boston: Beacon Press, 1998.

———. *Transgender Warriors: Making History from Joan of Arc to Dennis Rodman.* Boston: Beacon Press, 1997.

Ferrari, Marianne, ed. *Gay Travel A to Z.* Phoenix, AZ: Ferrari, 1998.

Ferrari International Publishing Staff. *Inn Places: Gay and Lesbian Accommodations World Wide* (13th ed.). Phoenix, AZ: Ferrari, 2000.

Finkelhor, David. "Current Information on the Scope and Nature of Sexual Abuse." In *Future of Children* 4(2) (1994): 31–53.

Fisher, Roger, and Scott Brown. *Getting Together: Building a Relationship That Gets to Yes.* Boston: Houghton Mifflin, 1988.

Fisher, Roger, and William Ury. *Getting to Yes: Negotiating Agreement Without Caving In.* New York: Penguin, 1983.

Fortune, Marie. *Sexual Violence: The Unmentionable Sin.* New York: Pilgrim Press, 1983.

Freeman, Pat. Personal communication. Seattle, WA, 1999.

Friedan, Betty. *The Fountain of Age.* New York: Simon & Schuster, 1993.

Fukuyama, M. A., and A. D. Ferguson. "Lesbian, Gay and Bisexual People of Color: Understanding Cultural Complexity and Managing Multiple Oppressions." In *Handbook of Counseling and Psychotherapy with Lesbian, Gay and Bisexual Clients.* Edited by R. M. Perez, K. A. DeBord et al. Washington, DC: American Psychological Association, 2000: 81–105.

Funderberg, Lise. *Black, White, Other: Biracial Americans Talk about Race and Identity.* New York: Quill, 1995.

Gage, Carolyn. "Hidden Disability," in *Restricted Access: Lesbians on Disability.* Edited by Victoria Brownworth and Susan Raffo. Emeryville, CA: Seal Press. 1999: 201–211.

Ganley, Anne L. *Understanding Domestic Violence: Preparatory Reading for Trainers.* San Francisco: Family Violence Prevention Fund, 1996.

Garcia, Norma, Cheryl Kennedy, Sarah F. Pearlman, and Julia Perez. "The Impact of Race and Culture Differences: Challenges to Intimacy in Lesbian Relationships." In *Lesbian Psychologies: Explorations and Challenges.* Edited by The Boston Lesbian Psychologies Collective. Urbana, IL: University of Illinois Press, 1987: 142–160.

Gaskins, Pearl Fuyo, ed. *What Are You?: Voices of Mixed-Race Young People.* New York: Henry Holt, 1999.

Gershick, Zsa Zsa. *Gay Old Girls.* Los Angeles, CA: Alyson, 1998.

Gibbs, E. D. "Psychosocial Development of Children Raised by Lesbian Mothers: A Review of Research." *Women & Therapy* 8(1–2) (1989): 65–75.

Gil, Eliana. *Outgrowing the Pain Together: A Book for Spouses and Partners of Adults Abused as Children.* New York: Dell, 1991.

Gillespie, Peggy (interviews) and Gigi Kaeser (photographs). *Of Many Colors: Portraits of Multiracial Families.* Boston: University of Massachusetts Press, 1997.

Golumbok, S., A. Spencer, and M. Rutter. "Children in Lesbian and Single-Parent Households: Psychosexual and Psychiatric Appraisal." *Journal of Child Psychology and Psychiatry and Allied Disciplines* 24(4) (1983): 551–572.

Gomez, Jewelle. "Across the Glittering Sea." In *Skin Deep: Black Women and White Women Write about Race.* Edited by Marita Golden and Susan Richards Shreve. New York: Anchor Books, 1995.

Gomez, Jewelle L., and Barbara Smith. "Taking the Home out of Homophobia: Black Lesbian Health." In *The Black Women's Health Book.* Edited by Evelyn C. White. Emeryville, CA: Seal Press, 1990: 198–213.

Gonsiorek, John C., and J. R. Rudolph. "Homosexual Identity: Coming Out and Other Developmental Events." In *Homosexuality: Research Implications for Public Policy.* Edited by J. C. Gonsiorek and J. C. Weinrich. Newbury Park, CA: Sage, 1991: 161–176.

Goodman, B. "Some Mothers Are Lesbian." In *Women Issues and Social Work Practice.* Edited by E. Norman and A. Mancuso. Itasca, IL: Peacock, 1980.

Gordon, Thomas. *P.E.T: Parent Effectiveness Training.* New York: New American Library, 1970.

Gottman, John M., and Nan Silver. *The Seven Principles for Making Marriage Work.* New York: Crown, 1999.

Gottman, John, et al. *A Couple's Guide to Communication.* Champaign, IL: Research Press, 1976.

Gould, Jean, ed. *Dutiful Daughters: Caring for Our Parents as They Grow Old.* Emeryville, CA: Seal Press, 1999.

Grady, Denise. "Lesbians Find Cancer Support Without Excuses (new breast cancer support group for lesbians at New York City's Beth Israel Medical Center)." *The New York Times,* Nov 23, 1999.

Green, G. Dorsey, and D. Merilee Clunis. "Married Lesbians." *Women & Therapy* 8(1–2) (1989): 41–47.

Green, Richard, et al. "Lesbian Mothers and Their Children: A Comparison with Solo Parent Heterosexual Mothers and Their Children." *Archives of Sexual Behavior* 15(2) (1986): 167–184.

Greene, Beverly, and Nancy Boyd-Franklin. "African American Lesbian Couples: Ethnocultural Considerations in Psychotherapy." In *Couples Therapy: Feminist Perspectives.* Edited by Marcia Hill and Esther D. Rothblum. New York: Harrington Park Press/Haworth Press, 1996: 49–60.

————. "African American Lesbians: Issues in Couples Therapy." In *Lesbians and Gays in Couples and Families: A Handbook for Therapists.* Edited by Joan Laird and Robert Jay Green. San Francisco: Jossey-Bass, 1996: 251–271.

Haines, Staci. *The Survivor's Guide to Sex: How to Have an Empowered Sex Life after Child Sexual Abuse.* San Francisco: Cleis Press, 1999.

Haldeman, Douglas C. "Ceremonies and Religion in Same-Sex Marriage." In *On the Road to Same-Sex Marriage: A Supportive Guide to Psychological, Political, and Legal Issues.* Edited by Robert P. Cabaj, David W. Purcell et al. San Francisco: Jossey-Bass, 1998: 141–164.

Hall, Marny. "Lesbian Families: Cultural and Clinical Issues." *Social Work* 23(5) (1978): 380–385.

————. *The Lesbian Love Companion: How to Survive Everything from Heartthrob to Heartbreak.* San Francisco: HarperSanFrancisco, 1998.

————. "Lesbians, Limerence and Longterm Relationships." In JoAnn Loulan, *Lesbian Sex.* San Francisco, CA: Spinsters Ink, 1987.

Hare, Jan. "Concerns and Issues Faced by Families Headed by a Lesbian Couple." *Families in Society* 75(1) (1994): 27–35.

Harris, M. B., and P. H. Turner. "Gay and Lesbian Parents." *Journal of Homosexuality* 12(2) (1985–86): 101–113.

Hart, B. "Lesbian Battering: An Examination." In *Naming the Violence: Speaking Out about Lesbian Battering.* Edited by K. Lobel. Emeryville, CA: Seal Press, 1986: 173–189.

Herman, Judith, and L. Hirschman. *Father-Daughter Incest.* Cambridge, MA: Harvard University Press, 2000.

Hertz, Frederick. *Legal Affairs: Essential Advice for Same-Sex Couples.* New York: Henry Holt, 1998.

Hill, Charlotte A. "Fusion and Conflict in Lesbian Relationships?" *Feminism and Psychology* 9(2) (1999): 179–185.

Hoeffer, B. "Children's Acquisition of Sex-Role Behavior in Lesbian-Mother Families." *American Journal of Orthopsychiatry* 51(3) (1981): 536–544.

Hollibaugh, A., and C. Moraga. "What We're Rollin' Around in Bed With: Sexual Issues in Feminism." In *Powers of Desire: The Politics of Sexuality.* Edited by C. Stansell and S. Thompson. New York: Monthly Review Press, 1983: 314–405.

Hopson, Darlene Powell, Derek S. Hopson, and Thomas Clavin. *Raising the Rainbow Generation: Teaching Your Children to Be Successful in a Multicultural Society.* New York: Fireside, 1993.

Huggins, S. L. "A Comparative Study of Self-Esteem of Adolescent Children of Divorced Lesbian Mothers and Divorced Heterosexual Mothers." *Journal of Homosexuality* 18(1–2) (1989): 123–135.

Huston, Ted, and Renate Houts. "The Psychological Infrastructure of Courtship and Marriage: The Role of Personality and Compatibility in Romantic Relationships." In *The Developmental Course of Marital Dysfunction.* Edited by T. N. Bradbury. New York: Cambridge, 1998: 14–151. Cited in A. Christensen and N. Jacobson, *Reconcilable Differences.* New York: Guilford, 2000: 35.

Jacob, Mary Casey. "Lesbian Couples and Single Women." In *Infertility Counseling: A Comprehensive Handbook for Clinicians.* Edited by Linda H. Burns and Sharon N. Covington. New York: Parthenon Publishing Group, 1998.

Jacobson, Neil, and Andrew Christensen. *Acceptance and Change in Couple Therapy: A Therapist's Guide to Transforming Relationships.* New York: W. W. Norton, 1996.

Jagose, Annamarie. *Queer Theory: An Introduction.* New York: New York University Press, 1996.

James, Steven E., and Blanca Cody Murphy. "Gay and Lesbian Relationships in a Changing Social Context." In *Lesbian, Gay, and Bisexual Identities in Families: Psychological Perspectives.* Edited by Charlotte J. Patterson, Anthony R. D'Augell, et al. New York: Oxford University Press, 1998: 99–121.

Jensen, Karol L. *Lesbian Epiphanies: Women Coming Out in Later Life.* Binghamton, NY: Haworth Press, 1999.

Johnson, Susan E. *For Love and for Life. Intimate Portraits of Lesbian Couples.* Tallahassee, FL: Naiad Press, 1995.

———. *Lesbian Sex: An Oral History.* Tallahassee, FL: Naiad Press, 1996.

———. *Staying Power: Long Term Lesbian Couples.* Tallahassee, FL: Naiad Press, 1990.

Johnson, Suzanne M., and Elizabeth O'Conner. *Your Guide to Helping Your Family Grow Up Happy, Healthy, and Proud.* New York: Guilford, 2001.

Jones, Teresa C., Nancy M. Nystrom, Karen I. Fredricksen, D. Merilee Clunis, and Pat A. Freeman. "Looking Back . . . Looking Forward: Addressing the Lives of Lesbians 55 and Older." Paper presented at the Council on Social Work Education Meeting, San Francisco, CA, March, 1999.

Kastner, Laura S., and Jennifer F. Wyatt. *The Seven-Year Stretch: How Families Work Together to Grow Through Adolescence.* Boston: Houghton Mifflin, 1997.

Kehoe, Monika. *Lesbians over 60 Speak for Themselves.* Binghamton, NY: Harrington Park Press, 1989.

Kelley, Patricia. *Developing Healthy Stepfamilies: Twenty Families Tell Their Stories.* New York: Harrington Park Press, 1995.

Kenney, Janet W., and Donna T. Tash. "Lesbian Childbearing Couples' Dilemmas and Decisions." In *Lesbian Health: What Are the Issues?* Edited by Phyllis Noerager Stern et al. Washington, DC: Taylor & Francis, 1993: 119–129.

Kirshenbaum, Mira. *Too Good to Leave, Too Bad to Stay: A Step-by-Step Guide to Help You Decide Whether to Stay In or Get Out of Your Relationship.* New York: Plume, 1996.

Klein, F., and T. J. Wolf. *Two Lives to Lead: Bisexuality in Men and Women.* New York: Harrington Park Press, 1985.

Kroeger, Otto, and Janet M. Thuesen. *Type Talk: The 16 Personality Types that Determine How We Live, Love and Work.* New York: Delta, 1989.

Landau, Carol, Michele G. Cyr, and Anne W. Moulton. *The Complete Book of Menopause.* New York: G. P. Putnam, 1994.

Larkin, Joan, ed. *A Woman Like That: Lesbian and Bisexual Writers Tell Their Coming Out Stories.* New York: Avon Books, 1999.

Larson, Per. *Gay Money: Your Personal Guide to Same-Sex Strategies for Financial Security, Strength, and Success.* New York: Delta, 1997.

Lechtenberg, Richard, MD. *Multiple Sclerosis Fact Book.* Philadelphia: F. A. Davis, 1995.

Ledray, L. E. *Recovering from Rape.* New York: Henry Holt, 1986.

Lerner, Harriet G. *The Dance of Anger: A Woman's Guide to Changing the Pattern of Intimate Relationships.* New York: Harper and Row, 1985.

Levin, Jack, and William C. Levin. *Ageism, Prejudice and Discrimination Against the Elderly.* Belmont, CA: Wadsworth, 1980.

Lewin, Ellen. *Recognizing Ourselves: Ceremonies of Lesbian and Gay Commitment.* New York: Columbia University Press, 1998.

Lipat, Christine T., Trinity A. Ordona, Cianna Pamintuan Stewart, and Mary Ann Ubaldo. "Tomboy, Dyke, Lezzie, and Bi: Filipina Lesbian and Bisexual Women Speak Out." In *Filipino Americans: Transformation and Identity.* Edited by Maria P. P. Root. Thousand Oaks, CA: Sage, 1997.

Lobel, K., ed. *Naming the Violence: Speaking Out about Lesbian Battering.* Emeryville, CA: Seal Press, 1986.

Loulan, JoAnn. *The Lesbian Erotic Dance: Butch, Femme, Androgyny, and Other Rhythms.* San Francisco: Spinsters, 1990.

―――. *Lesbian Sex.* San Francisco: Spinsters Ink, 1984.

Loulan, JoAnn. *Lesbian Passion: Loving Ourselves and Each Other.* San Francisco: Spinsters Ink/Aunt Lute, 1987.

Love, Pat. "What Is This Thing Called Love?" *Family Networker* 23(2) (March/April, 1999).

Love, Susan, with Karen Lindsey. *Dr. Susan Love's Hormone Book: Making Informed Choices about Menopause.* New York: Random House, 1997.

Luczak, R., ed. *Eyes of Desire: A Deaf Gay and Lesbian Reader.* Boston: Alyson, 1993.

Lustig, Harold L. *Four Steps to Financial Security for Lesbian and Gay Couples.* New York: Fawcett, 1999.

Lynch, Lee, and Akia Woods, eds. *Off the Rag: Lesbians Writing on Menopause.* Norwich, VT: New Victoria Publishers, 1996.

MacDonald, B., and C. Rich. *Look Me in the Eye: Old Women, Aging, and Ageism.* San Francisco: Spinsters Ink, 1991.

Mackelprang, Romel, and Richard Salsgiver. *Disability: A Diversity Model Approach in Human Service Practice.* Pacific Grove, CA: Brooks/Cole, 1999.

Mackey, Richard A., Bernard A. O'Brien, and Eileen F. Mackey. *Gay and Lesbian Couples: Voices from Lasting Relationships.* Westport, CT: Praeger, 1997.

Maltz, Wendy. *The Sexual Healing Journey: A Guide for Survivors of Sexual Abuse.* New York: Perennial Currents, 2001.

Maltz, W., and B. Holman, *Incest and Sexuality: A Guide to Understanding and Healing.* Lexington, MA: Lexington Books, 1991.

Mackoff, B. *Leaving the Office Behind.* New York: G. P. Putnam's Sons, 1984.

Marcus, Eric. *The Male Couple's Guide: Finding a Man, Making a Home, Building a Life* (3rd ed.). New York: HarperPerennial, 1999.

————. *Together Forever: Gay and Lesbian Couples Share Their Secrets for Lasting Happiness.* New York: Anchor Books, 1999.

Martin, April. *The Lesbian and Gay Parenting Handbook: Creating and Raising Our Families.* New York: HarperPerennial, 1993.

Martin, Del, and Phyllis Lyon. *Lesbian/Woman.* New York: Bantam Books, 1972.

Martinac, Paula. *The Lesbian and Gay Book of Love and Marriage.* New York: Broadway Books, 1998.

Matsakis, Aphrodite. *I Can't Get Over It: A Handbook for Trauma Survivors.* Oakland, CA: New Harbinger, 1992.

McCandlish, Barbara M. "Therapeutic Issues with Lesbian Couples." *Journal of Gay and Lesbian Psychotherapy* 1(3) (1990): 71–78.

McCloskey, Deirdre N. *Crossing: A Memoir.* Chicago: University of Chicago Press, 1999.

McConnell, P. A. *Workbook for Healing: Adult Children of Alcoholics.* San Francisco: Harper and Row, 1986.

McCubbin, H., and C. R. Figley, eds. "Stress and the Family, Volume 1: Coping with Normative Transitions." Cited in Janet M. Wright, *Lesbian Step Families: An Ethnography of Love.* New York: Haworth Press, 1998: 173.

McDaniel, Judith. *The Lesbian Couples' Guide: Finding the Right Woman and Creating a Life Together.* New York: HarperCollins, 1995.

McKay, M., P. Fanning, and K. Paleg. *Couple Skills: Making Your Relationship Work.* Oakland, CA: New Harbinger, 1994.

McKay, Matthew, Martha Davis, and Patrick Fanning. *Messages: The Communication Book.* Oakland, CA: New Harbinger, 1983.

McKay, Matthew, Peter D. Rogers, Joan Blades, and Richard Gosse. *The Divorce Book.* Oakland, CA: New Harbinger, 1984.

McWhirter, D. P., and A. M. Mattison. *The Male Couple: How Relationships Develop.* Englewood Cliffs, NJ: Prentice-Hall, 1984.

Middelton-Moz, Jane. *Shame and Guilt: The Masters of Disguise.* Deerfield Beach, FL: Health Communications, 1990.

Middleton-Moz, J., and L. Dwinell. *After the Tears: Reclaiming the Personal Losses of Childhood.* Pompano Beach, FL: Health Communications, 1986.

Miller, A. *Thou Shalt Not Be Aware: Society's Betrayal of the Child.* New York: Farrar, Straus, and Giroux, 1984.

Modrcin, M. J., and N. L. Wyers. "Lesbian and Gay Couples: Where They Turn When Help Is Needed." *Journal of Gay and Lesbian Psychotherapy* 1(3) (1990): 89–104.

Mok, Teresa A. "Asian American Dating: Important Factors in Partner Choice." *Cultural Diversity and Ethnic Minority Psychology* 5(2) (1999).

Molloy, Susan. *Handling It: You and Your Long-Term Disease.* Melbourne, Australia: Hill of Content, 1995.

Monroe, Peggy, Judy Gough, and Tim Grendon. *Circles of Care: Caring For and Remembering People with AIDS.* Seattle: AIDS Caregiver Support Network, 1998.

Moraga, Cherrie. *Waiting in the Wings: Portrait of a Queer Motherhood.* Ithaca, NY: Firebrand, 1997.

Moraga, Cherrie, and G. Anzaldua, eds. *This Bridge Called My Back: Writings by Radical Women of Color.* New York: Kitchen Table: Women of Color Press, 1983.

Muller, A. *Parents Matter: Parents' Relationships with Lesbian Daughters and Gay Sons.* Tallahassee, FL: Naiad Press, 1987.

Nestle, Joan, ed. *The Persistent Desire: A Femme-Butch Reader.* Boston: Alyson, 1992.

Newman, Felice. *The Whole Lesbian Sex Book: A Passionate Guide for All of Us.* San Francisco: Cleis Press, 1999.

NiCarthy, G. *Getting Free: You Can End Abuse and Take Back Your Life.* Emeryville, CA: Seal Press, 2004.

———. *The Ones Who Got Away: Women Who Left Abusive Partners.* Emeryville, CA: Seal Press, 1987.

Nichols, J. Randall. *Ending Marriage, Keeping Faith: A New Guide Through the Spiritual Journey of Divorce.* New York: Crossroad, 1991.

Nichols, Michael P. *Stop Arguing with Your Kids: How to Win the Battle of Wills by Making Your Children Feel Heard.* New York: Guilford, 2004.

O'Hearn, Claudine C., ed. *Half and Half Writers on Growing Up Biracial and Bicultural.* New York: Pantheon, 1998.

O'Keefe, Tracie, and Katrina Fox, eds. *Finding the Real Me: True Tales of Sex and Gender Diversity.* San Francisco: Jossey Bass, 2003.

Pace, Anita L., ed. *Write from the Heart: Lesbians Healing from Heartache.* Beaverton, OR: Baby Steps Press, 1992.

Parks, Cheryl A. "Lesbian Parenthood: A Review of the Literature." *American Journal of Orthopsychiatry* 68(3) (1998): 376–389.

Patterson, Charlotte J. "Children of Lesbian and Gay Parents." *Child Development* 63 (1992): 1025–1042.

———. "Children of the Lesbian Baby Boom: Behavioral Adjustment, Self Concepts, and Sex Role Identity." In *Lesbian and Gay Psychology: Theory, Research, and Clinical Applications.* Edited by Beverly Greene and Gregory M. Herek. Vol. 1. Thousand Oaks, CA: Sage, 1994: 156–175.

———. "Lesbian Mothers and Their Children: Findings from the Bay Area Families Study." In *Lesbians and Gays in Couples and Families: A Handbook for Therapists.* Edited by Joan Laird and Robert-Jay Green. San Francisco: Jossey-Bass, 1996: 420–437.

Paul, W., J. Gonsiorek, and M. Hotvedt. *Homosexuality: Social, Psychological, and Biological Issues.* Beverly Hills: Sage, 1982.

Pearlman, Sarah F. "Loving across Race and Class Divides: Relational Challenges and the Interracial Lesbian Couple." *Women & Therapy* 19 (1996): 25.

Peplau, Letitia A. "Lesbian and Gay Relationships." In *Homosexuality: Research Implications for Public Policy.* Edited by J. C. Gonsiorek and J. D. Weinrich. Newbury Park, CA: Sage, 1991:177–196.

Perry, Susan, and Kate O'Hanlon, MD. *Natural Menopause: The Complete Guide.* Reading, MA: Addison-Wesley, 1997.

Pharr, S. *Homophobia: A Weapon of Sexism.* Inverness, CA: Chardon Press, 1988.

————. "Two Workshops on Homophobia." In *Naming the Violence: Speaking Out About Lesbian Battering.* Edited by K. Lobel. Emeryville, CA: Seal Press, 1986: 202–222.

Pies, C. *Considering Parenthood: A Workbook for Lesbians* (2nd ed.). San Francisco: Spinsters/Aunt Lute, 1988.

Pitzele, S. *We Are Not Alone: Learning to Live with Chronic Illness.* New York: Workman, 1986.

Pogrebin, L. C. *Among Friends: Who We Like, Why We Like Them, and What We Do with Them.* New York: McGraw-Hill, 1987.

Rafkin, Louise, ed. *Different Mothers: Sons and Daughters of Lesbians Talk about Their Lives.* Pittsburgh, PA: Cleis Press, 1990.

Raphael, B. *The Anatomy of Bereavement.* New York: Basic Books, 1983.

Renzetti, Claire. *Violent Betrayal: Partner Abuse in Lesbian Relationships.* Newbury Park, CA: Sage, 1992.

Ricci, Isolina. *Mom's House, Dad's House: Making Two Homes for Your Child,* 2nd ed. New York: Fireside, 1997.

Robinson, Lori. *I Will Survive: The African-American Guide to Healing from Sexual Abuse and Assault.* Emeryville, CA: Seal Press, 2003.

Rofes, E. *"I Thought People Like That Killed Themselves": Lesbians, Gay Men, and Suicide.* San Francisco: Grey Fox Press, 1983.

Rohrbaugh, J. B. "Choosing Children: Psychological Issues in Lesbian Parenting." *Women & Therapy* 8(1–2) (1988): 51–64.

Rolland, John S. "A Conceptual Model of Chronic and Life-Threatening Illness and Its Impact on Families." In *Chronic Illness and Disability.* Edited by C. S. Chilman, E. W. Nunnally, and F. M. Cox. Newbury Park, CA: Sage, 1988.

————. "In Sickness and in Health: The Impact of Illness on Couples' Relationships." *Journal of Marital and Family Therapy* 20(4) (1994): 327–347.

Root, Maria P. P., ed. *The Multicultural Experience: Racial Borders as the New Frontier.* Newbury, CA: Sage, 1996.

————, ed. *Racially Mixed People in America.* Newbury, CA: Sage, 1992.

Rosenberg, Marshall B. *Nonviolent Communication: A Language of Compassion.* Del Mar, CA: PuddleDancer Press, 1999.

Rosenbloom, Dena, and Mary Beth Williams with Barbara E. Watkins. *Life after Trauma: A Workbook for Healing.* New York: Guilford, 1999.

Rothblum, Esther D., and Kathleen A. Brehony, eds. *Boston Marriages: Romantic but Asexual Relationships among Contemporary Lesbians.* Amherst, MA: University of Massachusetts Press, 1993.

Rubin, L. *Worlds of Pain: Life in the Working-Class Family.* New York: Basic Books, 1977.

Russell, D. H. *The Secret Trauma: Incest in the Lives of Girls and Women,* rev. ed. New York: Basic Books, 1999.

Ryneveld, Edna Copeland. *Menopause: A Gentle, Natural Approach.* St. Paul, MN: Llewellyn, 1998.

Saffron, Lisa. *Challenging Conceptions: Pregnancy and Parenting Beyond the Traditional Family.* London: Cassell, 1994.

———. *What about the Children? Sons and Daughters of Lesbian and Gay Parents Talk about Their Lives.* London: Cassell, 1996.

SAMOIS. *Coming to Power: Writings and Graphics on Lesbian S/M* (2nd ed.). Boston: Alyson, 1982.

Samuelson, Elliot D. *Unmarried Couple's Legal Survival Guide: Your Rights and Obligations.* Secaucus, NJ: Carol, 1997.

Sanford, Lynda T. *Strong at the Broken Places: Overcoming the Trauma of Childhood Abuse.* New York: Avon, 1992.

Sang, Barbara, Joyce Warshow, and Adrienne J. Smith, eds. *Lesbians at Midlife: The Creative Transition.* San Francisco: Spinsters, 1991.

Saslow, J. M. "Hear Oh Israel: We Are Jews, We Are Gay." *The Advocate* 465 (Feb. 3, 1987): 38.

Schnarch. David. "Constructing the Sexual Crucible." Workshop presented in Seattle, WA, 1997.

———. *Passionate Marriage: Love, Sex, and Intimacy in Emotionally Committed Relationships.* New York: Henry Holt, 1997.

Schulenburg, J. *Gay Parenting.* Garden City, NY: Anchor Press/Doubleday, 1985.

Sears, Vickie L. "Cross-Cultural Ethnic Relationships." Unpublished manuscript, 1987(a).

———. "Disabilities and Chronic Illness." Unpublished manuscript, 1987(b).

Shaul, S. et al. *Toward Intimacy: Family Planning and Sexuality Concerns of Physically Disabled Women.* New York: Human Sciences Press, 1978.

Sheehy, Gail. *The Silent Passage: Menopause,* rev. ed. New York: Pocket Books, 1998.

Sherman, S., ed. *Lesbian and Gay Marriage: Private Commitments, Public Ceremonies.* Philadelphia, PA: Temple University Press, 1992.

Shuman, Robert, and Dr. Janice Schwartz. *Living with Multiple Sclerosis: A Handbook for Families.* New York: MacMillan, 1994.

Silvera, M., ed. *Piece of My Heart: A Lesbian of Colour Anthology.* Toronto: Sister Vision, 1992.

Silverstein, Louise B., and Carl F. Auerbach. "Deconstructing the Essential Father." *American Psychologist* 54(6) (1999): 397–407.

Simons, Robin. *After the Tears: Parents Talk about Raising a Child with a Disability.* San Diego: Harcourt Brace Jovanovich, 1987.

Slater, Suzanne. "Approaching and Avoiding the Work of the Middle Years: Affairs in Committed Lesbian Relationships." *Women & Therapy* 15(2) (1994): 19–34.

————. *The Lesbian Family Life Cycle.* Champaign, IL: University of Illinois Press, 1999.

Smith, Barbara, ed. *Home Girls: A Black Feminist Anthology.* New York: Kitchen Table/Women of Color Press, 1985.

Snow, Judith E. *How It Feels to Have a Gay or Lesbian Parent: A Book by Kids for Kids of All Ages.* Binghamton, NY: Harrington Park Press, 2004.

Spring, Janis Abrahms. *After the Affair: Healing the Pain and Rebuilding Trust When a Partner Has Been Unfaithful.* New York: HarperPerennial, 1997.

Stanley, J. P., and S. J. Wolfe, eds. *The Coming Out Stories.* Watertown, MA: Persephone Press, 1980.

Steckel, Ailsa. "Psychosocial Development of Children of Lesbian Mothers." In *Gay and Lesbian Parents.* Edited by Frederick W. Bozett. New York: Praeger, 1987: 75–85.

Stiers, Gretchen A. *From This Day Forward: Commitment, Marriage and Family in Lesbian and Gay Relationships.* New York: Macmillan, 2000.

Stuart, Richard B., and Barbara Jacobson. *Second Marriage: Make It Happy! Make It Last!* New York: W. W. Norton, 1985.

Sullivan, Maureen. "Rozzie and Harriet?: Gender and Family Patterns of Lesbian Coparents." *Gender & Society* 10 (1996): 747.

Sutton, Linda. *Love Matters: A Book of Lesbian Romance and Relationship.* Binghamton, NY: Harrington Park Press, 1999.

Swallow, J. *Out from Under: Sober Dykes and Our Friends.* San Francisco: Spinsters Ink, 1983.

Takaki, Ronald. *A Different Mirror: A History of Multicultural America.* Boston: Little, Brown, 1993.

————. *Strangers from a Different Shore: A History of Asian Americans.* Boston: Little, Brown, 1998.

Tasker, Fiona, and Susan Golombok. "Adults Raised as Children in Lesbian Families." *American Journal of Orthopsychiatry* 65(2) (1995): 203–215.

————. *Growing Up in a Lesbian Family: Effects on Child Development.* New York: Guilford, 1997.

Teifer, Lenore. "The Opposite of Sex: A Conversation with Lenore Teifer." Interviewed by Moira Brennan. *Ms.* 9(5), (August/September 1999).

Tennov, D. *Love and Limerence: The Experience of Being in Love.* New York: Stein and Day, 1979.

Tessina, Tina, PhD. *Gay Relationships for Men and Women: How to Find Them, How to Improve Them, How to Make Them Last.* Los Angeles: J. P. Tarcher, 1990.

Tessina, Tina B., and R. Smith. *How To Be a Couple and Still Be Free.* North Hollywood, CA: Newcastle, 1980.

Tien, L., "Conjoint Work in Cross-Cultural/Cross-Racial Marriage." Workshop presented by the Washington State Psychological Association, Seattle, WA, April 1999.

*Tools for Diversity Training.* Portland, Oregon: TACS, 1994. (For more information, contact TACS, 1903 Ankeny, Portland, OR 97214.)

Trafford, Abigail. *Crazy Time: Surviving Divorce and Building a New Life,* rev ed. New York: HarperPerennial, 1992.

Triandis, H. C., et al. "Individualism and Collectivism: Cross-Cultural Perspectives on Self-Ingroup Relationships." *Journal of Personality and Social Psychology* 54 (1998): 323–338.

Trujillo, C., ed. *Chicana Lesbians: The Girls Our Mothers Warned Us About.* Berkeley, CA: Third Woman Press, 1991.

Turner, P. H., S. Scadden, and M. B. Harris. "Parenting in Gay and Lesbian Families." *Journal of Gay and Lesbian Psychotherapy* 1(3) (1990): 55–66.

Uhrig, Larry. *The Two of Us: Affirming, Celebrating and Symbolizing Gay and Lesbian Relationships.* Boston: Alyson, 1984.

Van Gelder, Lindsy, and Pamela Robin Brandt. *Are You Two—Together? A Gay and Lesbian Travel Guide to Europe.* New York: Random House, 1991.

Vaughan, D. *Uncoupling: Turning Points in Intimate Relationships.* New York: Oxford University Press, 1986.

Wadia-Ells, Susan, ed. *The Adoption Reader: Birth Mothers, Adoptive Mothers and Adopted Daughters Tell Their Stories.* Emeryville, CA: Seal Press, 1995.

Wallerstein, Judith S., and Sandra Blakeslee. *The Good Marriage: How and Why Love Lasts.* New York: Warner Books, 1995.

———. *Second Chances: Men, Women and Children a Decade after Divorce.* New York: Ticknor & Fields, 1990.

Walsh, Anthony. *The Science of Love: Understanding Love and Its Effects on Mind and Body.* Buffalo, New York: Prometheus, 1991. Cited in Janis Abrahms Spring, *After the Affair,* 1997: 71.

Weinstock, Jacqueline S., ed. *Lesbian Ex-Lovers: The Really Long-Term Relationships.* Binghamton, NY: Harrington Park Press, 2004.

Wells, Jess, ed. *Lesbians Raising Sons.* Boston: Alyson, 1997.

Weston, Kath. *Families We Choose: Lesbians, Gays, Kinship.* New York: Columbia University Press, 1991.

———. *Render Me, Gender Me: Lesbians Talk Sex, Class, Color, Nation, Studmuffins.* New York: Columbia University Press, 1996.

White, Evelyn C. *Chain, Chain, Change: For Black Women Dealing with Physical and Emotional Abuse.* Emeryville, CA: Seal Press, 1985.

Whitfield, Charles L. *Healing the Child Within: Discovery and Recovery for Adult Children of Dysfunctional Families.* Pompano Beach, FL: Health Communications, 1987.

Wilchins, Riki Anne. *Read My Lips: Sexual Subversion and the End of Gender.* Ithaca, NY: Firebrand, 1997.

Wilson, Melba. *Crossing the Boundary. Black Women Survive Incest.* Emeryville, CA: Seal Press, 1994.

Wisechild, Louise M. *The Mother I Carry: A Memoir of Healing from Emotional Abuse.* Emeryville, CA: Seal Press, 1993.

———, ed. *She Who Was Lost Is Remembered: Healing from Incest through Creativity.* Emeryville, CA: Seal Press, 1991.

————, ed. *The Obsidian Mirror: Healing from Childhood Sexual Abuse.* Emeryville, CA: Seal Press, 2003.

Woititz, J. G. *Struggle for Intimacy.* Pompano Beach, FL: Health Communications, 1985.

Woodman, N. J., and H. R. Lenna, *Counseling with Gay Men and Women: A Guide for Facilitating Positive Life-Styles.* San Francisco: Jossey-Bass, 1980.

Worden, J. William. *Grief Counseling and Grief Therapy: A Handbook for the Mental Health Practitioner.* New York: Springer, 1982.

Wright, Janet M. *Lesbian Step Families: An Ethnography of Love.* New York: Haworth Press, 1998.

Wright, Marguerite A. *I'm Chocolate, You're Vanilla: Raising Healthy Black and Biracial Children in a Race-Conscious World.* San Francisco: Jossey-Bass, 1998.

Ying, Yu-Wen, Mary Coombs, and Peter A. Lee. "Family Intergenerational Relationship of Asian American Adolescents." *Cultural Diversity and Ethnic Minority Psychology* 5(4) (1999): 350–363.

Zakarewsky, G. T. "Patterns of Support among Gay and Lesbian Deaf Persons." *Sexuality and Disability* 2(3) (1979): 178–191.

Zeidenstein, Sondra. "The Naked Truth." *MS,* 9(5), (August/September, 1999).

# Index

Trivial thoughts: 89
Troubleshooting negotiations: 102
Trust: closeness and risk 46; developing 44–47; money issues and 160; strong feelings and 46; trauma and 237; undermining 52
Turning toward each other: 27–28
Twelve-step programs: 232, 267
*Two of Us, The:* 207
Two-pot financial arrangement: 155, 156
Two-question rule: 79

## UV

Uhrig, Larry: 207
"Unfaithful" partners: 133
Unfinished business: 81–82, 292
Ury, William: 138
Vacations: decisions about 165–166; family holidays 203–204; time together as 141; vacation buddies 202
Validation: affirmation of bonding 207; communication and 72; couple friends as validation 201; disappointments and support 40; in adjusting to disability or illness 249; older lesbians and 266; women of color 226
Values: child rearing values 59–60, 63; cross-cultural relationships 229; differences in 59–61; money value differences 159–160; possessions and 55
Verbal abuse: 107
Videos: 3
Violence: 107–110; *see also* Abuse
Viral STDs: 130
Visitation rights: 186–187
Visual impairment: 253
Vocabulary of feelings: 83–85
Vulnerability: boundaries and 37; coming out and being out 195, 227; hiding 246; risks and intimacy 44, 46; sharing thoughts and 45

## WXYZ

Wallerstein, Judith: 13, 31, 103
Wants and needs: conflict about 92–94; desirable partners 300; expressing 85–87; negotiation and 138; new partners 299; reasonable expectations 19–20; self-esteem and 93; signs of caring 48–49
Warm-up step in negotiating conflict: 99
Warning signal of jealousy: 131
*We Are Not Alone:* 244
*Well of Loneliness, The:* 3
*What Do Women Want:* 46
White partners: "ethnic chasers" 229; dealing with racism 220–223; discussing racial situations 220–223; understanding outside friendships 226; white privilege 222, 228
White privilege: 222, 228
*Whole Lesbian Sex Book, The:* 2, 68, 123,124
Wills: 182, 184, 186, 210, 258, 276, 293–294
Withdrawal: coming out to children and 171; gridlock and 105; overwhelming feelings and 46
Women of color: adaptations made by 225–226; "armoring" behaviors 220; as label 218; "ethnic chasers" and 229; internalized racism 220; racism in public places 220–223; stereotyping partners 228–230; *see also* Race and racism
Worden, William: 291
Work: as source of conflict 103; being in business together 163–164; being out at work 151–154; children and 180; class and 54, 55; disabilities and 243, 252–253; dual-career couples 149; free time and; housework tasks and 149–151; jobs and careers 150; later years 261; older lesbians 270–273; part-time work 273; racial inequities in 224; relationship balance and 151; stages of work life 58; transitioning to home time 163–164; work-related separations 141, 151; *see also* Money
Wright, Janet: 3, 172
Zeidenstein, Sondra: 123–124

## About the Authors

D. Merilee Clunis, PhD, and G. Dorsey Green, PhD, are the authors of *The Lesbian Parenting Book: A Guide to Creating Families and Raising Children* (Seal Press, 2003). Merilee is also the coauthor of *The Lives of Lesbian Elders: Looking Back/Looking Forward* (Hayworth Press, 2004). Merilee and Dorsey are psychologists in private practice and have extensive experience counseling lesbian couples. They have published professional papers and led workshops and trainings on the topics of communication, couple relationships, and parenting. They live with their families in Seattle.

# Selected Titles from Seal Press

For more than 25 years, Seal Press has published groundbreaking books. By women. For women. Visit our website at www.sealpress.com.

*The Lesbian Parenting Book: A Guide to Creating Families and Raising Children* by D. Merilee Clunis, PhD, and G. Dorsey Green, PhD. $18.95, 1-58005-090-5. Drawing on real-life experiences of lesbian families and the latest information from family specialists and researchers, the authors cover each stage of parenthood and child development.

*The Lesbian Health Book: Caring for Ourselves* edited by Jocelyn White, MD, and Marissa C. Martinez.18.95, 1-87806-731-1. This invaluable resource highlights personal and community efforts to make health-care accessible and responsive to lesbians.

*Restricted Access: Lesbians on Disability* edited by Victoria A. Brownworth and Susan Raffo. $15.95, 1-580085-028-X. In looking at the intersection of sexuality and disability, this nonfiction anthology challenges readers to confront how America deals with difference.

*The Adoption Reader: Birth Mothers, Adoptive Mothers, and Adopted Daughters Tell Their Stories* edited by Susan Wadia-Ells. $15.95, 1-87806-765-6. With eloquence and conviction, more than 30 women explore this deeply emotional, sometimes controversial, and always compelling experience that affects millions of families and individuals.

*Out of Time: A Novel* by Paula Martinac. $12.95, 1-58005-020-4. A handsomely repackaged version of an award-winning debut novel that won the 1990 Lambda Literary Award for Best Lesbian Fiction and was a Finalist for the American Library Association Gay and Lesbian Book Award.

*Valencia* by Michelle Tea. $13.00, 1-58005-035-2. This is a fast-paced account of one girl's search for love and high times in the drama-filled dyke world of San Francisco's Mission District.